ADDICTION
TRAJECTORIES

EXPERIMENTAL FUTURES

Technological Lives, Scientific Arts, Anthropological Voices

A series edited by Michael M. J. Fischer and Joseph Dumit

ADDICTION
TRAJECTORIES

EUGENE RAIKHEL AND **WILLIAM GARRIOTT**, EDITORS

Duke University Press
Durham and London   2013

Library of Congress Cataloging-in-Publication Data
Addiction trajectories / Eugene Raikhel and William Garriott, eds.
p. cm.— (Experimental futures : technological lives, scientific arts,
anthropological voices)
Includes bibliographical references and index.
ISBN 978-0-8223-5350-8 (cloth : alk. paper)
ISBN 978-0-8223-5364-5 (pbk. : alk. paper)
1. Substance abuse—Research. 2. Addicts—Rehabilitation.
3. Substance abuse—Treatment. I. Raikhel, Eugene A., 1975–
II. Garriott, William Campbell, 1977– III. Series: Experimental futures.
HV5809.A335 2013
6.86 2—dc61   2012044751

CONTENTS

ACKNOWLEDGMENTS

We thank the contributors to this volume for the stimulating conversations that have helped to shape our thinking about addiction, as well as for their dedication and patience throughout the editorial process. Many of the chapters in this volume were originally presented at the workshop "Anthropologies of Addiction: Science, Therapy, and Regulation" at McGill University in April 2009, which was generously funded by an Aid to Workshops and Conferences in Canada grant from the Social Sciences and Humanities Research Council of Canada (SSHRC), as well as by the Division for Social and Transcultural Psychiatry at McGill University. We owe a particularly deep thanks to Sandra Hyde, whose collaboration was essential to our receiving the SSHRC grant and to the overall success of the workshop. This volume has greatly benefited from the careful readings, insights, and suggestions of a number of scholars who attended the workshop—as well as an earlier session at the American Anthropological Association conference in 2007—as participants and discussants: Nick Bartlett, João Biehl, Joe Dumit, Clara Han, Sandra Hyde, Nick King, Laurence Kirmayer, Barbara Koenig, Daniel Lende, Margaret Lock, Dawn Moore, Ronald Niezen, Michael Oldani, Tobias Rees, Lisa Stevenson, and Allan Young. We also thank the research assistants who have helped us in innumerable ways at various stages of this project: Emilio Dirlikov, Annie Heffernan, Roscoe Nicholson, Rachel Sandwell, Aaron Seaman, and W. Wilson Will. Finally, we are tremendously grateful to Ken Wissoker and his staff at Duke University Press for their support of this volume.

TRACING NEW PATHS IN THE
ANTHROPOLOGY OF ADDICTION

This volume provides a critical examination of "addiction"—a relatively new but increasingly prominent way of thinking about and intervening into the contemporary human experience. Rooted largely in Western ideas about health, illness, and comportment, addiction is now experientially, discursively, and geographically widespread. As it assumes the status of a "global form" (Collier and Ong 2005)—albeit a hotly contested one—it both shapes and is shaped by the contexts in which it takes hold and through which it passes. Addiction is particularly relevant as an object of anthropological inquiry because it sits at the crossroads of some of the issues that most define the world today: the role of scientific—and particularly bioscientific—knowledge in the shaping of identity, selfhood, and subjectivity; the mutual transformation of novel medical technologies and the cultural settings in which they are enacted; and the mediation of biological and psychological systems and social and political-economic ones by subjective and embodied meaning and experience.

The chapters in this volume were originally presented at a workshop on the anthropologies of addiction held at McGill University in April 2009. During our discussions, we found that while they reflected a range of geographical fieldwork locations and were written from a variety of theoretical perspectives, all of them examined addiction with an attention to a number of issues that speak to addiction's unique position in the contemporary world. These include shifts in the scientific understanding of addiction and the use of this knowledge for intervention (therapeutic and otherwise); new developments in addiction therapeutics, many of which (particularly in the case of pharmaceutical-based treatments) blur the lines between treatment and use; and the efforts by individual addicts, their families, and others to live with the effects of addiction while also making sense of changes in its therapeutic, scientific, social, and political management. We suggest that the affinity between these issues—and its significance for research on addiction—can be most clearly understood through a focus on what we call *addiction trajectories*. In highlighting the notion of trajectories, we aim to emphasize the directed (yet contingent) movement of people, substances, ideas, techniques, and institutions along spatial, temporal, social, and epistemic dimensions. More specifically, the chapters in this volume follow at least three principal types of addiction trajectories: (1) the *epistemic trajectories* traced by categories and concepts of addiction as they change over time and move across institutional domains; (2) the *therapeutic trajectories* of treatments as they move through distinct cultural and organizational settings; and (3) the *experiential and experimental trajectories* of lives constituted through the terrains of addiction and subjectivity.

To clarify what we mean by addiction trajectories, we first turn to an extended ethnographic example drawn from one of the contributions to this volume. In her chapter, Anne M. Lovell recounts her encounter with Pavel, a young man from Ukraine with whom she spoke while researching Eastern European drug users in Marseille. Pavel began injecting opium while still living in Ukraine. He found that, when dosed correctly, it helped him in his work as a computer programmer. But Pavel also found that his use had become an addiction, or *toxicomania*, the term generally used in French-speaking countries (and, with a more restricted meaning, in Russian-speaking ones).[1] "My toxicomania," he said, "was like a woman," suggesting that the experience simultaneously carried the passion and potential danger of a sexual relationship. "The needle," he continued, "was my brother," pointing to a level of intimacy with the means of injection rivaling that shared with a family member—a blood relative.

But Pavel's experience as an addict (or *toxicomane*) was not defined solely by these positively valenced experiences of productivity, pleasure, and intimacy. Still a young man, he had already seen friends overdose and die. One had been forced to have his leg amputated when gangrene set in at the injection site. Pavel himself started selling his parents' possessions to pay for opium—an act that prompted them to commit him to a forensic psychiatric hospital, where he would ultimately go through two rounds of treatment. At the institution, Pavel underwent a period of forced withdrawal combined with periodic injections of medications unknown to him, all while being strapped to a table—a form of treatment/punishment that reflects the hybrid penal and medical genealogy of post-Soviet addiction medicine (Elovich and Drucker 2008; Raikhel 2010).

Having suffered through commitment to a psychiatric hospital and the general depredations of his home country's punitive approach to governing drug use, Pavel left Ukraine. He traveled through Poland and Germany to Strasbourg, France, then on to Marseille, where he had friends. In Marseille, Pavel—along with an unknown number of other travelers from Russia and Eastern Europe—encountered a very different orientation to the management of addiction. There, as in many other settings, addiction was increasingly being framed using a neurobiological idiom, owing in part to decades of neuroscientific research into the condition (Campbell 2007; Vrecko 2010a). This biomedical model, which is the product of a different institutional and intellectual history than that which developed in Russia and other former Soviet states (described by Eugene Raikhel in this volume), has had a significant impact on addiction management in France. Specifically, it has both partially displaced an older model rooted in psychoanalysis and come together with local ideologies of citizenship, solidarity, and republicanism, leading to an approach that emphasizes the development of institutions and practices seeking to mitigate the harmful effects of drug use and draw drug users into the French social body (Lovell 2006). This hybrid model of addiction management provided Pavel, like other travelers from Eastern Europe, with a different identity through which he could envision a new future for himself. "In Ukraine," Pavel said, "the toxicomane, it's not like in France. In Ukraine, if someone is a toxicomane, he is already a criminal. If I am a toxicomane, I don't go to the hospital; I go to prison."

But it was also in France that Pavel started using drugs again—not opium this time, but heroin, as well as methadone, Rohypnol, and buprenorphine. Notably, methadone, Rohypnol, and buprenorphine are all legal medications marketed for their therapeutic effect, with methadone and buprenorphine being two leading medications used to treat addiction to opiates. Pavel was able to access these medications because opiate-substitution therapy plays a key role in the French approach to managing addiction, and drugs such as methadone are often available for free from local nongovernmental organizations (NGOs). Not surprisingly, perhaps, Pavel framed his use of these substances in strictly therapeutic terms as a form of self-medication that he could stop at any time.

While availing themselves of these opiate-substitution therapies and carving out new lives under a different drug-management regime, this contingent of Eastern European drug users provoked anxiety, frustration, and resentment among local drug users and public health workers in Marseille, not so much because they misused methadone and buprenorphine, but because—in an unexpected bid at biological citizenship—they seemed to use the harm-reduction services aimed at drug addicts primarily as a way to gain access to other social and health services that were not available to them in their home countries. Pavel and other addicted travelers thus continued to experience harassment and exclusion from the surrounding population by virtue of their addicted status (albeit a different kind from what they might have experienced at home). Perhaps in part because of this ambivalent reception in France, Pavel ultimately dreamed of returning home to Ukraine. "I want to live in my country," he said. "France is for the French. I'll find a job [in Ukraine]. I'll have a family, children—live!"

Pavel's story highlights the shifting place of addiction in the contemporary world. To be sure, this story has elements that are all too familiar. Pavel's is a story of the pain and pleasure that come with drug use, one in which drugs (both licit and illicit) offer a means to self-medicate the social misery caused by "reigning structures of social inequality" (Baer et al. 2003: 228). It is a story in which the awkward and often incompatible relationship between the medical and the political domains perpetuates the very inequalities that so often prompt the turn to drug use in the first place and hamper the prospects for therapeutic success. Finally, Pavel's is a story of sociality and marginalization, of being on the outside of not one but several social bodies while simultaneously forming new relationships and associations, often by means of the addiction itself.

Underlying and uniting these various facets of Pavel's experience, however, is something more fundamental: the simple fact of his movement as a result of his addiction. Through his addiction, Pavel is thrown into new contexts, new milieux. Indeed, these milieux emerge only as Pavel and his compatriots traverse the social, physical, and political landscapes in which their own experiences of addiction are embedded. Such movement is inherently productive, creating novel assemblages of people, ideas, interventions, and other constitutive matter—all of which recursively shape how individuals like Pavel come to experience and live with their addiction, even using it to make claims on the state for services, belonging, and care. Along the way, the lines that divide subject and substance, individual and environment, illness and treatment, and will and desire, among others, are reworked, blur, or evaporate altogether. This process works to refract and reframe the local impact of scientific research, therapeutic interventions, governance practices, even subjectivity itself, all of which are revealed to be inseparable from, rather than ancillary to, the contemporary experience and manifestation of addiction. Tracing the movement of Pavel and those like him brings into focus the work of addiction today: its role in shaping and being shaped by the trajectories along which individuals like Pavel travel and live.

Addiction: Anthropological Approaches

Before turning to the issue of addiction trajectories in detail, it is important to address an even more fundamental question: Why focus on "addiction" per se? Why not focus on "drugs" or "drug use" or "substance dependence"? Indeed, anthropologists have a long history of studying particular psychoactive substances, including alcohol, tobacco, "drugs," and, most recently, pharmaceuticals (Dietler 2006; Heath 1987; G. Hunt and Barker 2001; Kohrmann and Benson 2011; Mandelbaum 1965; Marshall et al. 2001; Page and Singer 2010; Petryna et al. 2006). Among other important findings, this literature has provided evidence for the cultural determination of distinctions between normal and pathological consumption (Linda Bennett et al. 1993; Colson and Scudder 1988; Douglas 1987; Eber 1995; Heath 1958; Marshall 1979; cf. Room 1984); furnished the basis for an influential argument on the cultural shaping of "drunken comportment" (MacAndrew and Edgerton 1969); documented local social and political-economic logics surrounding the use and exchange of substances (Agar 1973; Bourgois 1995; Bourgois and Schonberg 2009; Kunitz et al. 1994; Singer 2008; Spradley 1970; Waterston 1993); studied the intertwining of colonial (or postcolonial) domination, historical trauma, and stereotypy surrounding substance abuse in Native communities (Kunitz et al. 1994; O'Nell and Mitchell 1996; Prussing 2007; Quintero 2000; Spicer 1997, 1998); examined links between substance consumption and the construction of gender identity (Benedict and Benedict 1982; Marshall and Marshall 1990; Suggs 1996); analyzed the interrelationships between structural violence, harmful drug use, and infectious diseases (particularly HIV) (Bourgois et al. 1997; Rhodes et al. 2005; Singer 2006); theorized the transformation of self in treatment programs (Bateson 1972; Cain 1991); and examined the flow of substances as commodities in chains of production, exchange, and consumption (Mintz 1985; B. Roberts 2000; Stebbins 2001; Whyte et al. 2002).

While the papers collected here are deeply indebted to many of these earlier studies, they also move away from employing substance categories (alcohol, illicit drugs, pharmaceuticals) as the organizing rubric for research. Instead, they take up "addiction" as an object of anthropological study in its own right, all the while insisting on its contingency as a category of human experience. Both "addiction" and the notion of the "addict" in their contemporary meanings are of relatively recent origin. "Addiction" did not enter humanity's "grammar of motives" (Burke 1969: xvi) in earnest until the late nineteenth century. And its meaning continues to be revised and contested in light of new scientific knowledge, medical treatments, and subjective experience—as the various genealogies presented here demonstrate.

Returning to the question posed earlier, why, then, focus on "addiction" today? We suggest that a number of relatively recent developments have facilitated the emergence of "addiction" as an object of knowledge, intervention, identification, and contention in the contemporary world. One of these is the biologization of psychiatry and the emergence of a body of neurobiological knowledge which characterizes addiction as a dysfunction of normal brain systems involved in reward, motivation, learning, and choice (Campbell 2007; Kalivas and Volkow 2005; Vrecko 2010b). In addition to shifting much public discussion of addiction's roots from psychology, family dynamics, and social factors to neurotransmitters and brain functions, this research has produced a number of new pharmacological treatments for addiction, which may encourage forms of life that are radically distinct from those fostered by programs such as Alcoholics Anonymous (AA; see Lovell 2006; Rose 2003a; Vrecko 2006). Indeed, it should be noted that more than half of the chapters presented here discuss some form of pharmaceutical-based addiction therapy, with the majority focused on the drug buprenorphine.

But the contemporary story of addiction cannot be reduced to one simply of biomedicalization. The past decades have also seen a proliferation of technologies for addiction therapy and harm reduction, many of which openly eschew substance-based treatments. These range from mutual-help movements modeled on AA to therapeutic communities and needle-exchange programs. Such institutions are now being exported well beyond the countries of their origin, where they are transformed, adapted, and domesticated even as they seek to transform local ways of being (Borovoy 2001, 2005; Brandes 2002; Hansen 2005; Hyde 2011; Mäkelä et al. 1996; Saris 2008; Zigon 2010). Moreover, such interventions often exist alongside coercive institutions based on the criminalization of particular behaviors or substances (Garriott 2011; Moore 2007; Nolan 2001).

The increasing salience of "addiction" has been more, however, than simply the result of the global migration of ideas and interventions. A number of technological and political-economic factors have created conditions under which behaviors ranging from alcohol consumption to gambling are likely to become compulsive cycles. These include profit-making entities, such as the alcohol, tobacco, and gaming industries; narcotrafficking operations, which link compulsive desire to the circuits of consumer capitalism; and conditions of structural violence that undermine the forms of support people need to avoid such patterns (P. Benson 2010; Bourgois and Schonberg 2009; Gootenberg 2008; Jernigan 1997; Schüll 2012; Stebbins 2001; Vrecko 2008).

Appreciating the historically situated nature of addiction is essential for understanding its significance in contemporary life. Moreover, as the papers collected here show, to probe addiction is to examine simultaneously a series of distinctly modern forms of life, including patterns of consumption and production, sickness and health, normalcy and pathology, neglect and intervention, belonging and alienation—in short, the very "stuff" out of which the contemporary world is made. Thus, addiction is a category through which "anthropos today"—the contemporary human—has come to experience itself, one that is at once phenomenologically robust and historically contingent (Rabinow 2003).

Trajectories: Movement and Method

In writing of addiction trajectories, we seek to highlight a number of specific issues and problems evoked by the full range of meanings suggested by the notion of the trajectory. Trajectories can be spatial as well as temporal; in the cases presented in this volume, they are usually both simultaneously. Trajectories also can be charted over social and institutional dimensions. In addition, while the notion certainly suggests the temporality of a human life, addiction trajectories are not only about disease and illness processes as experienced by people. Categories, technologies, and institutional forms related to addiction also change over time and move from place to place. Thus, we mean simultaneously to evoke ideas of motion, temporality, and change, as well as the tension between forces that structure and determine social phenomena into well-worn paths and those that maintain the contingency and indeterminacy of those paths, allowing individuals to veer off into unexpected directions. In taking up this terminology, we also intend to signal a critical engagement with two broad and distinct literatures that have employed similar concepts: anthropological work on the spatial movement and mobility of people, things, and ideas and the often clinically engaged social science literature that examines "illness trajectories." Finally, the concept of addiction trajectories suggests a number of methodological choices, which we trace through the chapters in this volume.

In their emphasis on trajectory and movement, the contributions to this volume not only enrich our understanding of addiction but also bring greater analytic clarity to these themes in the anthropological literature more generally. Anthropologists have productively used movement, travel, and other action-oriented tropes and metaphors (flows, traffic, circulation) as heuristics through which to understand everything from the social lives of pharmaceuticals to the illegal traffic in human organs and the production of scientific knowledge (Petryna et al. 2006; Scheper-Hughes 2003; Whyte et al. 2002). We understand the notion of trajectory to refer not simply to movement, but to *directed movement*, thus implying the forces and processes—whether social, psychological or biological—which shape this directedness. Seen in this light, addiction cannot be reduced simply to a biological condition, a social affliction or the symptom of some deeper malaise. Rather, it must be seen as a trajectory of experience that traverses the biological and the social, the medical and the legal, the cultural and the political. Understanding addiction requires attention to how it inspires movement across these multiple domains, or, as Lovell puts it in her contribution to this volume, "tracing the trajectories of elusive travelers."

We are also indebted to the extensive literature on "illness trajectories," a concept widely used in longitudinal studies of illness in individual lives and across the life-course, and in related discussions about the social production of differential health outcomes (G. Becker and Kaufman 1995; Corbin and Strauss 1987; Strauss et al. 1982; Wiener and Dodd 1993). During the 1970s and 1980s, medical sociologists studying chronic illness developed the notion of the "illness trajectory" to refer "not only to the physiological unfolding of a patient's disease but to the *total organization of work* done over that course of illness plus the *impact* on those involved with that work and its organization" (Strauss et al. 1982).[2] This concept has been highly influential in qualitative health research, particularly in clinically applied studies in mental health seeking to understand "when, where and how to intervene" in order to achieve improved health outcomes.[3]

Many researchers working on addiction have used the related concept of "drug-use trajectories" in longitudinal and developmentally oriented studies (Hser et al. 2007). Much of this literature seeks to explain the finding that many people who use addictive drugs habitually for a period of time either "mature out" of heavy use or stop without therapeutic intervention (Chen and Kandel 1995; Robins 1993; Winger et al. 2005; Winick 1962). Anthropologically informed literature on drug-use trajectories has generally emphasized that norms, role expectations, and understandings of pathology are not only culturally determined but also differentiated across local conceptualizations of the life-course (Nichter et al. 2004; O'Nell and Mitchell 1996; Quintero 2000). The notion of trajectory is also implicit in discussions about conceptual frameworks for research and treatment that might move beyond the current dominance of diagnostic categories based on the *Diagnostic and Statistical Manual of Mental Disorders* (DSM), particularly among cultural psychiatrists and medical anthropologists concerned with the shaping or production of chronicity in psychotic disorders (cf. Good et al. 2010; Luhrmann 2007). In all of these uses of the term, "trajectory" signals a shift away from a synchronic focus on symptoms or markers toward a diachronic one on individuals undergoing changes and the relationship between individual experiences, life-course events, and environmental processes. Although we aim to draw on many useful elements of this discussion here, we also seek to inflect the concept of trajectory in somewhat different ways.

In particular, we draw attention to how the ideas of specific life trajectories with addiction work to perpetuate themselves—particularly when enacted in highly persuasive illness narratives. For example, numerous scholars, including Angela Garcia (2010), have argued that the overdeter-minedness of the AA or Twelve Step narrative—which plots a trajectory running from crisis to "hitting rock bottom" to redemption—may serve to reify or even produce the chronicity of addiction. Conversely, it is precisely an emphasis on the potential of open-endedness and contingency (what João Biehl and Peter Locke [2010], drawing on Gilles Deleuze, call "becoming") that distinguishes the notion of trajectory from that of the "career"—an idea that has been widely used in the ethnography of drug and alcohol use (e.g., H. Becker 1953; Kunitz et al. 1994; Waldorf 1973).

An emphasis on trajectories has a number of methodological implications as well. Specifically, concern with movement is rooted in a unique ethnographic sensibility that focuses on tracing or "following" subjects as they move through their everyday lives (de Certeau 1988; Le Marcis 2004; Marcus 1995). This approach has been central to ethnographers' ability to discover so-called hidden populations of drug users that typically remain outside the clinical gaze (Page and Singer 2010). But to follow someone in this way is not simply a matter of shadowing their every move. The approach here is a much broader enterprise. It involves attending not only to lived experience but also to the material out of which lived experience is made: the relations, knowledges, technologies, and affects, as well as the recursive impact of subjectivity itself (Biehl et al. 2007), which takes on particular significance given the "chronic" character of addiction. In his contribution, Todd Meyers argues that to "follow" one's subjects in this way includes "conversations with concerned family members, friends, parole officers, clinicians, and social workers—often in the absence of the 'study participant.'" Such a method also requires "documenting the work of clinicians" and the material administrative traces that remained after someone would disappear."

In tracing such trajectories, the contributors to this volume demonstrate the inadequacy of conceptualizing worlds or spaces—such as those of the clinic or of the "street"—as separate from one another. In her chapter, Anne Lovell notes that much of the addiction literature assumes a unilinear, uniform trajectory from use to treatment. However, the contributors to this volume suggest that subjectivities are forged and life patterns are shaped not so much in the clinic or rehabilitation center as an endpoint or exclusively in the domain of "use," but in the movement between them. Thus, in her chapter, Angela Garcia shows how the clinical logic of chronicity articulates with Hispano notions of endlessness to foreclose the possibilities for a particular patient's life. In a related argument, Meyers suggests some of the complex relationships between the aims and practices of the clinic and the ones that patients carry with them into non-institutional spaces. Here, patients' dispositions toward therapeutics are not adequately described by focusing on compliance or non-compliance; rather, they blur the more basic distinction between therapeutics and the pathology they seek to alleviate.

The remainder of this introduction will discuss the individual chapters in greater detail. It is organized around three kinds of addiction trajectories. The first section examines the *epistemic trajectories* of categories and concepts of addiction as they have transformed over time and moved across domains. Following this, we focus on the *therapeutic trajectories* of various treatments and related assemblages as they move between cultural and institutional settings. Finally, we attend to the *experiential and experimental trajectories* that emerge as subjects use substances, knowledge, and therapeutics and are used by them. In examining lives constituted through the terrains of experience and subjectivity, these contributions also show how addiction itself can be productively seen as a trajectory along which the subject travels.

Epistemic Trajectories

In using "addiction" as an organizing rubric for this volume, we aim to direct attention to what Ian Hacking (2002) has called the "historical ontology" of this category—its coming into being as an object of knowledge (and, importantly, self-knowledge) and intervention under a particular set of conditions—rather than to further naturalize it as a self-evident phenomenon.[4] This is not to discount the experiential reality of addiction. Rather, the contributors to this volume seek to understand how scientific and other expert framings of addiction are implicated in lived experience.

The etymology of the term "addiction" locates its earliest usage in Roman law. To be an addict in this context was to be in a state of slavery as a result of failure to pay a debt. In the Roman Empire, the addict was the debtor enslaved to his or her creditor; in the contemporary world, the addict is the person enslaved to a substance or process, whether it is alcohol, a drug, or an activity such as gambling (Gomart 2004).

Addiction in its contemporary meaning began to take shape in earnest in Anglo-American countries with the formation of the disease concept of alcoholism during the early industrial age. Here, the individual's desire to consume alcohol was framed as a chronic, progressive compulsion that led eventually and inevitably to a loss of control. This concept emerged at a time that drinking practices were increasingly problematized for their perceived incompatibility with the behavioral strictures then valorized, particularly those of self-reliance, independence, and productivity (Ferentzy 2001; Levine 1978; Room 2003).[5] Alcoholism and other such "diseases of the will," as they were framed throughout the nineteenth century, arose as a kind of shadow to the normative ideal of the freely choosing subject in much the same way that Foucault and others have argued that the concept of madness emerged in a mutually constitutive relationship to reason (Foucault 1965; Valverde 1998).[6] The cultural specificity of the relationship between person and substance figured by this idea is bolstered by several classic ethnographic studies, which together documented how valorized and socially constructive practices of heavy drinking in several indigenous communities transformed into more disruptive and painful patterns with the advent of markets and wage labor (Heath 1958, 2004; Marshall 1979, 1982).

The twentieth century saw a number of key shifts in how medical researchers understood the relationship between human biology, individual psychology, environment, and particular psychoactive substances. Moreover, researchers' conceptual categories and questions were deeply shaped by what states and social movements took to be significant problems of the day. For example, many late nineteenth-century physicians in the United States and Britain understood habitual drunkenness as a sign of "inebriety," a concept that drew upon contemporary theories of degeneration and understood alcohol as "racial poison" (Valverde 1998: 54). While inebriety was framed by some as an underlying condition that linked drinking with tobacco and opium use, as well as other so-called vices, the general idea of alcohol as inherently harmful meshed with the increasingly influential prohibitionist ideas of the temperance movement (Courtwright 2005; Valverde 1998). Following the repeal of Prohibition in the United States, AA articulated a conception of alcoholism as disease according to which some aspect of the particular drinker (rather than the substance itself) lent itself to pathological consumption (Gusfield 1996: 247–56). This general assumption about alcoholism, in turn, informed decades of studies on "predisposition" and "risk factors" that sought to identify the specific aspect of the drinker (social, psychological, or hereditary) or her or his environment to which addiction might be ascribed (Valverde 1998). In the meantime, at least until the 1970s, biological, public health, and social science research streams on alcohol, tobacco, and illegal drugs developed in relative isolation from one another, each influenced by a distinct field of actors with competing political, social, and commercial interests (Berridge 2001; Campbell 2007; Courtwright 2005).

The transformation of diagnostic categories and criteria has been similarly divergent, with different frameworks emerging from various institutional bodies, some of which have dropped the term "addiction" altogether. For example, during the 1960s, the World Health Organization, which publishes the *International Classification of Diseases*, replaced the related terms "drug addiction" and "drug habituation" with "drug dependence," which was defined to encompass both psychological and physiological dependence. By the 1980s, that had been loosened further still (Reinarman 2005: 311–12; Room 1998). The term "addiction" was similarly dropped from DSM-IV (the fourth edition of the American Psychiatric Association's authoritative *Diagnostic and Statistical Manual of Mental Disorders*), although arguments have been made for its reinstatement in the next edition (O'Brien et al. 2006). Finally, the entire Anglo-American addiction paradigm has been challenged in countries such as France and Russia, where different intellectual and institutional conceptualizations rooted in distinct national and political histories continue to hold sway (Lovell 2006; Raikhel 2010, this volume).

For nearly twenty years, neurobiologically oriented addiction researchers, led in the United States by the National Institute on Drug Abuse (NIDA), have publicly promoted the idea of addiction as a "chronic, relapsing brain disease"—a dysfunction of the brain systems involved in reward, motivation, learning, and choice (Hyman 2005; Kalivas and Volkow 2005; Leshner 1997). According to this model, addiction is generally understood as the behavioral outcome of this biological dysfunction, namely "compulsive seeking . . . and administration of a drug despite grave adverse consequences" (Nestler 2004: 698). This model, based on several decades of research conducted on the neural correlates of experiences such as craving and pleasure (much of it carried out on nonhuman animals), was strengthened and legitimated by the powerful imaging technologies that became widely available during the 1980s and 1990s, as Nancy Campbell discusses in her contribution to this volume (see also Campbell 2007; Vrecko 2010a). Specifically, the "chronic, relapsing brain disease" model replaced a narrative in which withdrawal and growing physical tolerance led the user to consume increasing quantities of a substance to maintain the same level of intoxication with one in which substances and particular behaviors "hijack" endogenous systems evolved to reward behavior that is necessary for survival—the so-called dopamine hypothesis (Hyman 2005; Kalivas and Volkow 2005). While the expansion of the addiction concept to behavior such as gambling, sex, and overeating may have been shaped as much by the burgeoning mutual-help and addiction-recovery movements as by biomedical research (Schüll, this volume; Sedgwick 1992; Valverde 1998),[7] the "chronic, relapsing brain disease" model has provided an important framing to this expansive notion of addiction by suggesting that certain behaviors not involving psychoactive substances nonetheless correlate with the activation and dysfunction of the same brain circuits (Block 2008; O'Brien et al. 2006; Petry 2006; Volkow and O'Brien 2007). On a more fundamental level, the neurobiological model shares certain basic assumptions with psychological models of addiction—for example, the notion that various behaviors associated with the repeated consumption of psychoactive substances are "symptoms" indicative of some discrete underlying condition, or, in other words, a disease entity rather than contingent outcomes of people interacting with particular milieux (Keane 2002: 568; Reinarman 2005: 308; Room 1983).

By briefly tracing these historical trajectories, we point to the contingent nature of their futures. While we have yet to see how the neurosciences will transform professional and lay understandings of addiction, it is clear that practices such as problematic drinking and drug use have not yet been biologized—or subsumed under the aegis of psychiatry—to the same degree as other forms of human suffering, particularly mental illness (May 2001; Valverde 1997, 1998). Some reasons for this may be internal to biomedicine. For example, Carl May (2001) suggests that we can speak only of a "quasi-disease model of addiction" in biomedicine, because a lack of clear organic disease markers makes physicians dependent on patients' self-reports for diagnosis, rendering diagnosis largely an issue of self-identification.[8] While some biomedical traditions have attempted to deal with this by associating addiction with certain discrete and observable behavioral markers, such as reflexes (as Raikhel shows in his contribution), the failure to identify clear biological markers has, at least until this point, meant that addiction has failed to live up to the evidentiary criteria of biomedicine. The issue of therapy is also important here, in that the success of psychopharmacological treatments seems to have helped to significantly legitimate biological accounts of mental illness, even in the absence of discrete biological markers, whereas pharmacological treatments for addiction have not yet been taken up as widely.

Moreover, while the neuroscientific framing of addiction enjoys widespread mainstream institutional support, rival conceptualizations persist. Active critiques of the brain disease model of addiction have been mounted not only by anthropologists, sociologists, and historians (whose work is described throughout this introduction) but also by researchers in other disciplines and by practitioners in various health professions. For example, psychologists, behavioral economists, and philosophers have argued that thinking about addiction as "disease" obscures how addicts continue to exercise choice, even under highly constrained conditions (Foddy and Savulescu 2010; Heyman 2009; Schaler 2000). Other psychologists have gone further, arguing that even defining addiction as a disorder amounts to a medicalization of conditions more properly understood as "problems of living," while some bioethicists have questioned whether a brain disease model will in fact reduce stigma around addiction, as is often claimed (Buchman et al. 2011; Midanik 2006; Peele 1989). Perhaps most notably, as Summerson Carr (2011) shows, the therapeutic and recovery fields in North America use a very different model of how addiction affects human subjectivity that foregrounds the inner depth and complexity of the human psyche. Other therapeutic techniques, such as motivational interviewing, display a conspicuous lack of interest in the specifics of addicted subjectivity or even in the phenomenology of addiction broadly conceived, focusing instead on the efficacy of the therapeutic encounter and the skill of the professional practitioner (Carr, this volume).

Disease models of addiction have also encountered significant resistance on the more general level of public understanding. As Jamie Saris suggests in his chapter, this may be true partly because disease models historically have been interpreted as underwriting a behavioral determinism that threatens Enlightenment notions of the subject with free will (Hyman 2007). Not surprisingly, in North America those who have argued in recent years against disease conceptualizations of addiction generally have offered some notion of "choice" as an alternative (e.g., Satel 1999).

In her chapter, Nancy Campbell demonstrates how the logics that dominate lay discourses on addiction in North America—largely those of the Twelve Step and recovery movements—can easily frame and undercut attempts to decouple addiction from notions of choice, responsibility, and self-control. Her chapter focuses on the appearance of Anna Rose Childress on *The Oprah Winfrey Show*. Childress, an addiction neurobiologist and clinician, sees her research—which represents an entire literature focused on "relapse" and devoted to understanding how particular settings and situations trigger drug cravings—as actively countering stigmatizing and moralizing interpretations of addiction as the result of an individual's failure to maintain self-control. Yet during the episode Campbell analyzes, Childress's work on the role of contextual cues that trigger certain states—often without a person's conscious awareness—sits very uncomfortably alongside—and, arguably, is drowned out by—the lay therapeutic discourse of personal choice and responsibility, as well as by the confessional register, promoted by Oprah. Moreover, in the shift to a popular arena, many common assumptions about the persuasiveness of scientific arguments are overturned. Even Childress's invocation of the supposedly ever seductive neuroimaging technology, with its brightly colored images, fails to prevail over the therapeutic discourse of confession and self-control. Ultimately, Campbell suggests, the "pharmacological optimism" of neuroscientists like Childress may index not a neurological determinism or reductionism but, rather, a "respect for the complexities represented by relapse" that is significantly greater than that expressed by those who see addiction as a matter of choice and self-control.

Jamie Saris similarly takes up the relationship between neurobiological models of addiction and the notion of the free-willing subject. Rather than abandon a notion of choice or will or agency, Saris argues for a more robust and better-theorized commitment to such notions. In concrete terms, this means ensuring that choice is conceptualized to allow it to be embedded in or emerge from contextual accounts of life and individual particularity. Moreover, these kinds of particularity are precisely what Saris sees as the interest of some scholars in pharmacology and neurobiology, as they turn from exploring the neural mechanisms underpinning addiction to examining more closely how these mechanisms interact with phenomena at other levels of complexity. For Saris, the current moment in the neurobiology of addiction provides anthropology with a specific point of entry or engagement, at which its insights can be invaluable for a potentially mutually transformative encounter with biologically based sciences. In fact, a growing number of social scientists studying addiction (some of them represented in this volume) have called for a robust and critical engagement with the biological sciences (Campbell 2010; Kushner 2006, 2010; Lende 2005, 2012; Singer 2001; Vrecko 2010a; Weinberg 2002).

Of course, debates about the nature of addiction are not limited to the medical and scientific arenas. As several of the contributors to this volume point out, legal and political debates have likewise had an impact on the development of disease models of addiction, often through policy practices that promote the criminalization of addiction. Indeed, this notion of an *inherent* opposition between the seemingly rehabilitative and therapeutic claims of a medical model and the coercive practices underwritten by a criminal one is often taken as an article of faith by professionals in the therapeutic arena. For example, proponents of the "chronic relapsing brain disease" model frequently argue that "scientific discoveries that substantiate the biological basis of addiction and improve treatment outcome should ultimately erode entrenched societal attitudes that prevent addiction from being evaluated, treated and insured as a medical disorder" (Dackis and O'Brien 2005: 1431). As a consequence, many proponents of therapy and rehabilitation see the propagation of biomedical models of addiction as a direct way to contest criminalizing approaches to the problem.

However, as William Garriott suggests in his chapter, a lack of acceptance of biomedical models of addiction is not necessarily the problem. Indeed, during his work on methamphetamine in a rural community of West Virginia, Garriott found that the prevailing NIDA model of addiction, which views addiction as a chronic, relapsing disease of the brain, was widely accepted by professionals working in the local criminal justice system. In the cases that Garriott documents, the model of addiction as a "disease" requiring treatment was seamlessly interwoven with an institutional logic that viewed addiction as inherently linked to criminal behavior, which privileged punitive responses to this behavior and foreclosed any possibility of therapeutic alternatives. In examining how the link between addiction as a criminogenic disease and incarceration as the only appropriate institutional response has come to be seen as self-evident, Garriott finds a number of ways in which the trajectory of this logic reinforces and embeds it in the institutions themselves.

Both Campbell and Garriott show what becomes of the neurobiological model of addiction as it is translated to different epistemic cultures, defined by particular discursive and institutional settings (Knorr-Cetina 1999). More specifically, their chapters suggest how, notwithstanding the assumption that knowledge of addiction's neurobiological basis will inevitably result in progressive social change, this knowledge may be radically transformed by the assumptions and imperatives of the domain to which it is translated—even though addiction knowledge can just as easily have its own transformative effects.[9]

Thus, what seems significant, beyond the sheer number of models purporting to explain what addiction is and how it works, is the recognition that each model carries with it a certain logic. This logic (albeit malleable) gives the model in question the capacity to have certain effects in certain contexts and under certain conditions. However, the dependence on context means that the effects are often difficult to predict in advance, and unanticipated consequences (e.g., the use of neurobiological knowledge of addiction by police officers to carry out police work) are the rule. In the terminology of the volume, we can say that different models of addiction are the product of different, highly contingent epistemic trajectories, and this particularity gives them unique capacities to launch new trajectories all their own. This dynamic is nowhere more apparent than in the realm of addiction therapeutics.

Therapeutic Trajectories

The sheer number of available addiction treatments is striking. They range from faith-based treatments rooted in Christian and other religious traditions to Twelve Step programs such as AA and any number of approaches rooted in psychology—everything from cognitive-behavioral therapies to family counseling. Although these treatments vary significantly in their approach and orientation—to say nothing about their working assumptions regarding the nature of both addiction and the human—it is not uncommon for individual addicts to combine or engage with them piecemeal based on availability or circumstance or to develop a therapeutic regimen tailored to their specific needs or desires (Schüll, this volume).

Such a motley approach can be seen as the product of insufficient access to appropriate treatment, the play of power relations, or (from the standpoint of medicine) patients' noncompliance, but it is also, in many ways, perfectly in step with mainstream medical recommendations, which emphasize that no single treatment is effective for everyone (even though most treatment regimens present themselves as singularly sufficient and efficacious). For example, NIDA states on its website that "the best treatment programs provide a combination of therapies and other services to meet the needs of the individual patient." This statement provides the caption to a chart titled "Components of Comprehensive Drug Abuse Treatment," which includes eighteen different components, ranging from "Substance Use Monitoring" and "Self-Help/Peer Support Groups" to "Legal Services" and "Child Care Services."[10] There seems to be a working assumption among medical practitioners that the number of interventions available is vast and that each addict will employ a unique combination of techniques based on his or her specific circumstances—or, at least, will experiment until he or she has found the treatment that works best. Conversely, this model seems to suggest that virtually any mode of intervention or therapy can be applied to addiction, mirroring the way that, today, almost anything can be figured as addictive (Schüll, this volume).

Employing the notion of trajectory, addiction therapeutics may thus be defined by the ongoing interplay between the discrete practices of specific therapeutic regimens, on the one hand, and those of addicted individuals who engage or are engaged by them, on the other. This process is itself mediated by institutions, politics, and public opinion, just to name a few. This ongoing interplay between therapeutic regimens and individual addicts creates a situation in which novel combinations are the rule and not the exception. Moreover, patients often bend therapies to their own purposes—for instance, to manage their use of a particular substance (Acker 2002). Like the models of addiction examined earlier, particular therapeutic regimens have their own historically and institutionally defined logics, which inspire trajectories based on the specific technologies they employ. For example, anthropologists have paid close attention to the social roles and models of self and personhood encoded in addiction diagnostics and therapeutics, as well as in less formalized lay models of or discourses on addiction. While certain kinds of treatment—particularly psychotherapy and self- and mutual-help programs—do this more explicitly by encouraging patients to experience themselves in particular ways, research carried out by anthropologists shows the subtle ways in which "even simple 'self-less' biomedical technologies [such as medications] inadvertently act as technologies of the self" (Lock and Nguyen 2010: 284).

One of the most significant recent changes in addiction therapeutics in this regard is the rise of new pharmaceutically based treatments. Once a domain occupied almost exclusively by methadone, such treatments now include drugs (used alone or in combination) such as naltrexone, disulfiram, acamprosate, bupropion, varenicline, and buprenorphine. This development cannot be explained simply by the vicissitudes of technoscientific innovation. Rather, it reflects more fundamental changes that have taken place in science and medicine over the past several decades, including the biologization of psychiatry and, more specifically, its reframing as a "clinical neuroscience discipline" (Insel and Quirion 2005). This shift, among others, presaged the movement of psychopharmaceuticals to the center of the contemporary clinical toolbox (Shorter 1998), a move that, in turn, created a market—and thus incentives—for producing medications to treat particular kinds of conditions. Disorders of a more chronic character are especially appealing from a market perspective because they hold out the prospect of patients' taking a particular medication not just until they are cured (understood as an impossibility in this case) but perpetually in pursuit of some semblance of normalcy. Health itself becomes something that is pharmaceutically mediated, and individuals grow accustomed to the idea of being on "drugs for life" (Dumit 2002, 2012).

One implication of this is that fairly longstanding distinctions are becoming increasingly blurred: between licit and illicit drugs, between products designed to addict and those designed to alleviate addiction, and, indeed, between "therapy" and "use." Of course, as numerous histories of psychoactive substances remind us, the distinctions between licit and illicit drugs, between those that heal and those that harm, have always been contentious and shifting. Heroin, after all, was developed and promoted during the early twentieth century as a safe alternative to morphine (Courtwright 2001). However, it does seem that a number of relatively recent developments have undercut what was—at least for much of the post–Second World War period—a strongly defined distinction between health-promoting and harm-inducing substances (even though this distinction often fell apart in practice, as demonstrated by the suffering that often accompanies addiction treatments such as methadone [Bourgois 2000]).[11]

This blurring of distinctions is evident in many of the chapters in this volume. Both Anne Lovell and Todd Meyers discuss the nonmedical use of buprenorphine and its circulation outside therapeutic settings—a phenomenon Lovell has referred to as "pharmaceutical leakage" (Lovell 2006: 146). Angela Garcia describes local framings of heroin as "medicine." And Natasha Dow Schüll examines how addiction therapy and machine gambling become part of a single circuit traveled by many residents of Las Vegas: "It is not only that gambling addicts' machine play is isomorphic with their therapeutic practices, but that a certain complicity and even interchangeability develops between the two, merging the zones of self-loss and self-recovery."[12]

Some of the drugs used to treat addiction are novel not only pharmacologically but also institutionally, socially, and culturally. For instance, buprenorphine has been approved in several countries for prescription by general practitioners partly as an attempt to reduce the stigma associated with clinic-based methadone maintenance therapy (Agar et al. 2001; Lovell 2006). Moreover, some observers have argued that various psychoactive medications, including the new addiction treatments and maintenance drugs, encode radically different notions of the self from those currently prevalent in North American and European folk psychologies: rather than teaching people to conceptualize behavioral problems as originating in a self or psyche shaped by the memory of personal experience, such medications may encourage their consumers to ascribe problems to neurochemical imbalances (Martin 2006; Rose 2003b; Vrecko 2006).

One of the most pronounced differences in this regard appears between talk-based and medication-based addiction therapies. Whereas psychotherapeutic interventions and the Twelve Step program employ what Carr (2006: 634) calls an "ideology of inner reference" to teach addiction sufferers to represent themselves as particular types of people—namely, alcoholics and addicts—pharmacological treatments encourage users to think of themselves as "targeting and controlling specific elements of neurochemistry" rather than resisting cravings through force of will or with the aid of fellow sufferers (Vrecko 2006: 302). Thus, the argument is often made that where the "psychological self" that underlies psychotherapeutic discourse and practice has depth and internality, the "neurochemical self" encouraged by pharmaceutical interventions is "flattened"; where the former encourages self-transformation, the latter facilitates self-modulation (cf. Rose 2003b, 2007). Such differences may partially account for some of the resistance that pharmacological treatments for addiction have encountered.[13]

But such binary distinctions between talk-based and pharmaceutically based treatment modalities are often overdrawn and neglect the ways in which such treatments, in practice, plot a trajectory that produces novel therapeutic regimens. Such regimens typically include a host of interventions, including those that are neither talk-based nor pharmaceutically based but are rooted in other institutional discourses such as religion, law, or alternative medicine. Philippe Bourgois (2000), for instance, documents how criminalizing and medicalizing discourses coexist within a methadone treatment program, each serving as a unique vector for the exercise of power to the detriment of those enrolled in the program. Moreover, although treatment is often discussed as a discrete, defined (or, at least, definable) event in an individual addict's life, it often occupies a much more circumspect position. One need only look at the life of Alma as presented by Angela Garcia to see how certain treatment experiences can come to be seen simply as one more component of the addiction rather than the means for alleviating it. Attending to such combinations provides an alternative context in which to examine how particular therapeutic regimens work in the shaping of subjectivity.

Therapeutic regimens work to shape subjectivity not just through combination but also through contrast, providing treatment modalities that are often quite at odds with others on offer and effectively forcing (or enabling) individual addicts to choose between two different models of patienthood. Many of the contributors examine the interplay between competing therapies, not as products of different historical epochs, but as models that coexist in the same temporal frame. In the process, they reveal both significant differences and unforeseen similarities.

Helena Hansen, for instance, examines opioid maintenance therapy based in primary care offices in the United States and Pentecostal addiction ministries in Puerto Rico. The basic differences between these models seem overwhelming: whereas the Puerto Rican addiction ministries view addiction as part of a moral struggle and cater largely to a socially marginalized population (Hansen 2005), buprenorphine treatment operates under the assumption that addiction is a neurochemical disorder and, at least in the United States, has been used primarily by a relatively middle-class and socially integrated population. However, rather than casting buprenorphine treatment as a new departure and addiction ministries as a return to tradition, Hansen emphasizes how each of these models is largely novel even as it echoes much older conceptions of personhood. Moreover, the two therapies have more in common than one might initially think. Hansen shows that both "evangelism and buprenorphine are products of a unique postindustrial form of dislocation, of a radical individualism and anonymity that reflects unstable social connections, and a thin sense of authenticity and purpose." Not surprisingly, then, although each model puts the focus on personal choice and individual change as keys to therapeutic success, in practice the users of both of these therapeutic modalities are trying to forge collectivities through ties of illness and self-recovery.

Summerson Carr's contribution complements other chapters in that it examines an incipient shift in the model of addiction underlying contemporary treatment practices. However, in this case the shift was brought about not by the development of psychopharmaceutical interventions for addiction but by the dramatic rise of another expert modality: motivational interviewing (MI). Carr notes that while the world of addiction treatment is itself vast and varied in North America, it has for several decades been unified around the notion of addiction as a "disease of denial." She begins by drawing on fieldwork in a treatment program for homeless women in the U.S. Midwest. She shows how counselors, in an attempt to dissipate denial and demonstrate "insight," work to elicit verbal demonstrations of accurate self-knowledge from their clients, beginning with the pronouncement that one is an addict. These clients are conceptualized not as having impaired volition but as being problematically willful, a condition that Gregory Bateson (1972: 313) identified as "an unusually disastrous variant of the Cartesian dualism, the division between Mind and Matter, or, in this case, between conscious will, or 'self,' and the remainder of the personality." Carr illustrates how the clinical formulation of willful denial plays out in highly confrontational methods, wherein therapists insist that clients speak the inner truths that they presumably deny.

In contrast to this still dominant way to define and treat addiction in North America, Carr then traces the rapid ascendance of MI, a modality that carries with it a strikingly different set of assumptions about language, personhood, and addiction. Not only does MI lack an elaborated theory of human interiority—in a manner somewhat akin to the Russian behavioral methods described by Raikhel—it also lacks an articulated theory of addiction. Instead, Carr argues, MI is an operationalized theory of clinical communication, one that bears striking resemblance to speech act theory. So, rather than enjoining clients to articulate emotions, intentions, and memories presumed to lay hidden beneath denial, MI practitioners subtly encourage clients to voice "change statements," which are conceived as speech that precipitates rather than references intentions to change clients' drug-related behavior. With these two prominent sites of American addiction treatment in focus, Carr suggests that "if American addiction treatment produces particular types of people, with a special interest in generating sober ones, it does so largely because it reproduces and refines the representational media available to American speakers." She adds that with the continued rise of MI, we will witness the "baptism" of a new group of drug users who are authorized to produce as well as denote truths when they speak, suggesting that anthropologists and practitioners alike listen out for what they might say.

Raikhel's study of addiction medicine in Russia—narcology—adds another dimension to how unexpected therapeutic trajectories result in the blurring and interrelation of different therapeutic models. The dominant modalities of treatment for alcoholism in Russia are suggestion-based methods developed by narcology, a subspecialty of psychiatry that was established during the Soviet period to deal with addiction—at the time, primarily alcoholism. A particularly popular method is the use of disulfiram, an alcohol antagonist, for which narcologists commonly substitute neutral substances. The chapter examines the epistemological and institutional conditions that facilitate this practice of "placebo therapy." Raikhel argues that narcologists' embrace of such treatments has been shaped by a clinical style of reasoning specific to a Soviet and post-Soviet psychiatry, itself the product of contested Soviet politics over the knowledge of the mind and brain. This style of reasoning has facilitated narcologists' understanding of disulfiram as a behavioral rather than a pharmacological treatment and has disposed them to amplify patients' responses through attention to the performative aspects of the clinical encounter and through management of the treatment's broader reputation as an effective therapy. Moreover, the methods of behavioral modification that make up the clinical armamentarium of narcology do not encourage patients to identify with their illness, as is common in many North American approaches to therapy. Rather than attempting to transform patients' subjectivities, these methods work by harnessing their preexisting ideas, beliefs, and affects, with an end result that is experienced as a change in behavior or practice without a change in self.

This chapter also reminds us that, like other technologies, therapeutic and administrative techniques for the management of addiction are increasingly tracing new spatial and cultural trajectories as they are exported to settings beyond their countries of origin.[14] Moreover, many of these modalities of therapy and harm reduction, ranging from mutual-help movements modeled on AA to therapeutic communities to methadone maintenance therapy and needle-exchange programs, are also embedded in or associated with larger institutional configurations and transnational projects (Walby 2008). These projects, in turn, can have profound effects on how issues are framed and addressed locally. To take only the most obvious example, the rise of the HIV/AIDS epidemic and the subsequent development of an assemblage of organizations, institutions, policies, and techniques to address it has had profound effects on the management of drug dependence, bringing the spectrum of harm-reduction approaches to the mainstream and, in some cases, shifting the moral valence surrounding intravenous drug users by reframing them as at-risk (Bourgois 2000).

Taken together, many of the chapters in this volume reveal how addiction therapeutics traverse the life of the addicted subject. The promises offered by therapeutics, typically framed in terms of self-management and ongoing recovery rather than "cure," are often at odds with the institutional imperatives that underlie treatment in practice. For example, Bourgois and Jeffrey Schonberg (2009) describe how homeless heroin users in San Francisco regularly expressed a desire to "go clean" and would enter treatment programs periodically for this purpose, particularly in the wake of sudden life crises.[15] Schonberg's extended account of his attempt to transport one key informant to a treatment program after she decided to go clean demonstrates in rich detail the multiple challenges and resistances addicts face when they attempt to enter recovery. Some of these arise from the addiction itself. But many others, as Bourgois and Schonberg show, are rooted more deeply in U.S. practices of drug management: inadequate funding for in-patient treatment programs, the lack of follow-up services for those trying to recover, the difficulties finding gainful employment in the licit market, and resistance to the expansion of methadone maintenance all complicate the efforts of those who want to address their addiction through therapeutic measures. Moreover, many of these challenges have been deepened by the restructuring of social-service provision according to a neoliberal logic of governance over the past decades (Fairbanks 2009).

The notion of therapeutic trajectories allows us to trace the often contradictory, always contingent existences of addiction therapies across individual lives, institutional spaces, and geographic contexts. By glimpsing the contradictions of the treatment system through the eyes of those trying to access it, we see how it is lived, employed, traversed. Moreover, highlighted through the lens of trajectory, we see an additional promise that therapeutics hold out to would-be recipients of treatment, perhaps the most fundamental: a possible exit from the cycle of addiction or, at the very least, the means to make life livable again, even if this means remaining within the confines of the addiction.

Experiential and Experimental Trajectories

Taking the historical contingency of addiction into account means that the "givenness" of addiction can no longer be taken for granted. While, again, not discounting the experiential reality of addiction, such a move forces us to look at this experience in terms of the wider systems of knowledge and practice from which the category of addiction derives its meaning and force. This includes efforts in science to define addiction, as well as efforts in the fields of medicine, law, and religion, just to name a few, to develop treatments and other forms of intervention targeting addiction. Indeed, the history of addiction in many ways is the history of its treatment as efforts to define this modern malady have taken place against the backdrop of its wider problematization. That is, addiction emerges as an object of inquiry and concern only when its associated behaviors become incompatible with the demands and expectations of modern life (Levine 1978; Vrecko 2010b).

From this perspective, addiction is revealed to be deeply implicated in questions of human vitality and what has come to be called "the politics of life itself" (Rose 2007). This politics includes the functioning of the life processes, the making of personal identities and connections, and even the "will to live" (Biehl and Eskerod 2007: 17). The continued pursuit of scientific knowledge of addiction has expanded our understanding of human vitality at the level of "life itself," shaping and reshaping how we understand ourselves and interact with the world (Campbell 2007; Franklin 2000; Rose 2007; Schüll 2012). This knowledge has, in turn, enabled numerous forms of intervention that give shape to "life as such," or life understood as "the course of events which occurs from birth to death, which can be shortened by political or structural violence, which can be prolonged by health and social policies, which gives place to cultural interpretations and moral decisions, which may be told or written—life which is lived through a body (not only through cells) and as a society (not only as species)" (Fassin 2009: 48). This orientation toward life reveals a politics centered less on "normalization" than on "deciding the sort of life that people may or may not live" (Fassin 2009: 48; cf. Bourgois and Schonberg 2009). It is thus a politics that understands that life (the vital) is never fully separated from its other—namely, death (the lethal).

Caught up in the interplay between the vital and the lethal, addiction can be seen, in two related ways, as a kind of "experimental system." The historian of science Hans-Jörg Rheinberger (1997: 238) has defined an experimental system as "a basic unit of experimental activity combining local, technical, instrumental, institutional, social, and epistemic aspects." Rheinberger used this term to describe the social context of laboratory science, and anthropologists have described as "experimentality" the enrollment of people living in resource- and institution-poor settings into clinical trials and treatment programs run by NGOs (Nguyen 2009; Petryna 2007). We see something that resembles this notion of "government-by-experiment" (Nguyen 2009: 211) and its associated assemblage of institutions, technologies, discursive practices, people, and capital in Lovell's account of the French state's attempt to pull drug addicts into the space of healthcare provision and social citizenship through the promotion of high-dose buprenorphine as an opiate-substitution therapy (see this volume and Lovell 2006). More broadly, the chapters by Schüll, Garriott, Meyers, Raikhel, and Hansen all trace unique configurations of the institutional, the social, the discursive, and the material through which experimental trajectories of addiction are forged.

However, recalling the etymological links between "experiment" and "experience," we might conceive of experimentality in a slightly different way (Desjarlais 1997; Cynthia Scott 1991: 781; Williams 1985: 126). Do we not see the same types of combination taking place as the drug user, gambler, or whoever throws himself or herself into a series of personal experiments with gambling or the drug—the kind of experiments that Walter Benjamin undertook with hashish to achieve a new orientation to the world (Benjamin 2006)? Should we not attend to this illicit form of experimentality, the combinations it produces, and its consequences?[16] In short, addiction, viewed along an experiential and experimental trajectory, is implicated in the "acting out" of technoscience (Biehl et al. 2001), as well as in forms of production and consumption, the effects of which are often unknown and unpredictable at the outset.

Thus, while addiction may indeed at times be an "unhealthy selection of a chemical solution to discomforting experiences" (Singer 2006: 10), as some have argued, it may also be understood as a form of experimentation or intervention at the level of life itself. From this perspective, so-called self-medication—and the idea that one is numbing oneself to the social world—is but one way to understand what is taking place when a person engages in substance use, gambling, or any other "habit-forming" behavior (Das and Das 2007). Another possibility is to see it as a way to harness the experiential or experimental potential of the body by means of a particular substance or activity (such as gambling or sex). From this perspective, social relations are significant not simply as contextual factors that explain a person's movement into substance abuse or addiction or as products of the hegemonic forces of unequal power relations, but as relational and experiential ends in themselves. These are part and parcel of the new trajectories of experience opened up—at least, initially—by means of the addiction.

This kind of illicit experimentality is not without risk. Deleuze has observed that such vital experimentation carries with it a lethal component, which tempers any celebration of substance use (or addiction) as an unqualified form of escape, enjoyment, or resistance. Indeed, accounting for this moment or process in which the vital becomes lethal remains a key challenge in the theorization of drugs and other objects of addiction (Deleuze 2007; cf. Biehl 2010). The analytic task from this perspective is to attend closely to the kinds of experimentation taking place and trace them back (and forward) to the subjective milieux from which they originate and (possibly) return. It means following the trajectories set in motion by this experimentation, even as they may lead the subject to self-destruction (Garcia, this volume). Deleuze defines this state abstractly as "the contrary of connections." He brings the question of drug use generally to that of addiction specifically when he asks, "Why and how is this experience, even when self-destructive, but still vital, transformed into a deadly enterprise of generalized, unilinear dependence? Is it inevitable? If there is a precise point, that is where therapy should intervene" (Deleuze 2007: 254).

Meyers examines the interplay of vital and lethal forces in the treatment experiences of adolescents in Baltimore. Cedric and Megan were both heroin users who became enrolled in a local treatment center. They were also enrolled in a clinical trial for the opiate replacement therapy Suboxone. Meyers's ethnographic approach in which he "followed" Cedric and Megan in their movement inside and outside the clinic across various sites of experimentality (both licit and illicit), revealed a number of distinct ambiguities in the experience of therapeutics. Among his most notable findings were the novel therapeutic practices Cedric and Megan developed in their use of Suboxone and management of their own addiction. This included the combined use of heroin, Suboxone, and sometimes OxyContin at various dosages. Cedric and Megan diligently recorded the date, time, and dosage levels involved in their efforts to slowly replace their heroin use with Suboxone. These practices, which functioned as a kind of "simulacrum of clinical reasoning," as Meyers describes it, did not fully comport with the rigorous expectations of the clinical trial process. Yet, as Meyers shows, these practices were not seen as novel or devious by Cedric and Megan. Rather, they were a faithful reproduction of the therapeutic process of replacement therapy they were learning about at both the treatment center and in the clinical trial. As Cedric himself put it, "It just like in group, you know, cut back a little, and a little more, and bad days less, and some day, you know, cured."

While the use of opiate replacement therapy to treat addicts like Cedric and Megan raised concerns in Baltimore about drug diversion and other forms of illicit use, Meyers shows that, in the lives of adolescents like Cedric and Megan, it carried several meanings and sustained various relationships. Perhaps its most significant impact on Cedric and Megan was that it held out the possibility of a future free from heroin. Cedric himself uses the term "cure" to describe the future he envisioned for himself and Megan, contradicting contemporary ideas about addiction as a chronic, relapsing disease in which cure is impossible. The stories of Cedric and Megan thus reveal the novel forms of experimentality at work in addiction and its treatment, as well as the blurred boundaries between the two as pharmaceutical interventions such as Suboxone move to the forefront of addiction therapeutics, replacing one object of habitual use with another.

Attending to the experiences of those whose lives have become defined by addiction offers a profound vantage point from which to view the interplay of vital and lethal forces that defines the addicted experience. Indeed, understanding experience as a driver of such trajectories (rather than simply a means of apprehending them) was a central tenet of some of the earliest important social science work on addiction (H. Becker 1953; Lindesmith 1938). Similarly, in focusing on the trajectories subjects trace in relation to addiction, such as those of Cedric and Megan, the chapters in this volume draw our attention to the motives driving this movement. A desire to locate and consume the object of addiction is a prominent motivation, as is the need to obtain resources, but so is the desire to avoid the substance and manage the addiction, to access therapeutic resources and achieve a sense of stasis. These trajectories typically intertwine and often in ways that make them difficult to distinguish.

As we see in these chapters, following subjects over the course of their trajectories opens up not only lives but milieux. Indeed, addiction itself can be seen both as a trajectory and as a milieu; it is both traversing and traversed. As described in Campbell's chapter, the contemporary science and treatment of addiction has attempted to come to terms with this quality of addiction through the discourse of "triggers"—those sights, sounds, smells, and people that are associated with using a particular substance and are understood to have the power to arouse the desire to use again. Those who have participated in AA will often discuss the need to change their "people, places and things" as an essential step in their recovery. These signal recognition of the importance of the milieux in which addiction occurs and into which subjects are "thrown" (see Campbell and Garcia, this volume). Moreover, such milieux may be shaped or structured in significant ways. As Daniel Lende aptly puts it, "Given how modern societies approach drug use—often demonizing it and confining its use to marginalized places of the social map—drug cues and drug availabilities come packaged together in specific environments" (2012: 349).

But anthropologists take this dimension further to show the broader impact of this highly charged relationship between addiction and its milieux. For example, in her chapter, Angela Garcia tells the story of Alma and her agonistic relationship with heroin. In following Alma's physical and imagined movements from a detox clinic to a Christian fellowship to the town of her childhood and, ultimately, to the local emergency room, Garcia reveals how the historical loss of land, culture, and integrity in the Española Valley provides the backdrop to what has become the area of the United States with the highest per capita rates of heroin overdose. Alma sees "no exit" (*no hay salida*) from her addiction, a view rooted in the dovetailing of local Hispano tropes of loss and endlessness and the clinical concept of chronicity, as well as in her own experience using and trying not to use heroin. These local sentiments of loss emerge from "structures of feeling" shaped by many decades of land loss and expropriation among Hispano inhabitants of the Española Valley, suggesting a structuring of affect that is spatial as much as it is temporal (Williams 1977).

In a similar vein, Lovell charts the experiences of *les russes* on their paths of medical travel as they are "caught up in biopolitical strategies of survival" that define our current age. In this way, she challenges contemporary paradigms of biological citizenship, particularly the idea that claims for citizenship and asylum based on illness carry more weight than those based on poverty, injustice, or violence, given the difficulty faced by those who try to make political claims using the illness of addiction (Fassin 2005; Nguyen 2005; Petryna 2002; Ticktin 2006).

Nowhere, perhaps, is the relationship between movement, trajectory, and milieu more evident than in the map drawn by Mollie and reproduced by Schüll in her chapter about video gamblers in Las Vegas. In this illustration, Mollie represents the various loci involved in her addiction to machine gambling. Notably, these include spaces of play and recovery—the casino and Gambler's Anonymous, respectively—as well as sites not so easily classified, such as the grocery store and the 7-Eleven. These spaces are linked to form a circle, at the center of which is Mollie herself, seated before a video gambling machine. Notably, this representation of her experience provides no point of entry or exit—only a closed system of spaces, routes, and locations she must traverse. In the same way, the system has no obvious end, no point at which Mollie might embark on a new trajectory (Schüll 2012).[17]

Mollie's map charts a territory at once external and internal to her experience. From a temporal perspective, it is a route she has traversed many times before but also anticipates traversing again. In its representation of routes, spaces, and places, it refers to "real" locations: the MGM Grand Hotel, the 7-Eleven, the electronic gambling machine. Indeed, along with other scholars inspired by actor-network theory, Schüll pays close attention to the materiality of these spaces and objects, and to the effects of their particular configurations (2012; cf. Duff 2011; Gomart 2004; Weinberg 2011). However, in Mollie's experience of them, and particularly in her experience of them as constitutive loci of her addiction, these spaces and places take on an imaginary quality. The trajectory she traverses over the course of her addiction signifies a space where the real and imaginary meet. Mollie's map thus charts the kinds of trajectories that emerge through the movement spurred on by addiction. These trajectories eventually become constitutive of the experimental system of addiction, blurring the distinction between addiction and subjectivity, trajectory, and milieu. This may even reach a point of lethality for the subject, as it did for Alma, where the only exit is death.

Conclusion

As we have suggested, addiction offers a particularly fruitful area for the advancement of anthropological theory today because it is a privileged site where individual experiences of desire, pleasure, and suffering; the expertise of professionals in medicine, psychotherapy, and the law; and the regulatory ambitions of the state intersect in ways that blur the distinction between the vital and the lethal, the normal and the pathological, illness and treatment. Although we make no claim to a unified theory of "the addicted subject"—indeed, such a claim would be at cross-purposes with the understanding of addiction presented here—the contributors to this volume nevertheless demonstrate a common concern with what we have called "addiction trajectories." This notion encompasses several distinct kinds of movement: that of ideas through time and space, of interventions through diverse institutional domains, and of subjects across the dimensions of experience and subjectivity.

As the story of Pavel with which we began the introduction shows, addicts are agents of the contemporary world trying to navigate its distinct contours. They are subjects seeking transformations at the level of their own personhood and experience; they are objects of knowledge for contemporary science and other epistemic cultures; and they are targets of a host of therapeutic interventions, from the medical to the punitive. The movement of those living with addiction depends on the kinds of trajectories—epistemic, therapeutic, experiential, and experimental—we have described here, bringing into being new configurations of people, ideas, and interventions.

Notes

1. Although "addiction" is the closest English translation for the term "toxicomania," the two should not be taken as strict synonyms. In the French context, "toxicomania" developed in a unique historical, institutional, and national context and has often been articulated self-consciously as an alternative to the Anglo-American addiction paradigm. A key distinguishing feature of the toxicomania paradigm is its largely psychoanalytic orientation (Lovell 2006). Narcology—the specialty of addiction medicine in post-Soviet countries—uses two terms: "narko-maniia" and "toksikomaniia," the former generally denoting dependence to illicit drugs and the latter to pharmaceuticals (Babayan and Gonopolsky 1985).
2. Much of this literature emerged from the work on "grounded theory" by the medical sociologist Anselm Strauss. Like the correlate and contemporary notion

of the "illness narrative," the concept of the illness trajectory was used partly to carve out a space for the study of both the social shaping of illness and the subjective experience of illness by its sufferers.

3. The NIMH lists one of the primary objectives of its 2008 Strategic Plan as "Chart Mental Illness Trajectories to Determine When, Where, and How to Intervene."

4. Hacking takes the term "historical ontology" from Foucault's "What Is Enlightenment?" (1984): "This could be the name of a study, [Foucault] said, that was concerned with 'truth through which we constitute ourselves as objects of knowledge,' with 'power through which we constitute ourselves as subjects acting on others,' and with 'ethics through which we constitute ourselves as moral agents.' He calls these the axes of power, knowledge and ethics" (Hacking 2002: 2). More specifically, Hacking (2002: 11) writes, "My historical ontology is concerned with objects or their effects which do not exist in any recognizable form until they are objects of scientific knowledge."

5. In his landmark essay "The Discovery of Addiction" (1978), Harry Levine attributes the first clear articulation of a disease model of addiction to the eighteenth-century physician Benjamin Rush of Philadelphia. Levine argues that Rush's model differed significantly from previous understandings of drunkenness in four ways: "First, he identified the causal agent—spirituous liquors; second, he clearly described the drunkard's condition as loss of control over drinking behavior—as compulsive activity; third, he declared the condition to be a disease; and fourth, he prescribed total abstinence as the only way to cure the drunkard" (Levine 1978: 152). Despite challenges to Levine's claim regarding the origins of the disease model, it seems that widespread medical consensus regarding alcoholism as a disease did not come until the nineteenth century (Porter 1985; Warner 1994).

6. Although notions of "willpower" are largely absent from most of today's biomedical conceptualizations of addiction, the same argument has been made in regard to the place of addiction under contemporary neoliberal conditions, particularly vis-à-vis the valorization of freedom (O'Malley and Valverde 2004; Reith 2004; Seddon 2007).

7. As Craig Reinarman (2005: 313) argues, "In 1942, the Alcoholism Movement was founded by Marty Mann, a public relations executive and former 'drunk,' and others. By 1944, she [had] joined with Dr. E. M. Jellinek at Yale to create an organization whose purpose was to popularize the disease concept by putting it on a scientific footing. Note the chronology: science was not the source of the concept but a resource for promoting it. This organization later became the National Council on Alcoholism. . . . Their goal was to create a new 'scientific' approach that would allow them to get beyond the old, moralistic 'wet' versus 'dry' battlelines of the Temperance and Prohibition period" (Reinarman cites Roizen 1991).

8. Even the "disease model" widely associated with AA and the Twelve Step movement stands in an ambivalent relationship to the medicalization of alcoholism in that it uses the notion of disease instrumentally as a means to alleviate stigma and counter notions of moral responsibility while simultaneously espousing an un-

derstanding of alcoholism that places a much greater emphasis on psychosocial and spiritual frameworks (Valverde 1998; Wilcox 1998).

9. Dingel and Koenig (2008) address what in some ways is the converse issue, examining how racial categories enter scientific discourse and practice in genetic research on addiction.

10. See the website at http://www.nida.nih.gov.

11. For example, addiction to prescribed drugs—in itself in no way novel—has grown in scale and become the object of increased focus in the public sphere along with the increasing prevalence of psychotropic medications. Thus, during the first decade of the twenty-first century, prescription and over-the-counter medications were reported to be the second most common class of drugs used for nonmedical purposes by U.S. high school students (after marijuana), and the issue of potential chemical dependence has been prominent in debates over the merits of selective serotonin reuptake inhibitors (SSRIs) and other common antidepressants (Haddad 2001; Johnston et al. 2009; Medawar 1997).

12. Additional blurring of previously distinct categories is taking place at the regulatory level. At the same time that tobacco is coming under the regulation of the U.S. Food and Drug Administration—and is thus framed in medicalized and public health terms—marijuana is increasingly coming under medical regulation, as well, although on different jurisdictional levels and in rather different ways (P. Benson 2010).

13. Just as various neurobiological disease concepts have encountered resistance in the form of choice-based ideas about the subject, so have attempts to develop pharmacological treatments for various addictions encountered particular kinds of resistance (Room 2004).

14. While many (though certainly not all) proponents of these methods assume that clinical and therapeutic technologies are discrete, portable, and transposable between contexts with little transformation, anthropologists have shown in great detail how various modes of treatment have been transformed in their encounter with local styles of clinical reasoning, medical traditions, and assumptions about illness and personhood. Anthropologists have examined Twelve Step groups in various cultural settings, including groups focused on co-dependency in Japan (Borovoy 2001, 2005) and AA in Mexico City (Brandes 2002). In ongoing work, Sandra Hyde (2011) examines the development of therapeutic community-type rehabilitation centers for heroin addiction in China, and Alex Golub and Kate Lingley (2008) have looked at the rise of Chinese discourses about "Internet addiction" as part of a moral crisis associated with a number of ongoing and profound social, economic, and technological changes.

15. Similarly, Caroline Jean Acker (2002) notes how heroin users in the first part of the twentieth century used treatment as a way to manage their addiction and bring their heroin use under control. Here the objective, from the subject's perspective, was not to stop using but to return use to a more manageable state.

16. We intend for our use of the term "experimental" not to be limited to the North American middle-class notion of "experimenting with drugs" but to refer more

broadly to the use of psychoactive substances or various practices in an attempt to open up horizons of possibility, whether affective, experiential, or social, albeit often in fleeting, compromised, and deeply constrained ways.

17. Natasha Schüll makes this argument in her discussion of Mollie's map in the introduction to her book: "The road that she drew features no exits, appearing instead as a closed circuit of stations where various vices—as well as their remedies—may be pursued. Inside this circuit, she hung with no clear grounding except the machine onto which she held. 'Where is that?' I asked when she had completed the sketch, pointing at the human-machine pair in the middle of the page. 'That's nowhere,' she responded; 'that's the zone'" (Schüll 2012: 26).

THE ELEGIAC ADDICT

Eternal Return

On the cusp of her thirtieth birthday, Alma Gallegos was discovered lying in the parking lot near the emergency-room entrance at Española Hospital. Like many patients who present at this particular ER, Alma was anonymously dumped by acquaintances who likely feared she might die or was already dead.[1] In fact, Alma was close to death: her breath was shallow; her heart rate barely discernible at six beats per minute; and, despite the intense summer heat, her skin cold to the touch. Upon quick inspection of her swollen limbs, the attending physician determined that Alma had overdosed on heroin, and she was treated with naloxone, an opioid antidote that, if administered in time, revives the body's central nervous and respiratory systems. Alma's vital signs were soon stabilized, and she remained in the hospital until the local drug court mandated that she be transferred to the very drug treatment facility from which she had recently discharged herself.

Four days after her overdose, Alma emerged from the facility's women's dormitory. With one hand against the wall for support, she shuffled unsteadily down a narrow hallway and entered her drug counselor's office with a groan. Having privately suffered through the initial torments of heroin withdrawal, it was now expected that she begin putting addictive experience into a social and linguistic frame—an exercise central to the clinic's therapeutic process. Alma pulled at her hair uncomfortably; her body twitched, and pebbles of sweat collected on her brow. For several minutes, she looked around the small, windowless office and stared blankly at the counselor. Finally, she asked in the Hispano manner (i.e., more statement than question): "Yo estuve aquí una vez, no?" (I've been here before, haven't I?)[2]

Indeed, it was Alma's second admission to the detoxification clinic in a year and her sixth admission to a drug recovery program in just five years. Addicted to heroin for half of her life, Alma's affective world—from her embodied pains to her cravings and the quietude she experiences during a heroin high—were as familiar to her as the institutions intermittently charged with apprehending or caring for her. It was a familiarity achieved through certain recurring personal and institutional fractures, indexed by long stretches of heroin use, arrest, mandatory treatment, and an eventual and ongoing return to heroin use, arrest, and treatment.

In clinical parlance, Alma's return to detox was a "relapse." Such a determination was in accordance with the logic of contemporary public health and addiction medicine, which understands and treats drug addiction primarily as a "chronic health problem, not a moral failing or a social problem" (McLellan et al. 2000). But Alma understood her presence at the clinic less as a "relapse," which connotes a period of remission, than as a "return"—a return to living "once more and innumerable times more" (Nietzsche 1974: 274) this particular aspect of Hispano life; these weary limbs, this room, this familiar and anticipated question now posed to her by the drug counselor: What happened?

For several moments, Alma pulled at her hair and let the question linger. Then she told the counselor that nothing had happened. "Es que lo que tengo no termina" (It's just that what I have has no end), she said. Yet almost two years later, Alma was rushed to the same hospital ER, where she was pronounced dead after overdosing on heroin.

This chapter considers heroin addiction and overdose in northern New Mexico's Española Valley as a vexing condition marked by the impossibility and the inevitability of an end. It reflects on observations and interviews I conducted with Alma between 2004 and 2006 and gives a sense of her struggle to reconcile this condition's inherent contradictions. Among its primary concerns are how recurring forms of personal and institutional experience configure the struggle—as well as the ways Alma would come to apprehend her world, her addiction, and, ultimately, the horizon of her future. The stress here is on the political and psychoanalytic, and I link local modalities of emotion, perception, and subjectivity—writ large as heroin addiction—to certain historical refrains.[3] My goal is to explore how ongoing political, economic, cultural, and biological forces constituted Alma's life—and her determination that it was not worth living.

The Melancholic Subject

The Española Valley is a rural network of poor, Spanish-speaking villages at the center of a triangle whose points are the tourist meccas of Santa Fe and Taos and the scientific center of Los Alamos. It encompasses the site of the first Spanish colonial settlement in the U.S. Southwest (where present-day Española resides) and is the site of centuries of colonial exploitation, resistance, and change. Since the 1990s, the region has had the highest rate of heroin overdose and heroin-induced death in the country. In a population of just over thirty thousand residents, nearly seventy people died from heroin overdose in one recent eighteen-month period—which is to say that nearly everybody knows somebody addicted to heroin or who has died because of it. The social and emotional wake of these deaths reverberates with the still tender wounds of recent history, such as the ongoing Hispano dispossession from, and longing for, ancestral lands and the consequent fragmentation of social order and intimate life. These constitute a recurring experience of loss that, if not directly assimilable, is nevertheless familiar in the sense of the very structure of recurrence and in the sense of the close connection this structure has to forms of loss: the loss of a tradition, a village, a daughter, a friend. My concern here is about these experiences of loss and memories of it, how intersecting forms of history come to bear on the present, and how heroin use—and overdose in particular— exposes the painful recognition that the future has been swallowed up by the past.

In "Mourning and Melancholia," Freud (1989 [1917]: 586) defines mourning as "the reaction to the loss of a loved person, or to the loss of some abstraction." It designates a psychic process to loss where the mourner is able to work gradually through grief, reaching a definite conclusion whereby the lost object or ideal is essentially let go and the mourner able to move on. Melancholy, by contrast, designates a kind of mourning without end. It entails an incorporation of the lost person or ideal as a means to keep it alive. Regarding its somatic features, Freud describes the sleeplessness of the melancholic, suggesting that it attests to the steadfastness of the condition. "The complex of melancholia," he writes, "behaves like an open wound" (S. Freud 1989 [1917]: 589).

In Freud's conception, the melancholic's sustained devotion to what is lost is pathological. He warns that the intensity of the "self-tormenting" condition can culminate in the melancholic's demise—most notably, via suicide (S. Freud 1989 [1917]: 588). More recent efforts to examine Freud's exploration of melancholia have been critical of his understanding of it as pathology and have offered important modifications to his theory—particularly the productive possibilities of melancholy in terms of subjectivity, art, and politics (see Butler 2004; Cheng 2001; Eng and Kazanjian 2003; Muñoz 1997). But here I want to pursue Freud's original suggestion regarding the danger to life melancholy may pose. In *The Ego and the Id*, Freud (1960 [1923]: 28) writes that melancholy possesses the power to shape the subject in a fundamental way—indeed, to determine the subject's very fate. The unrelenting nature of melancholy transforms the subject into one who mourns—transforms her, first and foremost, into a melancholic subject. But what if we conceive the subject of melancholy not simply as the one who suffers, but as the recurring historical refrains through which sentiments of "endless" suffering arise? How do we attend to these wounds?

The "melancholic subject" here is Alma and the structures in which her fatal overdose took root. And it refers to the all-too-familiar experiences of loss, articulated now as addiction, which have been shaped in part by the kinds of attachments that the logic of chronicity assumes. The recent work of anthropologists shows us how medical and technical forms of knowledge and intervention shape the experience and course of illness and more broadly affect subjectivity (Biehl 2005; Cohen 1999; Petryna 2002; Scheper-Hughes 2000; Young 1995). In the context of addiction, chronicity as knowledge and practice has become the ground for a new form of melancholic subjectivity that recasts a longstanding ethos of Hispano suffering into a succession of recurring institutional interactions. As Michael Fischer (2003: 51) describes, "We are embedded, ethically, as well as existentially and materially, in technologies and technological prostheses," and these take us into new models of ethics in which "our older moral traditions have little guidance or experience to offer." In the context of emerging technologies, he aptly describes us as being "*thrown* . . . to new forms of social life" (Fischer 2003: 51; emphasis added). But here, I want to suggest that the Hispano ethos of suffering is a social referent for addiction's recent biomedical turn, and the disparate technologies in which this turn is embedded (drug-treatment centers, research conferences, Narcotics Anonymous meetings, and so on) deepen this ethos of suffering in unexpected, even dangerous, ways. In the context of its preceding Hispano forms, I examine how these technologies not so much throw us but *bury* us beneath the weight of that which does not end.

A Work of Mourning

Anthropology has shown how following the life history of a single person can illuminate the complex intimate and structural relations that come to constitute a life, a community, and a social world (Biehl 2005; Das 2000; Desjarlais 2003; Pandolfo 1998). In following the plot of Alma's life, I also engage in this form of inquiry. I do so while recognizing that there are many elements of Alma's story that I do not know and other elements that could be told in the voice of Bernadette, Yvette, Johnny, Marcus, or any of the many other subjects I followed during the course of my research. They were all caught within the same cycle of trying to live their lives without heroin and surrendering their lives to it. I thus present Alma as embodying a condition that is more than hers alone.

While there are certain refrains between Alma's experience and the experience of Hispanos more broadly, one of my commitments here is to convey Alma as she appeared to me—generous, reflective, and deeply engaged in trying to find a way to live. In relating Alma's life, and in trying to reckon for her death, this chapter constitutes a kind of "work of mourning," but in terms that differ from recent anthropological works on violence and subjectivity, which examine discursive practices that seek to make possible the repair of injury and of the everyday (see Das 2000; Seremetakis 1991). Instead, this chapter constitutes a work of mourning in another tradition: the Hispano tradition, which commemorates the singularity of death while insisting on the inevitable repetition of it. It is a tradition that involves the creation of memorials called *descansos* (resting places) that are publicly placed at or near the site of death. The descanso does not seek to reinhabit the site of loss or repair the everyday; rather, it insists on death's essential relationship to life. Over the years, heroin-related descansos have gathered on the Hispano landscape. Frequently adorned with the used syringes that contained the lethal dose of drug, they highlight just how enmeshed heroin has become in physical space and everyday life, and they pose the question of whether and how "mourning as repair" is possible or even desired in the face of unrelenting loss. Rising along the edges of dirt roads and scattered among the valley's juniper-dotted hills, the undisturbed presence of the descansos constitutes a kind of ethical commitment to that which was lost. They keep vigil over it; they coexist.

One day, while we were sitting together in my parked car in front of the Española Public Library, a certain memory flashed up for Alma, urgent and unannounced. It was a cold afternoon, already dark despite the early hour. I turned on the car's ignition and was ready to return Alma to the halfway house in which she resided following thirty days of heroin detox-ification. To my surprise, Alma grabbed my hand and told me to wait; she wasn't ready to go back. For a few moments, we stared quietly at the library's iron-barred windows, our breath visible in the chilly air. Alma broke the silence and told me that her older sister Ana, whom she had never mentioned to me before, loved to read. Ana had been killed by a drunk driver four years earlier. She had been on her way to work, Alma recalled, driving along the winding two-lane highway that connects Es-pañola to Chimayó. Days before her death, Ana had called Alma to share the news that she was pregnant.

Following local custom, the Gallegos family put up a handmade de-scanso in the very spot that Ana was killed. Alma told me that afternoon in front of the library that it still marked the spot of her sister's death and asked if I'd seen it. She described the plastic yellow flowers and fading family portrait that adorned Ana's wooden cross. I told Alma that I knew the descanso and offered to drive her there. Alma shook her head no and added that for years she had to turn her head away every time she passed the cross during the trip to Chimayó to meet her dealer. She confessed that she still turned her head away but was able to conjure the image of the descanso in her mind. She said, "Ahí está, mirándome" (There it is, look-ing at me).[4]

In his examination of the English elegy, Peter Sacks (1985) notes that the traditional forms and figures of the genre relate to an experience of loss and the search for consolation. The passage from grief to consolation is often presented in the form of repetition—that is, through the recur-rence of certain words and refrains. Take, for example, Theocratis's "First Idyl," the poem said to have initiated the elegiac genre: "I weep for Adonis; lovely Adonis is dead. Dead is lovely Adonis; the Loves join in weeping" (quoted in Sacks 1985: 23). According to Sacks, the elegy's repetitive structure functions to separate the living from the dead and forces the bereaved to accept a loss that he might otherwise refuse. He goes on to suggest that the reiterative structure of elegy mirrors one of the psychological responses to trauma, whereby the psyche repeats the traumatic event to retroactively alleviate the initial shock it caused. In this way, the repetition creates a rhythm of lament that allows grief to be simultaneously conjured forth and laid to rest. But what if the structure of repetition creates not a working through grief but the intensification of it? What if the demarcation between the living and dead instead reinforces the shock of loss and represents a refusal to "properly mourn"? How might the structure of repetition become a constitutive force for a kind of mourning that does not end?

Alma's past returned to her in feeling and image, inducing a never-ending tension—not a resolution—between today and yesterday, between the dead and the living. Like the descanso that marks her sister's death, the elegiac character of Alma's narrative offers a continuous double-take on thinking about the relationship between history, loss, and the present: what is lost *is* what remains. In Alma's words, it is "sin fin" (without end), forging the patterns of her experience.

The Entanglements of Time

In thinking about the temporal dimensions of loss and sentiment, I have found Raymond Williams's concept of "structure of feeling" particularly useful. Structure of feeling roughly describes the interaction between experience and memory that relate cultural identities to a particular place and a time; it refers to a constellation of "specifically affective elements of consciousness and relationships; not feeling against thought, but thought as felt and feeling as thought." (Williams 1977: 132). This constellation is derived from lived, material histories that become embodied in changing cultural practices, in meanings, and in emotional resonances. According to Williams, at any given time, multiple structures of feeling are in operation, corresponding roughly to the generations living at that time. Each generation creates its own structure of feeling in response to the world it inherits—taking up or abandoning the value, sentiments, and practices of its predecessors. A particular structure of feeling thus has elements of the dominant, the residual, and the emergent. His way of thinking about "the living substance of perceptions and relationships" (Williams 1977: 34) thus has a temporal dimension that helps elucidate the historical and interlocking nature of experience and affect.

Consider, for instance, expressions often repeated among elder Hispanos: "Todo es historia" (History is everything). It is a saying that simultaneously acknowledges the loss of times past and the longing for continuity in a precarious and changing world. Another, "La historia es una herida" (History is a wound), is frequently evoked in the context of expressing the material and cultural losses that resulted from the region's past. And another, "Chiva es el remedio para todo" (Heroin cures everything), is repeated by the addicted. Thus, while elders worry that the younger generation is all too willing to forget the past, the young are just as likely to understand the heroin problem as a contemporary consequence of it while still offering heroin as a remedy for the pain that accompanies the past. In this way, young and old insist that to meaningfully address the heroin problem, one must also address the region's deep historical scars.

There are other kinds of scars, such as those on the skin. The needle marks and abscesses that mapped Alma's body—open wounds in the literal sense—powerfully attested to how addiction is also a historical formation and immanent experience. These are wounds in which the future, the present, and the past commingle through the force of recurring need: the need to score heroin, the need to get high, the need to find a vein. Alma once described it to me this way: "The thing about being hooked is you're always thinking ahead, thinking about your next fix, how you're going to get the money, where it's going to come from. It goes on and on. . . . And now, I've been using so long, nothing ever lasts. The high . . . it's over before you know it, and you're back to it, thinking about the next fix, making calls. It never stops."

Byron Good notes that in the context of illness narratives, the autobiographical narrator is telling a story that is not yet finished—that more than one temporality is woven together in a narrative (Good 1994; see also Garro 1992). Indeed, in the context of talking about her addiction, Alma expressed all of the following: the experience of past heroin use; her current condition, which she identified as being worse than before and therefore foreshadowed a grim future; and the inevitability of further heroin use. Such entanglements show how time and the Hispano trope of endlessness are reworked through the experience of addiction. And it is mediated again through the explanatory model of chronicity.

Briefly, the model of chronicity likens addiction to a lifelong disease process, such as asthma, diabetes, or hypertension. From this perspective, addiction is enduring; relapses are an expected occurrence; and treatment is long term and partially effective. The chronicity model initially emerged as a response to the high incidence of repeated relapse seen among addicts who entered publicly funded treatment programs (and, as an aside, thus neutralizes the failure of these institutions to care for the addicted poor). It also corresponds to developments in bioscientific knowledge that point to the genetic or neurological basis of addiction, usually described in terms of "adaptive changes" or "habituation" (D. Brewer et al. 1998; Camí and Farré 2003; McLellan et al. 2000). Mediated by a new set of medical and scientific translations, the current vision of addiction is deeply biological.

The ideologies and practices associated with addiction's biomedical turn, and the institutions in which they are embedded, have generated new affects and narratives of those struggling with addiction. Heroin addicts I spoke with frequently expressed that they had little or no chance of recovery and often explained their pessimism in biological terms. Their addiction, they said, was *in the blood, like a virus*, something they could not eradicate or recover from, even if they wanted to. But this locally biologized understanding of addiction differs from the medico-scientific view. In the Hispano milieu, the family is often the primary domain of heroin use, and heroin is frequently shared by fathers and sons or mothers and daughters. In this context, heroin addiction is conceived of as a kind of contemporary "inheritance"—an intergenerational and intersubjective experience that literally accesses the bloodline.[5] Thus, while addicts I spoke with emphasized the biological language of "chronicity," particularly when talking about their "lifelong struggle" with heroin, their experiences revealed profound differences in the symbolic ordering of addiction and time, whereby the "lifelong" struggles of an addict might exceed that which is traditionally conceived of as "a life." Here, "lifelong" may represent several related lives, entangled together in ways that make a biologized and individualized approaches to treatment futile.[6]

Despite the increasing reliance on metaphors of chronic disease, the motivating factor behind drug recovery, in practical terms, is invariably understood as personal choice or will. This is largely due to two factors: first, the prevailing Twelve Step model of recovery, which emphasizes personal power over addiction (made possible through the sustained reflection and vigilance over past behavior—what is described as a "moral inventory"—as well as the personal act of "surrender" to a "higher power"); and second, the ever expanding punitive approach to addiction, which emphasizes the addict's capacity to reason and, therefore, control her drug-using behavior. Whereas from a medical perspective, relapse may be seen as understandable and even expected, from a juridical perspective, the relapsed addict is ultimately assigned the blame for relapse and is seen as lacking the will to recover (cf. Garriott, this volume).

Increasingly, the mechanism through which addicts enter publicly funded treatment is the drug courts, which leverage the threat of imprisonment if the "offending addict" does not comply with treatment. Here, the traditional boundaries between the therapeutic impetus of medical and social services and the state's authority to control "criminal" individuals and populations are further blurred, even eradicated. More than 80 percent of the heroin addicts I encountered during my research had been appointed or sentenced to detox and treatment by courts—a finding that mirrors national statistics of publicly funded treatment programs (Office of Applied Studies 2005). Those with the highest rates of "relapse" were eventually incarcerated one or more times for not complying with prior treatment sentences. Alma, for example, spent a total of eighteen months at a women's detention center for two separate sentences related to drug possession. At the time of her death, she was awaiting a court date for "offenses" relating to her failure to comply with an earlier round of court-appointed treatment. The great irony is that her relapse was expected, even innocent—at least, from a medical perspective. From the juridical perspective, however, it represented a failure of will and was to be reckoned—through a sentence for further treatment, incarceration, or both.

How have the seemingly incompatible discourses of "chronicity" and "choice" supplanted alternative ways to understand and treat addiction? What are the psychic effects of these discourses on the addict, particularly those who have been through repeated cycles of recovery and relapse? How do medical and juridical responses to addiction lock addicts into an incommensurate "medical-moral identity" (Young 2007), in which the outcome of relapse is not only expected but produced?

Jean Jackson (2005) has written about the uncertain ontological status of the chronically ill. She describes how this status provokes stigma and forces the patient into deeper modes of suffering. Many of the heroin addicts I interviewed—addicts who in today's lingo would be described as chronically ill—talked not about uncertainty, but about fixity. Alma, for instance, described her life and the struggles and losses that defined it as being "sin fin." She echoed the sentiments of many addicts I spoke with when she told me that the only way she could exit the cycle of endlessness was through a heroin high. Alma once said to me, "The only time I feel really OK is when I don't feel *anything*. When I'm high, it's like . . . it's hard to explain, but just for a little while everything goes away. But that feeling of nothing . . . it's gone before you know it."

New Day

The Nuevo Día Recovery Program was established in the early 1970s on the outskirts of Española.[7] Nuevo Día, which means "new day" in Spanish, initially provided peer support for male alcoholics, many of whom were returning from the war in Vietnam. Former clients and staff recall those early years of operation as fraternal. "It was like a house," one staff member remembered. "We all lived together and helped each other out. We were like family." Over time, an increasing number of younger men sought services for heroin addiction. In the 1980s, heroin addicts were being transferred to Nuevo Día upon release from the local hospital or the county jail. The once comfortable facility became cramped, and the waiting list to gain entrance grew longer still. In 1998, a separate women's support group was established, and women, long overlooked, began to gain access to the program's limited services. With the rising caseload, the recovery home took on an increasingly institutional feel. A thick Plexiglas wall was added in the lobby, separating staff "on the inside" from the increasing number of addicts *afuera* (on the outside). Male and female heroin addicts and alcoholics in varying phases of detox suffered along side each other. Most stayed for only a few days; many returned within months. Still others died after they were released from the program or while waiting to get in.

In 2004, Nuevo Día established a medically monitored detoxification clinic, which focused on the unique and growing needs of heroin addiction. Located in a nearby village, the detox clinic was composed of a group of small adobe houses that surround a larger building, once a state mental institution for Hispanic adolescents called Juniper Hills. According to local rumors, in the final year of Juniper Hills' operation, a young girl diagnosed with schizophrenia set fire to the main building, culminating in her death and the facility's closure. For years, the facility sat vacant, its exterior walls still scorched from the long-extinguished flames. County officials considered condemning the building, but a special congressional hearing on the region's heroin problem in 1999 identified it as a potential site for a needed drug-treatment center. Five years later, Nuevo Día's detoxification clinic opened its doors.

The detoxification clinic signified certain cultural, economic, and medical advancements in a historically impoverished and drug-weary region. It was the first facility in the region specifically for heroin addiction; it was also the first to promote a medical model for detoxification by offering anti-opioid medications and what it considered a "clinical setting." At the opening of the clinic, musicians performed traditional *rancheras* as journalists and state politicians toured the facility, carrying with them paper plates heavy with tamales. County officials spoke movingly about the opportunity to stem the endless tide of heroin overdose, and many recounted their own struggles with alcohol and drug addiction. A prayer for healing was murmured. With the cutting of the yellow ribbon, the troubled memory of Juniper Hills was laid to rest and Nuevo Día was born.

The year Nuevo Día opened, the Española Valley saw forty fatal heroin overdoses. I had just been hired as a detox attendant at the newly opened facility, a job I took as a way to get closer to my subject of research. I was on duty the morning Alma was admitted. She had no personal belongings, other than the clothes she wore, and was in a state of acute heroin withdrawal. Alma immediately began to beg for medications to ease her pain. The male counselor on duty explained that she needed to undergo a drug search before she could receive a dose of Robaxin, a muscle relaxant that would ease the spasms in her legs. As the only female attendant on duty, I was instructed to lead Alma to the women's dormitory and perform the routine search.

I had observed drug searches in the past, but this was the first I would carry out. We stood in a room the size of a school bus beside one of six narrow beds, which would briefly become Alma's. Alma was familiar with the procedure and began removing her clothes. I hastily combed through her sweaty garments, my fingers tracing the inside seams of her jeans, her tank top, the crotch of her panties, the underwire of her bra. When I was finished, I told Alma that I could arrange to have personal belongings delivered to the recovery center. Alma responded in complete sincerity that she had no personal belongings.

She would sleep in that bed for only a fraction of her "drug sentence," leaving early on her third morning because she said there were mice in the women's dormitory and she did not feel safe when there were no women on duty. I asked the head counselor if he knew where Alma had gone; he responded with a shrug and added that he knew Alma—she'd be back soon enough. I was struck by the counselor's sense of the inevitability of her return, which I came to understand as similar to the hopelessness and "burnout" that many clinicians and mental health professionals feel, particularly those who work in resource-poor hospitals with high caseloads (see Raviola et al. 2002). I witnessed this among drug counselors and mental health professionals working in the region—a kind of moral detachment to which one succumbs after working too long in an environment of mounting need and repeated loss.

In fact, I would see Alma again a few months later, during the counseling session recounted at the beginning of this chapter. She had just been readmitted to the detox clinic following an overdose, for which she was hospitalized for less than twenty-four hours, and then transferred to the detox clinic, as directed by her parole officer. According to her patient file, Alma's heroin overdose was labeled "accidental poisoning," the circumstances of which remained unclear. The attending physician recommended that she begin a regimen of antidepressants to treat what was described as "underlying emotional issues," the nature of which also remained unclear. I shuffled through the other papers in Alma's patient file and learned that she was thirty years old and married and had no reported children. Her mother was listed as her emergency contact, and her permanent address was in the village of Tierra Amarilla.

I began to see Alma regularly in the evenings, at the start of my shift. She would linger around my "station"—a child-size desk positioned at the crux of an L-shaped hallway that led to the patients' dormitories, which were separated by sex. As a detox attendant, my primary duties were to watch and record the activities of patients between 6 PM and 8 AM, details that might become significant in case of legal issues, which were common. I also dispensed medications supposedly according to the orders of a clinic nurse, but there was no such nurse. The clinic could not afford to maintain one.

During her second stint at the detox clinic, Alma would lean on my desk and fill me in on the details of the day's events—which patients had walked out, which had been kicked out—stressing, it seems, the hard-won fact that *she had made it, she had stayed.* She became, in a way, my friend. Each time I returned to the clinic and found she was still there, I felt something akin to relief. She grew uncomfortable, though, if I commended her in any way for staying or if I asked her about *la vida afuera* (life outside). "I don't like thinking about that," she would say, referring to her future, to what existed beyond the clinic walls. Or, "Don't throw me a party yet!" suggesting that, any day, she might just lose it. In the end, Alma remained in detox for thirty days. She was then transferred to Nuevo Día's ninety-day Community Integration Program—a kind of halfway house where she would begin the process of "finding one's feet," to use the language of the program's mission. Alma liked to joke that, after fifteen years of heroin use, she had no feet, only collapsed veins.

The Community Integration Program was a chaotic, rundown facility on the edge of Española. There were more bodies than beds, and residents spent most of their days watching television, usually one of the many *Cops*-like reality-based programs or Court TV, in both of which clients essentially saw themselves criminalized on-screen. Alma and I saw each other only occasionally during this time—sometimes over lunch or sometimes during shopping trips to the Super Wal-Mart, where she briefly worked while a resident of the program. During these visits, it became apparent to me that Alma was growing demoralized and anxious. She considered moving back into the trailer she had shared with her estranged husband or to the family home in Tierra Amarilla. Neither of these options appealed to her. She didn't know what to do.

Yellow Earth

"Sometimes I shoot up and I'm sure it's gonna be the last time. The needle'll be in me, and I'll be pushing the plunger in thinking, *this is it! ¡Se acabó!* [It's over!] But I wake up all sick, and life for me . . . [*pause*] it doesn't stop. Even when it should, you know? There's no reason to live a life like this. Not one like this." It was 2:45 in the morning when I recorded these words. Shortly after the incident at the public library, Alma went on a four-day heroin binge. She passed out at a laundromat in Española, where she had sought shelter from the cold, and was arrested for heroin possession. After two nights at the county jail in Tierra Amarilla, Alma returned to the detoxification clinic—her final opportunity, as her parole officer put it, to "straighten up." It was Alma's third admission to Nuevo Día in fourteen months. Upon admission, the intake counselor asked why she had "sabotaged" her recovery yet again. Alma responded that there wasn't anything to sabotage; this was her life.

On her second night back, Alma remained with me in the clinic's common room. Plagued by memories, she couldn't sleep. I suggested her sleeplessness was related to heroin withdrawal and, in the absence of more effective medications, suggested a warm bath. Alma shook her head no, said it was the thoughts "messing with" her head, thoughts she needed to get out, lest she explode.

And it was a tangle of thought and memory that she related to me that night. She talked about her home in Tierra Amarilla, the village where her family has lived "forever," and where she had just spent two nights at the county jail, trembling alone in a windowless cell. She had left her village when she was seventeen years old, a year short of high school graduation, because she said she was choking on the memories of her elders—*las memorias de los viejos de antes* (memories of the elders of bygone days)—memories of a time that had preceded her, that did not concern her. Her retreat from their memories, she said, was drugs.

Several weeks later, I began the process of transcribing Alma's recorded narrative. She spoke about her sister, about Tierra Amarilla, about memories that were her own and memories she had inherited. At one point in the recording, she paused for a long time and then said, "It all keeps me awake at night." Minutes later, she said: "It weighs heavy on my heart." Alma repeated the phrase "It weighs heavy on my heart" throughout the recorded narrative. Detective-like, I kept rewinding the recording and replaying it, trying to locate all of the events that explained such heaviness. But Alma's admission of *feeling*, her moving descriptions of her embodied pains, were usually temporally disconnected from specific recollections of the past. For example, in one segment of her narrative, Alma talked about her sister's death, then digressed about a recent trip to Albuquerque, and *then* talked about a heavy heart. Throughout her recorded narrative, such phrases of pain dangled precariously, isolated utterances that seemed to speak, as it were, for themselves.

I tried to understand the nature of this seeming disconnection between feeling and event. Perhaps it was a consequence of heroin withdrawal, where orientations to time shift according to the process of detox and to the organizational structure of clinical life (on temporal perspectives of patients in drug treatment programs, see Klingemann 2001). Perhaps it was an effect of the pre-dawn hour and the dimness of the room, which created an otherworldly environment. Whatever the reason for this apparent disconnectedness, one of the themes that Alma kept returning to in her narrative was the sense that nothing changes, that life and its ensuing pain is unalterable—"sin termina" (without end). Indeed, it was within such terms that she explained her relapse and at one point acknowledged that she *knew* she would return to the clinic, as if her relapse and readmission were simply part of the order of things, cause and effect. Referring to the so-called responsibility and challenge of staying clean—which is stressed by counselors at the clinic—Alma said, "It's not that I wasn't *ready*. . . . It's that there's nothing to be ready *for*."

Shortly after I transcribed Alma's narrative, I drove up Highway 84 to Tierra Amarilla. It was fall, and the cottonwoods along the Chama River were in full yellow bloom. As I climbed higher into the San Juan Mountains, tall, full-bodied ponderosa pines flanked the road. Set back from the highway were clusters of adobe houses and trailers and, adjacent to them, neat stacks of firewood ready for the coming chill of winter.

As I entered Tierra Amarilla, Alma's words began to echo in my mind. I imagined that she was in the passenger seat beside me, accompanying me with her memories. What memories might she have of that empty lot or the burned-out trailer next to it? Did she know who had scratched Reies Lopez Tijerina's name on the historical marker that welcomes visitors to the infamous mountain village? Among the abandoned lumber mills, dilapidated corrals, and boarded-up houses I imagined events Alma might have participated in or witnessed: parties, marriages . . . overdoses, deaths. She had spoken to me about some of these things that night at the detox clinic; told me, for instance, about the suicide of a trusted schoolteacher who had tutored her in reading. "She slashed her wrists in the woods and didn't leave a note," Alma said. "My brother's friends found her when they were out partying. The only thing we could think is that her son died in Desert Storm."

Tierra Amarilla: "Yellow Earth." Perhaps more than any other *norteño* (northern) New Mexican village, it is the symbolic ground of the Hispano history of dispossession and longing for land and times past that has inspired decades of political struggle—by turns mainstream and underground, through means violent and not. Tierra Amarilla was first settled as a land grant in the mid-1600s. Like all land grants in northern New Mexico, Spanish and, later, Mexican settlers were allotted land for an individual home, an irrigable plot for personal farming, and the right to share common land with other settlers for pasture, timber, and hunting. According to the deeds, personal allotments could be sold as private property, but common lands could not. The commons were just that—collective property—and were to be used and preserved for the community's well-being.

Since 1848, when New Mexico became part of the United States, generations of land-grant heirs have found themselves struggling to regain lost lands. Even today, they continue to argue that the United States broke the Treaty of Guadalupe Hidalgo, which was intended to protect titles secured before the war, thereby preserving the economic and cultural integrity of Hispano people. The heirs of the Tierra Amarilla land grant, who include Alma, alone lost more than a half-million acres, much of it now part of the Carson National Forest.

Here, the idea that the land was "lost" is no mere exercise in nostalgia; over generations, it has given rise to a constant stream of rebellion, most famously in Tierra Amarilla forty years ago, when Reies Lopez Tijerina and a group of armed insurgents stormed the local courthouse, a symbol of an "outsider" authority that drove a wedge between the people and the land. The "Courthouse Raid"—as it is now known—prompted the governor to activate the National Guard and send in tanks to suppress the rebellion. A five-day manhunt by five hundred law enforcement agents ensued. The rebellion was successful in symbolizing how deep passions run on the issue of the land and who has rights to it.[8] In an interview following the raid, Tijerina exclaimed, "These people will always remember how they lost the land. . . . They have not forgotten after hundreds of years. . . . They will never forget" (Kosek 2006: 344). Indeed, memories and sentiments regarding land loss remain powerful tropes, particularly among elders. The ultimate irony is that which was "lost" is still *there* for Hispanos to see—it's all around them in the mountains, rivers, mesas, and buttes. One wonders how Freud's conception of melancholy can be extended to address such material losses—losses like land that remains present but out of reach, particularly in a context where land is constituent to cultural identity and economic survival.

As I drove through Tierra Amarilla on that fall day—through the plaza anchored by the infamous courthouse—Alma's narrative was fresh on my mind. I couldn't help but wonder what role "the land" plays in memories of women like Alma: women who, in her words, "no existia" (didn't exist) during the most militant phase of the land grant movement; women whose lives have been dominated not by the loss of land, but by the loss of people. Certainly, these forms of loss intersect in powerful ways. Alma's insistence that there is "nothing there . . . nothing but memory" speaks to tragedies of earlier generations that are indelibly linked to the present. And the material legacy of land loss in northern New Mexico is the very stage for losses associated with heroin use. Indeed, the first time Alma shot up was deep in the forest, in a crumbling adobe on a large parcel of land that once belonged to "la familia Mascaranes," a shepherding family who lost their land-use rights when much of the common land was designated a national forest, a transformation that erased their livelihood. Their old adobe is still locked in the forest and is the site of many of Alma's heroin-related memories, including the first time she witnessed a heroin overdose.

I wanted to talk to the Mascaranes family, but I didn't know how to find them. I thought about asking a clerk at the general store, but the general store no longer existed; it was boarded up. I drove to the county offices—a new complex painted the color of adobe and the only building in the plaza that wasn't in a state of complete disrepair. Although it was a weekday afternoon, even it was closed.

As I drove home, I thought about Alma's words: "There's nothing up there no more. Nothing but memories."

Intolerable Insomnia

Alma left the heroin detox clinic three days after our pre-dawn interview. According to the detox attendant on duty at the time of her departure, she simply walked out at approximately 2 AM. I asked to see her discharge papers, which patients are required to sign to acknowledge they have received counseling on the potential consequences—legal and not—of leaving detox before "successful completion." Alma signed her name in bubbly, childlike script. In response to the question "Reason for Self-Discharge," she wrote (this time in awkward block letters) "CANT SLEEP."

Jorge Luis Borges (1998: 98) writes about the "unbearable lucidity of insomnia." He describes sleep as a state in which one is able to forget oneself. When one awakens, however, time, places, and people return—the self returns. One of the many words in Spanish for "to awaken," and which Borges regularly employs, is *recordarse*, which translates literally as "remember oneself."[9] In this sense, when one awakens, one remembers oneself. By extension, in the absence of sleep, the self never leaves, never forgets, and thus remains vigilant over itself and its memories. Borges understood that this vigilance can lead one to a state of despair. In his short story "The Circular Ruins," a man who suffers from insomnia walks miles through a jungle in the hope that he will tire himself, lose himself to sleep. "In his perpetual state of wakefulness," Borges (1998: 98) writes, "tears of anger burned the old man's eyes."

According to the attendant who was on duty the night of Alma's departure, no one picked her up at the clinic, suggesting that she had walked fifteen miles of dark highway to reach Española. I called the only phone number that I had for Alma, which was for the trailer that she shared with her on-again, off-again husband. There was no response. Over the next week, I tried calling again and again. Eventually, a recorded voice answered, curtly informing me that the number I was trying to reach had been disconnected.

Several weeks after my visit to Tierra Amarilla, Alma called me. She wanted me to know that she was OK and that, although she knew what people must have thought regarding her discharge, she hadn't "screwed things up yet." Her tone was casual, even happy. She told me that she was living alone and working at the local Subway sandwich shop. She also told me that she had begun to attend services at Rock Christian Fellowship, a growing evangelical church in Española. She said she liked the music, as well as the upbeat message of the congregation, particularly its focus on rebirth. I wondered how Alma's transition from Catholicism to evangelical Christianity might be understood as a reflection of her complicated relationship with her own past and of a desire to forget.

The following afternoon, I drove to the trailer Alma had shared with her husband. When she answered the door, she was still wearing her work uniform: baggy khakis and a green pullover. Although it was still light outside, it was almost completely dark inside the trailer. Alma invited me in, informing me as she did that her home currently lacked phone service and electricity. But she quickly added that she was confident that her utilities would be reconnected within the week, thanks to help from the fellowship. I asked Alma if she was warm enough, worried that winter was on its way and the trailer would get terribly cold. Did she need anything? Alma told me that she was OK and laughed that her recent weight gain—a benefit of quitting heroin and eating on the job—was helping to keep her warm.

Votive candles flickered on a small coffee table in the living room, where I waited for Alma to change out of her work clothes. Aside from a threadbare couch, the coffee table, and a large wall hanging depicting the Virgen de Guadalupe, the living room was bare. I wondered whether this was a consequence of her husband's departure or simply amplified by the absence of heat and light. I looked at the votives and the Virgen de Guadalupe. Alma had not entirely let go of her Catholic roots, her ties to the past. I was curious about her foray into evangelicalism and wondered about her desire to be "born again" for a future.

Positioned between a discount grocery store and a mobile home showroom, the Rock Christian Fellowship is a sprawling cinderblock complex located in the center of Española. It can be spotted from some distance because of an enormous neon billboard depicting the face of Jesus that reads, "Rock Christian Fellowship: Making Disciples." In addition to traditional church services, the fellowship offers a childcare center, a men's recovery home, a "spiritual university," and a restaurant. The Solid Rock Café sits on the northern edge of the complex. Alma suggested we go there for a light dinner. When we arrived, the café was nearly empty. We sat at a small table near the window and watched the evening rush hour traffic gather along Riverside Drive. To my surprise, Alma pulled out two Subway sandwiches from a backpack. I ordered each of us a soft drink, and we ate our sandwiches—which had grown soggy with time—in comfortable silence.

Alma told me that the fellowship was helping her and added that she didn't know what she would do without it. It was the first time since we had reestablished communication that she acknowledged that things had been difficult. I asked her about the night she had left the clinic. She told me that it was a mistake to have been sent back—that the clinic didn't work because its focus on the past made life unbearable. "They want you to always be thinking about what you did, why you did it, how you're always gonna be an addict and you got to stay clean, fight the temptation. You're always 'ceptible to heroin, and there's no cure. . . . [That's why] I like it here [the fellowship]. They're not always looking back, you know? Pastor Naranjo talks about the future; he says that's what counts. The future —so you can be blessed and go to heaven." Alma continued, "At Nuevo Día, with Twelve Steps . . . it's like with Luis [her husband], always reminding me of the fuck-ups, you know? The things I've done. It's like, you don't have to keep reminding me! I know better than anyone else what I've done and where I've been. I can't forget. But don't keep pushing me down there, you know? I have a hard enough time dealing with it."

Alma's account of being "pushed" into remembering that she is at perpetual risk of relapsing into "past" addictive behavior provides a powerful critique of the model of chronicity, an approach that began, in part, as a well-meaning attempt to dispel the moral implications of being a drug addict. But Alma's framing suggests that there are, in fact, moral and psychological repercussions to approaching addiction as a chronic, unending process. Anthropologists have described how the uncertain ontological status of the chronically ill—whether they are depressed, asthmatic, or addicted—can provoke stigmatizing reactions in others (Jackson 2005; Luhrmann 2007). This is true in Alma's experience, although I would add that the idea that her addiction is chronic—that is, its chronicity, its unendingness—may provoke other, perhaps more dangerous, responses, including a deep sense of hopelessness. And while some might read Alma's appeal for "the system" and her husband to stop "pushing [her] down there" as "denial" (cf. Carr, this volume), an alternative reading may be that it is a genuine plea for a new understanding and approach to addiction. I began to understand Alma's turn toward evangelicalism as an attempt to carve out such a response. "I don't want to go through this anymore," she said of the seemingly perpetual cycle of treatment and relapse. Perhaps it was in evangelicalism and through the promise of being "born again" that Alma was able to envision putting an end to chronicity as such and to seek for herself a true and lasting recovery.

Indeed, that evening in the restaurant, Alma quietly swore to me that she hadn't used heroin since leaving the clinic, crediting the fellowship and her new, forward-looking perspective for her sobriety. The only problem, she said, was that she still couldn't sleep. I could see by her eyes that this was true. Bloodshot and watery, Alma's eyes conveyed the culmination of too many sleepless nights. She told me she hated nighttime because she worried, even before getting into bed, that sleep would not come. I asked her how many nights it had been since she had slept. "Nights!" she laughed. It had been so long since she'd slept that she didn't even remember what it felt like.

True insomnia is not merely tossing and turning on a bad night. Rather, it is sleeplessness night after night, a mind and a body in revolt against itself. Alma described wanting sleep like a hungry person wanting food;

her insomnia was a kind of starvation or another kind of withdrawal. It had reached a point at which normal patterns of wakefulness and sleep no longer made sense, or they seemed permanently unavailable to her. During the hours that preceded her departure from the clinic, Alma said her mind had started "playing tricks":

> I kept going over things in my mind, you know? I'd tell myself to stop, but I couldn't. My thoughts were, like, separate. I can't control it. It's always been like this for me.
>
> [That night at the clinic,] I was thinking about my parents and how they're getting old and are probably going to die. How I messed things up and, like, my mom hates me now and she's up there in [Tierra Amarilla], and I don't go there no more. I don't. I don't even like to call. But mostly, I kept thinking about Ana and how fucked up everything is, how she died with her baby inside of her. Did it die first? Did she, like, *know* she was going to die? Did she feel it? I mean, did she feel her baby die and that she was going to die, too?
>
> This is what I kept thinking that night.

"Insomnia," the Romanian philosopher Emil Cioran (1992: 140) writes, "enlarges the slightest vexation and converts it into a blow of fate, stands vigil over our wounds and keeps them from flagging." Night after night, the same thoughts appeared to Alma. She asked me why that is—asked me why, during the day, she was able to get by, but at night the same thoughts and memories swelled up, always in the same way.

Alma asked the social services coordinator at the fellowship for help, hoping that she would be referred to a physician who could write her a legitimate prescription for a sleep aid. Her request was denied. She admitted to me that she had resorted to buying prescription meds, mostly tranquilizers, off the street. But they were too expensive, costing up to $10 a pill, and the effect was too temporary. The thoughts, Alma told me, always returned. They were, in her words, without end. "The only time I can sleep is with *chiva* [heroin]. That's the only time, and it's the best sleep, because you forget everything. There's nothing, just this quiet. I can't explain it to you. It's the best medicine."

I asked Alma that evening whether she was worried that she'd start using again—if her insomnia would cause her to return to heroin. "Yes . . . always," she said. It was always on her mind.

Perpetual Peace

Last Christmas, Alma's estranged husband found her lying on her couch, alone and unresponsive. Within minutes, she arrived at the Española Hospital, a short distance from the trailer they once shared, and was pronounced dead. A toxicology examination performed by the Office of the Medical Investigator determined her cause of death to be a lethal combination of heroin and the prescription medication diazepam (Valium). Her death was classified an "accidental poisoning," the standard classification given an overdose with no corroborating evidence of intent.

However, an overdose surveillance report examining the characteristics and intent of overdose events at the Española Hospital Emergency Room in 2004–5 suggests otherwise (Shah 2006). It found overdoses resulting from a combination of prescription medications (i.e., benzodiazepine, diazepam) and heroin—that is, overdoses like Alma's—to be the routine presentation in the emergency department. Nearly half (47 percent) of these overdoses were determined to be attempted suicide, with women being the most significant covariate among those who attempted suicide via overdose.

Alma's death might have been a suicide.

There is an overwhelming sense of despair that staff at the Española Hospital feel, witnessing the same men and women cycling in and out of the ER; several have described to me their terrible premonitions that the next time will be the last for this or that individual (in such a sparsely populated region, staff and patients are likely to be friends or family). The clinicians ask overdose patients whether they "meant to do it," a question meant to begin the process of rewriting the script of the "accidental overdose." At the same time, the clinicians acknowledge that the intermittent triage care they provide and even the answering of the question of intentionality in and of themselves do not constitute even the possibility of recovery. Collecting these data merely ensures that intentional overdoses will be recognized as such. The clinicians thus partake in their own work of mourning—one that does not suppose it can heal the inevitable recurrence of these events but that nevertheless is committed to marking them as they occur, seemingly without end. They, too, keep vigil over loss.

Since Freud, an implicit understanding has remained that the melancholic subject is trapped in affect and incapable of sublimating the pain of past loss to live meaningfully in the present. Even melancholia's contemporary interlocutors tend to agree that such sublimation can occur only through the process of narrativization, such as in elegy, through which the past is resurrected, but only with the intent to vitalize the present (Ruti 2005; Silverman 2000). In this conception, the past, though unearthed for its potentiality in the present, is simultaneously laid to rest. To tend to the past as such, to remain loyal to it without this presentist perspective, is to remain its prisoner and to live a life as a partially realized subject.

The idea that the past must be relinquished or appropriated to serve as the foundation for the present echoes Nietzsche's work on the liberatory uses of forgetting. In "On the Uses and Disadvantages of History for Life," Nietzsche (1997: 67) writes that when the past "attains a certain degree of excess . . . life crumbles and degenerates." He calls for the abandonment of the past, because it "returns as a ghost and disturbs the peace of a later moment" (61). Much like contemporary melancholy theorists, Nietzsche suggests a critical discourse on the past that would be attentive to the needs of the present and proposes that one "actively forget" those haunting moments—again, so as not to disturb the potential of the later moment.

Alma's past remained a fundamental force in her everyday experience, and it was not a force that was "appropriated" in the goal of defining a future or to learn how to self-actualize or even heal. Rather, her past, which was undeniably filled with the sorrow of loss, was experienced *as such*: painful, heavyhearted, and seemingly endless. Does it mean that, to be passionately engaged with the past on its own terms, one necessarily sacrifices the potential for a present and even sacrifices the self? Can one live a melancholy life that is meaningful on its own terms?

Before her death, I believed so. I believed that it was through the experience of melancholy that Alma lived what Arthur Kleinman (2006) calls a "moral life"—that is, a locally and interpersonally engaged life, however precarious these engagements may be. Before her death, I believed that seeing and experiencing the world and the past as painful—and not forgetting or sublimating this pain for other purposes—is likewise a way to live in the world. In other words, there is meaning in melancholia, meaning in wounds that haven't healed, and perhaps never will.

But I am left wondering whether Alma believed this, for it seems to me now that she wanted to forget, wanted to heal—and desperately so. That is, above all, what heroin offered her: an ahistorical frame in which to finally sleep. But the various relational, cultural, and institutional processes in which she was embedded kept reminding her of the past; that the painful moment *would* return and disturb whatever momentary peace she achieved.

There is nothing accidental about Alma's death. It was forged out of the forms of endlessness in which she lived.

Notes

I thank the participants of the Anthropologies of Addiction Workshop held at McGill University for their careful engagement with my work. A version of this chapter appeared as "The Elegiac Addict: History, Chronicity, and the Melancholic Subject," *Cultural Anthropology* 23, no. 4 (2008): 718–46. Reprinted with permission of the American Anthropological Association.

1. The names in this chapter are pseudonyms.
2. I use the term "Hispano" to refer to the Spanish-speaking people of northern New Mexico, many of whom trace their ancestry directly back to the region's original Spanish settlers. They thus consider themselves Hispano or Spanish.
3. In this sense, this work could be described as a critical phenomenology. For works that make the link between the phenomenological and the political, see, e.g., Desjarlais 1997; O'Nell 1996; Scheper-Hughes 1992.
4. The continuing pain of past losses, especially those that are enshrined in the Hispano landscape, offers an alternative perspective to the notion of "triggers," avoidable "temptations" that can lead to the return to drug use (see Campbell, this volume). For Alma, "triggers" are spatial and psychic, unavoidable and unshakeable. Her narrative highlights the insufficiency of the popular and clinical understandings of triggers and the discourses of choice and self-responsibility on which they are based.
5. Addiction as inheritance in this sense is more than a reworking of a substantialist conception of descent, and it is more than the encroachment of medicalizing discourse on addicted families. Rather, it is a way to conceptualize one's relation to another and the kinds of practical and moral obligations this relation entails. This conceptual complexity raises critical questions about the nature of personal "will" and its limits in the context of addiction: see Saris, this volume.
6. In engaging with these very different, but intersecting, figures of biology and temporality, I have found the work on the relationship between the subjective experience of psychotic illness and political subjectivity by Byron Good and his colleagues (2007) helpful.
7. Nuevo Día is a pseudonym.
8. For more on Tijerina, land grants, and the courthouse raid in Tierra Amarilla, see Gardner 1970; Nabokov 1970. For more on Hispano land grants in northern New Mexico, see Ebright 1994; Gonzales 2003.
9. The Latin root is *re* (to repeat) and *cordis* (heart), as in "to pass through the heart again."

BALANCING ACTS
Gambling-Machine Addiction and the
Double Bind of Therapeutics

Terry's Machines

Terry, a small woman in her early sixties with short gray hair and deep-set blue eyes, lives in a ground floor studio unit of the Archie Grant Projects in North Las Vegas. It is evening, and the only light in the apartment comes from the lamp between our two chairs and the television screen in front of us. Terry smokes 120s, tapping the ash into a large, black tray on her lap; it seems as if every fiber of the carpeted, curtained apartment has been infused with smoke. Her nasal oxygen inhaler is held in place by thin plastic tubing that ropes up around her ears and joins beneath her chin. The tubing runs down the folds of her housedress and winds around her feet, then off in the direction of a motorized, gurgling noise that I assume to be a component of her oxygen equipment, humming from an area of cluttered shadows at the other end of the apartment. A large box of medications rests atop a pyramid of three television sets.

"Addiction runs in my family," she begins. Between drags, she catalogues the dependencies of her six children. Her youngest boy is an alcoholic and former drug addict; her oldest daughter is a bingo fanatic and plays the lottery; another daughter goes from man to man; two other daughters have overeating problems; her youngest girl is multiply addicted—to crack cocaine, alcohol, abusive men, keno machines, and video poker. "Maybe I have most of these addictions myself," she muses, "just in different degrees."

I had met Terry the week before, at a Gamblers Anonymous (GA) meeting she regularly attends at the Triangle Club, a Twelve Step meeting center and café off Boulder Highway near the Sam's Town casino. She moved to Las Vegas from Illinois in 1983 when her doctors recommended a dry, desert climate for her chronic lung disease. She had just completed an accounting degree and speculated that Las Vegas would be a good place to use it. For a while, she worked as a bookkeeper, as she had planned. "Then I was terminated at my job because everything got computerized, and I never got training on computers," she said. She began to gamble every day. For the past ten years, Terry has struggled to get her gambling losses under control. This struggle has involved Gamblers Anonymous, individual counseling, and fee-for-therapy groups that she learned about on the radio—but all to little avail. "It doesn't help that the technology keeps advancing," she tells me, "and that I'm surrounded by it."

"It would probably be good for me to move away from all the triggers," she reflects, "but then I'd be without all the support I have, because Las Vegas is the boot camp of problem-gambling recovery. So I'm kind of stuck here."

As the population of Las Vegas has grown, the gambling industry has increasingly set its sights on city residents as a potential market. A full two-thirds of those who reside in metropolitan Las Vegas gamble. Of these, one study finds, two-thirds gamble "heavily" (defined as twice a week or more, for four hours or longer per session), or "moderately" (one to four times a month, for up to four hours per session [Shoemaker and Zemke 2005: 395]).[1] Known in the industry as "repeat players" (as opposed to tourists or "transient players"), they typically gamble at neighborhood casinos that offer easy parking, childcare facilities, and other amenities. They also play at gas stations, supermarkets, drugstores, car washes, and other local outlets that have inspired the term "convenience gambling" (see figure 2.1).[2] "Our local players are very discriminating," observed a slot manager at one venue that is popular among residents. "They know what they want, and they're there five to seven days a week."

What local players want is machines, and this preference has closely tracked the evolving appeal of slot machine technology. While only 30

FIGURE 2.1 An AMPM gas station in North Las Vegas. Photograph by the author.

percent of residents identified machines as their preferred form of gambling in 1984, just ten years later the figure had sharply risen to 78 percent (GLS Research 1995: 14). Generating impressive revenues for gambling establishments through the collective, steady repetition of their play, low-rolling local machine gamblers displaced high-rolling tourist table gamblers as the heavyweights of the gambling scene in Las Vegas. "This is machine city," a cocktail waitress remarked as she led me through aisle after aisle of gambling devices at Palace Station in 1999. That year, the property's director of slot operations identified Las Vegas as the most "mature" of domestic machine markets.

Whether or not repeat machine play represents a form of "market maturity," it has a darker side. Machine gambling is associated with the highest rates of addiction of all forms of gambling, and this holds true among Las Vegas locals.[3] By the mid-1990s, the vast majority attending the self-help group GA played machines exclusively—a striking change from the 1980s and earlier, when the typical GA member bet at cards or on sports. Although the establishment of "pathological gambling" as an official psychiatric diagnosis in 1980 encouraged a focus on individual gamblers and their inability to resist internal impulses (American Psychiatric

Association 1980),[4] a growing number of researchers and clinicians believe that the machines themselves share in the addictive process.[5] In 2002 the first in a line of studies found that individuals who regularly played video gambling devices became addicted three to four times more rapidly than other gamblers (Breen and Zimmerman 2002). While all forms of gambling involve random patterning of payouts, machine gambling is distinguished by its solitary, continuous, and rapid mode of wagering. Without waiting for "horses to run, a dealer to shuffle or deal, or a roulette wheel to stop spinning," it is possible to complete a game every three to four seconds (Eggert 2004: 227). To use the terminology of behavioral psychology, the activity involves the most intensive "event frequency" of any existing gambling activity (Griffiths 1993, 1999).

Gambling addicts in Las Vegas describe their city as an environment of continual technological stimulation and themselves as particularly susceptible to this stimulation. "It feels dangerous out there," a middle-aged real-estate agent told me. "Something might push my buttons and trigger me to play at any moment. I'm not sure what would set me off." "The [GA] rules say don't be around [gambling] machines," said one man, "but I live in Vegas, so how is that possible? I like to go to a bar to have a drink sometimes, but I can't seem to do that without there being a damn machine there staring back at me. Hell, you go to the drugstore and they have them. Every time I fill my prescriptions I run the risk of getting stuck for hours at the machines." The wife of a successful banker recalled praying in parking lots outside a Lucky's grocery store, repeating to herself "I have to eat, I have to eat," then hurrying past the video poker machines that flanked its entranceway. A young single mother, on excursions to buy milk and baby formula, would close her eyes and rush by the machines. "You need complete vigilance, every moment of every day," commented a long-time machine gambler.

Terry called Las Vegas the "boot camp of problem-gambling recovery." As her words attest, the city's extensive gambling infrastructure is overlaid with a robust therapeutic network for those who become compulsively caught in its devices.[6] Tacked to the wall above a bank of video poker machines in a gas station serving a residential neighborhood that I visited in 1998, flyers advertised self-help groups, fee-based clinics, and other locally available therapies to treat those who gamble to excess (see figure 2.1). The machines themselves bore stickers indicating the toll-free number for GA, a fellowship that offered approximately a hundred meetings per week in Las Vegas and its suburbs.[7] In 1997 a for-profit group called Trimeridian Resources for Problem Gambling opened a clinic in Las Vegas that offered a range of individual and group counseling options.[8] As locals learned through radio advertisements, the Eli Lilly pharmaceutical company had commissioned Trimeridian to recruit local video poker players for a double-blind experimental trial involving the drug Zyprexa, a widely prescribed antipsychotic that researchers hoped might also reduce cravings to gamble.[9] The trial was based at Charter Hospital, which housed an in-patient treatment clinic for problem gamblers from 1986 until the national collapse of its hospital chain in 1998. After Charter closed, the clinic's former director, Robert Hunter, founded the nonprofit Problem Gambling Center in a blighted downtown neighborhood. The center, which charges only $5 for a group counseling session, was established with financial support from Station Casinos and other local gambling businesses.

At first glance, therapeutic enterprises would appear to operate at cross-purposes with commercial gambling. While the gambling industry designs techniques and technologies to induce extended consumption, the recovery industry—comprising researchers, funding bodies, in-patient and out-patient therapy groups, and purveyors of individual counseling— designs techniques and technologies that promise to weaken the bind of this consumption. Given the pursuit of objectives so precisely at odds, one might expect the methods of the two industries to differ also—yet they share two crucial traits. First, both are geared to the idea that behavior can be modified through external modulation; like gambling machines, therapeutic products are designed to be "user-centric" and amenable to custom tailoring. Second, both work by bringing about in their users a state of affective balance that insulates them from internal and external perturbations.

The resonance between machine gamblers' employment of gambling technologies and their employment of therapeutic technologies evinces the blurring of the line that might otherwise cleanly separate recovery from addiction; in both, gamblers seek means of self-modulation that can produce a continuous, homeostatic state and keep risk at bay. As we will see, the attentive state of balance they characterize as "recovery" bears an uncanny resemblance to the tensionless state they call "the zone." "The kind of serenity I feel when I'm doing my [therapy] exercises comes closest to the serenity I felt at the machines," Terry told me. As we will also see, it is not only that gambling addicts' machine play is isomorphic with their therapeutic practices, but also that a certain complicity and even inter-

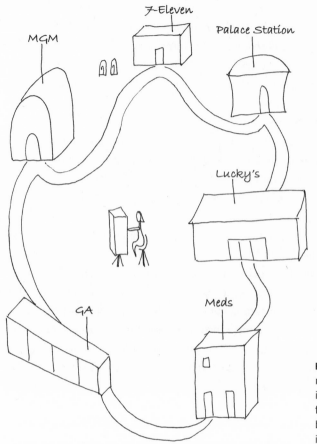

FIGURE 2.2 Mollie's map of everyday life in Las Vegas, drawn for the author in 1998 by a gambler residing in Las Vegas.

changeability develops between the two, merging the zones of self-loss and self-recovery. "It's tricky," a local therapist recounts, "because I've seen people use their anti-anxiety medications to heighten the sense of escape they feel playing machines."

Recovering gamblers in Las Vegas, plugged simultaneously into two sets of "self-medicating" technology, find themselves in a double bind: the point that appears to be the end of their addiction seems to circle back to its source. This circling back is thrown into visual relief in a map drawn by a gambler named Mollie, in which her clinic and the site of her GA meeting lie on the same road that takes her to the casino and the supermarket slots (see figure 2.2). Like Terry and others who wish to stop gambling, Mollie's challenge is to navigate this no-exit road in a way that partakes of its remedies while dodging its risks. Here I explore that challenge and its consequences.

Taking Inventory, Managing Risk

On a Saturday morning in the windowless conference room of Trimeridian's office suite, a longtime therapist of gambling addicts named Julian Taber handed out copies of a four-page document to the participants in his group therapy session. The document was a catalogue of addicting items to which he alternately referred as the Consumer Lifestyle Index and the Inventory of Appetites.[10] The items were listed in no apparent order, each followed by boxes to check for "6–12 month use" and "lifetime use" (see table 2.1). The ten of us in attendance proceeded together through the list and marked each weak link in our respective chains of will, adding new items along the way.

A vocal young woman proposed that "spending just for the sake of spending" and "searching for, buying and collecting certain items" be clustered together with two new categories—"shopping for shopping's sake" and "buying and returning things," compulsive tendencies that she considered to be in the same family but slightly different from the two already included in the index.[11] Underlining the nonproductive, circular character of addicts' conduct, Taber suggested that "buying *for the sake of* returning" might make a more accurate phrasing of the second habit, and it was added to the list. Half the people in the room, including the author, gave themselves a check for that behavior.

An older man named Daniel thought that "carbohydrates" and "vitamins/other health foods" should be included on the index, musing that although the first was bad for his body and the second good, he was nevertheless addicted to both. A younger man pointed out that "video games" and "Internet use" were obvious missing items, and a soft-spoken woman volunteered the less obvious "taking care of your child," an idea that produced a quiet pause before it was added to the list. Everyone agreed that "self-help"—a blanket category covering tapes, literature, techniques, and self-directed as well as group programs—belonged on the handout. At that point, it seemed there was nothing left to say, and the collective inventory-taking exercise that had begun an hour earlier came to a close. We stood to stretch, to visit the washroom, to step outside and smoke.

The lessons imparted by the exercise we had performed on ourselves reflected both the "expanding inventory of everyday risks" facing consumers (as the sociologist Alan Hunt [2003: 185] has written) and the ever

TABLE 2.1 Consumer Lifestyle Index/Appetite Inventory

Cocaine
Heroin
Amphetamine or similar "pep" pills
Morphine or related opium-like drugs
Gambling for money
Marijuana
Pipe, cigar, cigarette, snuff or chewing tobacco
Alcohol, beer, wine, liquor, whiskey, etc.
Barbiturate and similar sedative drugs
Hallucinogenic drugs (LSD, PCP, mescaline, etc.)
Caffeine (tea, coffee, cola beverages, etc.)
Exercise, jogging, playing sports or working out
Seeking and having sex with another person
Seeking and using pornography
Watching television
Talking for talking's sake
Searching for, buying and collecting certain items
Lying (for no good reason)
Aspirin or other non-prescription pain medications
Controlled (prescription only) pain medications
Laxatives
Nasal decongestant sprays and inhalants
Stealing, shopping, petty theft, etc.
Sugar-based foods (candy, baked goods, ice cream)
Fatty, oily or greasy foods
Salt from the shaker and/or salty foods
Highly seasoned or spicy foods
Spending just for the sake of spending
Work for the sake of being busy
Anger, fights and arguments
Trying to manipulate and/or control other people
Trying to get attention for attention's sake
Reading for reading's sake
Trying to get others to care for me/to do things for me
Antihistamine pills or other decongestant pills
Antacids, stomach remedies
Fast and/or reckless driving (not including DUI)
Valium, Librium and related "minor tranquilizers"
Physical violence
Cough and/or cold medications
Religious activity

Created by Julian Taber for use in the treatment of gambling addiction.

broadening scope of addiction that had come into cultural circulation since the 1980s.[12] The first lesson, communicated by the sheer number and diversity of items on the list, was that *anything can addict*. Although no substance or activity was bad in and of itself, any consumer behavior—no matter how necessary, benevolent, or life enhancing it might be when practiced sparingly or even regularly—could become problematic when practiced in excess, or "for its own sake." "Anything that's overly done is not good for us; if you get excessive with running, it's an addiction," remarked Daniel. "Religion, too—there are people who just have to go to church all the time, and that's an addiction." This lesson was confirmed when participants unanimously voted self-help itself into the catalogue of addicting items. The implications were dizzying: if the potential for addiction lay even in the remedies intended to treat it, then where did addiction start and end, and how could it ever be arrested or recovered from?

The second lesson was that *anyone can become addicted*. An older participant in the group commented: "Aren't we all born with addictive tendencies, to some degree? For one person, it's shopping; for another person, it's cleaning or working. For me, it's gambling and cigarettes." Daniel concurred. "It seems like addiction or compulsion is in everybody," he said. "Some of us do one thing, and some of us do another—even normal people have addictions." Rocky, a nuclear scientist, went as far as to suggest that susceptibility to addiction was a constitutive part of normalcy: "I think we all have the potential for some behavior to become extreme—it's just that most of us have another behavior to counterbalance it. The idea [of health] I've been fiddling with—that certain behaviors balance out other behaviors in some complicated way—is an equilibrium concept."[13] Health, as he construed it, was a function of balance between behaviors that were neither inherently good nor inherently bad. The potential to become addicted was not an aberration, we learned, but a liability that all humans carry.[14] Determined neither by constitution nor environment alone, addiction was an outcome of the interaction between the two; accordingly, it was a mercurial and circumstantial condition, unhinged to specific objects and open to a proliferating chain of attachments and substitutions. A subcomponent of this second lesson was that individuals were likely to have more than one susceptibility—or, as Taber put it, "a variety of possible dependencies." (Participants in GA meetings frequently expanded the typical self-identification of "compulsive gambler" to "compulsive person" or, even more expansively, "compulsive everything.")

These two lessons—that the world is a field of potentially addicting elements and the human being a field of potential dependencies—set the ground for the third and most important lesson, on how we should understand our own role in addiction. At the close of the session, Taber summed this up: "Addiction is a problem of you governing your own life—not the government doing it for you." By "govern," he did not mean that gamblers should *abstain* from all potentially addictive activities—an impossible task because this would be to abstain from life—but that they should vigilantly *monitor and manage* themselves, adjusting their behavior and applying treatments when necessary. This last lesson falls neatly in line with the more general demand of neoliberal society that individuals participate robustly in consumptive markets while assuming responsibility for their conduct—from the economic to the legal and medico-psychological. Following a behavioral template that one scholar has called "privatized actuarialism" (O'Malley 1996: 198),[15] gamblers in recovery were expected to engage "in the continual inspection of their internal states and modifications of their own behavior," as the sociologist of gambling Gerda Reith (2007: 48) notes.[16] A narrative posted by a gambler to an Internet recovery forum resonates with this injunction:

> At the moment, I am in remission, keeping my illness maintained, contained—just like my son does with his ADHD meds, just like my husband does with his diabetes meds, like my mother in law with her cancer support groups. Like someone with cancer, diabetes, or even the common cold, I MUST take care of myself, I MUST take my medicines. I take my meds every day—counseling, prayer, reading posts, emailing with my fellows, going to meetings, learning about myself, helping my fellows, and even taking a medication for anxiety/compulsive behavior. Now I have the "medicines" to keep me from ever being that sick again.

More than simply reiterating the familiar rule of Twelve Step programs that individuals assume responsibility for their own recovery,[17] the personal catechism articulated in the post specifies that responsibility means availing oneself of an array of therapeutic techniques and technologies, all of which fall under the sign of "medication." The task is to discern which of these techniques and technologies, at any given moment of behavioral risk, might enable a needed adjustment.[18]

This technologically inflected vision of addiction recovery correlates not only with neoliberal directives but also with a broad shift in the conception of health. Health is increasingly regarded as a balancing act that requires ongoing monitoring and modulation via medico-technological interventions, rather than as a default state or as something that can be definitively accomplished or "recovered." Echoing Rocky's earlier comment that health is an always precarious equilibrium, Joseph Dumit aptly terms this formulation of health "dependent normality." The "pharmaceutical self," as he names the subject of this mode of health, experiences his symptoms "as if he is on bad drugs, too little serotonin perhaps, and in need of good drugs . . . to balance the bad ones out and bring both biochemistry and symptoms to proper levels" (Dumit 2002: 126).[19] The recovering gambling addict is similarly exhorted to pursue the different techniques and technologies by which the balance of health—a sort of homeostatic zero state (not altogether different from the zone, as we will see)—can be maintained.[20]

The understanding of addiction recovery (and health more broadly) as a question of technological self-management owes much to the self-enterprise culture of contemporary capitalism. The daily and weekly "Craving Scales" with which the counselors at Trimeridian armed their clients, for example, explicitly borrowed from the larger set of calculative tools that consumers are encouraged to make use of to plan their futures and govern their lives (cost-benefit analysis, the financial audit, budget forecasting, and other accounting and actuarial techniques) (Valverde 1998: 175).[21] The scales asked addicts to numerically rate the duration, intensity, and frequency of their gambling urges according to a set of subjective measures so they could better assess the current state of their risk for addictive behavior (see figure 2.3).[22] As on a financial balance sheet, zero was the target rating for such measures as "Gambling will make me feel better" and "Gambling would get rid of any discomfort I am feeling." Like the inventory-taking exercise recounted earlier, this self-rating technique was meant to help addicts detect the symptomatic imbalance of their addiction—not so they could remove it, but so they could keep it in check.

Daniel's story of how he came to enroll in Trimeridian's recovery program exemplifies the sort of calculative self-inspection that gambling addicts were encouraged to undertake. After calculating that he could afford to spend $2,400 a year, or $200 a month, on the machines, he consulted his carefully kept ledger of gambling sessions and saw that he had more than surpassed that limit, having played on 25 percent of the days in the year, for

PG CRAVING SCALE
100 mm Visual Analog

"0" = Not at all   "100" = Most ever

0_____100
"I would like to gamble"

0_____100
"I intend to gamble in the near future"

0_____100
"Gambling will make me feel better"

0_____100
"Gambling would get rid of any discomfort I am feeling"

0_____100
"I feel I can control my gambling"

FIGURE 2.3 "Pathological gambling daily craving scale." Form used by Trimeridian Problem Gambling Consultants.

an average of five to seven hours per session. Upon further investigation he found that his year-end gambling expenditures fell between $15,000 and $20,000; based on a cost-benefit analysis, he concluded that it would be worth the treatment cost to enroll in Trimeridian's five-week intensive outpatient program, which charged an average of $1,000 for twelve sessions, on a sliding scale. Once enrolled, the self-audits he had produced using Trimeridian's craving scales were supplemented in individual and group therapy with guided strategizing on how he might avoid or remove particular addiction "triggers" from his life and which counteractive behaviors—exercise, medications, hobbies, prayer, activities with family and friends—he could employ to move himself back toward zero, or "out of the red and into the black," as he phrased it.

The remainder of this chapter explores how gambling addicts' therapeutic projects are complicated by the fact that "zeroing oneself out" also characterizes the zone of their machine play. Although the project of recovery would appear to be an instantiation of actuarial selfhood while the zone would appear to be a rejection of it, gamblers describe both as states of dynamic equilibrium that they maintain through constant acts of self-modulation; the microtechniques of the recovering subject, like those of the practicing addict, work to quell perturbations in the system and "zero out" excess affect. This likeness undermines the divide between the two and implicates each in the other. As I will show, the "balancing act" of addiction recovery rehearses the very escape mechanisms it is meant to overcome.[23]

Circuits of Self-Medication

Gamblers describe their machine play and their application of therapeutic practices in terms of self-medication. In their stories, it is not always clear which instances of self-medication follow a line of self-destructive escape and which follow a line of self-attentive recovery; the kind of affective balance sought and the means to hold that balance are similar enough in each case that they seem to blur into each other. This blurring comes to the fore in a comment made by Mollie. "A very common 'slip' when we read aloud from our GA handbook," she noted, "is to say that we have *Sought through prayer and mediCAtion*—instead of *mediTAtion*—which is laughable but truthful, because we have all self-medicated so much."[24]

Janet described this self-medication as a constant tuning and retuning of the various technologies that modulate her inner state. A young woman who wears thick glasses and a hearing aid, she feels near-constant anxiety because she is ashamed to ask people to repeat themselves when she has not heard them clearly, fearing she will seem stupid. At the time of our interview she played video poker every day at the grocery store to gain relief from this anxiety. She had learned that she could enter the zone most efficiently when she turned her hearing aid off or to "another frequency." When she combined video poker and this re-frequencing of her hearing aid with the amphetamines her husband was dealing or the Ritalin her son was taking for his attention deficit disorder, she achieved this relief even more readily.

It is not unusual for gambling addicts to describe the effects of their machine play itself as pharmaceutical-like. "The machine is like a really fast-working tranquilizer," said Randall. "Playing, it takes two minutes to disappear, to forget, to not feel. It's a wonderful way to alter my reality—an immediate mood shifter." Machine play can also shift bodily sensation. A nurse in her late thirties recounted how she felt sudden cramps one day while driving down Boulder Highway and pulled into a gas station to gamble. As she began to play, a numbness overcame her that remained until her last quarter ran out, whereupon she felt severe pain, looked down, and saw that she was hemorrhaging. "It interferes with the pain receptors or something," she told me, speaking of the machine in an analgesic idiom.

The fact that machine gambling is used, as are most addictive substances, for self-medication makes it difficult to distinguish its effects from those of the remedies applied to treat it. It is not simply that the technologically enabled, self-medicating equilibrium of the zone and that of the recovery model just examined are alike but that the two become intertwined. The following pages consider how addicts' machine gambling practices can play into and even abet their experience of therapy, and conversely, how their therapeutic practices can play into and sometimes intensify their experience of machine addiction.

Mollie approaches the project of self-recovery with the same combinatory drive at play in her self-loss, assembling an arsenal of tools and techniques to bring herself into balance: "Some say I need different meds. Some say I should connect with the Anxiety and Social Phobia message boards. Some people tell me I need God in my life. Others say if I just do the Twelve Steps I'll be OK. They're all probably right. A combination of group and/or individual therapy, meds, GA, and virtual therapy on the Internet, is what counts."

Mollie's statement, posted to an online forum for gambling addicts, prompted other gamblers on the forum to share their own therapeutic assemblages. A man named Geoff had cobbled together the following techniques to manage the physical and psychological disquiet that drove his addiction: "Meditation—a simple breath-watching exercise—gets the mind-chatter under control for about two hours. Same with exercise. I need a large endorphin-rush, so I play handball now and then. I also lift weights and swim at a local gym. That gym also offers yoga classes. All of these help." Meditation, diverse forms of exercise, and yoga were all components of Geoff's custom-tailored armamentarium of self-care strategies, designed to bring his endorphins, mind chatter, and willpower into a state of balance that could keep him out of the zone and in the world.

For others responding to the thread, psychotropic medications figure more prominently. Gambling addicts participating in online forums frequently exchange what amounts to quasi-professional advice on the different medications they have been prescribed—Xanax, Neurontin, Paxil, Zoloft, Prozac, Percocet, Ritalin. "It sounds like you should try adding an anti-anxiety medication to your recovery," writes one woman. "If I ever get medical insurance, I think I need Neurontin," writes another.[25] Many have developed exact insights into how to measure and modulate their dosages. "I keep a meticulous record of the medications I take," Rocky told me. "I've gotten to the point where I can cut my Xanax dosage in half and take it every four hours."

As gambling addicts describe it, addiction treatment is not unlike a user-oriented game whose elements, like the machinic object of their addiction, can be configured and reconfigured to accommodate their immediate affective requirements. Counterintuitively, equilibrium-oriented therapies such as meditation, yoga, exercise, and pharmaceutical management may work for machine gamblers *because of*—and not despite—their skill at accessing the zone state of compulsive machine play.[26] The catch, as we will see next, is that these therapies can also provide a route back to the zone.

Given that their treatments so frequently operate according to virtually the same principles as their addiction—that is, ongoing technological self-modulation to maintain equilibrium—perhaps it is not surprising that gamblers like Mollie, Geoff, and Rocky are so devilishly difficult to treat; the very protocol that promises to lead them out of their addiction risks turning into a game in which they can become lost. "Sometimes I get so carried away with a certain exercise or step that I lose track of where I'm going with it," said Mollie, noting that her therapeutic practice can take on a compulsive quality similar to that of her machine play. At every moment, her treatment trajectory is susceptible to diversion from its intended end. As Gilles Deleuze has observed of drug addiction, that which is vital can "turn" self-destructive: "The drug user creates active lines of flight. But these lines roll up, start to turn into black holes" (Deleuze 2007: 153; see also Raikhel and Garriott, this volume).

This susceptibility is at the crux of the dilemma that confronted Maria, a social worker in her early forties who was wary of using either medication or meditation as a recovery tool, fearing they could lead her back into addiction. She had begun gambling to dampen her distress over a divorce and an unwanted pregnancy. She experienced panic attacks when she attempted to stop and assumed these were part of her "withdrawal from the machines." When they did not subside, she visited a doctor and was offered pharmacological treatment, but Maria "refused to be medicated," worrying that she would become as addicted to the drugs as she had been to the machines. "Medication was liable to become part of the problem," she told me. Even the nonpharmacological, meditative therapies that remained at her disposal struck her as dangerous—because of the way she had "used" them during her addiction:

> One recovery step says "Seek through prayer and meditation to improve your conscious contact with God as you understand him." Spirituality plays a big role in the recovery steps, but my dilemma is that gambling itself was linked to spirituality from the start. I would meditate at night to try to see the cards that were going to come up on the machine the next day; it was never an out-of-body experience, but I'd be flying and all of a sudden I'd be somewhere in front of a machine, and it was like a vision. I'd see a certain card combination. So I was afraid to pray and meditate during my recovery because I made a connection to what I had done when I gambled. I'd think, *I'd better not do that step.*

In the very act of meditation, Maria ran the risk of addiction—for the activity risked producing a state she too closely associated with that of the machine zone.

Another example of this risk can be found in Mollie's relationship to the antianxiety medication Zoloft, a drug that originally was prescribed to help her cope with the social interactions she sought to avoid through her machine play but that ultimately enabled her further withdrawal from the world. Mollie, who wears a full prosthetic leg and walks with a cane, was frank in her admission that video poker functioned as a mechanism for escaping from others, and from her own body. She nevertheless found that play could stimulate pleasurable bodily sensations: "I would have what you might call mini-orgasms at the machines—kind of a tightness but just very small, an exciting kind of release. It would happen when I got certain card combinations." Within the protected space of play, Mollie was able to experience her body in a way that she found difficult to do in social situations or moments of intimacy with others. The Zoloft she took to help her overcome her social isolation ended up compounding it, for she learned that the medication prevented her from having orgasms during sex with her husband, further compromising their intimacy. After she began taking Zoloft, sex became "strictly mechanical"—which she preferred given that sensations left her feeling dangerously exposed and overstimulated: "too close." In this way, the very drug prescribed to help her reconnect with and abide social ties ended up working in tandem with the gambling technology she employed to disconnect from others and experience her body in a controlled and private manner.

Pharmaceutical drugs most clearly "turn" from conditions of recovery into elements of addiction when gamblers discover, in the course of administering them, how well they can supplement the act of gambling and even facilitate the zone experience. Patsy, for instance, first took the medication Paxil to "even out" her moods and regulate the anxiety that led her to play machines: "Before Paxil, I would medicate myself with machines—but then, after playing, I would have strange pains in my jaw and my ears, and my menstrual cycle and appetite were irregular. Paxil was wonderful, an absolute miracle—I could feel it go to my brain and stop the anxiety from forming, and all the pains stopped, too." As she recounted, her machine play began as a form of medication to treat her emotional and bodily disequilibrium; although video poker alleviated this to some extent, it had the effect of aggravating and even producing new imbalances and irregularities, amplifying the need for more "medicine"—this time, pharmaceutical rather than machinic. But what appeared initially as Paxil's successful therapeutic outcome became more complicated when the drug began to flatten her mood to a point where she found herself gambling without guilt; she also found that she could more easily access the zone state while on the medication: "On the drugs, it didn't take as long to get there."

An even more striking example of how drugs prescribed to dampen cravings for machine play come to function as intensifiers of its effects presents itself in the case of Amy. A recently divorced small-business owner in her late fifties, Amy was prescribed Xanax to counteract the same anxiety she sought to neutralize through gambling. Almost immediately, she incorporated the drug into her play:

> I'd get so anxious when I was playing machines, I'd have panic attacks. My doctor prescribed Xanax, and I never felt so good in my life. I was hooked for eight years. I'd take them while I was gambling. I'd feel the panic if I'd start losing, and also if I'd win—it was like an overload of excitement—and I'd pop two Xanax, or three, and it would calm me

right down. I was taking four a day, I was supposed to be taking one. The doctor never knew about the gambling and how I used the pills with it. I'd just have him call in my prescription. If my prescription ran out, I knew somebody who lived in North Las Vegas who could buy them for one or two dollars a pill.

Amy's story, in which the administration of a therapeutic drug comes to augment the addictive effects of machine gambling, illustrates what Anne Lovell (2006: 138) has called "pharmaceutical leakage," whereby a prescription pharmaceutical migrates from a treatment context to "an informal, illicit network (the drug economy)." In the course of this leakage, the two "drugs" are joined in mutually reinforcing action.[27] When Amy learned that Xanax could efficiently cancel out the "the overload of excitement" she felt when she won or lost at machines (for her, the two events carried the same perturbing value of an affective remainder), the drug became part of her play process. At the same time, her machine gambling modulated the calming effect of Xanax and in so doing entered the pharmacological process.

The unexpected interdependencies that form between the affect-regulating properties of drugs and machines short-circuit distinctions between self-care and compulsion. The concept of the *pharmakon* as Jacques Derrida elaborates it describes this no-win predicament in which remedies double as poisons and vice versa. "The *pharmakon*," he wrote, "can never be simply beneficial . . . [for] what is supposed to produce the positive and eliminate the negative does nothing but displace and at the same time multiply the effects of the negative, leading the lack that was its cause to proliferate" (Derrida 1981: 100). As gamblers recognize, the therapeutic remedies they self-administer—medicinal and meditative alike—carry multiple, indeterminate, and ultimately risky effects. They can rupture the zone's equilibrium, reinforce the reasons it is being sought, or simply strengthen its effects in a vicious, anaesthetizing circle.

Although this chapter has focused on instances of therapeutic failure, or "turning," it should be noted that gambling addicts' projects of self-care do not always or necessarily fail. Nevertheless, even their moments of triumph tend to bear the traces of the double bind at stake in our discussion. In a post to an Internet forum, for example, a gambler once addicted to online video poker observed that her computer had morphed from a vehicle of addiction into a vehicle of recovery. "I spent most of the last several months of my gambling in total isolation in front of the computer," she wrote. "That is where I reached my bottom and that is why the online recovery sites are so important to me." As she told it, the conditions of her recovery were rooted in the conditions of her addiction. Another gambler on the forum described the implicit challenge this double bind posed for him: "I tried filtering out gambling sites using key words such as gamble, gambler, etc., but that prevented access to online recovery sites such as this one which have become so very important to me and my own personal recovery. So it's a constant struggle."

Las Vegas locals carry out this struggle in everyday living spaces rather than online. To repeat Terry's comments, "it would probably be good for me to move away from all the triggers, but then I'd be without all the support I have, so I'm kind of stuck here." At the close of our meeting she recounted a recent gambling episode in which she had walked a distance to Sav-On Drugs with her oxygen tank to fill a prescription she needed for her lung condition. Having forgotten to bring cigarettes, by the time she arrived she was so desperate that she picked up a butt from the ground to smoke: "The only place to sit and smoke that butt was in front of a poker machine. Just going near that machine was unwise—before I got up I had dropped a hundred-dollar bill and I was broke again. I couldn't get the medication I'd come for, couldn't get a cab home, couldn't walk home either, and I was almost out of oxygen." She asked a woman in the parking lot for a ride home, and it turned out they knew each other from GA. During their car ride the woman, who like Terry also had a lung condition, told her about a casino that offered its regular players free oxygen tank refills and another that gave away free prescription drug refills based on the number of credits players had "earned" on their slot club cards.[28] Terry was stuck, it seemed, between pharmacies that doubled as casinos and casinos that doubled as pharmacies (figs. 2.4–2.5).

As we have seen, gamblers' and treatment programs' wish to "filter out" the toxic from the vital, to remove links to illness while preserving links to cure, carries a high risk of failure. Recall the Consumer Lifestyle Index exercise, in which each new element of addiction that participants added rehearsed this wish to separate negative from positive, unhealthy from healthy. The final lesson of that exercise—unwittingly clinched when therapy itself was included in the list of perilous conduct—was that the two cannot be clearly distinguished in a context in which addiction and the means to control addiction move on a continuous circuit.[29]

FIGURES 2.4–2.5 Drugstore signs in Las Vegas advertising video poker, 2002. Photographs by the author.

Actuarial Addicts

Some months after my first meeting with Terry, I visited her home a second time. When I asked about developments in her life, she gestured at the dim shapes crowding her apartment and answered by way of a technological inventory. She had a new oxygen tank from which she didn't dare venture far, but it was such an effort to drag around that she wasn't going out much. The car she had managed to buy had been stolen, making it difficult to refill her medical prescriptions. The microwave on which she "had become quite dependent" had stopped working a week earlier. She didn't own a computer, only a broken typewriter, and her radio no longer functioned. She didn't have the money to replace these appliances, but she was "learning to adjust." Only one of her three television sets worked, somewhat: "If it goes out—and I won't be surprised if it does—I'll have to learn to get along without that, too."

The technologies among which and through which Terry lived—some of them defunct or nearly so—were alternatively sources of depletion and resuscitation: video poker machines promised reward and control while draining her finances; the new oxygen tank kept her alive but restricted her movement; casinos offered her free meals and oxygen-tank and prescription refills, but only if she racked up enough credits on her player card; a pharmacy provided medication and a place to rest in front of a machine. In a world where potentially addicting elements were tactical components in the task of self-care and palliative elements were potentially addicting, she was challenged to configure and reconfigure her technological interactions in order to "adjust."

The double bind of the recovering gambling-machine addict resonates with the more general predicament of consumers as they struggle to make and manage choices from within a field of goods and services whose effects are often difficult to predict. Machine addicts exemplify the sort of adjustability required of actuarial selves in the face of this predicament. At first glance such a claim may seem counterintuitive, for addicts are typically defined as lacking the skills of self-adjustment that healthy selves require to successfully navigate the world; they are an "outcast sector," writes the sociologist Nikolas Rose (1999: 259, 263), "unable or unwilling to enterprise their lives or manage their own risk, incapable of exercising responsible self-government."[30] The "government of addiction," he observes, thus takes the form of interventions that "enable the individual to reenter the circuits of everyday life, where he or she will re-engage with the cybernetics of control built into education, employment, consumption, and leisure" (Rose 2003: 431).[31] Yet the experience of gambling-machine addicts, while certainly at odds with ideals of enterprise and responsibility, is by no means marginal to the "cybernetics of control" built into everyday life. In fact, their conduct—not only in their practice of recovery but in their practice of addiction itself—makes them more fitting representatives of contemporary actuarial selfhood than the mythic figure of the "consumer sovereign" who masterfully and rationally maximizes a pristine, coherent, and unconflicted set of desires in a world whose chorus of consumptive appeals do not affect him or her.[32] Gambling addicts, like other consumers in "risk society," act not so much to maximize as to manage; to this end, they continually recalibrate their actions in response to environmental feedback, flexibly adjusting themselves to changing circumstances and contingencies.

Notes

This chapter benefited from the generous feedback of Vincent Crapanzano, Duana Fullweily, Stefan Helmreich, Andrew Lakoff, Emily Martin, Heather Paxson, Rayna Rapp, Stephen Rosenberg, Jonathan Tresch, Scott Vrecko, and the participants in the Anthropologies of Addiction workshop. It includes sections of chapter 9 from Natasha Schüll, *Addiction by Design: Machine Gambling in Las Vegas* (Princeton: Princeton University Press, 2012). Used by permission.

1. A study by GLS Research (2009) similarly found that two-thirds of Las Vegas residents gamble "at least occasionally." Of those, 44 percent gamble at least once a week and 27 percent do so twice a week or more.

2. The term was used as early as 1995 (Goodman 1995), to distinguish it from "destination" or "tourist" gambling. One-fifth of Clark County residents who gamble do so in convenience stores, grocery stores, or gas stations. One-quarter gamble in local bars or restaurants (GLS Research 2009: 6, 36–37).

3. "The academic literature on electronic machine gambling is, with few exceptions, faultfinding," write two scholars of gambling. "While there is unanimity about the superior revenue generating capacity of electronic gambling machines for both the state and gambling venue proprietors, there is also concurrence on the distress these machines can visit on the public" (Smith and Wynne 2004: 54).

4. Although the American Psychiatric Association (1980) officially listed pathological gambling as an Impulse Control Disorder Not Elsewhere Classified, most psychiatrists and clinicians felt that the condition was best conceived as an addiction and the category of psychoactive substance dependence was used as a model when the criteria for pathological gambling were modified in a revision of the manual to include preoccupation, tolerance, loss of control, withdrawal, escape,

and denial (American Psychiatric Association 1994; see also Castellani 2000: 54; Lesieur and Rosenthal 1991). The *DSM-V* will change "pathological gambling" to "disordered gambling," and will classify it under "Addiction and Related Disorders." The diagnosis is associated with job loss, debt, bankruptcy, divorce, poor health, incarceration, and a high rate of attempted suicide. Despite the considerable difficulties of accurately measuring its prevalence (see, for instance, chapter 4 in Abbott 2006; Volberg 2001), there is broad consensus among researchers that 1–2 percent of the general population fits the criteria for the diagnosis; an additional 3 percent qualify for the somewhat milder "problem gambling" (Shaffer et al. 1999). Yet whatever the percentages of pathological and problem gamblers among the *general* population, they are a good deal higher among the *gambling* population and higher still among *regular* (or repeat) gamblers—20 percent, by some estimates (MacNeil 2009: 142, 154; Productivity Commission 1999: 6.1; Schellinck and Schrans 2003: xi).

For critical discussions of the pathological-gambling diagnosis and its "individual susceptibility" framework, see Borrell 2008; Castellani 2000; Dickerson 2003; Livingstone and Woolley 2007; Orford 2005; Reith 2007; Volberg 2001; Wakefield 1997.

5. For a more complete discussion of machine design and its implication in gambling addiction, see Schüll 2012.

6. Although Las Vegas has the most robust GA group nationally, state funding for problem-gambling programs is only a fraction of that provided in many other states and was not implemented until 2005, when a $2 annual fee on each slot machine was contributed to treatment and prevention programs (Skolnik 2011). Recently, senators have moved to redirect these funds toward plugging the budget deficit and providing other services to citizens. The funds to problem-gambling programs have been cut in half (Patrick Coolican, "Severing Lifeline for Gambling Addicts Would Be a Shame," *Las Vegas Sun*, February 18, 2011, http.lasvegassun .com/news/2011/feb/18/severing-lifeline-gambling-addicts-would-be-shame/, accessed February 2011).

7. Meetings are offered from as early as 8 AM to as late as 9 PM. Fifteen meetings are in Spanish. They are held at hospitals, strip malls, VA clinics, churches, and even power plants.

8. "As in many a capitalistic country," wrote one of the company's spokespeople in a press release, "the private sector has stepped to the forefront in treatment design and implementation": Joanna Franklin, "Problem and Pathological Gambling: A View from the States," n.d.

9. Although Zyprexa (Olanzapine) was not shown to reduce gambling behavior among video poker addicts and the results of the study were never published, Trimeridian accomplished its chief aim of proving to a major drug company (Eli Lilly) that it could run a competent drug trial.

10. The handout, written by Taber (2001) in the 1990s, was inspired by "a need to take an inventory of all addictive behaviors," as he put it. His use of the word "inven-

tory" echoes the tradition of the "moral inventory" in Alcoholics Anonymous and the financial inventory as a means of "taking stock" of one's worth.

11. Contributors to the volume *I Shop, Therefore I Am* (A. Benson 2000) similarly distinguish between disorders of spending and disorders of buying, among other forms of pathological shopping.

12. The earliest use of the word "addiction" was in Roman law, where the word indicated a sentence of enslavement of one person to another, usually to pay off debts. (Because these debts were often incurred through gambling, some in gambling studies have claimed that gambling addiction was the very first addiction.) Later, the word was used to indicate a strong devotion to a habit or pursuit. It was only during the eighteenth century that "addiction" was used in association with psychoactive drugs (Shaffer 2003: 1). The term was extended to a wider and wider range of drugs during the twentieth century and, eventually, to all forms of human behavior (Sedgwick 1993: 584; see also Berridge and Edwards 1981; Courtwright 2001b; Brodie and Redfield 2002; Keane and Hamill 2010; Kushner 2010; Vrecko 2010b). By the 1990s, more than two hundred self-help groups modeled on Alcoholics Anonymous had been formed to help those who believed they were addicted to such activities as shopping, watching television, exercising, eating, using computers, and having sex. A number of scholars have approached the expansion of addiction as a lens through which to consider the broader predicaments of late capitalism. Eve Sedgwick (1992: 587), in her essay "Epidemics of the Will," notes "the peculiarly resonant relations that seem to obtain between the problematic of addiction and those of the consumer phase of international capitalism." Along similar lines, Fredric Jameson (2004: 52) has written about America that "no society has ever been quite so addictive, quite so inseparable from the condition of addictiveness as this one, which did not invent gambling, to be sure, but which did invent compulsive consumption."

13. The concept of equilibrium as Rocky uses it here evokes a diverse set of expert meanings, from thermodynamics in physics to economic concepts such as the Nash equilibrium, cybernetic theories of control and regulation, ecological notions of systemic balance, and psychoanalytic understandings of how the pleasure principle and the death drive work to extinguish excitation and restore a state of rest (Bateson 1972; S. Freud 1961 [1920]). Although the state of equilibrium would seem at first glance to be contrary to the condition of addiction (which is associated with excess), in fact it plays a critical role in the addictive process.

14. The idea of addiction as a liability continuous with normal human propensities is reflected in contemporary neuroscience, where dependency is increasingly understood as a potential all humans possess. This scientific normalization of addiction proposes that drugs and certain activities addict because they stimulate or "hijack" the same reward pathways as survival-linked behavior such as sex, eating, and the formation of attachments to people and places (Bozarth 1990; Breiter et al. 2001; Vrecko 2010b). As Nikolas Rose (2003a) argues, there has been a "mutation in the logic of the norm" so that addiction no longer carries the moral weight

of deviancy; rather, is understood as an error in neurochemical machinery (Rose 2003a: 419, 439).

15. Following "privatized actuarialism," individuals reflexively apply to their own lives the same techniques used to audit and otherwise ensure the financial health of corporations and government bureaucracies. As in the spheres of insurance, finance, and global politics, the application of risk-assessment techniques at the scale of individual lives is a means for controlling—and even profiting from—the particular contingencies of post-Fordist, finance-based capitalism. Specifically, the model actuarial self is expected to indemnify itself against the increased risks of unemployment and lack of health that has accompanied the emergence of "flexible," short-term regimes of service-based employment and the eclipse of social welfare programs, while simultaneously reaping the economic rewards that come with exercising their own flexible and sometimes risky responses to this field of contingency.

16. The anthropologist Emily Martin (2004, 2007) makes a similar argument in her work on therapeutic engagements by individuals with mood disorders. The responsible citizen must engage in a "constant monitoring of health," writes Rose (1999: 58).

17. Twelve Step programs require recovering addicts to take certain steps to overcome their addictions. The first step, for example, is "to admit one has a problem."

18. The self-modulation that recovering gamblers are expected to pursue is different from the self-transformation expected in classical Greek and Christian modes of self-care as Michel Foucault (1988: 18; see also 1990) has described them, involving "technologies of the self" that allowed individuals to "transform themselves in order to attain a certain state of happiness, purity, wisdom, or immortality." Rose (2003a) has noted the shift from self-transformation to self-modulation. For further discussion of how the classical ethical question of "how to live" gets re-posed in contemporary technological societies, see the discussion of "regimes of living" in Collier and Lakoff (2005; see also Biehl et al. 2001; Fischer 1999, 2001; Collier and Ong 2005: 8; Rabinow 1996, 1999).

19. For a similar argument using the term "neurochemical self," see Rose 2003a. As Scott Vrecko notes, contemporary psychotropic medications are not meant to *cure,* but to modulate the intensity and frequency of impulses (2010b: 45).

20. In her analysis of mood charts as a means of self-regulation for those with mood disorders, Martin described how a visiting guest introduced himself at a support group following a protocol in which speakers choose a number on a scale from –5 to 5 to indicate their mood status: "I'm Brad, and I guess I must be zero" (Martin 2007: 187). Brad's statement registers the conception of health as a kind of homeostatic zero state.

21. Peter Miller (2001) has described how the inculcation of management accounting practices has extended to the subjective domains of life such that subjects deploy them to manage their inner states in a kind of responsible "self-accounting" (see also Martin 2004, 2007). The self-auditing that Taber's inventory-taking exercise encourages exemplifies this.

22. Upon intake, each new client would undergo a battery of tests and diagnostic instruments that were used to code, evaluate, and manage their behavior. The dossier included the Human Behavior Questionnaire, the Addiction Severity Index, the Family Environment Scale, the Barratt Impulsivity Scale, the State-Trait Anxiety Inventory, the Beck Depression Inventory, the Dissociative Experiences Scale, and a variety of gambling-specific testing instruments.

23. Elsewhere (Schüll 2012), I elaborate the corresponding argument that gamblers enter the "zone" of machine gambling by rehearsing the very same actuarial modes of behavior from which they seek escape.

24. As Gregory Bateson (1972: 309) noted in his research among alcoholics in the 1960s, their use of alcohol was a "short cut to a more correct state of mind." Bateson's idea that equilibrium is related to addiction shares qualities with the "need state" theory of gambling addiction (see Jacobs 1988, 2000), which proposes that gamblers seek to escape personal troubles and self-medicate negative feelings through gambling.

25. The medications that gamblers mentioned target symptoms ranging from anxiety to depression, pain, and attention disorders. There was not yet any mention of opiate antagonists (such as "naltrexone") that were then beginning to be tested and prescribed specifically to manage addictions, including pathological gambling. As Scott Vrecko has noted, this development has been "paradigm-shifting" (Vrecko 2010b: 42; see also Grant et al. 2003; Grant et al. 2006; Potenza 2001). Trimeridian's drug trial, in which Zyprexa was tested on video poker addicts, was the only application of an antipsychotic medication to gambling addiction that I came across during my research. (Even in this case, it was not clear whether the trial's designers hoped the drug's antipsychotic properties or its mood-altering side effects would alleviate compulsive gambling.)

26. For a similar analysis concerning the case of anorexia nervosa see Gremillion 2001. The same self-control and calculative practices that allow the disorder to flourish (calorie counting, choosing from menus, constant surveillance and manipulation of intake) are those called on in the treatment process: "Medical practices can recreate forms of bodily control that help constitute anorexia in the first place" (Gremillion 2001: 385).

27. Philippe Bourgois (2000: 170, 180) describes how methadone patients "mix" the drug with a range of others, including "cocaine, wine, prescription pills, and even heroin. . . . By strategically varying, supplementing, or destabilizing the effects of their dose with poly-drug consumption, methadone addicts can augment the otherwise marginal or only ambiguously pleasurable effects of methadone" (see also Lovell 2006: 153).

28. Given that seniors make up 20 percent of the Las Vegas population, casinos oriented toward locals find it in their interest to operate jitneys that shuttle back and forth to assisted-living centers. One property transports eight thousand to ten thousand seniors per month. "We're happy to take the people that are handicapped in any way, oxygen tanks, walkers. We do a lot of that. We have a lot of wheelchairs," said a shuttle driver for the Arizona Charlie's casino (quoted in

Geraldo Rivera, "Las Vegas—The American Fantasy," *Geraldo Rivera Reports*, NBC News, 2000).

29. In his history of "limbic capitalism," David Courtwright draws our attention to the many new goods and services that derive secondary profit from bad habits associated with consumer products such as food and drugs (e.g., the diet industry, drug rehabilitation, and nicotine patches), noting that "logically, the demand curves for the two sorts of products are correlated" (2005: 121).

30. Helen Keane (2002: 8) has similarly characterized addiction as the "constitutive outside to domains of health."

31. Vrecko (2010b: 45) calls such interventions "civilizing technologies," for they work to "produc[e] states in which individuals are healthier, more responsible and more able to adhere to the duties, expectations and obligations of their families and societies."

32. Colin Gordon (1991: 43) reminds us: "Whereas homo economicus originally meant that subject the springs of whose activity must remain forever untouchable by government, the American neo-liberal homo economicus is manipulable man, man who is perpetually responsive to modifications in his environment." We might call this model *homo addictus*, in pointed distinction to the self-interested figure of *homo economicus* (Schüll 2006).

A FEW WAYS TO BECOME UNREASONABLE
Pharmacotherapy Inside and Outside the Clinic

Between July 2005 and May 2008, I conducted an ethnographic study of opiate-dependent adolescents in a drug rehabilitation treatment center in Baltimore.[1] There, I followed a small cohort of young men and women from the time they entered residential drug treatment. Once they were discharged, I continued to follow them into their neighborhoods, homes, and other clinical and nonclinical institutional settings—including, too often, back into drug rehabilitation. The backgrounds of the adolescents I followed varied widely, not only in terms of their economic situations or demographic characteristics, but also in how they came to use and abuse opiates and the paths that eventually led them into treatment. Despite the variation, I came to recognize an experience they shared, a common element in the therapies they received. They each had been either enrolled in a clinical trial or were currently being treated with a relatively new drug for opiate withdrawal and replacement therapy: buprenorphine. What emerged was a focus on buprenorphine—specifically, two pharmaceuticals developed under the trade names Suboxone (a combination drug consisting of buprenorphine and naloxone) and Subutex (buprenorphine). Through long-term ethnographic engagements inside and outside the clinic, I sought to trace out patterns of pharmaceutically mediated experience and to better understand the mutual shaping of addiction and treatment for adolescents. In this chapter, I consider how clinical reasoning comes to rest on other forms of individual reasoning during pharmacotherapeutic treatment, inside and outside the clinic.

Over the past few decades, the sharp divide between the licit and illicit use of pharmaceuticals has become increasingly blurred, both epidemiologically and through forms of individual reasoning associated with use (Bourgois and Schonberg 2009; Campbell 2007). Self-medication, the abuse of prescription opioids, and prescription sharing are each characteristics of use that require detailed accounting. In the following pages, such accounting takes direct issue with the assumption that adolescents remain forever institutionally (legally and clinically) visible and moves sharply away from the claim that adolescents' experiences of drug use and abuse are largely unvaried.[2] Likewise, no one "picture" can satisfy an understanding of the experience of a therapy. Not all of the adolescents I followed lived in unstable households, though many did. Some lived in the suburbs, and some lived in the city. Not all had parents or guardians who were abusing drugs, though some did. Some, in the time I knew them, experienced recovery from dependence, though these cases were few. In the cohort of adolescents I followed, patterns of serious drug abuse were episodic and more often described than observed.

I followed twelve adolescents for more than two years.[3] "Follow," however, may be too strong a word. At any given time, I had consistent contact with three or four adolescents. Following would have to include conversations with concerned family members, friends, parole officers, clinicians, and social workers—often in the absence of the "study participant." Rumor, too, was a form of following. Rumors passed between adolescents at the treatment center, between staff members and nurses, and, at home, between friends and family. Following would include documenting the work of clinicians and the material administrative traces that remained after someone disappeared—a "file self," to use Roma Chatterji's terminology (Chatterji 1988). Following would also need to account for and blend the moments of impaired and unimpaired interaction with adolescents using drugs. As such, the method of retention in the study consisted of multiple phone calls, dropping in unexpectedly, missteps, chance, and, very often, disappointment. In my work, the technical terms "attrition" and "loss to follow-up," which are so often heard in human subjects research, do not easily find a place in the grammar of lived experience.

When an existing pain medication—Buprenex (buprenorphine)—was made available for the treatment of opiate dependence, it marked a dramatic change in public policy directed at the regulation of drug-dependence treatment and new clinical possibilities in the treatment of a set of difficult disorders relating to drug abuse.[4] Once the drug was approved and the strict criteria for success in early clinical trials claimed less attention, the long-term clinical effectiveness of its short-term efficacy generated concern. The questions asked during a clinical trial are not designed to anticipate concerns beyond their scope. Said another way, the duration of research and the measure of a therapy's efficacy are finite and highly specific in the context of a randomized control trial (Marks 1997; Matthews 1995). There is a fundamental tension between the efficacy of a therapy during a clinical trial and the clinical effectiveness a drug may have outside the parameters of research, especially within highly diverse populations. At its core, the approach of a clinical trial is direct: Does some *thing* (either a pharmaceutical or behavioral intervention) satisfy the questions asked of it during a specified timeframe? Of course, every question cannot be answered by a clinical trial, or even by many trials. No one drug is the key to unlocking addiction. How could it be? The nature of drug dependence is cyclical and lifelong—a disorder or set of disorders as much chemical as behavioral that carries a tremendous moral and social weight even in its aftermath (Campbell 2007; Castel 1981). In the case of buprenorphine, the desired clinical outcome of the pharmacotherapy is straightforward: to lessen discomfort associated with withdrawal symptoms, to lessen craving for other opiates, and, eventually, to reduce therapeutic replacement dosages over time.

However, patients and their families have other expectations (demands) of the therapy. The "evidence" of success is not always the same inside and outside the clinic. The way evidence is used to judge the success of the therapy through a process of clinical reasoning at times runs alongside—and at other times completely counters—individuals' experiences with the therapy. It needs to be made clear that my concern is not to call into question the criteria for evidence in a clinical trial or to say that the conclusions drawn from the existing research are false. My aim—and the aim of the chapter—is to pick up where research questions end and examine other types of questions that relate to the experiences of individuals under therapy, particularly at the point where the *clinical* and the *social* become difficult to distinguish.

Technologies of Suspicion

In December 2007, the *Baltimore Sun* published a series of feature articles profiling the relatively recent use of buprenorphine to treat opiate addiction in Baltimore.[5] The articles spanned the use of the drug in sub-Saharan Africa, France, and a number of cities in the United States to contextualize the local impact of the treatment. In addition to offering a short history of the drug and its implementation, the *Sun* reported that the police had seized twenty-four and a half buprenorphine "pills" from a man selling them along Pennsylvania Avenue on Baltimore's west side. Self-medication and drug diversion were subjects discussed by the reporters in anonymous "street interviews" conducted throughout the city. The basic narrative of the articles was clear: the therapy was clinically promising but suffered from widespread abuse and misuse. The main concern centered on new markets for the illegal sale of the drug for nontherapeutic ends: "buprenorphine's wide availability is starting to create some of the problems it was meant to solve. An investigation by the *Sun* has found that patients are selling their prescriptions illegally, creating a new drug of abuse that some people are injecting to get high."[6]

A few days after the *Baltimore Sun* ran the stories, the *City Paper*, a local alternative weekly, ran a similar story, echoing claims of growing abuse in Maryland.[7] Indeed, there were many physicians in Maryland prescribing the drug to treat opiate-dependent patients—at the time, slightly more than four hundred doctors were signed up to prescribe buprenorphine, and the prescription volume was the seventh highest in the country.[8] Despite the volume, few—if any—physicians in the Baltimore area reported grave concern about patients' misusing or selling their prescriptions.[9]

The *Baltimore Sun* articles provoked an immediate response. Rolley "Ed" Johnson, vice-president for scientific and regulatory affairs at Reckitt Benckiser Pharmaceuticals, wrote an official letter from the company responding to the characterization and extent of the problem suggested in the reports, emphasizing its intentions to thwart continued misuse.[10] The letter conceded poor surveillance. The company acknowledged incidences of abuse but failed to deepen the discussion of the drug's potential for abuse or of how prescribing practices and surveillance might be improved. The aim of the letter was to assure a concerned public that everything was being done to prevent abuse. The drug manufacturer avoided a vehement defense of its product, opting instead to maintain a picture of integrity while promising increased scrutiny of existing mechanisms for surveillance.[11]

Joshua M. Sharfstein, Baltimore's commissioner of health, was considerably less deferential in his response to the articles. In a strongly worded letter to the editor, Sharfstein wrote that the articles had worked to "obscure the enormous good that ha[d] already come to hundreds of thousands" and ignored the fact that the treatment "saves lives."[12] Even in the face of potential abuse and misuse, the benefits outweighed the problems—and, he noted, compared historically with the illegal sale and diversion of methadone, that of buprenorphine paled (Joseph et al. 2000). Close to the time of the articles, Sharfstein asked the Maryland General Assembly to expand funding for buprenorphine treatment by $5 million. The request was empirically warranted. Only a few months before the *Baltimore Sun* published its articles, MedChi, the Maryland State Medical Society, produced a study in which it found that the biggest hurdle related to effective treatment was not misuse and diversion but cost (Center for a Healthy Maryland 2007). Nevertheless, the *Sun* articles continued to generate concern. Only a few days after the first article in the series had been published, the Maryland State Senate called for a probe into the abuse of buprenorphine. The legislators were concerned about misuse of the drug, although they were equally concerned about the misuse of tax dollars to support what seemed like a problematic form of treatment.[13] The claims regarding poor surveillance leading to diversion and the alleged incidences of illegal sale were at the core of the debate. The findings of the Senate probe two months after the articles first appeared described the problem of abuse as "serious" and "dangerous" and suggested that the problem might be due largely to "negligence" on the part of the medical community.[14]

Apprehension about abuse and diversion of buprenorphine was not a new topic; it had existed from the beginning. In 1978, while Donald Jasinski and his colleagues were scrutinizing the treatment potential of the analgesic Buprenex, they were also examining the analgesic's abuse potential (Jasinski et al. 1978). They found the potential for abuse—as well as the potential for negative outcomes such as respiratory distress—to be far smaller than that for existing treatments—namely the full μ-receptor agonist therapy, methadone. The Substance Abuse and Mental Health Services Administration (SAMHSA) first became aware of "anecdotal" cases of abuse and diversion in December 2005, outlined in a report based on the findings of a post-marketing surveillance mandated by the U.S. Food and Drug Administration (FDA) and set up by Reckitt Benckiser Pharmaceuticals—post-marketing surveillance that had been in place since 2003 (Center for Substance Abuse Treatment 2006). In his oversight of the buprenorphine initiative, H. Westley Clark, director of the Center for Substance Abuse Treatment under SAMHSA, was determined to keep the focus on the therapeutic effects in the treatment of heroin abuse and dependence (understanding drug addiction as a public health problem) and not on potential abuse and diversion.[15] Charles R. Schuster, a physician who gave congressional testimony in 2002 during the hearings on the drug's approval and a past director of the National Institute on Drug Abuse (NIDA) who conducted clinical trials on the buprenorphine and naloxone combination drug Suboxone, maintained that only a very small percentage of opiate-dependent abusers have experimented with the drug based on the collection of national statistics on abuse and diversion (Schuster 2004). Nevertheless, public concern persisted.

Some people believed that the problem was significant and that it rested primarily with physicians. David Fiellin, a professor at Yale University who directs the Physician Clinical Support System, has proposed that the problem with misuse and diversion of buprenorphine lies with physicians who practice outside the standards of care (Fiellin and O'Connor 2002). He suggests that the combination of a lack of active surveillance and practices of over-prescribing by physicians obscures the ability to discover whether patients are selling their prescriptions or are crushing and injecting the drugs themselves for nontherapeutic ends. Although physicians are limited in the number of patients they are allowed to treat (currently, one hundred patients per physician), perceptions that prescribing practices have gone off the rails pervade (R. Johnson et al. 2003). In an outline of strategies to reduce misuse and diversion, Reckitt Benckiser planned to train doctors in how to improve prescribing practices to reduce the abuse of buprenorphine and to increase awareness of crushing and injecting practices.[16]

Doug Donovan and Fred Schulte, the two reporters responsible for the *Sun* series in 2007, continued to write about the abuse of buprenorphine in Baltimore throughout 2008. In April, they reported on police seizures and evidence of increasing illegal sales. They associated the increase with a national trend but argued that Baltimore warranted special attention. Donovan and Schulte described the contents of an internal Baltimore

Police Department document noting that Suboxone was "widely available" on the street, ranging in price from \$5 to \$10 per pill. The report documented 182 cases of buprenorphine seizures in 2007 and offered anecdotes about the arrest of a thirty-one-year-old woman holding two dozen Suboxone pills and a prescription bottle with a scratched-out label, as well as about a fifty-three-year-old arrested man who possessed "a bottle with an 'obliterated' label containing 38 Suboxone pills and \$302 in cash," to support its claims.[17] However, it is unclear how many of these seizures were made from individuals who possessed legal prescriptions. The article ends with a quote from Elinore F. McCance-Katz, president of the American Academy of Addiction Psychiatry: "We must address this issue of diversion. If this drug is seen as something that is potentially harming the public, we want to get in front of that. As physicians we need to look at this very carefully."[18]

Many details remain puzzling about the *Baltimore Sun* articles and the reactions they provoked. There was little effort on all sides to differentiate between the two treatment drugs. Subutex and Suboxone (the drug most commonly prescribed in Baltimore) were consistently conflated in the debates. It was "bupe" (as buprenorphine is called in Baltimore) that came to denote both treatment drugs. While both drugs are partial μ-receptor agonists, Suboxone—a combination of buprenorphine and naloxone—is also a partial μ-receptor antagonist, making its abuse by opiate users with long careers of dependence nearly impossible (or, at least, improbable). Christopher Welsh of the University of Maryland School of Medicine wrote in a letter to the newspaper that "the *Sun* sensationalizes claims of abuse—no serious addict would seek this drug out for abuse."[19] The ceiling effect provided by naloxone in the drug Suboxone is simply prohibitive. In France, Subutex is the most commonly prescribed treatment and is given by the *Sun* as an example of an analogous experience of growing abuse and diversion (Feroni and Lovell 2007).[20] But the frontline treatment in Baltimore is not the same, and the different drugs (Suboxone and Subutex) do not have the same potential for abuse (Lovell 2006). Moreover, the evidence in the articles citing Subutex abuse in the urban United States were drawn almost exclusively from Worcester, Massachusetts, not Baltimore. Finally, the articles link the epidemic of heroin abuse to the risk for HIV infection through injecting practices (thus creating a very specific picture of the type of abuse—and abuser—imagined). However, not one example is given of an individual crushing tablets and injecting the drug or even a combination of drugs. Moreover, the articles fail to distinguish between the problems of heroin addiction and the increasing abuse of prescription painkillers such as OxyContin.

It is not surprising that the articles failed to address these close though arguably crucial details. Only so much can be asked of a journalistic account. What is surprising, however, is that nowhere do we find detailed arguments offered in response to what can only be described as damning indictments of the therapy. The articles make it seem as though the treatment of opiate dependence using buprenorphine offers little more than new possibilities for abuse requiring attenuation. But how accurate is that perspective? Where does it find its empirical ground? Even a Baltimore City Grand Jury found that the abuse and diversion of buprenorphine was minor, even as the problems associated with addiction are so great. The jury suggested that efforts should be made to significantly increase treatment offerings in the city.[21] In the face of overwhelming evidence suggesting the benefits of the treatment, the *Sun* still fomented public concern. As Sharfstein and Peter Luongo, director of the State of Maryland's Alcohol and Drug Abuse Administration, point out, the *Baltimore Sun* did so, successfully, without addressing the larger social and economic dilemmas associated with drug abuse, without citing interviews with anyone in Baltimore whose primary problem is buprenorphine abuse, and by citing unnamed critics. In the letters to the editor responding to the first series of feature articles, Diana Morris, director of the Open Society Institute of Baltimore, writes that the *Sun*'s characterization "distorts the picture of a promising therapy, with no focus on high social costs."[22]

Other People's Problems

How does the potential for individual misuse lead to fears of new or renewed forms of public harm? The issue is not whether the pharmaceutical is or has ever been used nontherapeutically, rather, the issue is how a conception of therapy and therapeutics against abuse is itself imagined, and how categories of *licit* therapeutic opiate use and *illicit* nontherapeutic uses become unstable. The public consumption of private danger represents a shift away from individual behavioral risk toward a generalized anxiety regarding the collapse of regulation and the threat of unchecked abuse under the sign of medical expedience (Lovell 2001). The anthropological concern—at least in my work—is not about new forms of drug abuse. It is, instead, about how drug-addicted people are viewed and imagined in relation to therapy and how that imagining often does not match individual experience (Boltanski 1968; Bourgois 2007).[23] What interests me the most in the media account of "medication leaking" is the idea that opiate-dependent individuals being treated via replacement therapy might actually be using other opiates simultaneously. Asked simply: can medicine absorb the individual as both addict and patient (see Bourgois and Schonberg 2009; Gandhi et al. 2006; Christy Scott et al. 2005)?

A complex calculus is at work in negotiating harm, risk, and danger in relation to a new therapy, including concerns about potential misuse and abuse and the possibility that new underground markets of illicit use will take hold. Situated within this complexity is a persistent question: What happens when patients are thought to be working against a given therapy? How, then, is noncompliance factored into (or seen to depart from) clinical reasoning? As Jeremy Greene (2004: 329) argues in his essay on the nomenclature of noncompliance (what he calls "therapeutic infidelities"), ideas about noncompliance are not only about patients doing (or not doing) what they are told by physicians; they are also ways to manage the uncertainty of therapy itself. Noncompliance assumes a very clear idea of how and why interventions—in this case, pharmacological interventions—are effective and how they should be properly used, and how the risk of misuse is managed (Rosenberg 1997). However, a lived reality remains outside the laboratory or the clinic—a reality in which individuals make choices beyond the scope intended by medicine and where not only drugs but also forms of reasoning seem to be diverted.

Cedric and Megan

While following adolescents inside and outside the clinic, I spent a considerable amount of time with a young couple, Cedric and Megan. Their lives (together and individually) over the period I knew them wove (swerved) in and out of residential drug-dependence treatment and various other clinical environments (most notably, short-term psychiatric hospitalizations). Through their stories, I began to see more clearly the processes and logics of self-medication that bind a sense of social, bodily, and intimate security while exposing social and medical concerns regarding the individual danger of drug misuse.

Cedric and Megan were assigned different designations of patienthood at different times, determined largely by the environments through which they passed. But it was the designation of the drug-dependent person that held constant meaning. Dependence for both Cedric and Megan was not only a label but something felt internally: dependence was an ache and a hurt and a pleasure and a bodily habit—but also something they believed needed intervention externally.

I followed Megan and Cedric, who were both sixteen when I met them, from in-patient drug treatment through outpatient treatment and into Cedric's mother's house, where they both were living—which was a period of about eighteen months all together.

Diverting Drugs and Reason

I was surprised that the photo on the cover of the church program from Cedric's brother's funeral, placed next to a small collection of silk flowers on the coffee table, looked so much like Cedric. My gaze lingered a little too long on the photograph as I sat in an oversize couch across from Cedric and Megan in Cedric's mother's living room. "My mom said we were like twins she had two years apart," he said. I smiled, though the image was uncanny—more like an object from a not-so-distant future impinging on the present. Another teenager had stabbed Cedric's brother to death during an argument about stolen drugs—drugs allegedly stolen by Cedric's brother (who was a low-level dealer) from a main stash to support his own habit. Cedric gave some indication that he knew the boy who had stabbed his brother, but his description lacked any current of anger or judgment. "You looking at what I ain't, or ain't going to . . ." His words trailed off as though he had lost the thread of his thought, hoping to turn attention elsewhere. Cedric had been using prescription painkillers and heroin (smoking and snorting, although he insisted that he never shot heroin intravenously) for at least three years; Megan had been doing so for considerably less time. Cedric had been in residential treatment only once, the time that I met him. After an arrest for assault, he had been ordered into treatment instead of being sent to a juvenile criminal facility. While in treatment, he was one of the last patients to be enrolled in a clinical trial for Suboxone opiate-replacement therapy.

By all accounts, Cedric was successful during his time in the treatment center. He had minimal withdrawal symptoms and reported less craving during his stay. He was "diligent" (to borrow a word from one of the clinical staff when I discussed Cedric with her). He continued (now with Megan, also a treatment-center patient and trial participant) to see the clinical staff once every few weeks for a supply of pills (little orange sublingual tablets) and attended outpatient group therapy based loosely on the Narcotics Anonymous Twelve Step model but tailored to adolescents and young adults.

Cedric was a tall, lanky teenager with a deeply rutted face that seemed too old for his body. He wore the same oversize green-and-yellow warm-up suit for months on end, and given his slight frame, it was hard to imagine his body swimming beneath the clothes. His eyes were always heavy during our conversations, something I mistook for boredom, only to realize later that it was part affect and part exhaustion. Cedric was exhausted by the simplest tasks. He would slowly peel himself off the couch when his mother called to him from another room. Cedric acted very much like an adult, a middle-age man, though his mother called him "baby" and made him "do chores" every day. I resisted the urge to attribute his fatigue to some underlying medical condition and at times would forget that his slow movements were also the effects of a steady accumulation of drugs in his system.

The more I came to know Cedric, the more I felt I was able to discern how well (or poorly) he was doing. He looked remarkably changed from the Polaroid photograph that was stapled to his research study file, taken a year before. He was older and thinner and his features were more intense. In the photograph taken three days into his hospitalization (detoxification) at the treatment center, his eyes are floating as if they are trying to maintain a focus on something, anything. His hair is partially braided, with the combed-out half extending outside of the frame of the photograph. It was not long after his hospitalization that he met Megan through a mutual friend.

Megan was a thin girl, blonde and fragile in her appearance. She shared Cedric's weathered look, and though she still passed as a young girl, her hands were rough and covered with healed-over scars from cigarette burns. She had been in treatment several times and had dropped out only to reenroll in the clinical trial, twice. She eventually dropped out altogether after expressing vague paranoia that she was being "dosed" by the research staff. "I'm not a chimp," she told me between long drags from her cigarette while cradling a cup of coffee from McDonald's.

Megan's distrust of the treatment staff did not stop her from attempting to treat her own addiction. Cedric and Megan described in great detail how they were managing their dependence on opiates: "We just cut a little, snort a little [heroin] and then take the 'bupe' pill [Suboxone]."

Megan added: "Sometimes, a little [OxyContin] sometimes, you know, to balance." Cedric was emphatic every time I wanted to discuss their therapeutic regime: "It just like in group, you know, cut back a little, and a little more, and bad days less, and some day, you know, cured." They had indeed been reducing the amounts and proportions throughout. A small spiral notebook was produced as evidence: "We keep a chart."

Cedric's statement is ironic, but this is precisely the point. It was a clinical record of a closely self-monitored process of replacement therapy. Of course, when it came to heroin, the *stability* (purity) of each dose varied—wildly—and "tapering" was more akin to minute increments. But the rationale was the same: a simulacrum of clinical reasoning (Epstein and Gfroerer 1997). What is more, for Cedric and Megan there was a picture of a future free of dependence. Somehow that future was not as potent as the present moment—one filled with an attitude of success and the resistance to a shared fate of his "twin" brother.

When I saw Cedric on his own, which was rare, he told me about his suspicion that Megan was using heroin not only when they were together but elsewhere. Megan and Cedric often hung out with Wayne, a close friend of Cedric's who was a few years older and whose affection for Megan was clear. Megan caught rides with Wayne to her mother's house to collect clothes, and occasionally money and food, but mainly she went to visit her younger siblings. I never brought the subject up, but I was curious about why Cedric elected to stay at his house rather than ride to Megan's house with Wayne and Megan.

"If we'd just stay with the 'rehab,' we'll be fine," he said, implying that this was not happening with Megan. Strangely, when I went with Megan to get food at the corner store after the outpatient treatment meetings at the clinic, she shared the same suspicions about Cedric. "The mother-fucker doesn't think I can count," she said, referring to the number of pills that remained between the times that they used together. Only once did she offer a window into her deep anxiety and jealousy over Cedric's relationship with Wayne. Megan had borrowed my cell phone, called Cedric, and screamed "get a fucking room" into the phone—shoving it back into my hand, on the verge of tears.

The "chart" Cedric and Megan kept was some means of monitoring each other, however imperfectly. The chart was *clinical* in the strictest sense, but it was also *social* and *intimate*: a document of multiple fidelities, including *therapeutic fidelity*, to reverse Greene's formulation. So what are the issues? Here is a case of self-medication, noncompliance, and patterns of substance abuse seen and unseen. How do we begin to truly contend with the lived realities of *therapeutics*? It is not enough to say that Cedric and Megan are mirroring clinical reasoning, because clinical reasoning and social life dissolve into each other, remaking therapeutics. Personal formations of healing are at odds with therapeutic practices as determined by the clinic (and, indeed, the clinical trial in which Megan and Cedric were participating). Said (or asked) another way: What is the picture of healing shared by Cedric, Megan, and the clinician researchers they saw regularly? Despite the assumption that opiate-dependent adolescents are in a sense "futureless," in the case of Cedric and Megan we are forced to contend with personal forecasting and an almost overdetermined picture of a dependence-free future. Cedric and Megan actively work against the idea that substance abuse is a chronic, lifelong condition, but they acknowledge the pitfalls of recovery through suspicion of each other. The commonly held notion of an addiction-treatment career cycle (periods of relapse, treatment re-entry, recovery, incarceration, abstinence in the community, and possibly death) was something they were aware of but resisted when considering their own experiences (Office of Applied Studies 2001). Instead, they held on to something singular: a future directed by their commitment to the therapy.

. . . Wayne

The relationship that Wayne had with Cedric and Megan is hard to characterize as any one type. He procured drugs for them, but in strict terms, he was not their drug dealer. He was a friend but remained aloof and seemed to take pleasure in straining the relationship between the two of them. He drove a wedge between Cedric and Megan in one moment and was the person who held them together in the next. I overheard more than one telephone conversation in which it was clear that Wayne was on the other end convincing either Megan or Cedric that one was in love with the other. When he came into their lives, Megan had just begun using pills and heroin. Wayne was part of an initiation into drug use, and Cedric passively followed Wayne's direction.

Speaking with Wayne was difficult. He rarely made eye contact, and when he did engage, it was almost always to challenge or to manipulate. He insisted that I give him money (I refused repeatedly), and when I offered Megan and Cedric rides to the clinic or elsewhere, he either tried to tag along or asked to be taken to some outlandish place ("Drive me to D.C., OK? Just tell 'em it's for your work").

While the tension that Wayne caused between Cedric and Megan was very real, there was also something profoundly intimate about their mutual relationships. Wayne could be calming to both Cedric and Megan when they were around him. Each shared the suspicion that the other was having sex with Wayne. It was never entirely voiced as such, but there was a history within the relationship to which I could never gain access and that was somehow out of bounds for discussion.

The role that Wayne played in "schooling" Cedric and Megan about drug use was bound up with the precision of their self-medication, *self-therapeutics*. He offered advice to both of them throughout. He also seemed to have knowledge of the treatment center and of how replacement therapy worked—and, perhaps more important, of what should be "said and not said" when Cedric returned for counseling and to refill his buprenorphine prescriptions. Concealment and the management of what others are able to see were strategies Wayne used both socially and institutionally. Wayne helped Cedric and Megan manage the frequency of dosage, and so on, which cannot be taken for granted even in the clinical context (Marsch et al. 2005). Not knowing the long-term outcomes of the treatment included a lack of clear understanding of the best dosage and tapering of the drug over time (Gandhi et al. 2003). In many ways, Cedric and Megan were managing the uncertainty of the treatment in a fashion similar to that of the clinic (test, observe, change), although many more substances and circumstances were in play.

In the one conversation I had with Wayne, as I drove him to a repair shop to pick up his frequently broken-down car, I asked for his thoughts on Cedric's and Megan's program of recovery. "You know, they trying something, so that's better than most of these fuckers out here. Junkies be junkies. If they [Cedric and Megan] junkies, they'd be junkies already. You born with the gene, you know? Someday they'll walk into that fucking rehab and say, 'Hey, I'm clean, so fuck you!'" I also asked Wayne what he thought about the "chart" Cedric and Megan kept. He laughed: "Don't believe everything you read."

Reading the Paper

The media accounts regarding the abuse and diversion of buprenorphine became a technology of suspicion, and a hugely effective one at that.

When I discussed the articles with many of the actors who either wrote or publicly commented on them, their stories remained almost entirely the same. I expected more nuance, more ambiguity, and, in some way, a less polemical stance on all sides. A well-known addiction medicine specialist in Philadelphia (whom the reporters had sought as a source) told me that "the reporters were on a crusade" and little could detour them from the kind of story they wanted to tell. Moreover, the local media accounts in Baltimore moved outward into national media outlets, reestablishing and amplifying the story again and again.

I carried the articles around for weeks after they were published, hoping to share them with the clinicians and residential staff at the treatment center. I even mentioned the articles in my telephone survey with health-care providers certified by SAMHSA to prescribe buprenorphine on an outpatient basis. At the residential treatment center, the articles seemed universally to represent a threat to the standard of care that had been created with the new therapy and an indictment of the program itself. A psychiatrist at the treatment center, who later became a friend and collaborator, was very direct in her response—"They [the reporters] have no idea what they're talking about. It's good fiction, but bad fact"—simultaneously signaling absurdity and recognizing the impact the articles seemed to have. As simple as it was, her response was the most reasonable I had heard. She had little patience to respond to the details of diversion and abuse that the articles claimed. "We've got bigger problems to deal with— namely, how to keep kids on the medication and off street drugs," she said. I asked whether she ever suspected that any of the adolescents she treated were selling or abusing buprenorphine. "No, I don't ask," she answered. "I really don't need to. . . . You can tell if they're staying away from other opiates or staying on the meds. . . . I always have the urinalysis."

There are many ways in which the body (in all its forms and iterations) and the measure of fidelity (romantic, social, therapeutic) become intermeshed. But it is worth pointing out that the body here is not simply a metaphor or a placeholder to be filled with some undisclosed value. As Angela Garcia so eloquently shows in her chapter in this volume, biological forces are situated alongside (and bound up with) social, political, and cultural forces in the constitution of subjectivity in addiction. Along similar lines, Eugene Raikhel and William Garriott rightly point to Nikolas Rose's notion of a "politics of life itself" when they problematize the paradigmatic view that social structures of inequality are the only lens through which to view addiction, which can be read as a caution against the evacuation of the subject, as well as a redirection toward corporality. In this chapter, my aim has been less to reinsert the subject into a conception of therapeutics than to make the subject present—again, sounding off of Angela Garcia's chapter, a presence with all of the vanquished features of a lived past to make the present possible.

Multiple forms of suspicion circulate around buprenorphine that have been put into operation by different technologies. The chart that Cedric and Megan kept was a technology of suspicion, however faulty, about drug use outside the arrangement they had made for themselves. The chart found in the clinic offers another technology, although the fidelity in this case is wedded to clinical medicine and lacks the intimate features of Cedric's and Megan's relationship to each other and to Wayne. It is not completely unheard of for patients to keep a diary. Often in studies, patients' diaries are used to gain information about aspects of a treatment that are not necessarily discussed in the clinic (Zanni 2007).[24] The "chart" that Cedric and Megan kept was different, however. It was not to be shared; it was meant to record something that was delicate in their relationship: a shared conception of therapeutics.

Shortly after the *Baltimore Sun* articles were published, I took them to Cedric's house to hear his thoughts and, perhaps, to complain about the contents. Cedric quietly read the articles, with some interest at first, then handed the small stack of papers back to me. "Figures that some fiends be doing that," he said. "Drug addicts are stupid and criminal." After returning the articles to me, Cedric asked whether I wanted to go to his next outpatient therapy session with him and whether I would take him to refill his prescription. Knowing that he planned to continue "diverting and misusing" the medication, I could not help but comment on the dissonance. "Isn't what you're doing kind of similar to what the paper is complaining about?," I asked. Without hesitation, he responded, "No." Staying on the prescribed Suboxone—in whatever form—paradoxically gave Cedric and Megan the sense that their drug use remained faithfully under the sign of therapeutics. Between public and private dilemmas, between the extremely porous categories of licit and illicit drug use the newspaper articles seemed to miss, there was nothing ambiguous about therapy for Cedric and Megan.

Notes

I thank Eugene Raikhel and Will Garriott for inviting me to be part of the Anthropologies of Addiction workshop at McGill University, where I greatly benefited from the thoughts, insights, and interventions of the other participants. This chapter was presented in various stages of development as seminars and lectures at the Department of Social Anthropology, University of Edinburgh; École des Hautes Études en Sciences Sociales, Paris; Substance Abuse Research Center, University of Michigan; University of Wisconsin, Milwaukee; and Le Médicament comme Objet Social research group, Université de Montréal. I am grateful to the individuals at each of these venues for their input. I am indebted to Richard Baxstrom, Jonathan Ellen, Stefanos Geroulanos, Lori Leonard, and Pamela Reynolds for their personal and intellectual support and to Harry Marks, who is missed very much. At the clinic, I appreciated the encouragement of Philip Clemmey and Geetha Subramaniam. Perhaps most of all, I thank Cedric and Megan for tolerating my constant intrusion into their lives.

This chapter is adapted from my forthcoming book, *The Clinic and Elsewhere*, to be published by the University of Washington Press.

1. The research was supported under a training fellowship from the National Institutes of Health, National Institute on Drug Abuse (F31-0202039; sponsor: Dr. Jonathan Ellen, Department of Pediatrics, School of Medicine, Johns Hopkins University). The Homewood Institutional Review Board of Johns Hopkins University approved the research (HIRB no. 2006021 "Therapeutic Contexts for Substance Abusing Adolescents"). The names of the informants are pseudonyms.

2. The adolescents I followed—even in the context of a small cohort—varied so widely in terms of their initiation to drug use and the patterns of use during their short careers that it was virtually impossible to talk about the "adolescent experience of drug abuse" as a singular construct—at least, as one that held much meaning. This, however, does not imply that no very broad "patterns" of use and abuse were present. The point I am attempting to make is that individual patterns are more useful than a wholesale retreat into general categorizations or totalizing statements in understanding the impact of treatment.

3. I use the term "adolescents" throughout the chapter. In some ways, it is technically correct, at least in a developmental sense. However, I followed these young people for several years, and during that time they moved (developmentally) from adolescents to young adults—not to mention that their life experiences went well beyond their years. I have maintained "adolescents" to distinguish them from adults, to avoid the confusion of moving between terms, and to keep the focus centered on the institutional and clinical situations in which they found themselves.

4. In her chapter in this volume, Helena Hansen describes the highly specific social aspects of buprenorphine's history from the 1990s on—a history that is both transformative and productive of a reimagining of the ideal treatment population. Here I will simply reiterate some details. In 1978, Donald Jasinski conducted a

small clinical trial using Buprenex, an analgesic licensed for the treatment of moderate to severe pain, in an attempt to treat opiate dependence in adults addicted to heroin. Jasinski and his colleagues conducted their work at the Bayview Hospital in Baltimore, one of the Johns Hopkins University medical centers. A series of randomized controlled trials followed comparing the efficacy of buprenorphine (a partial μ-receptor agonist) with that of methadone (a full μ-receptor agonist). A number of trials were also conducted comparing buprenorphine to placebo-controlled groups. As part of the Drug Addiction Treatment Act in 2000, buprenorphine was rescheduled by the U.S. Drug Enforcement Administration from a Schedule IV and Schedule V drug to a Schedule III drug, which allowed physicians to prescribe it privately (albeit in regulated fashion) rather than in monitored settings such as methadone clinics. The FDA approved two new drugs —Subutex and Suboxone—for use in opiate-dependence treatment in 2002.

5. "Success, Setbacks in France," *Baltimore Sun*, December 17, 2007; "Drug Earning Millions despite 'Orphan' Label," *Baltimore Sun*, December 18, 2007; "Not a Cure-All," *Baltimore Sun*, December 18, 2007.

6. "The 'Bupe' Fix," *Baltimore Sun*, December 16, 2007.

7. "Drug Disabuse," *City Paper*, December 19, 2007.

8. The number of physicians does not include those working in treatment programs authorized under Title 21 U.S. Code (USC) Controlled Substances Act, sec. 823(g)(1), to dispense (but not prescribe) opioid-treatment medications. Treatment programs registered under 21 USC 823(g)(1) are not subject to patient limits. The prescribing volume in Maryland does include these treatment programs. The SAMHSA provider locator is available online at http://buprenorphine.samhsa.gov/bwns_locator (accessed October 12, 2007).

9. In March 2008, I conducted a randomized phone survey with physicians ($N = 126$) in the Baltimore area who had received certification from SAMHSA after 2000 to prescribe buprenorphine. In the brief, eight-question phone survey of physicians who were prescribing Subutex or Suboxone to outpatients at the time ($N = 86$), none reported that he or she believed his or her patients were selling or distributing the drugs illegally, and none knew of any reports of illegal distribution or sale (other than the *Sun* articles, which were specifically mentioned). When I asked the physicians whether they believed their patients were abusing the drugs, in several cases they asked, "You know how the drug works, right?," referring to Suboxone's dose-response threshold and thus its low potential for abuse. I used the word "believe" because I was interested in the physicians' perceptions of abuse and diversion rather than in empirically identified cases.

10. In the letter (*Baltimore Sun*, December 17, 2007), Johnson states:

> We are totally committed to reducing the harm of this devastating and misunderstood disease state, and to helping as many individuals as possible into successful, long-term treatment. To this end, we have worked closely with the government, the addiction medical societies, and key thought leaders in the field of addiction to bring this medical treatment forward for the millions of everyday Americans who need treatment. . . . Our objective is for buprenor-

phine treatment to be a powerful intervention to what has become a public health threat. Certainly we as individuals and as a company are concerned about any possible misuse and/or diversion of our products, and from the beginning have worked to establish mechanisms that enable us to work with the government, law enforcement, and indeed the clinical community to curb the likelihood and extent of such illegal activity. . . . Additionally, the company has made and continues to make significant investments in creating an abuse-resistant distribution network. We also have and continue to maintain a proactive and open communication with our physician base to educate them as to their role in minimizing potential diversion and misuse. The company's extensive and ongoing additional financial investments were anticipated at the outset as part of the cost of doing business in a disease . . . that is as highly stigmatized and inherently risky as addiction treatment. Any treatment of this type will carry an additional corporate burden; the patient population is at higher risk of misuse and/or diversion by the very nature of their chronic medical condition, and one must have realistic expectations. But despite the risks, it is a testament to the value of this medical treatment that the vast majority of patients are receiving a safe and effective, FDA-approved treatment for a condition (and a social public health threat) that has defied so many previous attempts to overcome it.

11. In addition to problems with surveillance, he acknowledged problems such as children sickened by accidentally ingesting pills in a report submitted to the FDA on January 8, 2008.

12. "Addiction Poses Greater Dangers," letters to the editor, *Baltimore Sun*, December 22, 2007.

13. "Senators Urge Action to Reduce 'Bupe' Abuse," *Baltimore Sun*, December 20, 2007.

14. "Bupe's Misuse on Rise, Report Shows," *Baltimore Sun*, February 3, 2008; "Agency Sat on 'Bupe' Study," *Baltimore Sun*, February 12, 2008.

15. "Buprenorphine: Patient Limits Increase," *SAMHSA News*, January–February 2007.

16. "Strategies to Control Bupe Abuse Outlined," *Baltimore Sun*, February 23, 2008.

17. "Bupe Seizures Rise as Treatment Use Grows," *Baltimore Sun*, April 18, 2008.

18. The quote in the article is from a "Buprenorphine in the Treatment of Opioid Addiction: Expanding Access, Enhancing Quality," paper presented at the CSAT workshop, Washington, D.C., February 21–22, 2008.

19. "Addiction Poses Greater Dangers."

20. "Success, Setbacks in France."

21. Report of the Grand Jury for Baltimore City, January 7, 2008, through May 2, 2008, and Baltimore Substance Abuse Systems, "The Baltimore Buprenorphine Initiative: Second Interim Progress Report," available online at http://www.baltimorehealth.org (accessed December 2, 2008).

22. "Addiction Poses Greater Dangers."

23. Regarding individual and familial experience in a different context, see Garcia, this volume.

24. The assumption is that clinical diaries provide a way for patients to assess their own health status without clinicians' bias or interpretation. Cedric and Megan, however, did not keep their chart to map symptoms or experiences unaccounted for in the chart at the clinic. Their chart's significance existed outside the document itself.

PHARMACEUTICAL EVANGELISM AND
SPIRITUAL CAPITAL
An American Tale of Two Communities of Addicted Selves

The year is 2001. George W. Bush has just won a U.S. presidential campaign that owed much of its success to an evangelist voting constituency. He reveals to the media that he found his own sobriety from alcohol by being born again in Christ and announces his Faith Based Initiatives for government funding of religious addiction treatment, catapulting evangelist addiction programs into the national limelight. Puerto Rico, a territory of the United States whose governor aspires to make it the fifty-first state, implements a new Mental Health Law that defines addiction as a spiritual-social rather than a psychiatric condition and opens the door for government funding of evangelist programs. Meanwhile, Reckitt Benckiser Pharmaceuticals and addiction treatment advocates have successfully lobbied Congress to pass federal legislation legalizing opiate-replacement treatment in primary care offices, and the U.S. Food and Drug Administration (FDA) gears up to approve buprenorphine as the first opioid maintenance therapy to be prescribed by U.S. generalist physicians since the era of the Harrison Act of 1914.

It is ironic that these two federally sanctioned treatments for addiction, one faith-based and the other neurochemical, gained U.S. national attention in the same year. On the surface of it, they represent polar opposite models of what addiction is. They also invoke different images of who an addict is and lead to different responses to addiction as a society. This contrast is highlighted by two clips that aired on television in the early 2000s, one representing a faith-based concept of addiction treatment and the other an office-based opiate maintenance concept of treatment. The first is a public service announcement by the Partnership for a Drug Free Puerto Rico, which opens with a weathered Latino man in a tattered T-shirt who asks drivers at an intersection for change. He enters a dark stairway, takes coins out of his pocket, puts them on a table, and rolls up his sleeves, apparently to inject drugs. The camera pans out to reveal that he is actually in a church, placing coins in a donation basket and freeing his arms for prayer in front of a great cross.

The second television clip is from the HBO special series *Addiction*. It profiles a young white couple in Maine who are starting buprenorphine maintenance as a treatment for their OxyContin dependence. They greet the cameraman in sweatshirts with college logos as they prepare breakfast in their suburban ranch-style home. Justin, twenty-three, explains that his growing prescription opiate habit was interfering with his ability to work as a cook, and Amanda, twenty, offers the hypothesis that people like her who struggle with anxiety and depression tend to use opiates because "they make you feel very comfortable and relaxed." Justin and Amanda then drive to the substance abuse treatment program in a colonial house, where they will get buprenorphine. They are greeted by an addiction specialist who explains that "ninety percent of the people who don't use replacement therapy relapse, because they can't stand how they feel."

In these clips, we have two sets of people with an opiate problem, but the first represents the addiction as a moral struggle, portraying the addict as a homeless street beggar in San Juan who has fallen to the depths and margins of society. He is dark-skinned, hardened, silent, and nameless. His ultimate solution is Christian salvation; he gives his few coins to a church, employing his forearms in prayer rather than in injection. The second clip represents addiction as biological and somatic and the addicts as a collegiate pair attempting to self-medicate. They are fair-skinned, youthful, articulate, and identified by name. Their solution is a wise consumer choice: they select a technician who tailors pharmaceutics to their neurochemical imbalance. The contrasts abound, yet both clips speak to a larger narrative of social reintegration and self-direction.

In this chapter, I trace the origins of these apparently divergent narratives, then follow their logics to an unexpected convergence. The individualist focus of the characters in both clips on their personal, inner states—formerly addicted evangelist and biomedically maintained—belies the degree to which substances, spiritual or molecular, are the medium for new, imagined global collectives in which ex-addicts and pharmaceutically maintained addicts place themselves. To generate these collectivities, pharmaceutical manufacturers and prescribers engage in medical evangelism—testimonials and ritual consecration of molecular technology as the source of salvation—while evangelist addiction ministries market moral authority through membership in a virtual spiritual network to socially displaced postindustrial consumers.

The Marketing of Spiritual Capital

During fourteen months of fieldwork among Puerto Rico's street ministries in the era of Faith Based Initiatives, I found that most Puerto Rican addiction ministries were ambivalent about accepting government funding (Hansen 2005). Yet President Bush identified a real phenomenon: evangelical addiction ministries were and are multiplying across the United States and Latin America. Evangelical Protestantism is the fastest-growing religious movement among Latinos in the United States and Latin America (Cox 1994), and abstinence from substances is a primary focus of the movement's appeal (Brusco 1995). One-third of Puerto Ricans identify themselves as Pentecostal evangelists (Cleary and Stewart-Gambino 1997). On the U.S. mainland, a nationally representative survey in 2003 found that 37 percent of all Americans identified themselves as born-again Christians.[1] So this seemingly esoteric topic—evangelism as a treatment for addiction—actually relates to national and international struggles over what kind of problem addiction is and how the problem should be addressed.

The currents of drug trade and Pentecostalism converged and cross-fertilized especially well in Puerto Rico, a Caribbean island of three million people. As a U.S. territory since 1898, Puerto Rico has long been a portal for North American Protestant evangelists to enter the rest of Catholic Latin America, and Pentecostals have had a native ministry there since 1916. The narcotics trade became a major industry in Puerto Rico sometime after the Second World War, and by 1997, the island had been named the major Caribbean point of transfer to the United States for Latin American cocaine and heroin (U.S. Drug Enforcement Administration 1997). This reflected economic shifts on the island. Starting in the 1970s, manufacturing plants were moved to cheaper labor pools overseas, and in the past few decades, Puerto Rican unemployment has run twice the U.S. median; male workforce participation has been less than 50 percent; and 70–80 percent of the population has qualified for food stamps (Dietz 1986, 2003). Puerto Ricans are U.S. citizens, and customs procedures are minimal for goods entering the United States, so the drug economy has grown to fill a void left by the decline of manufacturing. As a result, the rate of AIDS contraction via drug injection in Puerto Rico exceeded that of New York (Centers for Disease Control 2001). Yet Puerto Rico is behind all fifty states in funding for drug treatment (CASA 2001). Evangelists have moved in to fill the niche: by the last count, three-fourths of all state-licensed drug treatment programs in Puerto Rico were faith-based (Melendez et al. 1998).

Most addiction ministries in Puerto Rico are founded by ex-addicts who converted, some of whom then attended Bible school. They offer residential treatment that caters to working-class men, with a curriculum of a year or more during which recruits participate in daily prayer, Bible study, and worship services. Ministry leaders enforce extreme bodily discipline, including abstinence from sexual activity, cigarettes, and in some cases even caffeine, praying several times daily beginning before dawn, and undertaking hours of physical labor. Participants are required to take on leadership roles; seasoned recruits counsel newer ones, teach Bible classes, and coach others in evangelism during street outreach and revivals.

Ministries define addiction as the result of a moral choice rather than a disease. Evangelists would not acknowledge the main criterion of the DSM-IV diagnosis of substance dependence: loss of control. The idea of loss of control, in biomedicine, implies that a person is unable to choose whether or not to use substances in a logical way. In contrast, evangelists see addiction as the outcome of a choice—the choice of whether or not to accept the will of God. This choice is open to all and is often framed in individualist economic terms, as a wise investment. As one convert said, "It's spiritual Wall Street!"

Yet exercising this individual choice leads to a loosening of boundaries around the self and a letting go of control. Most addiction ministries practice two types of baptism. The first is baptism in the Holy Spirit, a conversion experience in which worshipers are overtaken by the presence of God and give over their bodies and minds to the Spirit. People converted by this possession experience follow up with ritual baptism in water, to mark their death as a sinner and rebirth as a person of God.

This series of baptisms means several things from the point of view of addiction. First, the convert himself chooses to follow God. Second, to choose to follow God is to choose an entirely different life and identity. The convert is literally a new person with new behavior, new relations (that is to say, a new family in Christ and the church), and new social roles (those of an evangelist). Third, if he achieves this new identity, the convert is no longer a hedonist or homeless failure but, rather, a disciplined holy man entrusted by God with special gifts. The convert finds himself providing counsel and sacred rites to family members who had judged him harshly in his addicted past. He is no longer a pariah but instead claims moral authority over the unconverted (albeit authority by proxy, as a medium of the Holy Spirit). He achieves what Victor Turner called symbolic inversion (Babcock and Turner 1978).

The metaphor of baptism in water also alludes to a washing away of difference, of barriers between self and other. As an ex-addict pastor and Vietnam veteran told me, after his baptism, "Suddenly I read the Bible. I saw my wife and children differently. I didn't see myself as Puerto Rican. I didn't see Vietnam. I didn't see racism." Other converts speak as he did, of a reimagined timeless, universal self unmarked by ethnicity or class—a self that was no longer a Puerto Rican, a Vietnam veteran, or an addict, joined, through immersion in the Holy Spirit, with the rest of humanity.

Further washing away the social distinctions between themselves and others, ex-addict evangelists do not distinguish between alcohol, cocaine, or heroin dependence, because in their view, the basis for the addiction is not biochemical. They equate addictions with other sins such as adultery or greed, citing corrupt businessmen and celebrities as alienated from the Holy Spirit, just as they were during their drug use. Successful conversion leads to a social leveling—a rejoining of ex-addicts with nonaddicts—as addiction ministries aspire to have ex-addict converts recognized simply as Christians in the evangelist mainstream. At times, they succeed. I saw some ex-addict converts become pastors of general community congregations.

While biomedical practitioners often treat patients suffering withdrawal symptoms with pharmaceuticals, the Pentecostal convert's suffering has a spiritual purpose. Pentecostals eschew substances of all kinds and engage in ritual fasts while continuously studying the Bible and praying, denying the body to enhance the spirit. In their frame, suffering strengthens faith. Bodily discipline is one of many evangelical practices designed to cultivate a sense of union with the Holy Spirit, a state that

Tanya Luhrmann calls "metakinesis." She argues that the compelling effects of evangelism come not just from Bible reading, but also from the physical and emotional habituation that helps evangelists embody their faith (Luhrmann 2004). In addiction ministries, fasts are followed by emotionally evocative worship services, called *cultos*, that employ live music and rhythmic movements such as "Jumping for Jesus" to cultivate this ethereal, metakinetic state of spiritual union.

Suffering, bodily and mental discipline, and emotive worship all build a convert's spiritual power, enhancing what Pierre Bourdieu would call social and cultural capital (Bourdieu 1986). This is particularly salient for the economically displaced working class, African American and Latino ex-addicts who make up the bulk of addiction ministries in U.S. and Caribbean cities. For instance, one of my study participants, Juan, found that his avid reading of the Bible and uncanny ability to cite chapter and verse were prized skills among evangelists, as was his extreme sensitivity to the moods and signals of other people, which evangelists saw as gifts of telepathy and prophecy. By mentoring young recruits and earning the trust of the mission's leadership, Juan built social capital. Juan's enrollment in a seminary was then made possible by supporters at the mission.

Men like Juan, who gain authority in the ministry, talk about their positions in terms of the respect they receive, especially from family members. For instance, Abel, a young man who became assistant pastor at the New Faith Bible Academy (Academia Nueva Fé) after years on heroin, felt especially proud when his seven-year-old daughters told their friends, "My daddy is a pastor!" Another ex-heroin user, Paulo, who converted in his fifties, was ordained as a pastor in the academy's ministry and opened a new center on the eastern coast of the island. His nieces came to him for advice and asked him to christen his grandniece at a family reunion. Paulo later presided over his mother's conversion from Catholicism to Pentecostalism at her tender age of eighty-six.

Abel and Paulo see their spiritual power as the result of inculcation of spirits; they use prayer and meditation to tap into a realm in which converts literally converse with benevolent spirits that move freely between bodies to inhabit and possess them. The Holy Spirit itself passes through the most fervent converts, primed by fasting, hours of Bible study, and ecstatic worship at culto, leaving them "slain in the Spirit," passed out on the floor of the worship hall. Ironically, the individual, lonely act of choosing to be born again in Christ and thereby leaving behind nonbeliever family and community members, former dealers, and drug-using partners is an act that opens the boundaries of the individual, making the individual more permeable to outside influence. Spirits inhabit the individual and become the medium for communication of knowledge about self and others, both intimate (learning to read signs from God regarding personal conduct, receiving prophecy) and cosmological (sensing the suffering of people close by or thousands of miles away, seeing one's essential connection to the whole of humanity). Spirits (as in disembodied social beings) become the vehicle for establishing a collective spirit (as in prevailing mood) in an era and a place in which so many describe turning to narcotics out of a sense of loss, of disconnection, from a faltering service economy that excludes them and an informal drug economy that violently consumes them.

Pharmaceutical Evangelism and Clinical Rites

Let us return to the year 2001. It is the end of President Bush senior's Decade of the Brain, during which federal agencies such as the National Institute of Mental Health and National Institute on Drug Abuse (NIDA) pushed researchers to identify the biological basis of addiction and other mental health problems and intervene on the biological level—both pharmaceutical and genetic. A widely cited article by leaders in addiction research has just been published in the *Journal of the American Medical Association* (McLellan et al. 2000). On the basis of data showing similar heritability and treatment outcomes of narcotics dependence compared with hypertension and diabetes, it urges clinicians and policymakers to reframe addiction, addressing it as a chronic, neurophysiological illness that can be treated in the same manner as diabetes or hypertension—in a physician's office, with pharmacological intervention. The authors' hope is that this chronic illness model will reduce the stigma associated with addiction treatment.

The one pharmacological development that NIDA was able to claim as a success, coming out of the decade of the brain, was none other than buprenorphine (Vocci et al. 2005). A synthetic opiate-receptor agonist/antagonist, buprenorphine was approved by the FDA as a Schedule III medication for opiate dependence in 2002. Its manufacturer, Reckitt Benckiser, had successfully lobbied Congress to change federal law, passing the Drug Addiction Treatment Act of 2000, which allowed generalist physicians to prescribe approved Schedule III opioids in their offices for maintenance treatment of opiate dependence (Jaffe and O'Keeffe 2003).

Prior to this act of Congress, generalists had been banned from prescribing opiates for maintenance of dependent patients in the United States since the Harrison Act of 1914. Federal agencies prosecuted doctors who maintained their addicted patients on opiates. The government had thereby shut down the morphine prescription mills that had dotted the American landscape since the nineteenth century, when housewives, soldiers, and many others developed dependence on opiate-based nonprescription elixirs and widespread medical morphine and heroin (Musto 1999). Heroin, which by 1914 was generating widespread dependence, had been introduced by the Bayer pharmaceutical company just sixteen years earlier, in 1898, as a "nonaddictive" pain reliever and a treatment for morphine dependence. It was one in a series of opioids marketed with such claims. In the 1990s, OxyContin and buprenorphine (marketed as Suboxone and Subutex) would be its later chapters.

By the 1960s, an upsurge of heroin use related to veterans returning from Vietnam, and aggressive heroin marketing by organized crime in turbulent inner cities, brought new pressures to develop effective treatments for heroin addiction. Vincent Dole, a metabolic disease researcher at Rockefeller University who conceived of opiate addiction as opiate deficiency syndrome that could be treated with opiate replacement in a manner akin to insulin replacement for diabetics, collaborated with the psychiatrist Marie Nyswander to test dolophine (or methadone), a synthetic opioid developed in Second World War–era Germany, for the long-term maintenance of heroin-addicted patients (Courtwright 1997). The ability of their early research subjects to hold jobs and to stop committing crimes received national attention. By 1970, the psychiatrist Jerome Jaffe had been recruited by the Nixon administration as the nation's first "drug czar," to construct a network of federally regulated specialty clinics to dispense methadone for the maintenance of "hard core," treatment-resistant, heroin-addicted patients: the methadone maintenance treatment model that we know today.

While the history of the buprenorphine maintenance model in the United States has yet to be written, researchers involved in its early development told me in interviews that buprenorphine, publicized with fanfare in 2002 as a breakthrough in the pharmacological management of opiate dependence, was actually developed in 1973. Reckitt Benckiser, known then as Reckitt Coleman, isolated the synthetic opiate receptor agonist/antagonist in the search for a potent, nonaddictive opioid analgesic. Early publicity for Buprenex, the initial, injectable form of buprenorphine, claimed that participants in clinical trials experienced no tolerance, dependence, or withdrawal from the drug, although this was later disproved. Yet buprenorphine (marketed as a sublingual tablet under the name Subutex) did have a lower potential for lethal overdose than methadone, and its oral form could be combined with the opiate antagonist naloxone (marketed under the name Suboxone) to limit its abuse by injection. Despite the efforts of key addiction researchers, who lobbied Reckitt for support to test buprenorphine as an opiate-maintenance medication, the company warded off any association with addiction, holding on to hopes of marketing the drug as a minimally addictive opioid pain reliever.

By the 1990s, the global HIV epidemic had added urgency to the search for new opiate-maintenance treatments, and activist primary care doctors in France pushed their government to disseminate buprenorphine managed by general practitioners (Lovell 2006). Within a few years, buprenorphine overtook methadone in France (Fatseas and Auriacombe 2007). In the United States, Reckitt Benckiser, having had little luck with Buprenex as an analgesic, was coaxed into pursuing the addiction market by attractive offers from the federal government. During the 1990s, Reckitt Benckiser received $23 million in research subsidies from NIDA to test the drug as a treatment for opiate dependence, and by 2002, the company had secured orphan drug designation from the FDA, granting it license exclusivity until 2009 (for a drug developed in 1973), empowering the company to set the price for the medication untrammeled by competition from generic manufacturers.[2]

Reckitt Benckiser saw the opportunity to "change the face of addiction" in the minds of Americans, in their words—to work against the stigma of addiction treatment by promoting images of people in treatment that challenged stereotypes of addicts as unemployed and criminal. This public relations agenda fit neatly with what the company likely saw as a growing middle-class market for opiate-maintenance treatment. The 1990s were marked by two trends of increased middle-class consumption of nonmedical opiates in the United States. The first was a middle-class heroin epidemic in urban centers including New York City, fueled by pure, cheap Latin American heroin that made sniffing, and heroin chic, fashionable among the middle and upper classes (Hamid et al. 1997). The second, and most significant, was the prescription opiate epidemic of the late 1990s, brought to a head by Purdue Pharma's aggressive marketing of OxyContin as a "nonaddictive" pain reliever. Approved by the FDA in 1996 as a slow-release form of oxycodone, a formulation that the company claimed carried a "less than one percent" risk of addiction, OxyContin was marketed among primary care providers as a safe alternative in the treatment of chronic pain. Users soon learned to crush the slow-release casing and inhale, ingest, or inject its contents for an intense high. By 1999, widespread misuse of OxyContin was being reported, and by 2005, prescription opiates had surpassed heroin as a drug of abuse, second only to marijuana among illicit drugs of abuse (Van Zee 2009).

Reckitt Benckiser was thus well positioned to crack the volatile and often unprofitable addiction market. The company saw two challenges ahead, however: winning generalist physicians over to the model of office-based addiction treatment and breaking the stigmatizing association of opiate-maintenance treatment with criminal, impoverished, and uneducated (and, implicitly, ethnic minority) addicts. So the company worked to associate buprenorphine maintenance with mainstream, respectable people. It targeted an affluent clientele with Internet-based provider-referral networks, consumer blogs, and consumer education as shown in a video public service announcement on the company-sponsored website for the "National Alliance of Advocates for Buprenorphine Treatment." Mike, the middle-aged white man in the video, is apple pie: a diner owner, soccer league coach, and former church choir member supporting his blonde wife and two children in Ohio. He unwittingly became dependent on OxyContin painkillers prescribed for a back injury. A year after starting buprenorphine with a doctor he can trust, he is comfortable being interviewed in his business, flanked by two American flags hanging on his wall.

With this ethnic marketing, Reckitt-Benckiser captured its target audience. According to a nationally representative survey of buprenorphine users and prescribers published by the U.S. Substance Abuse and Mental Health Services Administration (Stanton et al. 2006), 91 percent of U.S. buprenorphine users are white; more than half are college educated; and more than half are employed at baseline. In addition, 50 percent of buprenorphine patients are exclusively dependent on prescription opiates; only one-quarter exclusively use heroin.

Buprenorphine use in New York City in 2007 followed the same patterns when mapped by neighborhood and accompanying social class and ethnic indicators. Using data collected by the U.S. Drug Enforcement Administration from community pharmacies on the number of people living in each Zip code of New York City and its five boroughs, I found that buprenorphine users live in white neighborhoods, neighborhoods with the highest incomes and most college-educated residents. This was consistent with what New York City health officials described to me as an evolving two-tiered system, in which patients able to afford it receive buprenorphine from a private office, while others are directed to methadone maintenance programs with requirements for daily attendance, urine drug screens, surveillance, and control. Moreover, there is little overlap between areas with a high density of methadone programs and those with significant buprenorphine usage (Hansen et al., n.d.).

I first encountered buprenorphine while working in a primary care clinic under the leadership of an early buprenorphine researcher, who advocated "changing the culture of medicine" by getting physicians themselves to see addiction as a physiological disease that is within their ability to treat rather than as a moral problem. I was intrigued by the fact that a pharmaceutical had prompted physicians to attempt cultural change from within medicine.

To understand how users and prescribers are managing the social symbolism of buprenorphine, I spent eleven months as a participant observer in hospital-based clinics that offered buprenorphine. I found that despite buprenorphine's promise of treatment that enhances patients' autonomy, buprenorphine patients are still preoccupied with the locus of control around their prescriptions and how they take their medication. Patients obsess over how often they schedule visits to doctors, who decides how many times a day they take buprenorphine and at what dosage, and whether and how they take other medications or drugs along with buprenorphine. The visual artists among them experiment with "drug holidays"—going off buprenorphine to enhance their creativity and counteract a pharmacological deadening of their senses. Most patients struggle to reconcile feeling "normal" on buprenorphine with being physiologically dependent on a powerful opioid, and thus socially dependent on its manufacturers and prescribers. They harbor fantasies about being drug-free; many attempt to taper themselves off buprenorphine to be drug-free against the advice of their doctors.

Working-class patients in the only public New York City hospital that offers a buprenorphine clinic tell stories about prior institutional violence by hospital staff outside the clinic. Several Latino patients told me that they never mention their addiction when they go to the emergency room for physical problems, because they know that once they are identified as addicts, the staff will not treat their pain and may not even examine or treat their presenting condition. As one man learned when he was hospitalized for phlebitis from injecting heroin: "rounds is when the doctor comes in with ten students first thing in the morning, yanks off my gown, points to the huge boil on my naked butt, and tells them I'm an addict, without even looking me in the eye."

In contrast, buprenorphine prescribers in this public clinic are a unique group. They come out of a harm-reductionist, HIV-prevention, social-advocacy tradition and do not practice clinical business as usual. The buprenorphine program staff in the primary care clinic are available to new patients by cell phone around the clock; patients receive personalized follow-up. The chemical-dependence clinic offers a peer-led community in which patients are invited to participate in groups ranging from art, yoga, and meditation to documentary filmmaking, and they are invited to plant and harvest in the sobriety garden next to the main hospital tower. An echo of the nineteenth-century pastoral care model in psychiatry, of moral therapy that led to the construction in 1929 of the "Narcotics Farm," the federal prison-cum-pastoral rehabilitation center on one thousand acres in Lexington, Kentucky (Campbell et al. 2008), the importance of community gardening to the sobriety of buprenorphine patients was underscored in 2006, when the city hospital proposed to turn the garden into a parking lot. A number of chemical-dependence clinic patients relapsed after the proposal was announced, and the hospital later retracted it.

These clinic doctors are embroiled in a continual struggle to convince buprenorphine patients to stay on their medications for the long term, to help them see that pharmaceuticals return patients to their natural state, to their true self, rather than pharmacologically maintain them in an artificial state. As one prescribing psychiatrist says many times a day to her buprenorphine patients, "When you bang your endorphin receptors— your natural opiate receptors—over and over again over the years with high doses of heroin, your body produces fewer and fewer receptors, they wither, and even if you stop using heroin they may never come back. So the 'bupe' is like insulin for a diabetic; it just replaces what is no longer naturally there." Primary care physicians down the hall work to redefine buprenorphine as a medication (as opposed to a drug of abuse) in the minds of the patients. They remind their patients to take buprenorphine only as prescribed, once a day, like a vitamin, not in response to their mental or physical state but as something preventative and not requiring self-adjustments by the patient. Other prescribers sidestep this struggle, giving control to their patients, supporting them in decisions to divide doses or take more on stressful days or even crush and snort buprenorphine if that makes them feel secure. Nonetheless, buprenorphine is offered as a prosthetic device—a technology for maintaining homeostasis.

These public clinics have an enviable patient-retention rate, which reflects the efforts of their staff to give buprenorphine patients a more positive institutional encounter than they have come to expect. As one staff member told me, given the level of discrimination against drug users in most hospitals, it is no wonder they hesitate to take new medications like buprenorphine that require them to go into withdrawal for induction and to rely on a prescriber to prevent withdrawal thereafter. Her point leads to another insight about biomedical framings of disease: if biomedical institutions have systematically stigmatized particular social groups, members of those groups will not feel less stigmatized if their condition is medicalized. So the success of buprenorphine maintenance at certain clinics may have to do with how the clinic is made atypical by buprenorphine and by how buprenorphine prescribers induct patients into a biochemical order, rather than how buprenorphine is mainstreamed into typical clinics. As Ronald Niezen (1997: 465) writes about medical evangelism among the James Bay Cree Native Americans in colonial Canada: "We can see parallels between biomedicine and evangelical religion: 1) Each carries a conviction of access to vital knowledge . . . 2) This conviction of truth implies the necessity to communicate belief and to change the behavior of those who lack fundamental knowledge . . . reinforced by 'total institutions': boarding schools and hospitals were parallel institutions through which cultural knowledge was communicated and behavior closely observed and corrected." Buprenorphine is the ritual object around which an institutional realignment and a reweaving of the social fabric of care is performed.

Spirit Possession and Receptor Saturation

I finish work late one night at the hospital and offer Bart soup in the diner. He is a carpenter, and I ask how he learned the trade. He describes leaving home in Britain at sixteen, being the last of his peer group to try heroin, and picking up an apprenticeship during the era of Prime Minister Margaret Thatcher, when none of his friends could find work. Bart is politically minded: born to a blue-collar Irish family in the British Isles, he relates that although buprenorphine helps him stay focused on his work, he hates the thought of enriching a multinational pharmaceutical company while on a lifelong maintenance therapy for a so-called chronic disease. In the conversation that follows, Bart charts his mental map of opiates: their cultivation and processing in the Near East and Latin America distribution networks through Eastern Europe and Southern Europe to land in Britain or through Mexico and the Caribbean to the United States. He places himself within these circuits of bodies and substances, imagining himself as a tiny capillary in an enormous opiate-driven organ that has grown new vessels for buprenorphine. And although he is ambivalent about buprenorphine, he finds a sense of social purpose in helping young addicts in his neighborhood shake off withdrawal by sharing his tablets and giving them his psychiatrist's number.

Damian, a former journalist whose penchant for drama led him to report to his last day of work at a newspaper with a needle and syringe stuck in his neck, describes his present life as domesticated. Having supported his past injected-heroin habit as a nighttime cab driver, and having mastered shooting up while driving, he admits that his current routine of psychotherapy for his personality disorder and afternoon classes in social work geared toward counseling other addicts lacks a certain thrill. He is trying to enjoy more subtle forms of satisfaction. His life is reoriented by therapy, social work class, and writing about life on opioid maintenance.

I flash back to Puerto Rico, to my evening with Juan at Misión de Salvación. We sit outside the chapel where sixty ex-addicts are fervently clapping and hopping at culto, giving their emotions and bodies over to the Holy Spirit. Juan explains that he feels called to bring Christ to people outside Puerto Rico. "I want to be a missionary, go to Africa, help the people," he says. "I can do that through the Pentecostal church." His ambition is not so far-fetched: at Academia Nueva Fé a few miles away, the ex-addict Carmen and her husband, Ruben, are preparing for a mission to South America to take the Holy Spirit and a home for addicts to parts of the world that the pastor deems even needier than Puerto Rico.

Addiction links both neurochemically maintained and spiritually maintained people together in an emerging biosociality (cf. Rabinow 1992), marked not only by the physiological memory of escalating opiate use and withdrawal but also by the social memory of skating the margins of the informal economy, of reentering ailing late capitalist service economies as pastoral care providers for other addicts. The alternately hyper-therapized and hyper-evangelized space of their pastoral routines becomes their new magnetic pole, reorienting their senses and energy away from street economics. They take part in major social movements to redefine previously addicted selves as biological or spiritual agents, armed with the self-disciplinary tools of molecular biology or of exorcism and communion. With these tools, Juan, Carmen, Bart, and Damian are working not only within their person but also between persons, conveying spirits, neurotransmitters, and related humors that ebb and flow between somatic and social bodies—bodies that, in the past, strained their boundaries only to be violently snapped into place with diarrhea, bone pain, joblessness, and arrest.

These two versions of agency have obvious differences. The biomedical, therapeutic rituals of buprenorphine clinics ultimately locate the pathology of addiction in the sufferer's body. Although their approach to the biological disorder of addiction implies a host of social interventions—from doctor-patient relationships to the manufacture, marketing, and sale of medication by one of the largest suppliers of household products in the world—the goal of treatment is transformation of the addicted person's body. Although successfully treated addicted people become spokespeople for buprenorphine, and at times become peer counselors, their pharmaceutical evangelism begins and ends with bodies that are "biologically vulnerable" to addiction and relapse.

In contrast, evangelical addiction ministries start with the spiritually vulnerable—people who have descended into the moral depths of addiction and now look for salvation—as an entry point for recruiting "soldiers in God's army" in a war for worldwide spiritual revolution. For evangelists, addicted people are not fundamentally different from other people: all humans are stained by sin, both original and contemporary. The sermons of pastors in addiction ministries center not on addiction but on the moral degradation rampant across society, from adulterous businessmen to a popular culture that treats everything, from consumer goods to young people in poor neighborhoods, as disposable. Addiction ministries locate the pathology of addiction not in individual biologies, but in an imagined global society. This is a fundamental shift from the individualism of pharmaceutical intervention.

Yet both addiction ministries and office-based buprenorphine offer forms of agency that are simultaneously self-disciplinary and social. And they are local end points of international corporate structures—structures with prominent coercive elements. Pastors in addiction ministries, on one hand, are moral authorities ordained not only by their communion with the Holy Spirit but also by global networks of Pentecostals who host teleconferences and missionary campaigns in Latin America, Africa, and Asia. With this international sanction, pastors take disciplinary action against those who question their leadership. I saw many ministry apprentices dismissed from membership altogether for lack of complete obedience in their "discipleship."

Buprenorphine prescribers, on the other hand, are gatekeepers for a patented substance that is manufactured on three continents under exclusive corporate license and that, by 2009, had earned Reckitt Benckiser nearly $1 billion per year in sales.[3] Buprenorphine's physician gatekeepers enforce a clinical discipline based on both the threat of physiological withdrawal from the drug and emotional withdrawal from the relationships and routines of the clinic. In buprenorphine clinics, I observed that the most common reason for physicians to stop writing prescriptions for patients was the patients' unwillingness to keep appointments and adhere to doctors' recommendations. Yet converts and patients in ministries and clinics do not always experience this discipline as externally imposed. Reminiscent of Foucault's biopower (Lemke 2000), the potential oppressiveness of ministerial and clinical corporate structures is also the basis for their transformative value: addicted people's altered sense of self emerges in relation to these structures. João Biehl and his colleagues (2001: 90) write about the "technological prosthesis" of HIV testing among Brazilians who use testing as a route to self-definition, as a route to existential and material forms of social life that emerge from new technologies (such as HIV testing) that create "reification and affective absorption of bio-technical truth and the engendering of a *technoneurosis.*" The "technoneurosis" that Biehl and his colleagues describe among those seeking repeated HIV testing could also apply to opioid-maintained buprenorphine patients, who search for signs of their individuality, agency, and personal worth in relation to the collective through a course of pharmacological treatment.

Evangelists and buprenorphine-maintained people bridge the highly personal, individual states of possession, or neuroreceptor activation, with a view of themselves as part of a worldwide network sharing in a medium, whether of molecules or spirits. They are adapting to a post-Enlightenment, postindustrial struggle of individualism and locality within an unwieldy meshwork of global interdependence. The cultural work that they undertake is an attempt to craft and position the self. Addicts entering evangelical ministries and buprenorphine treatment are told that they are deficient, that the shell of their social existence needs filling, whether with neurotransmitters or spiritual power. They learn that the deficiency is not visible or audible to the naked eye or ear; it is molecular, of opioid neurotransmitters, or ephemerally nonmaterial—"of the spirit." They are inducted into a web of surveillance and monitoring systems, co-pastors and counselors, Bible study leaders and neighborhood pharmacists, but they are also alert to their own signs of progress, monitoring themselves for authentic communion with Christ; for normal energy, sleep patterns, and productivity.

As Mariana Valverde (1998: 28, 127) has put it, early twentieth-century technologies of recovery such as mutual-help groups (e.g., Alcoholics Anonymous) and disease models of addiction (e.g., substance use disorders) were evolutions of "various ways of governing the soul's relation to itself," a way to cultivate a "new relation of self to self." Contemporary evangelism and buprenorphine are recent innovations in the evolution of American addictions that reflect a "tension between desire and will" (Valverde 1998: 33), the manifestation of a neo-Calvinist struggle between cultural motifs of predestination and agency, both personal and social. Evangelism and buprenorphine are products of a unique postindustrial form of dislocation, of a radical individualism and anonymity that reflects unstable social connections and a thin sense of authenticity and purpose. Adherents to both take totalizing phenomena—opiate addiction itself, biomedical subjectivities, neo-evangelist revivals—and attempt to achieve local stewardship of them. Biomedicine and Pentecostal rebirth, apparently individualist models of self that involve somatic uniqueness and personal choice, leverage institutional and cultural materials to create clinical and congregational forms of life.

Notes

This research was supported by Medical Scientist Training Program/National Institutes of Health Training Grant GM07205, the Social Science Research Council Dissertation Field Research Fellowship, the American Psychiatric Association/Substance Abuse and Mental Health Services Administration Minority Fellowship, the Center of Excellence for Culturally Competent Mental Health of the New York State Office of Mental Health and the Nathan Kline Institute, the Robert Wood Johnson Health and Society Scholars Fellowship Program at Columbia University, the Yale Center for International and Area Studies, Yale University's John Perry Miller Fund, and Yale's Council on Latin American Studies. I thank Carmen Albizu, Ann Finlinson, Sara Huertas, Nancy Martinez, Irene Melendez, Salvador Santiago, and the directors and staff of Escuela Bíblica Nueva Fé and Misión de Salvación for making this study possible, as well as Carol Bernstein, Philippe Bourgois, Kathryn Dudley, Mindy Fullilove, Marc Galanter, Ze'ev Levin, Annatina Miescher, Patricia Pessar, Linda-Anne Rebhun, Stephen Ross, and Mary Skinner.

1. *The Economist*, "Therapy of the Masses," November 6, 2003, 12–16.

2. Reckitt Benckiser's vice president, Charles O'Keeffe, and Jerome Jaffe himself later proudly recounted this exemplary "public-private partnership" in disseminating effective new treatments in the article they cowrote for *Drug and Alcohol Dependence* (see Jaffe and O'Keeffe 2003). The resulting financial windfall—earnings of over $3.4 billion between 2005 and 2010 in the United States and Australia—was more discreetly reported in the company's annual report (Reckitt Benckiser 2009, 2010).

3. Simon Bowers and Ian Griffiths, "How a Heroin Substitute Helped to Fuel Profits for Reckitt Benckiser Chief," *Guardian* (London), May 5, 2010, available online at http://www.guardian.co.uk.business (accessed July 13, 2010).

FIVE ANNE M. LOVELL

ELUSIVE TRAVELERS

Russian Narcology, Transnational Toxicomanias, and
the Great French Ecological Experiment

Marseille, the multicultural city whose inhabitants pride themselves on being "not French" (*marseillais pas français*) turns its
back to Paris, as a local expression has it, and faces the other
shore of the Mediterranean, constantly reinventing itself from
the steady stream of "foreigners," their cultures, and their economies (Temime 2006). This popular understanding of the city's
origins inhabits the social imaginary of Marseillais and has produced a vast local and foreign literature, a creolized music (Bordreuil et al. 2003) and cultural cinema, and a colorful yet contradictory political scene.[1] Drugs, too, penetrate this imaginary. In
the past, the maligned "French Connection" evoked Mediterranean trade corridors reaching as far as the ports of North America (Paillard 1994). More recently, cocaine travels to Marseilles
from Northern European platforms, and the hashish grown in
Morocco's Rif region flows to the patchwork of housing projects
and village-like neighborhoods of northern Marseille.[2]

Hence, it is not without some astonishment that, in the first
decade of this century, I sensed vast discomfort among public
health officials and drug treatment workers and social workers
with regard to recently arrived non-Marseillais, whom they
called *les russes* (the Russians). They were described as an elusive
group of undocumented youths regularly "spotted" in the city

center, a triangle that connects the St. Charles railway station and the port with the now heavily West African and Maghrebian Noailles and Belsunce neighborhoods—the very area that for two centuries has served as a transit zone for immigrant groups that make up present-day Marseille.

The staff of a bus dispensing free methadone, run by a nongovernmental organization (NGO) in the area, also made "spottings," only to learn that the Russians were in fact Eastern European: Russians, yes, but also Chechen separatists, Belarusians, Ukrainians, Poles, Czechs, Romanians, and even Bosnians. At first, workers surmised that these newcomers were after methadone or Subutex (high-dose buprenorphine, or HDB) during local heroin shortages. But they came from "somewhere else . . ." and had "no plan, no money," the workers claimed. "It's an enormous problem" (Observatoire Français des Drogues et des Toxicomanies 2003). Here was a new type of drug user. While clients of the bus took methadone for its physical effects—to detox, avoid withdrawal, or just "get loaded" (*se défoncer*)—the Russians and Eastern Europeans were manipulating the methadone program as a way to gain access to health and other services, workers said. Not long afterward, the director of a drug treatment program based at a local hospital confirmed the "arrival of Eastern Europeans . . . presenting themselves as *toxicomanes* [drug abusers]" just so they could receive social services (Observatoire Français des Drogues et des Toxicomanies 2004). In other words, the travelers looked to gain access to drug treatment services for everything except that for which they were primarily intended.

Then, during the summer of the deadly heat wave—the *canicule* of 2003—an official with the Marseilles Public Health Department described to me with horror how abandoned large-gauge syringes, of the sort used in masonry, had been found behind the railway station, under the overpass where homeless people and drug users congregated. Someone was injecting "non-injectable" methadone, too thick for the gauge of syringes provided by outreach workers and needle-exchange automats. The presence of numerous abandoned syringes suggested a group of injectors who, given the urban wasteland setting, would be engaging in unhygienic and hence high-risk practices. Simultaneously, veterinary offices had been broken into, and animal tranquilizers had been stolen. My interlocutor attributed these events to the Russians. But how did she know? Most of them spoke Russian, and according to the bus staff, the occasional ones who knew French would not discuss their drug use.

Local drug users never injected methadone. In fact, methadone is commercialized in France with a chemical security mechanism built in: it is produced in the form of syrup that is too thick to inject. Under these conditions, pharmaceutical leakage (Lovell 2006), or the diversion of methadone to illicit markets and practices such as injection, becomes—in theory—technically impossible (Lovell and Aubisson 2008). The image public health workers purveyed of self-mutilation with a non-injectable medicine using devices for penetrating concrete and stone could only correspond to some elusive "other."

At stake in this narrative for public health officials and drug treatment workers is the success of a municipal drug policy and harm-reduction philosophy that redeemed Marseille from a "sinister" reputation as a mafia-ridden drug platform, a city rife with banditry, corruption, and violence. In the late 1990s, Marseille capitalized on both its relatively early and unique—for France—citywide harm-reduction approach and the promotion of opiate-substitution treatments, primarily Subutex, to position itself in the avant-garde of enlightened drug treatment policy among Mediterranean cities (Lovell and Feroni 1998). Throughout France, from the late 1990s on, Subutex could easily be obtained through universal health coverage from general practitioners' offices, a situation sometimes called France's great ecological experiment.[3] In Marseille, Subutex treatment existed side by side with the free methadone bus, needle-exchange automats on sidewalks, street outreach programs, and an emergency shelter for drug users only—an assemblage of techniques of tolerance to attract drug users largely outside mainstream treatment. Such "hidden populations" (Rhodes et al. 2007), so construed through users' concealment of illicit and stigmatized practices, are the bane of epidemiology and public health efforts, which require practices that make users visible so they can be counted, predicted, and surveilled (Observatoire Français des Drogues et des Toxicomanies 2007).[4] Elusive travelers, then, could only trouble such an assemblage by manipulating its elements for their own purposes, resisting being made visible and introducing contagion in the form of new drugs, diverted medicines, and uncommon means of consumption.

At a more general level, the introduction of transnational drug users to this assemblage reveals how drugs, drug users, drug workers, police, and other officials become entangled not only in diverse ways of managing consuming habits, but also in associated practices of social inclusion, citizenship making, and identity making. Tracing the trajectories of elusive travelers backward, then forward in real time, and observing interactions with the social world of drug prevention and treatment in Marseille —the milieux that contribute to the materialization of those trajectories— allows us to conceptually link contrasting regimes of drug management: the narcology-influenced policing methods used in Russia and other Eastern European countries and the addiction-based yet resolutely social techniques and policies of contemporary France.[5]

Movement, or users' attachment at different points that constitute the assemblage, avoids falling under the totalizing effects of a single regime, though, as we shall see, rules and tools of both regimes, as well as the contingencies of movement, contribute to the subjectification of travelers themselves. The conceptual juxtaposition of regimes also reveals discursive spaces that counter at least two contemporary master narratives: the successful transformation in France of drug dependence as an object of treatment into addiction, which is grounded in modern medicine and the neurosciences, and the postmodern discourse of drug addiction as an end state, or what Gilles Deleuze and Félix Guattari (1987: 285) call the rigidification of drug, dealer, and dependence. Contrary to these master narratives, the trajectories reveal a complex play of constantly reconfigured elements, without closure.

This chapter, then, presents a transnational phenomenon of drug users as an analytic to further our understanding of the specific heterogeneity of addiction as epistemic object and the more general relationship between individual drug users, institutions, and states in the contemporary, globalized era of biopolitics and biological citizenships. First, I discuss the potential of trajectories and movement as heuristic devices (albeit undertheorized ones in medical anthropology) for understanding addiction. Then I present a range of trajectories drawn from narratives of the so-called Russians, elusive travelers whose movements link two drug-management regimes: a medical, legal, and social regime based on Soviet narcology and a solidarity-based hybrid of harm reduction and biomedical treatment particular to France. I will use the term "drug management," which is neutral as to whether the object being managed is drug consumption, a medical condition, or an individual. Similarly, throughout the chapter I use the terms "toxicomania" and "toxicomanic" instead of "drug dependence" or "addiction" to reflect local biologies and etiologies. Toxicomania terminology inhabits everyday language in both the contexts from which the elusive travelers depart and the drug-management nexus they encounter in France.

I also examine how toxicomania, as a "constituent matter of life," troubles current theses of biological and therapeutic citizenship. Finally, I show how, far from being autonomous, entrepreneurial individuals or "unencumbered selves" (Ong 2006), the Russians cannot escape processes of subjectification in the discursive spaces of Marseille any more than local users can. The exterior world of drug management they move in and out of folds back onto these travelers, engaging them in identity making and resistance. In conclusion, I will suggest what this analysis contributes to the new anthropologies of addiction.

The Logics of Circulation
Flows and Parts: Theorizing Travel in Medical Anthropology

Underlying recent anthropological contributions to understanding biologicals, pharmaceuticals, therapeutics, biocapital, and bodies are phenomena of movement: global flows of objects, internal flow of bodily substances, individuals tracing trajectories. The social lives perspective posits medicines as substances whose meanings and social uses are shaped by multiple logics and practices that transform them as they trace paths across time and space (van der Geest et al. 1996). The anthropology of science and science studies both deepen and broaden the analysis, revealing the pertinence of the movement of medicines through overlapping spheres, such as research, development, and production (Gaudillère 2005); marketing and regulation (Feroni and Lovell 2007; Lovell and Feroni 2005); and consumption. More recent work reveals how forms of global health depend on the capacity to decontextualize and recontextualize objects and human subjects across diverse geographies and spheres of life (Ong and Collier 2005). The trafficking in organs is an early and outstanding example of this work, as body parts, donors, willing and unwilling victims, and medical tourists cross paths, reproducing global inequalities and regimes of life on a large scale (Scheper-Hughes 2000). "Immutable mobiles" such as therapeutic regimes, standardization procedures, clinical trials, and other elements of global medical assemblages cross borders between "growth regions" and geopolitical sites of available bodies and other resources, reappearing in the production of scientific knowledge and harnessing of medical markets (Petryna 2009). Medical humanitarianism as a form of traveling sovereignty embeds these movements in processes of biological and therapeutic citizenship that bypass borders in numerous problematic ways (Nguyen 2005; Pandolfi 2001).

Movement as a heuristic device contributes to understanding drugs in new ways, as well. Within the individual body, such substances configure spatially, temporally, and functionally in complex ways with potentially competing effects, as has been conceptualized for psychotropic medications such as stimulants, sedatives, anxiolytics, and even antidepressants (Kirmayer and Raikhel 2009). For psychoactive substances to transform themselves into catalysts for and objects of pleasure and desire, they must circulate not only through blood, brain, and other body sites but also through social settings. For example, the same addictive pharmaceutical circulates between sites of therapeutic legitimacy (e.g., factory, pharmacy, physician's office) and through informal and illicit networks (e.g., the drug market). In doing so, the pharmaceutical morphs from clean to "dirty" commodity in a social space that is beyond the grasp of medical deontology and state regulatory mechanisms (Lovell 2006). While neuroscience and cognitive models recognize the relationship between site and effect (see Campbell, this volume), such models cannot address the hierarchy of values, the practices, and the collective symbolization that determine the meaning of drugs according to setting—that is, they cannot access the social. However, they provide another model of addiction based on knowledge of where bodies flow and with what they form conjunctions—and not simply the flowing of a substance within a body for understanding drugs.

At the other end of these connected elements—pharmaceuticals and other substances, treatment modalities, illicit markets—drug users are in movement. Old studies depicted the Skid Row alcoholic caught in repetitive movements between places of drink, sustenance, and recovery (see, e.g., Wiseman 1970); today's addiction can be mapped onto circular movements between domesticity, resources for recovery, and gambling (Schüll, this volume). None of these accounts examine movement across expanses of space, let alone transnational displacement. Philip Lalander, for example, studied heroin users in local "drifting cultures"—taking days as they come, refusing schedules imposed by authorities, focusing on the here and now. The drama of drug use—"plans," "deals," transgressions, accidents, contingencies—fuels restlessness. Drifting reinforces a drug culture that promotes the illusion of equality, with its own history and codes

(Lalander 2003). Postmodern accounts focus on desire flowing through bodies and bodies linked up with other elements, such as heroin, needles, or a certain aesthetic or milieu. Bodies reconfigure these elements, moving around in different processes of territorialization: the drug user in an "ordalic" experience of extreme risk taking,[6] or contained within a public health discourse, by an addiction treatment, in a prison cell. Postmodernists disagree, however, about the possibilities in an assemblage of drugs, pleasure, therapeutics, and repression. Deleuze and Guattari (1987) posited the drugged body as a body without organs, a configuration of collapsed possibilities, emptiness, sickness, and alienation. Current cultural analysts turn this vision around, reinvigorating the drugged body as always capable of changing territories and relations: to the drug, to treatment, to the law, but also to music, to aesthetics, and—why not?—to drifting (Boothroyd 2006; Malins 2004).

All of these approaches undertheorize the movement of bodies in global biopolitical assemblages. Because they rarely consider different drug-management regimes within a globalized world, they allow only partial analyses of how regimes affect one another, even coexist. Yet even a seemingly unvarying addiction treatment, such as Suboxone or Subutex in general practice, will differ according to the assemblage to which it is attached (as an implicit comparison between this chapter and the chapters by Meyers and Hansen in this volume attests). Conceptualizing movement toward an endpoint rather than through points along an assemblage, multiple and changeable in their effects, decomplexifies the *pharmakon*-like nature of the substance, the multiple actors, materials, and symbols involved. Grasping a global movement requires us to view not only the flow of body parts, therapeutics, and drugs but also the movement of bodies that consume them, from the global flow of substances that shape cosmopolitan medicine and illicit consumption where they touch down to the transnational flows of people (as intensive drug users, curious partiers, pharmaceutical consumers, patients). In this view, the controversy over the neuro-biologization of problem drug use in France, thanks to opiate substitutes such as buprenorphine and methadone, and the struggle to introduce these addiction pharmaceuticals into Eastern Europe must be seen as they affect other parts of the world and, as I will show later, in quests for biological citizenship.[7] As we shall see, subjectivities are shaped and identities are contested in a space of becoming that lies between competing and sometimes hybrid cultural identities suspended between drug use and heterogeneous addiction therapeutics and in the relation between the two.

In Europe since the mid-1990s, not only drugs but users themselves have traveled along the corridors of illicit traffic, much likes the hippies who headed toward Asia thirty years earlier, but with different objectives. *Traveleurs*, or drifters for whom a nomadic rave scene mutated into a permanent lifestyle of drugs and often violence, social precariousness, even disease, crossed the United Kingdom, Germany, France, and Spain.[8] The wealthy ones flew to Switzerland or New York to "withdraw"; the poor ones sojourned in villages and small towns where drugs were often hard to come by. In Marseille, Maghrebi families sent their sons back to the *bled*—in Arabic, one's village or country of origin, but also a sort of moral topology of kin networks and purity associated with healing and the return to traditional values. In a period of rising racism in France, Andalusian and Catalan gypsies living along an arc from Spain through France and Italy were rumored to apply their *savoir-circuler* (nomadic know-how) to the heroin trade, becoming users themselves (Messaoui 2002; Tarrius 2001). State policymakers redefined these gypsies as communities in decay, identifying high rates of AIDS as resulting from father-son injecting dyads, the weakening of the traditional patriarchal structure, and the subsequent out-marrying of gypsy women in large numbers (Messaoui 2002). Hence, the flow of bodies in conjunction with imagined or real addictions were fixed categorically through a biopolitical othering (Fassin 2001). It is in this context that we can place the arrival in Marseille of elusive travelers from Eastern Europe.

Elusive Travelers and Drug Management Regimes

Shortly after the methadone-injection rumor started, our ethnographic team first encountered the "Russians." Pavel, a tall and wiry, well-dressed twenty-four-year-old from Kiev, told me that he and his Ukrainian friends had been given doses of methadone at the methadone bus. They had frozen it into ice cubes and, once it separated, melted off the active component. It was so thick that they had to acquire masonry syringes. "It was disgusting! I could never do it again," Pavel said. Some of his friends continued experimenting with the substance, however, in the collective construction of tacit knowledge that elsewhere I call the "pharmaco-associative" (Lovell 2006).[9]

Like Pavel, the twenty or so other Eastern European men we encountered between 2002 and 2004 (female travelers were rare and quickly moved on) frequented the central-city triangle, the site of the NGO's methadone and needle-exchange bus and of "the Room," an emergency shelter for drug users situated down the street from the railway station. Why did they come to Marseille? Some said they had come because friends were already there. Others had heard it was easy to meet Russians in Marseille. Russian, in fact, is often heard on the Canabière, the once stately boulevard visible from the station that leads to the port. Approach Russians when you step off a train from Paris and they will explain everything, we were told: where to sleep, where to eat for free, how to apply for papers. If you spot toxicomanes—and you can tell who they are—they will tell you what is around and how to use it. In Marseille, the atmosphere is easy: "You have the cops next to you, the needle exchange machine, the guys smoking dope, the café, the dealers. They're all there at the same time." You make friends with other Russians—not drug users—who let you stay in their apartments. You learn how to steal upscale clothes from stores that you can sell in the streets and at the open market of Noailles. You can make 30–40 euros a day. The Room costs 1.5 euros. You can get Subutex for 10 euros. You will have plenty of money left over to buy beer or food if you do not want to eat at a cafeteria run by some nuns. You can work "black," too, at parking lots or building sites. Then you can chip in with compatriots to buy a used car for about 600 euros and travel to Nice and to Spain—until you are stopped because you do not have drivers' licenses or insurance and the car is confiscated. It is not a bad life.

Pavel, the son of a military officer and a mother who worked as an accountant, grew up near Kiev with a brother and sister. He was trained as a computer programmer, a skill he later honed in the army. As a teenager, he hung out on the ground floor of his apartment building with friends who trafficked in home-concocted opium, or *chorny* (black), made from raw poppy straw.[10] After watching them consume opium a few times, Pavel joined in. At first, the chorny was free. Eventually, he started injecting opium he purchased. He became a "toxicomane"—the Russian and French terms are etymologically similar, implying passion for or uncontrollable attraction to the effects of a particular substance. "My toxicomania was like a woman," he recollected, and "the needle was my brother."[11] When I met him, he extolled opium as a drug that, if taken at the correct dose, allowed him to work at his computer job; it was "not like cocaine, where if you don't pay attention, it explodes the heart," and, he would later surmise, it was not like heroin, which overcomes you. But he also described a downside: although he was still young, he had seen friends overdose and die. One had had his leg amputated because of gangrene (Pavel points to the inner thigh, where the friend injected). When Pavel started selling his parents' possessions to buy opium, they committed him to a forensic psychiatric hospital in Ukraine. He was strapped to a table to withdraw "cold" and injected with drugs. He did not know what they were. "You crave [opium]; you crave," he said. "Then they inject you. You hallucinate, you hallucinate. For ten hours. Then no craving." He was sick. The first time, he escaped from the hospital. Another time, he was forced to stay for three weeks. But each time he left, he started injecting opium again within weeks.

Pavel left Ukraine in 2000. His cousins and aunts and uncles had already dispersed to different parts of Russia and to Moldova, wherever they found work. Their pattern was common in Ukraine, as young people in particular crossed borders to find jobs or buy merchandise to bring back and trade (K. Roberts et al. 2003). Pavel himself had found little work after the army. Because he had been hospitalized for opium abuse, he was marked. "In Ukraine, the toxicomane—it's not like in France. In Ukraine, if someone is a toxicomane, he is already a criminal. If I am a toxicomane, I don't go to a hospital; I go to prison." He and several other Eastern Europeans we spoke to explained that their names were entered into a registry simply because they were caught for using drugs. They were harassed whenever they were suspected of stealing or consuming drugs, and the police often had to be paid off.

Pavel knew that friends from Kiev lived in Marseille. He rode buses and trains through Poland and Germany and obtained a tourist visa for France. He crossed into Strasbourg and worked his way to Marseille. That is where he started using again—heroin and methadone (briefly), then Rohypnol and Subutex—but always as a temporary sort of self-medication that, he convinced himself, he could "psychologically stop" whenever he wanted. "I was obliged to come to France, [but ultimately] I want to live in my country," he said. "France is for the French. I'll find a job [in Ukraine]. I'll have a family, children—live!"

Vladimir came from a better-off family in Vladivostok (Russia). His father had been an instructor for the merchant marine but had died young. We met Vladimir one afternoon at the NGO's office, where a social worker was filling out a request so he could see a doctor to get hepatitis-C treatment. After his father died, Vladimir had quit school to work on ships sailing around the world. He dabbled in heroin, mostly sniffing, and was accused of a robbery he said he did not commit. Back on Russian territory, he was drafted but did not want to fight in Chechnya. So at twenty, Vladimir flew to Moscow, then on to Paris, before the police could catch him. He joined the Foreign Legion and was stationed near Marseille. After being kicked out for fighting, he went to Switzerland, thinking it would be easier to obtain identity papers. He was allowed to stay for three months, with an allowance. At his shelter, Georgians "taxed" the residents, he told us, and Kosovars brought in brown heroin. He started sniffing again with the other travelers who shared his room, until his time in Switzerland ran out. He returned to Vladivostok, where, he said, Tadjiks were trafficking in very pure and inexpensive white heroin. He bought it from them and became a small-time dealer, selling just enough to pay for his personal supply. Eventually, he left on a ship, hoping to get off heroin "cold." When the maritime company he was working for went bankrupt, he returned to France. In Marseille, he replaced heroin with injected Subutex, and then cocaine. Stealing has taken him in and out of French jails, which he, like other Eastern Europeans, describes as "Club Med." But, he says, "give me 2,000 euros and I'll go back to Russia tomorrow. I'll start a little business."

Vladimir's and Pavel's trajectories and points of origin may differ, but they resemble each other in their transnational character. Their migration is impermanent, with the relationship between "here" and "there" maintained, however fragile it may be. In this sense, they are transnational drug consumers. Several other threads run through their tales and those of other elusive travelers, rendering the very act of travel thick with meaning and, sometimes, crossed intentions. Being "tracked," "marked," or registered as a toxicomane and a criminal—the two are often the same, as we shall see—becomes a major push to leave. Experiences of harrowing and ultimately ineffective drug treatment—or the equally frightening lack of such treatment in jails or prisons, without medication to relieve the sickness—were recounted in other narratives, as well. Andriy, a registered toxicomane who had been arrested many times for petty theft in the mining town near Donetsk that was his home represented an extreme example of such despair. He described himself as totally taken over by his need for opium. His parents scrimped together enough money to send him over the border; leaving became the only means to help him live.

Traveling can also express a therapeutic quest. In Romania, Christian became addicted to heroin, which had come through Iran and Iraq from farther east. Like those who sold heroin to him in Bucharest, Christian would become an undocumented migrant. He had already served almost a year in prison for possessing a syringe by the time his parents committed him to a "hospital for the mad," where he was given "medicine to make [his] brain forget." Christian's experience resembled Pavel's, and Christian, too, escaped, sleeping in a friend's car or on the streets and soon injecting heroin. When his distraught mother found him, filthy and sick, she sent him to an uncle in Marseille to stop using drugs. His uncle blamed lack of willpower for Christian's drug use and locked him in a room for a month while his aunt brought him daily meals.

Intentionally or not, traveling broadens the palette of drugs and drug-related experiences. After finishing his military service, Vitaly, an ethnic Russian from Ukraine who had been trained in the building trades by his father, left to find better work in the Czech Republic. He lacked working papers, but not skills, and soon found an abundance of jobs, which he took using someone else's name. He had money to spend and frequented clubs where "the drugs moved around." He liked to inject the amphetamine perventine, which, he said, bonded people so that strangers could talk together for hours. His girlfriend also used the amphetamine, however, and they soon spiraled downward together. He left his girlfriend to go to the Netherlands, where he tried hallucinogens, but France appealed to him more. He landed in Marseille, where he quickly found Russian-speakers and methadone users who were receiving treatment from the free bus but got more than they needed and were able to sell the excess. He bought methadone from them and carefully self-medicated with oral doses in the absence of more attractive drugs.

Thus, traveling opens up numerous possibilities and follows various logics of consumption and rejection of substances. Illicit drug-management regimes linked by these individual trajectories further open up or, on the contrary, constrain these possibilities. Such linkages tie individual bodies to one or the other social body—or to several social bodies at once—in different ways. Conceptualized as ideal types, the two regimes between which the "Russians" circulated, illustrate this.

From Narcology to the Solidarity-Biological
Nexus of Addiction Management
Narcology and the Criminalization of Opiate Substitution Therapy

Although Eastern European countries are undergoing massive transformations in their drug-treatment and drug-prevention regimes (Sarang et al. 2007), Soviet-era Russian narcology, a subspecialty of psychiatry, continues to exert much influence on drug treatment and to serve as a point of departure for the trajectories I have just described. Narcology arose at a time that Soviet officials viewed alcohol-related morbidity as a widespread social problem (which it remains today) but touted the absence of morbidity related to illicit drugs. They drew a sharp contrast between "misuse of prescription drugs," which was a recognized problem in the Soviet Union, with the widespread "toxicomanias" of the capitalist West (Babayan and Gonopolsky 1985). In this chapter, I discuss neither the origins of narcology nor its relationship to particular types of personhood (but see Raikhel, this volume). Instead, I draw on the *Textbook on Alcoholism and Drug Abuse in the Soviet Union* (Babayan and Gonopolsky 1985), an official teaching tool of narcology, whose first author, Eduard Babayan, promoted its perspective at the level of Russian social policy until his death in 2009 (Elovich and Drucker 2008) and on additional observations in the international literature to highlight elements that correspond to the fragments of experiences brought forward in the narratives we gathered.

Soviet narcology represented a centralized management system for all toxicomanias, whether they were related to alcohol or illicit drugs, as well as a conceptualization of substance-linked morbidity and social phenomena. The underlying concept of narcology, and of the apparatus of services and surveillance of individuals who consume illicit drugs, rests on three dimensions. The first is the medical dimension, which incorporated an understanding and response to the effects of narcotics on the central nervous system—such as sedation, stimulation, and hallucination—that render the substance attractive for nontherapeutic uses (Babayan and Gonopolsky 1985: chap. 36). It also implied the need for medical treatment, the essence of which I discuss later. The second, or legal, dimension was embedded in a tautological definition of the object of narcology: that class of drugs legally defined by national laws and international convention as "narcotics" and, hence, illicit. Finally, the social dimension referred to the potential scale of illicit use of narcotics, which can reach proportions great enough to be recognized as a social problem (Babayan and Gonopolsky 1985). This last dimension depicted patients under the influence of narcotics as lacking self-control and awareness of the danger they pose to self and society or the state. This problem of social volition was the justification for necessary incarceration—either forced hospitalization or prison. Simply using narcotics, then, was a basis for criminalization. At a surface level, these dimensions do not differ from the assumptions behind the French "master" Law of 1970, which also criminalized drug use. However, as we shall see, the 1970 legislation is configured differently, resulting in contrasting relationships between state and drug users in each of the two drug-management regimes.

To this somewhat abstract explication, two practical translations should be added. First, during the Soviet period, narcology operated through an alliance of the Ministry of Health and the Ministry of the Interior. In particular, personal information on individuals entering treatment was entered into a national registry, marking them as toxicomanic and providing data for public health monitoring, but with the aggregate effect of making visible a stigmatized and hence vulnerable population.[12] Families and sometimes individuals were caught between wanting to treat an addiction and rejecting the possibility of marking the toxicomanic in this way.[13] Treatment without registration has become available since the early 1990s but only at a cost that has made it inaccessible to many. Second, treatment throughout the 1990s and 2000s was limited mostly to heavily medicated detoxification and, when resources and staff were lacking, "cold turkey" withdrawal. Therapy is available only in private clinics, which most people cannot afford. Treatment based on opiate substitution with synthesized medication, particularly methadone, continues to be interpreted as the legalization and promotion of another narcotic rather than as a medical means of addressing the question of substance abuse or dependence (Bobrova et al. 2007; Elovich and Drucker 2008).

When borders opened after the collapse of the Soviet Union, drugs flowed in from Central Asia and Afghanistan, and drug dealing came to constitute somewhat fluid "ethnic businesses," a survival means for groups with little access to work and residence permits in Russia. At the same time, widespread unemployment, especially among youths, has been associated with a propensity for narcotics consumption (Orlova 2009). Outside analysts concluded that if drug policy in the former Soviet Union targeted trafficking, it was drug users who became the target of policing.

The focus on users, coupled with their continual surveillance through toxicomania registries and ubiquitous police corruption, led to the widespread harassment and payoffs (Elovich and Drucker 2008; Orlova 2009) that are so evident in the narratives of Pavel and others. Furthermore, researchers with Human Rights Watch reported that police in several countries of the former Soviet Union subjected drug users to physical and psychological pressure, including severe beatings, electroshock, partial suffocation with gas masks, and threats of rape, as a means to extort money or information from them (Human Rights Watch 2006). Reformers intent on replacing criminalization of drug use and addiction with humane medical forms of treatment have also been persecuted and imprisoned (Parfitt 2006b).

Since the mid-2000s, countries such as Ukraine have introduced opiate maintenance (Schaub et al. 2009), but not without a struggle. The absence of a "modern" therapeutic regime in some countries of the former Soviet Union became a source of international contention, similar to the case for many years in France, which for different reasons opposed opiate-substitution therapies until the mid-1990s (Lovell 2006). For example, the World Health Organization (WHO) pressured France to shift from a nonmedicalized to a biological treatment for opiate dependence (Bergeron 1999). More recently, WHO placed similar demands on the Russian Federation, Ukraine, Belarus, and neighboring countries, decrying the lack of opiate substitution for drug users and their marginalization and discrimination as an obstacle to obtaining anti-retroviral treatment,[14] intravenous drug use being the major route of HIV transmission in these countries (Poznyaka et al. 2002). The originators of Marseille's free methadone bus and other NGOs promote similar harm reduction and citizenship projects (which I discuss later) in the countries of the former Soviet Union, but with variable success, given this institutional context.

Although opiate-substitution programs have since been introduced in Ukraine and some former Soviet and Eastern European countries (Bruce et al. 2007; Schaub et al. 2009), during the early 2000s, the period when the Russians left their country of origin (one to two years, on average, before we encountered them), the narcology perspective still governed the management and treatment of drug users. Ironically, about the time I met Pavel, a Russian medical delegation visiting Marseille to learn about the drug treatment and harm reduction system and eventually transfer the technology, concluded by vehemently rejecting the "enlightened approach" on which the city of Marseille prides itself.[15] It is to this approach that I now turn.

National Solidarity and the Biologization of Toxicomania

When the Russians arrived in Marseille, French health-policy makers and practitioners had already accomplished the process of biologizing "toxicomania," a practical category rooted in pre-biological, social, psychoanalytic, and moral understandings of the relation between drugs and the person who consumes them. But toxicomanes have not been magically transformed into addicts with a chronic disease. Not only do traces remain of the old toxicomania model, but the responses to problem drug use extend beyond biology to a particular solidarity practice.[16] Hence, biological treatment becomes inseparable from questions of solidarity and, ultimately, citizenship, thereby producing a hybrid model. And, as we shall see, the transnational phenomenon of Eastern European drug users arriving in Marseille intersects with drug treatment in ways, albeit contradictory, made possible by these solidarity practices.

At the level of the individual user, nineteenth-century psychiatric notions and psychoanalytic theory have long posited toxicomania as the object of passion, as well as a question of volition. From the 1980s to the mid-1990s, professionals competed for control over the care of toxicomanes. Psychiatrists, psychoanalysts, and social workers displaced the medicalized interventions of general practitioners with psychosocially and psychoanalytically oriented approaches. Their use of medication was limited to the management of withdrawal and the prescription of psychotropics. The master Law of 1970, still in force, established compulsory treatment as an alternative to prison for indicted drug users. Paradoxically, in the absence of standardized treatment interventions, the courts continued to be the main route into treatment. With methadone limited to a few experimental slots and buprenorphine not yet authorized as a treatment for opiate dependence, interventions tended to be psychosocial or psychoanalytic, rather than medical, well into the mid-1990s.

Parallel to this tendency, "biologization" emerged as activator and effect of the often contentious twenty-year process catalyzed by a small network of French and Belgian physicians, drug users and activists, and researchers in the French pharmaceutical industry. In the end, Subutex, a sublingual form of HDB, was authorized in general medical practice,[17] and methadone was permitted under more restricted conditions. But the mere availability of a biological treatment does not suffice for it to be used, as pharmaceutical companies know (Barry 2005).[18] Toxicomanes themselves, many of them without identification papers after long periods on the streets and outside the social protection network, first had to be legitimized as subjects for treatment. Thus, as I will show, this biologization is only partial, constituting an element within the larger assemblage that eventually led to a hybrid biosolidarity.[19] To understand its emergence, we must examine the notion of solidarity itself, which is so central to French personhood.

French solidarity is rooted in the organicist idea of society conceived by political thinkers of the early Third Republic (1879–1940). Although influenced by Catholic understandings of solidarity grounded in charity and compassion, the French Revolution ideal of *fraternité*, and nineteenth-century mutual aid, solidarism is firmly entrenched in French republicanism, an almost sacred notion of the state as the expression of the general interest of the nation and the embodiment of the greater good of its citizens. Republican solidarity emerged around the "social question," or the mid-nineteenth-century debates over the social and economic problems of industrialization, urbanization, and capitalism (Nicolet 1982; Silver 1994). Out of the ideological opposition between market liberalism and socialism, solidarity forged a third way, positing the individual not as a monad but as a citizen, part of a larger body to which he (women did not obtain suffrage until 1944) contributes and that, in turn, both recognizes him and guarantees his protection. These protections would later be conceptualized as *social property*, a form of social citizenship. While capitalists and landowners possess material property, the wage earner of industrial capitalism possesses this nonmaterial social property in the form of assurances or guarantees, or, paraphrasing Alfred Fouillée (1884, cited in Castel 2009), the minimum human capital necessary for the citizen to live freely and equal to others. Émile Durkheim's theory of organic solidarity and the division of labor provided the "scientific" basis for this solidarity, in a dual sense: not only did Durkheim's vision of society draw directly on natural science models of the era (Berthelot 1999), but political thinkers naturalized social solidarity on the basis of Durkheim's theory of social forms of reciprocal dependence constitutive of a whole. That social organism became conflated with the political body of the Republic.

The founding of France's compulsory health insurance system, the *régime général* (commonly known as Sécurité Sociale), in 1945 was anchored in social solidarity. Robert Castel's history of the "social" illustrates the extent to which the justification for this massive pillar of France's system of social protection rests on *corporatist* solidarity (theorized in Durkheim's social division of labor). The citizen benefits from national health insurance (and other manifestations of social protection) on the grounds of being a (legal) worker, his or her dependent, or someone officially recognized as unable to work. In fact, the so-called *régime général* is actually a fragmented system, with about 20 percent of its beneficiaries enrolled in a profession-determined state insurance system, such as those for agricultural workers or employees of the national railroad. But the point here is that the beneficiary is a citizen socially integrated into the Republic by virtue of work affiliations that contribute to maintaining the social body.

The treatment and management of toxicomanes in France is inseparable from considerations of solidarity. But the transformation of the social figure of the toxicomane (along with the construction of youth as a social category in and of itself) from a marginal issue to a widely felt social problem during the late 1970s shook the ideology of Republican solidarity. Alain Ehrenberg argues that the status of the drug user threatened the Republican notion of the citizen by setting off new tensions between private and public spheres of life. Whereas American drug treatment, including the then widespread therapeutic communities, rested on the idea of a society composed of individuals, French approaches to toxicomania could not be imagined outside a policy of state-determined, collective emancipation (Ehrenberg 1995). If toxicomanics are citizens, the logic goes, it behooves them to distance themselves from any particular interests or social groups (like that of fellow drug users) and to accept the general interest incorporated in the law (and, for politicized Lacanians, the Law). By pursuing individual pleasure and passion in a heretofore unthinkable manner, the toxicomane exemplified a new kind of individual, outside the well-worn paths of class-based, normative trajectories.[20]

But toxicomania threatened Republican solidarity in a less abstract way, as well. By the 1990s, the appearance of large segments of the population— initially, the "new poor"—tested the limits of the French social protection system. For one, they were seen as outside, and often as never having entered, the world of official work to which the welfare system is connected. "Poverty" did not exist in the language of the Republican solidarity model—although Fourth World and other Catholic solidarity movements in France embraced the term—because theoretically all citizens are already in a reciprocal dependence with the state. The growing numbers of poor and disenfranchised people were seen as proof that the social bond (*lien social*)—in fact, a political relationship created by interdependence within the Republican body state—had broken.

Government reports and official texts began to classify toxicomanics under the rubric of the excluded (*exclus*), alongside the chronically unemployed, the disabled, and so forth. Although sociological studies were slow to include toxicomanics among the victims of social disqualification (see, e.g., Paugam 1996, which does not mention drug addiction), toxicomanes themselves described the bottoming-out experience of marginality as *la galère* (a nightmare or painful ordeal),[21] as opposed to the ordalic pleasure of initial drug consumption. Through this process, they, like other socially disqualified people (e.g., the so-called new poor), fell through the administrative net woven from the information contained in identification papers, national health insurance cards, taxes, and other institutions that permit counting and categorizing and thus make them *visible* to state workers.

National responses to the rise of exclusion in France completed the transformation of the meaning of solidarity. Two new elements materialized this transformation by extending solidarity beyond citizens linked to the state through work. The first, the Revenu Minimal d'Insertion, a tax-funded guaranteed minimum income (recently replaced by the Revenu de Solidarité Active), is available to citizens age twenty-five and older and sought by drug users, as well as by others outside the workforce. The second is the less visible (to the toxicomane) Contribution Sociale Générale, a flat tax on all income, investments, and social benefits paid by all "integrated" citizens to support those outside the safety net. Some commentators interpret these innovations as a new humanistic understanding of solidarity (Béland and Hansen 2000). For the French intellectual who has most contributed to imagining these reforms, they correspond to a national solidarity in which the state, always the legitimate expression of the community of citizens, has the obligation to protect all of its citizens— not simply in relation to work (Rosanvallon 2000 [1995]). Finally, in the healthcare arena, this solidarity translates into the universal medical coverage approved in 2000, which extends the general regime of social security to French citizens without links to the world of work.

Besides guaranteed minimum income and the special tax,[22] everyday practices in Marseille extend this enlarged Republican notion of solidarity and connect it to the social world of drug use, treatment, and management. The way in which outreach and other workers conceptualize "harm reduction" (usually translated into French as "risk reduction") illustrates one set of solidarity exchanges. Harm reduction in public health usually refers to practices and policy oriented to the possible damage engendered by taking substances and by their means of administration. Harm reduction interventions often frame substance use practices in terms of a series of choices around consumption along a range of possible actions, from the most harmful (e.g., sharing needles) to the least harmful (abstinence). In principle, harm reduction policy transmits knowledge and the means to make those choices in what I have elsewhere termed a manifestation of the (then) new public health, articulated on the assumption of an autonomous individual and his or her responsibilities for self-care (Lovell 2001).

Service providers in Marseille, however, practice risk reduction as an *interpersonal relationship* that diminishes the social distance between themselves and drug users. Not only does each party exchange knowledge, but it behooves the provider to demonstrate his or her acceptance of the drug user. This approach—now codified (Richaud and Febvrel 2005)—stemmed from numerous practices we observed: use of the familiar *tu* form of address and first names (including aliases) between worker and user; the tendency of providers to discuss their own personal situations or problems with users; and the ritual exchanges of the *bise* (kiss on the cheek), a gendered greeting common among men in Marseillais but more restricted to heterosexual contact or contact among women in other parts of France. These solidarity practices bond worker and user, an initial step toward including bodies in the larger social body.

Simultaneously, the biologization of toxicomania through the introduction of Subutex was envisioned at the national level as a way to provide access to medical care for all—a reflection of Republican values in keeping with the modified meanings of solidarity. Workers employed by NGOs explicitly used their services as a conduit—and not as an alternative—to le *droit commun*, or the ordinary rights and services that apply to every citizen. In other words, rather than supporting the idea of exceptional arrangements, such as special services for toxicomanics, they sought to integrate them into the healthcare system. The term *droit commun* literally translates as ordinary or common law, but a more technical meaning differentiates the exception in matters of rules, laws, forms of societal support, and programs from those ordinarily applicable or available to all citizens. For example, the Law of 1970 that defines procedures and penalties for drug users falls outside the droit commun because it requires a longer pretrial detention than that spelled out in criminal law for other types of suspected crimes. In the Marseille social world of drug prevention, treatment, and harm reduction, social actors use the expression "le droit commun" to refer to nonspecialized housing, healthcare, and minimum guaranteed income, as opposed to resources for special groups, such as the Room, the emergency shelter that accepts only drug users.

This opposition is illustrated by an exchange I had with a nurse, Valérie, who had just returned from accompanying Taufik, whose arms were badly swollen with abscesses from shooting up Subutex, to the public hospital. The emergency room had released Taufik without treating him, and Valérie feared he might develop gangrene. I asked her what she could do. "The problem is to get the toxicomanes into le droit commun," she responded, as if that required a visa. Instead, for now she could only offer individuals such as Taufik the (inadequate) health services of NGOs, like the bus, the unintended effect of which was further stigmatization as both an *exclu* and a recipient of a service for drug users rather than citizens. Taufik, she insisted, had a right to be treated like any patient, and ordinary patients are not turned away from public emergency rooms. I asked where services provided by the bus begin and end. The NGO's mission, she responded, was to promote the acceptance of toxicomania as a disease like any other so that drug-specific services would no longer be needed. Her NGO's job was to create the necessary conduit, obliging change on the part of the healthcare system and eventually making their own drug-specialized services obsolete.

We have now seen how two drug-management regimes are linked through the travel of the Russians. At one end, at the beginning of the twenty-first century, networks of narcological dispensaries and obligatory surveillance systems manage and treat toxicomanics in the countries of the former Soviet Union, with similar approaches in other Eastern European countries. At the other end, France deploys a hybrid of exceptional and ordinary biosolidarity approaches centered on harm-reduction techniques and voluntary office-based opiate-substitution therapy with Subutex to attract toxicomanes into the health system of the droit commun. In their trajectories, we could suppose, elusive travelers come to substitute the latter regime for the former. To consider this possibility would require us to identify at least two elements: the logics and articulation through which elusive travelers might link up with the biosolidarity nexus and the acceptance of that linkage by the travelers themselves. Both involve the question of therapeutic citizenship: whether stateless, transnational, or a combination of the two. We now turn to these possibilities and the explication of their forms.

ZONES OF SOLIDARITY AND THE TRIALS OF BIOLOGICAL CITIZENSHIP

Much medical anthropology today analyzes the biopolitical processes through which suffering bodies in and of themselves provide the legitimacy for acquiring therapeutic citizenship. The arrival of uncontrollable and unknowable toxicomanes from Eastern Europe (and not even the other side of the Mediterranean, from which many of the older addicts in Marseille originated), their tinkering with supposedly secure methadone, and their passing as patients to obtain Subutex and social services could only trouble the carefully constructed drug treatment hybrid, as we gleaned in the responses of service providers and government researchers. Yet the elusive travelers were engaging in a project of what Adriana Petryna (2002) calls biological citizenship, centered on "the very constituent matter of life" itself as the differentiating criterion that legitimizes ethical demands placed before authorities and their representatives—in this case, the social workers and clinicians of Marseille's drug treatment world. Although undocumented foreigners in medical need may use public hospitals freely and anonymously in France, the mechanism that allows the particular exercise of biological citizenship on the part of the elusive travelers came into practice shortly before they began arriving in France. Since 2000, nonresident foreigners have been able to gain access to healthcare beyond free and anonymous hospital emergency services through a universal illness protection known as the Aide Médicale Etat (AME).[23] Undocumented foreigners living in France can apply for the AME if they have been on French territory for three consecutive months, plan to stay, and have resources at or below the poverty level (at the time of this writing, 587.16 euros [$822] per month for a single person). The Room, the NGO methadone bus, and other programs for drug users provided letters certifying the three-month residency of elusive travelers, thus accomplishing a first step in providing them with administrative and legal papers while strengthening their ties to the biosolidarity nexus.

However, this linkage does not suffice to legitimize a continuing presence of elusive travelers in France. That would require a second, far more complicated step, of applying for asylum on the basis of sickness. Didier Fassin (2001) has observed that, in the past decade, the suffering body has displaced political persecution as the rationale for which the majority of cases of asylum are granted in France. At the other end of the asylum process, Vinh-Kim Nguyen (2006) describes from his fieldwork in the Ivory Coast how people with AIDS build networks across state boundaries (and with the former colonizer) through sociability, community associations, and international NGOs to gain access to a stateless therapeutic citizenship, or guaranteed healthcare, in France, sometimes remaining for years. The asylum mechanism behind both the statistical transformation Fassin reports and the stateless therapeutic status Nguyen observed, a statute known as the CESEDA,[24] allows illegal entry into or presence in France to be regulated on the basis of the need for healthcare. While social workers or healthcare workers may submit the application on behalf of the candidate, the regional medical inspector ultimately determines whether the candidate's state of health would be severely compromised or life-threatening should she or he be returned to the country of origin. To reduce arbitrariness, the Ministry of Foreign Affairs maintains a list of countries and the level of healthcare provided for specific diseases.

Although NGO workers told me that addiction qualified as a chronic, life-threatening condition, I was not able to identify any Russians who had obtained asylum on that basis alone. Theoretically, the absence of opiate-substitution treatment in their countries of origin as I was making my ethnographic observations would suggest that the treatment criterion for asylum was being met. But biological constructs prove inadequate here, for addiction is not seen as a disease. Rather, the body racked by the effects of opiate dependence remains unworthy, if not untrustworthy, compared with other bodies.[25]

The biopolitical exception of the addicted body despite the tolerant biosolidarity nexus reveals the larger assemblage with which drug-management regimes connect up. Not only Soviet-style narcology but also the French hybrid regime is inseparable from acts of inclusion and exclusion through state definitions of which type of citizen and noncitizen will potentially trouble the larger social project of cohesion. The stakes involved in constructing this articulation with the biosolidarity nexus of drug care are illustrated by two separate events. One concerned a Russian I never met but who, shocked NGO workers told me, had deliberately injected himself with another drug user's blood tainted with the hepatitis-C virus, in the hopes of developing a "legitimate" condition for asylum. About the same time, another Eastern European drug user tried to immolate himself on the sidewalk in front of the stately Marseille Police Prefect's palace. He was stopped before he hurt himself, but this dramatic incident contrasted with the perceived self-control and relative nonchalance of modern elusive travelers. Both examples also suggest the degree to which questions of toxicomania and addiction are entangled with larger biopolitical issues.

One night, shortly after the Russian narcology delegation visited Marseille, I went to the Room to interview Nikolai. A tall, tanned twenty-three-year-old man, still damp from a shower and dressed only in black jeans and white sneakers with a towel draped over his chest, greeted us. His muscular build and confident posture contrasted with his agitated movements, as he repeatedly opened and closed the door to the interview space, entering, leaving, then entering again. He finally told our interpreter, Magdalena, in Russian that he did not wish to be interviewed, adding, "Do you come from the police?" We assured him that we did not and that his interview was completely voluntary. Only later did we learn that the Russian delegation had recently visited the Room. They had been highly critical of this harm reduction shelter that did not require abstinence, and they had asked to talk to the young Russians. After they left, Nikolai, Pavel, and others told the staff of the Room that the delegation had come from the police.

On the one hand, Nikolai's fears probably reflected the ambiguity between treatment and surveillance set up through the registry system back home. At the same time, he had been explicit about wanting to ask for political asylum. Fellow travelers, such as Dima, had put in asylum claims as ethnic Russians persecuted in Ukraine. (Dima had also commented that Ukrainians and Russians get along just fine in Marseille.) Whether or not the asylum applications worked, applicants could continue to appeal the decisions at different levels, buying time in France. But Dima, Nikolai, and others seeking asylum on medical or political grounds would have to provide papers of some sort.

Not unlike many older French drug users who have spent long periods of time on the streets of Marseille, Nikolai's identity and other administrative papers had been lost or stolen at different points. He had to juggle with numerous national identities. He had literally buried his first passport, then, after new identity papers were stolen, obtained an identity card from a migrant network. "But," he complained, "it has been years since I lost myself, because I use so many different IDs. I can't do what I have to do."

Yet he did not want to reconstitute his real identity. Eventually, he told us that like Valentyn, who also slept at the Room, he had barely escaped from Ukraine. Nikolai had been beaten into a coma by police during a major commemoration and demonstration for a nationalist patriarch, whose party was now represented in the Ukrainian Parliament. With his background in military service and connections with military intelligence, he had quickly worked his way into the ranks of the party militia. But while he was being hospitalized for the coma, he was sentenced to eighteen months in prison. Valentyn had applied for asylum as a political refugee, but Nikolai feared such a move. In fact, white-supremacist backgrounds like his were not likely to gain the sympathy of French courts.

Nikolai was stuck living a dog's life in Marseille, or so he put it. Later the same evening, he pulled us aside again. Behind the closed door of the interview room, he told us he had tested positive for hepatitis-B, hepatitis-C, and HIV. "Don't tell Pavel or Valentyn!" he pleaded. None of his "brothers" knew of the infections and, hence, possible contagion. He self-medicated with Subutex every night; now he wanted healthcare for its own sake, but that might threaten his relationship with Pavel and the brothers—and engage him in a sensitive paper chase.

Articulations with the biosolidarity regime of drug management thus produce—or threaten to produce—different effects according to the other elements with which they combine. Claims of biological citizenship lack force on the basis of addiction alone, despite efforts to transform toxicomania into the disease of addiction. Hence, other somatic and political claims are put forth, eliciting resistance from outreach and other drug treatment workers, who perhaps are equally confused and concerned about the uses to which their services are being put. At the same time, putting claims into action makes elusive travelers visible not just as drug users within a larger hidden population, but in multiple ways linked to their own trajectories of political and criminal (petty or not) activity, as well as mere drug consumption. But even the mere articulation with the biosolidarity regime, in which elements of visibility (such as identities) are held back, encloses elusive travelers in ways that they themselves attempt to resist, creating subjectivities other than the "unencumbered selves" they often project.

SUBJECTIFICATION AND THE STAGING OF DIFFERENCE

In many ways, the Russians constitute a social body within the larger body of toxicomanes in Marseille. At the Room, they slept, whenever possible, in the same six-bed box or dorm, looking out for each other. They referred to each other as brothers, a referent with numerous meanings. Some were actually blood brothers; others were related to Russian or Ukrainian family members, not necessarily drug users, who had migrated to Marseille earlier. But Pavel projected a larger meaning, explaining that in his hometown, "the toxicomanes, we know them all. We're like a family. It's not like in France."[26] They passed around their names in Marseille, which confused drug treatment and social service workers. It was not uncommon at the Room for a social worker to call out one man's name and for three or four to stand up.

Relations with local drug users also were not simple. Dima and two brothers had approached the psychologist at the Room to tell her Mehdi had stolen her wallet. She checked her purse, and the wallet indeed was gone. Who had stolen it? In different contexts, Taufik and others at the Room complained that the Russians were thieves, a believable accusation because whenever one was arrested and imprisoned, the other "brothers" spread the news. These accusations came to a dramatic head one night at the Room, when Dima tried to slit Taufik's throat with a broken bottle in retaliation for Taufik's stealing from him. The idea of shared protection took on a new meaning after that.

The NGO bus, the Room, and the triangular city center through which elusive travelers pass is also frequented by a sedentary group: men and women in their thirties and forties, most of whom were addicted to heroin and now are treated or self-medicate with Subutex or combine it with other substances. Unlike younger or well-to-do drug consumers, they are particularly visible. Their dependence on places like the Room reflects momentary family conflict—even the director of the Room, an experienced drug services professional from Paris, remarked on the solidarity of extended family networks in Marseille—as well as extreme poverty. On some evenings, as users line up on the sidewalk hoping to get a bed at the Room, the scene evokes local domesticity. A woman wheeling a baby carriage argues with her ex, who is standing in line, and friends discuss whether to wait for a bed or go get a beer.

What transpires between the nomadic young Eastern Europeans and sedentary older Marseillais calls into question any simple contrast between intact, self-entrepreneurial subjects, on the one hand, and excluded, dependent subjects, on the other. At the same time, it reveals a tension between the ways in which elusive travelers position themselves vis-à-vis the biosolidarity nexus and how the elements of the larger assemblage actively reconstitute them in ways they resist.

It is past 7 PM at the Room; the slots for beds have long been filled. The bouncer closes the front door against a crowd of shouting men. A smell of vomit pervades the open area between the door and the three, large adjacent rooms beyond. Someone complains about an older Algerian man, in a fishnet shirt and skinny jeans, who "can't keep his Subutex down."

Beyond the entrance, the older men have taken paper plates of lumpy spaghetti, poured on lots of vinegar and harissa, and eat at a table. One, whom I recognize as Momo, nods off, his gold chain and fishnet undershirt falling into the pile of food on his plate as his head rests on the table. His neighbor Ahmed slips from the bench onto the floor, semiconscious. Mehdi, to whom I had been introduced earlier outside the building, provides a running commentary. "They should be ashamed!" Earlier, Mehdi had told me, "I'm not a toxico," meaning that, one, he's not from Marseille, and two, he grew up in the bled in Algeria and moved to Paris. Not like these two losers.

Now Momo and Ahmed are crawling slowly under the table, motioning at the floor. In front of them sit the "Russians," in a large sitting area with the TV set that they always appropriate for themselves, choosing the channel and monopolizing all of the chairs, night after night. Tall, blond, tanned, dressed in top brand-name sneakers (as opposed to the generic or "fake" ones of the Marseillais), new jeans and designer T-shirts, most of them exude health and youth next to the toothless, balding, and skinny Marseillais. Nikolai strides over to the counter, where the cook hands him a plate with the lumpy spaghetti and some strips of processed cheese. Nikolai takes one taste and swears in Russian, shaking the fist of his free hand. He holds the plate up, disgusted, pointing at the cheese. The cook is explaining in French (which Nikolai doesn't understand) that the pasta is not lumpy, just "al dente." He passes him a bottle of sauce. Nikolai, now seething with anger, throws the pieces of cheese, one by one, into the garbage can. The cook, swearing back, comes out from behind the counter and picks each strip out of the garbage. More "Russians" come into the sitting area, freshly showered and wearing clean clothes. Vlad picks out a chair against the wall in front of the TV and nods off from his nightly Subutex, all the while seated straight up. At some point, Mehdi turns to me as if to confess: "Well, I am a toxico, you know." Marek is now back from outside; he and Kamel had come to blows recently because Marek was stealing personal items from the dorm.

Suddenly, the man who had vomited his Subutex wakes up. He rises from the bench and turns to Nikolai shaking his fist. "Come here, come here, you fag," he screams, cupping his crotch. "*Viens, viens!* Come over here and I'll get you fucked in the ass."

At first glance, the tension expressed in this violent scene appears to resonate with what some outreach, shelter, and other drug workers had complained about during the months leading up to it: the elusive travelers were "eating" resources meant for poor Marseillais. Other workers and even some Marseillais drug users also voiced resentment to me that I (and my fellow fieldworkers) were studying the transnational drug consumers rather than the (to them more deserving) older and broken-down Marseillais. (That I had written, published, and lectured on Marseillais drug users for both user groups and professionals was irrelevant to them in this context [see Lovell and Aubisson 2008; Lovell and Feroni 1998].) Furthermore, limited resources at once undercut the solidarity dimension of the drug-management nexus and reinforce the misgivings expressed earlier about the so-called Russians manipulating drug services.

But more is at hand is this tension, in which the Russians resist becoming lost addicts, like the sick and emaciated Marseillais. As a theory of subjectification, Keiji Yoshino's "weak theory of performativity" (Yoshino 2002) works well here, because it allows for the materiality of the Subutex and its strong effects on the bodies on-stage. In a triangulation—Mehdi "cleaner" because of his closeness to the bled; Momo and his buddy crawling on the dirty floor; Nikolai, Marek, and the other "blonds" striding about, scorning the soup kitchen food—each gesture, type of dress, or word expresses the subject position of their agent through the contrast with the identities of the others. Borrowing Yoshino's schema, we could say that the older toxicomanes are "converted" through these interactions to their status of aging drug users, whose bodies are further ravaged by injected buprenorphine. Mehdi "passes," pretending not to be a tox—until his presence in a special place for toxicomanes leaves no other possibility as to his identity. And the Russians "cover" as not-addicts, taking over calm spaces in the shelter, wearing the same clothes as their non-toxicomane compatriots from the Canebière, and trafficking openly in a palette of medicines and drugs—agitated today from amphetamines; nodding the next night from Subutex.

In this scene and others like it, despite the mutual distancing between strong, healthy "white bodies" and sick, emaciated "dark bodies," the subjective "interior" of elusive travelers, too, are affected by the folding over of the outside, of that combination of special shelter, strong substances, administrative papers, and such. Until they leave Marseille—and Nikolai, Vladimir, and many others were eventually expelled from France, as their various schémes fell through or asylum appeals ran out—they have become, to some extent, part of the biosolidarity hybrid.

Conclusion

As epistemic object and practice, addiction defies stability of definition or effects. The worlds brought together through the trajectories of elusive travelers belie a simple categorization of practices and perspectives into modern and less modern, biological and social, medical and criminal. Rather, they reveal how apparently radically different drug-management regimes inevitably combine legal-juridical, biological, and political (in the sense of citizenship) perspectives in various ways. Neither narcology, as a counter-example, nor a solidarity-biological framework fits with current grand narratives of a biologizing science of addiction that will whittle away, once and for all, the stigma, prejudices, confusions, and types of control surrounding drug consumption in its most problematic forms.

The elusive travelers locally characterized as "the Russians" occupy an intermediary space between consumption of substances and disease-consumed or disabled bodies of medical traveling. Rather than simple drug tourists, like the hippies of the previous century, they are caught up in biopolitical strategies of survival. Their narratives provide a corrective to the notion that illness claims for citizenship and asylum carry more weight today than claims based on poverty, injustice, and structural violence. While the force of somatic suffering may work generally to gain access to asylum, problematic drug use—be it called toxicomania, drug dependence, or addiction—does not suffice as an illness claim.

However, recent researchers portray a hybrid of addiction treatment and policing (see Garriott, this volume), and the French sociologist Albert Ogien (1995) has long argued that addiction can never be separated from its hybrid medical-juridical-social register. Whether or not these observations will hold over time, the movement as heuristic—elusive travelers—illustrates the degree to which toxicomania has not completed its transformation into a biological model. In a larger sense, the biopolitical framework presented here reveals how travel and mobility as part of the construction of medical knowledge and markets, therapeutic quests, and biological or therapeutic citizenship link disparate worlds while reproducing the social inequalities that both link up and divide them.

Notes

In memory of Mohammed, Eve, Mansour, Toufik, and the two Nassers, Marseillais and brave pioneers all.

Some data on which this paper draws were collected with the support of National Institute on Drug Abuse Grant R03 DA14719 ("Network Risks among New IDUs in New York and Marseilles") to Alan Neiagus and Anne M. Lovell. Ali Benrezkellah and Cyrielle Orenes conducted some of the interviews and observations, and Magdalena Sow acted as Russian-French interpreter. I thank Eugene Raikhel for his critiques and for opening up my horizons. Clara Han and Sandra Hyde provided thoughtful readings of an earlier version; I regret only my inability to address all of their suggestions within the context of this chapter. Samuel Bordreuil brought his usual critical attention to a first draft. Thanks also to Anna Leppo in Helsinki, to Didier Febvrel and his staff and to Béatrice Stamboul for our exchanges.

1. This literature is too vast to list, but see non-French writers such as Anna Senghers, Sembene Ousmane, and Claude McKay, as well as numerous literary journalists. Regarding films, Robert Guedjiguan's are the best known of this genre; more recently, the popular television series *Plus belle la vie* stereotypes Marseille for national audiences. And regarding the political scene, although the non–French-born constitute 14 percent of the population, few hold elected offices. Elected officials in Marseille are split between socialist/communist and conservative affiliations, with the right-wing nationalist and xenophobic National Front party always present.

2. Amina Haddaoui, unpublished manuscript, Laboratoire Méditerranéen de Sociologie.

3. In 1986, France became the first country to allow Subutex in general medical practice, without requiring training in addiction medicine. A meeting of Euro-

pean addiction researchers that I attended in Lausanne, Switzerland, in October 2003 epitomized the intense debate around this policy. Some depicted French policy as irresponsible and premature for authorizing Subutex without social (e.g., directly observed treatment) or molecular-level (e.g., naloxone) controls against abuse. Clinicians and other drug treatment professionals had become aware by then of widespread Subutex injection (Lovell 2006). French participants heatedly questioned one of their country's main buprenorphine researchers and the conference's only visible link to Schering-Plough, the French distributor of Subutex and the funder of the researcher's studies. At the same time, harm reduction advocates turned criticism of buprenorphine misuse around, complaining that syringes in government-sponsored needle-exchange kits were too large for the liquid derived from Subutex tablets, causing abscesses and even gangrene. At this celebrated psychiatric hospital in Lausanne, French participants played out a controversy often repeated at home. But under the gaze of German, Swiss, and Belgian colleagues, they were on the spot to publicly defend their experiment with biological and social treatment.

A psychiatrist representing the American Society of Addiction Medicine who had supported the introduction of Suboxone in the United States inadvertently came to the rescue. Unlike the United States, he explained, France was engaged in a *massive ecological experiment*. In essence, by authorizing mono-buprenorphine without the built-in control of naloxone or the external control of certified addiction doctors, France had succeeded in attracting addicts into treatment, bringing them out of the woodwork. While Americans would not replicate that experiment, it succeeded on its own—French—terms. But he left those terms unspecified. As I suggest in this chapter, those terms refer to the social and historical dimension of the treatment, grounded in French debates about solidarity and exclusion (October 2, 2003).

4. A French solution to hidden populations is TREND, a monitoring system that employs anthropologists, former drug users, and community-based workers (*travailleurs de proximité*) to gather local information on drug users and practices and feed it up the pipeline to the Observatoire Français des Drogues et des Toxicomanies.

5. For a different merging of addiction treatment as police science, see Garriott, this volume.

6. Some French psychoanalytically oriented clinicians, even after the introduction of buprenorphine, viewed heroin use as an *expérience ordalique*—metaphorically, ordeals by fire.

7. For example, until buprenorphine was approved in Finland, Finnish heroin users traveled to France to purchase buprenorphine. When Estonia introduced buprenorphine prescription in general practice, Finns ferried to Tallinn for their supplies: Anna Leppo, personal communication, September 13, 2010. French buprenorphine exists on the black market in many areas, from Georgia to former colonies such as Madagascar.

8. In French, traveleurs include "gypsies," "tinkers," those who live in caravans or

trailers, and, more recently, musicians and self-made entrepreneurs who criss-cross Europe organizing electronic (formerly "techno") festivals, and their followers.

9. Pavel spoke French, but, as the TREND reports note, most Eastern Europeans did not. Magdalena Sow acted as the interpreter for most of the interviews on which this chapter is based, most of which were audio recorded. We conducted twelve formal interviews.

10. Similar preparations are called *cherniarka*, *cherniagua*, or *khanka*. I thank Eugene Raikhel for bringing the last term to my attention.

11. The gendering is different for Marseillais. Like others, they compare the effects of opiates to orgasm but call the needle their "woman."

12. Medical registries are devices used to create risk categories and monitor populations. They exist for a variety of conditions, such as cancer and cardiovascular disease, as well as surveying the prevalence and incidence of a number of diseases over the lifetime. (Compare the case of locally constituted population databases—for example, those in Denmark.) Hence, it is not the existence of the registry per se that determines its use but, rather, its exploitation for particular purposes. The Soviet narcology model, including its current applications, combines health surveillance and policing but is weighted toward the latter.

13. Such an alliance exists in France, of course, and probably in a majority of Western countries. However, it is not institutionalized in the same way.

14. "Ukraine: Summary Country Profile for HIV/AIDS Treatment Scale-up," Country Office for Ukraine, World Health Organization, 2005.

15. Mylène Frappas, Département de Santé Publique, Ville de Marseille, personal communication, September 1, 2004. The first delegation included a proponent of opiate-substitution therapy. By the second visit, that physician was no longer with the delegation, which eventually transformed an announced public health mission into an economic mission between Marseille and a Russian city, but without concrete results, such as import-export exchanges.

16. For the moment, "problem drug use" should be taken to mean drug consumption that creates controversy, in a public sense. Although health researchers and psychiatrists in particular now harness the language of addiction, "toxicomania" is more commonly used in French media, policy, and nonmedical research; even the scientific literature is prone to translate the English term "addiction" as "toxicomanie." Hence, the French inter-ministerial group on substance abuse and dependency is still called the Mission Interministérielle de Lutte contre les Drogues et la Toxicomanie (Interministerial Mission against Drugs and Toxicomania), and the statistical drug surveillance agency remains the Observatoire Français des Drogues et des Toxicomanies. *Toxicomanie–hépatites–SIDA* is the journal of the professional organization by the same name, although it belongs to the French Fédération d'Addictologie. A report by Jean-Philippe Parquet (1998) first brought attention to the distinction between "use," "abuse," and "dependence." Although surveillance studies by the Observatoire Français des Drogues et des Toxicomanies later adopted a similar typology for measuring drug use, I rarely saw those distinctions made by

outreach workers, nurses, and doctors during my fieldwork. Harm reduction seemed to outweigh such distinctions.

17. Here I am concerned only with the French history of buprenorphine.

18. It is interesting to remember the importance to methodological individualism of the opinion leader model of diffusion of medical innovation. Pharmaceutical companies apply this model to create prescribers. For example, a former researcher with the pharmaceutical company that commercialized Subutex in France explained that the research-and-development branch identified the same opinion leaders the marketing branch would later target as researchers to carry out industry-funded studies: François Boillot, personal communication, June 4, 2006.

19. In the mid-1990s, an earlier hybrid, SIDA-toxicomanie, emerged from the social worlds, a resultant shift of French policy and practice away from the judicial corrections approach toward a sanitary one (see Lovell and Feroni 1998). But this period precedes both the French ecological experiment with buprenorphine and the laws and decrees concerning exclusion. Elsewhere, I have described the conditions, contingencies, and actions that led to the widespread office-based treatment of toxicomanes with HDB by general practitioners, beginning in 1996. This was the first such experiment in the world, and HDB remains the major treatment modality in France for opiate addiction. But such a modality, in a medical system that until then had rejected methadone maintenance as "American pragmatism" that chemically masked the underlying problems in the opiate user, required acceptance of a different paradigm of drug dependence (Gomart 2002). The advantages of HDB and Subutex (the commercial name) as a new wonder drug were marshaled throughout the late 1990s and early 2000s in France. Despite controversy, most interested parties, from professionals and paraprofessionals to user groups and government representatives, eventually agreed that Subutex was both a less dangerous alternative to methadone and a substance that drug users would willingly take (Conférence de Consensus 2004). Clinicians and researchers cited scientific findings that explained the buprenorphine compound's uniqueness in its ability not only to block the κ-receptor (its antagonist effect) in the brain, but also to activate the μ-receptor (its partial agonist effect). This agonist effect, unlike that of other μ-agonists such as morphine and methadone, appears to create a ceiling effect on respiration and is thus thought to lower the risk of severe respiratory depression. The partial agonist also lessens euphoria, without completely eliminating it, and is said to be less likely to cause dependency (Vocci and Ling 2005). I should emphasize the role of consensus is establishing Subutex's efficacy and the dependence on findings—versus evidence—in synthetic scientific papers, such as the one cited, written by one of the most important actors in the effort to approve buprenorphine-based treatment for opiate addiction in the United States.

20. The necessarily paternalistic role of the state with regard to problematic drug use was quite literally reinforced by the categorization of toxicomania as an epidemic. Under the centralized French public health system, epidemics are matters of the

state. Hence, drug prevention and treatment until recently were funded by the state, and state ministries were responsible for the drug problem.

21. This colloquialism, which translates loosely into the English expressions "a hard life," "the pits," and "difficult circumstances," is etymologically related to the life sentence of laboring in ships' galleys, to which convicts (*forçats*) of the seventeenth century and eighteenth century were condemned. A similar expression, *ramer* (lit. to row, but colloquially to struggle, work hard) also refers back to the forced labor of French criminals and of enslaved Africans.

22. Drug users with an illness, such as AIDS, that prevents them from working full time are also eligible for a disability-related indemnity that provides higher monthly revenues than the Revenu Minimal d'Insertion or Revenu de Solidarité Active and does not require beneficiaries to apply for work, training, or other social insertion programs.

23. Code de l'Action Sociale et des Familles, art. L 251-1, Law of July 1999. The AME provides nonresident foreigners 100 percent coverage, according to the French national health insurance program's fee schedules for office-based physician care, prescriptions, lab tests, some dental care, and termination of pregnancy.

24. Code de l'Entrée et du Séjour des Étrangers et du Droit d'Asile (CESEDA), art. L 313-11.

25. At the time of this writing, Gerard Coruble, medical inspector for the regional Department of Social Services in Marseille, confirmed for me that no asylum request on the basis of addiction alone had been successful. Drug users who were given asylum included veterans from the Russian-Chechen war, which suggested that political asylum could be justified for severe psychiatric problems, including post-traumatic stress disorder from their war experience.

26. Eugene Raikhel brought to my attention the term *bratok* (pl., *bratki*), often used to refer to the members of a gang (*brigada*), criminal or otherwise. Bratki is a variation on *brat*, which literally means "brother." Raikhel notes that these terms have long since entered mainstream argot in Russia yet retain their association with the criminal world and its language. It is not clear in what sense Pavel meant "brother," as, unaware of the polysemy, I did not ask for the Russian term. But what he described sounds very much like a loose network or gang.

SIGNS OF SOBRIETY
Rescripting American Addiction Counseling

We do not object to the drug user's pleasure per se, but a pleasure taken in an experience without truth.
—Jacques Derrida, *Points . . . Interviews, 1974–1994*

It has long been an American cultural conviction that drug addiction severs one's ties to reality as the sober properly know and experience it. This politically loaded concern is clinically expressed in the resonant terms of "addicted denial." One need only peruse the vast clinical literature on addiction and addiction treatment, published since the 1930s, to learn that "addiction is a disease of denial" (Paolino 1991: 219), and, moreover that "client denial *distinguishes* addiction" (Rasmussen 2000: 114; emphasis added).[1] As the prominent addiction psychiatrist Edward Kaufman (1994: 54) notes, "Denial has become so widely acknowledged as a hallmark of alcoholism or drug abuse that to deny substance abuse is frequently considered diagnostic of the disease." In other words, the American client's denial of a drug problem is commonly the American professional's evidence of it. So whether or not one agrees with the premise of Sigmund Freud's statement that there is "an intimate connection between special forms of defense and particular illnesses" (Freud 1973 [1926]: 163–64), it is nevertheless clear that denial enjoys the privileged status of American addiction's "special" defense.[2]

Indeed, despite their general disregard or abjuration of fundamental psychoanalytic concepts, contemporary American addiction specialists almost invariably agree that "denial of entire segments of reality, especially behavior concerning drug use, is typical [of the addict]" (Davidson 1977: 165). And, significantly, this agreement cuts across otherwise distinctive theoretical orientations. For instance, casting their textbook overview of addiction in distinctly behaviorist terms, David McDowell and Henry Spitz nonetheless devote significant attention to denial, defining it not only as a "primitive psychological mechanism for dealing with reality" but also as a "focused delusional system" in which the addict avoids the realities that are "obvious to everyone else" (McDowell and Spitz 1999: 121; see also Rothschild 1995: 193). Terrence Gorski (2000: 2) identifies twelve types of denial that can be addressed with "traditional cognitive therapy," and the Eriksonian therapist John Lovern (1991: 11–12) writes, "[The denial] system allows a chemically dependent person to become more and more out of touch with reality, while somehow hanging onto the ability to convincingly appear competent, rational, and right."

While the political rhetoric of addiction charges that the addict cannot accurately see and therefore productively participate in the world as it is (Derrida 1995), it is the concern that addicts cannot see *themselves* that drives the clinical discourse of addiction. Consider, for example, the widely known and still commonly exercised family-confrontation model, otherwise known as the "intervention" and recently popularized by the A&E show of that title. Under clinical direction, friends and family are gathered to "confront" an addict, often in emotionally charged terms, and persuade her or him to enter treatment. Suggesting that it is the addict's impoverished insight that must be targeted, Vernon Johnson, the father of the intervention, once noted, "We are most useful as confronters when we are not so much trying to change another person as we are trying to help him see himself more accurately" (quoted in Flores 1997a: 346).

According to these otherwise diverse clinical texts, denial is not merely a symptom of addiction. Denial is the very antithesis of sobriety, which is conceived as a state of accurate self-insight. So whereas the addicted putatively deny inner signs, the sober can accurately see them. And, given that addiction professionals' primary evidence of sober insight is sober speech, mainstream American addiction treatment entails retooling drug users' relationship to language as much as it involves reworking their relationship to drugs. More specifically, addiction professionals train clients to clearly identify and cleanly verbalize the inner states that are presumably denied in active addiction—that is, to use language as a mode of pure inner reference. Indeed, the ethnography of American addiction treatment demonstrates that American sobriety is a way of speaking as well as a way of being.

Notably, the definition of sobriety as demonstrable self-insight circulates well beyond strictly clinical terrains. For while we might most readily associate the term "sobriety" with abstaining from the excesses of alcohol and drugs, the term has historically enjoyed a much broader application, connoting dispassionate, solemn, and serious self-recognition. As Max Weber famously posited in his portraiture of "the sober, middle-class, self-made Man" (1958: 163), the production born of *self-restraint* is ideologically dependent on the rationality born of transparent *self-knowledge*. In this sense, the clinical texts and practices highlighted in this chapter must be understood as fundamentally cultural in that they instantiate a model of personhood by prescribing a set of constitutive practices by which we can recognize and render ourselves, and thereby be recognized by others.

Drawing on extensive ethnographic engagement in the world of American addiction treatment, this chapter elaborates three distinct if interconnected claims. First, I propose that "addicted denial" is a clinical articulation of a dominant ideology of language, which privileges the referential function of language to denote already existing inner truths. I call this "the ideology of inner reference" (see Carr 2006, 2011). By visiting Fresh Beginnings, an intensive outpatient addiction-treatment program in the midwestern United States where I conducted fieldwork between 1997 and 2002, we will see how therapists work to make people sober by getting them to speak in sober ways.

Second, I demonstrate that the ideology of language that undergirds mainstream addiction treatment has far-reaching symbolic and material consequences—for the clients who are analyzed and treated, for the professionals who accordingly fashion and circulate forms of expertise, and for the cultural figuration of the addict as a politico-therapeutic type. This will become evident as we visit a second site where an increasing number of contemporary American drug users are currently treated, a site that I have studied for the last several years. This is the relatively new therapeutic field of motivational interviewing, where addicts get sober not because they learn to see and say what they once denied, as mainstream programs like Fresh Beginnings would have it. Espousing a philosophy of language that highlights the performative or productive function of language, motivational interviewing instead proposes that with the proper therapeutic direction, drug users can talk themselves into sobriety regardless of whether or not they originally believe what they say to be true.

As these innovative practitioners make clear, the clinical formulation of addiction and its treatment transform along with professionals' ideas about language and its functions. Accordingly, my third and overarching aim is to demonstrate the intimate relationship of language ideology and clinical ideology, a relationship that is often overlooked in the anthropology of addiction's tendency to focus on the constitution and experience of addicted subjectivity. Taking off from the idea that there are multiple—if not equally legitimate—ways of rationalizing language in any cultural milieu, I suggest that competing clinical approaches for treating addiction draw from, mobilize, and significantly elaborate competing ideologies of language. Given that these ideas about language spawn specific therapeutic rituals, they also profoundly shape what drug users can felicitously say about themselves and their circumstances during, and often well beyond, the course of treatment. It follows that we cannot understand American ways of theorizing addiction and formulating treatment, nor can we adequately capture the experience of addiction, without appreciating American ways of theorizing language.

Inculcating Insight: Mainstream American Addiction Treatment in Practice

On any given morning, inside an unassuming gray house lodged on a densely populated, middle-class street in a midwestern town, the mostly African American and uniformly poor women that composed Fresh Beginnings clientele gathered for their daily group therapy session. The fact that these women were required to participate in the group in order to keep their much coveted spots in temporary housing or retain the other critical services administered by local social service agencies would not be readily apparent to an interested onlooker as the women sunk comfortably into a circle of cushy donated loveseats and took turns weaving the day's designated theme (e.g., shame, codependency, responsibility) into personalized narratives of early trauma, accelerated denial, rock bottom, and willful recovery. Nor would one initially suspect that the therapist, who oversaw the group's narrative practice with warm prompts and sympathetic nods, could readily place a phone call to a parole officer or child-welfare worker should she suspect that something was amiss in a client's talk that day. Though following uncannily predictable plotlines, the narrative rounds of group therapy generally seemed so intimate that the cold fact that the speakers were continually at risk of landing in jail, losing their beds in the domestic violence shelter, or having their children removed from their custody seemed odd if barely possible. But, as all Fresh Beginnings clients would eventually learn, their therapists were always listening for evidence of denial in the circulating signs of sobriety, and were poised to act accordingly.

Indeed, at Fresh Beginnings, as in the vast majority of addiction treatment programs across the United States, program therapists grounded their therapeutic practice in the belief that their clients suffered from a distinctly linguistic malady: the inability to read their inner states and render them in words—a malady glossed by the clinical term "denial." Accordingly, therapists prescribed a well-delineated set of principles for producing verbal acts of transparent, or sober, inner reference.

This semio-therapeutic project started from the moment clients initiated treatment. All incoming clients were handed a treatment contract, which foreground the importance of demonstrable self-insight to the recovery process and which required their signature. The document read: "Our immediate purpose [at Fresh Beginnings] is to discover and identify in order to see clearly who I am and what needs to change. Acceptance of *what is* precedes change." Yet normatively tethering behavioral change to self-insight was not enough. Therapists also felt obliged to explain how the pathology of addiction blinds the afflicted, thereby foreclosing on the possibility of sober or otherwise productive behavior. Along these lines, Fresh Beginnings clients received another document once they began attending group therapy. It read:

> The purpose of this paper is to discuss the assumptions and techniques we are using in conducting group therapy. To begin with, let's look at some of the similarities within the group. In addition to chemical dependency we all have two things in common. First, before we came to the point of seeking outside help, we each tried our own *Do It Yourself* program in an effort to change ourselves or someone else. The second similarity is that we all failed. A basic assumption of group therapy is that a major reason for this failure is that our most determined efforts can't change what we can't see, and there is a great deal we are not seeing clearly.

Reading further, Fresh Beginnings clients learned that their eyes were not just unfocused but that they suffered from extreme farsightedness—the

FIGURE 6.1 "Denial," as pictured in "My Ego" (1986), by Mary K. Bryant.

inability to see what is closest to them. In this vein, the document continues: "For this reason our goal in group therapy is: TO DISCOVER OUR-
SELVES AND OTHERS AS FEELING PERSONS AND TO INDENTIFY [*sic*] *THE
DEFENSES THAT PREVENT THIS DISCOVERY.*" Accordingly, throughout the
course of treatment, Fresh Beginnings therapists reminded their clientele
that "secrets keep you sick." They even periodically scrawled "D-E-N-I-A-L
(Don't Even Notice I Am Lying)" on the dry-erase board in the group room
in the hopes that it would prompt the spoken signs of self-awareness. Such
speech—after all—was therapists' primary evidence of clients' therapeutic
progress. For if Fresh Beginnings clients' recovery hinged on self-insight,
then their therapists' expertise hinged on the verbal demonstration of it.

This professional preoccupation with insight challenges much of the critical scholarship on American addiction therapeutics, which has charged
that addiction has been culturally understood and professionally treated as a
disease of the will (Keller 1972; Levine 1978; Rush 1805; Valverde 1998).[3] In
fact, American addiction specialists have long underscored the extreme
willfulness of addicts (see Meyers, this volume), including the tenacity with
which they practice denial. For instance, consider Leon Wurmser's explanation of the "psychophobia" typical of addicts: "the disregard for the importance of introspection of any kind and its resolute self-righteous avoidance
—in fact, not rarely a disdain for any approach to it" (Wurmser 1985: 92). In a
group therapy session, Fresh Beginnings therapists imparted this very same
thesis, if in lampooned form, when they circulated a cartoon among their
"psychophobic" clientele, hoping it would lead to an enlightened discussion
of their disease (see figure 6.1).

Clearly, the portrayed problem is not that "My Ego"—as the figured
addict—lacks a strong will. Quite to the contrary. Despite his buckling

knees, dramatic trembling, and sinking feet, he believes that he can "handle" a colossal boulder that has evidently rolled downhill. Significantly, the cartoon's punch line is not that "My Ego" cannot *do* what he *wills*. Instead, even after having been crushed into the ground, he fails to see "why" he cannot do it (notice, by the way, that "My Ego" has been given ears but no eyes by his artist). Eventually, client consumers of the cartoon learned to explain that "My Ego" has a crushing problem that is much bigger than he initially thought it was, and there is no conceivable way to "handle it" on his own. Fresh Beginnings was there to help, but program therapists were careful to underscore that sobriety would come only to those who willingly engaged the central therapeutic task of seeing and saying what they usually, presumably, denied.

Denial on Arrival

If "My Ego" provided some comic relief, Fresh Beginnings therapists Laura and Susan nevertheless took its underlying message quite seriously. Accordingly, they prepared themselves not just to encounter but also to confront the willfully blind egos that they believed composed their clientele.

The confrontation often began even before clients initiated treatment at Fresh Beginnings. Laura and Susan first encountered prospective clients during assessment interviews, which were initiated by referrals from social workers at one of the local social service agencies affiliated with the treatment program. All of these agencies required that clients abstain from drugs while receiving their services, which included shelter, transitional housing, child care, legal aid, psychiatric care, and some educational services and job training. If clients betrayed evidence of drug use, either through required urinalyses or in conversations with their case managers, they would be referred, as a matter of policy, to Fresh Beginnings for a clinical assessment. And since even casual use of drugs, once registered on lab or case reports, could threaten their status as service recipients, there was invariably much at stake in clients' first encounters with the addiction professionals who assessed them.

Notably, by the time they met Fresh Beginnings therapists, most of these clients had already accrued plenty of experience negotiating professional investigations into various aspects of their lives. For as these clients sought entrance into one of the agencies with which Fresh Beginnings was affiliated, they were greeted by case workers and shelter managers armed with long lists of questions—about finances, romantic relationships, use of prescription and illicit drugs, family history, legal history, educational history, employment history, and mental and physical health—that most Americans would characterize as private or, at least, highly personal.[4]

However, there was a fundamental difference between these relatively standard social work interviews and the assessments conducted by Fresh Beginnings therapists—indeed, an epistemological difference rooted in the professionals' respective philosophies of language and communication. Namely, while the shelter and case managers understood that they might not get the "full story" when conducting assessments, and would have to sort through a variety of half-truths, strategies, tricks, and evasions spawned by their interviewees' desperate circumstances, Fresh Beginnings therapists labored in a far simpler semiotic economy—one in which only inner truth and its denial were recognized.

Thus, every client referred to Fresh Beginnings for an assessment was met by both a therapist and a therapeutic expectation that the only positive sign of addiction might be the absence of signs (i.e., denial). As Laura explained in an interview with me:

> Laura: This is a classic example of kinda how it went: there was a woman at [the domestic violence shelter] who had used cocaine and alcohol right before she came into the shelter.
> ESC: OK.
> Laura: And she couldn't hide the alcohol, because it *smells*.
> ESC: Right.
> Laura: But she denied the cocaine use, and another woman stayin' at [the shelter] who knew her and knew that was an issue for her identified her to me in treatment. . . . And so I made an inquiry to the case managers . . .
> ESC: Umhm.
> Laura: Saying, "You've got somebody in here that one of our clients is worried about, but is afraid to come to you about it, so could I do an evaluation?

Here, Laura describes a fascinating taxonomy in which active users hide and deny, naive case managers ignore obvious signs (if not scents), worried clients in treatment knowingly identify, and inquiring therapists keenly evaluate, ultimately identifying the etiology of cocaine and alcohol use. In so doing, Laura positions herself in the epistemological life of the institution as closest to the furtive truth of clients' experiences (second only to her well-trained client informant). She continued:

Laura: So I interviewed this woman.

ESC: Uh-huh.

Laura: She is completely denying to me that she's used cocaine, but she agreed to do a urinanalysis.

ESC: Umhm.

Laura: And it came back positive. . . . And I'm sitting there with her with the results showing the positive cocaine.

ESC: Umhm.

Laura: And she's like, "I did not!" "I *have not* used cocaine!" And so to try to help her feel safer, I'm like, "Nothing bad is gonna happen to you. This is just denial."

Pitting the client's specious protests against her own disciplined knowledge—bolstered as it seemed to be by a positive urine screen—Laura describes a discursive coup in which she can declare, unequivocally, "This is just denial." Well-assured of her own position relative to the client's still unspoken truth, Laura initially greets what she reads as denial with assurances, telling her client that "nothing bad will happen," a statement reportedly rendered in the name of therapeutic safety.

Yet if Laura was ultimately interested in making her assessee "feel safer" so that she would admit the thing that she had presumably denied (i.e., recent cocaine use), she also wanted her prospective client to recognize denial itself as a pathological practice and propensity (i.e., symptomatic of addiction). After all, for Fresh Beginnings therapists, assessments had a pedagogical as well as a diagnostic function. Thus, faced with a typical assessee, Laura shifted strategy, taking a more didactic approach:

Laura: I explained denial. And, I suggest perhaps she's repressing it . . .

ESC: Umhm.

Laura: Ya know. And she asked me what that means, and I explained what [denial] means.

ESC: OK, what did you say?

Laura: I prefaced it with "a lot of people think denial is lying. And denying is not lying. When we are in a state of denial, it's because we cannot deal with the *reality* or the consequences of something that is happening or has happened in our life. And it's not *conscious*, so there's no control over it . . ."

ESC: Oh.

Laura: "And if and when it becomes safe, for us to accept it, then it comes to our consciousness."

ESC: I see.

Laura: And for a lot of people, including a lot of the women that came into my program, they thought: "Oh, that's *bullshit* . . . [chuckle] that's just lying."

In familiar clinical terms, Laura's lesson on denial emphasizes its unconscious, protective, and uncontrollable qualities. Note that Laura is also careful to clearly discriminate between "the state of denial" and *reality*, which she emphatically insists will emerge into consciousness (and then, presumably automatically, into words) once the denier can accept and deal with it. With apparent amusement, Laura also implies that her clients' rejection of her learned explanations of denial, which they confused with "bullshit," only further demonstrated their resolute lack of awareness. So when I asked, "When you explained these things to her, then what happened?" Laura gave another knowing chuckle and responded, "She continued to deny."

Having been trained to recognize and confront psychophobia, Laura accordingly upped the interactional ante, shifting from a pedagogical register into a medical one. Without a hint of apparent regret, she recounted:

Laura: I got this woman sitting in front of me denying that she's ever used cocaine and thinks I'm full of shit and I've got these cocaine results from her urine . . .

ESC: OK.

Laura: Saying that she used cocaine, so I figured what the hell, ya know? This is the last trick in my bag, I'm gonna pull it out. [I] said, "Well . . . you're tellin' me you haven't used cocaine for six months, that you did not use cocaine the night you came in here, . . .

ESC: Hmmhm.

Laura: Yet your level shows that you had this much cocaine still circulating in your urine two days ago. So either your liver isn't working and your body can't process cocaine that you used six months ago . . .

ESC: Umhm.

Laura: Which means you're in *really* bad shape physically or you're repressing.

In the face of a client who thinks she is "full of shit," Laura now gives her two choices: to admit that she has fallen victim to denial and repression or to face liver dysfunction and imminent death. What is striking is not only Laura's seeming abandonment of her mission to create "safety" but also the explicitly theatrical terms she used to describe her own linguistic actions: Laura reaches down to retrieve the "last trick in [her] bag," and, as if thinking aloud, quickly calculates and decides, "What the hell . . . I'm gonna pull it out."

Importantly, for Laura there was no contradiction between her genuine care for clients, her insistence that they speak the truth, and these "tricks," grounded as they all were in the effort to dismantle denial. And while she did not believe for a minute that her assessee was immediately at risk of dying of liver dysfunction, Laura *did* believe that the woman would ultimately have to choose between denial and death—an idea she introduced in the reported dialogue in a concretized way. In fact, the equation of denial and death was not at all uncommon at Fresh Beginnings. For instance, in a letter, the therapist Susan admonished one client who did not show up for treatment on several occasions: "Addiction is a disease which is progressive, chronic, and fatal and that denial is part of your disease. If you do not stop using mood altering chemicals, you can expect that your life will continually become unmanageable."

It is also important to recall that Laura's assessment methods are well supported by the addiction counseling literature. For example, Karen Derby (1992: 118) provides Laura with ample support: "The therapist must juxtapose the stark contradiction of the reality of the patient's life with the patient's view of that reality. This can be done gently, although technically it is a 'confrontation.' The patient must be helped to examine critically the ways in which he or she continues to act to bring about his or her own destruction ('self'-destruction)." Even with the now fairly widespread critique of the extreme confrontational methods that characterized many early addiction treatment modalities (see Morgan 2006), there is still precious little professional debate that firm and persistent persuasion to enter treatment is required precisely because addicts do not recognize themselves and their problems nearly as clearly as their therapists do (see Paolino 1991).

In light of this literature, Laura felt justified in laying out only two possible answers to her insistent questions: death or denial. And, according to Laura, the fact that when given these options, the assessee chose "death" further proved the therapist's point. She explained:

Laura: And rather than take the opportunity to say, "OK, maybe I'm repressing it," she decided that she was dying. . . .

ESC: She *decided she was dying!?*

Laura: That her body was not processing it.

ESC: I see . . . hmmm.

Laura: And then she was able to get mad at me because I was so insensitive to her physical well-being and she was just really pissed that I was telling her that she's dying and . . . ya know, she's had enough shit to deal with, she just got beat up, she's in shelter, and here I am telling her she's dying . . .

ESC: Yeah.

Laura: So I just had to go with it and said, "Well, while you're getting that checked out and seeking medical attention, why don't you try our program?"

In reaction to my stunned question ("She *decided she was dying!?*"), Laura makes the ethical trajectory of her actions clear: she allows the assessee to continue with the misguided premise that she is dying, and encourages her to seek medical attention and to "try" Fresh Beginnings while she is at it. And though the assessee-turned-client reportedly responds by charging her new therapist with insensitivity,[5] Laura maintains that her coercive means are justified by the therapeutic ends of getting another denier into treatment.

Therapists' symbolic authority to assign truth value to assessees' self-reports, coupled with their institutional authority to require forms of treatment by way of their "recommendations," meant that they clearly had the upper hand in these initial encounters. One might imagine that this made some clients angry. However, note that Laura does not portray her verbal manipulations as "mak[ing] her client mad." Instead, she implies that she merely incited the anger that she presumed was already lodged in the addicted client's psyche. Anger—like denial—was considered a purely intra-psychic property, a leftover layer of drug use, rather than a reasonable response to a coercive interaction. So when Laura says that the assessed client was "able to get mad," she is likely suggesting that therapeutic progress had been made in the course of the confrontational exchange.

As Laura and Susan would readily admit, these "classic" confrontations were a less than ideal way to establish a therapeutic alliance. Nevertheless, they stood their ground, firm in the well-supported conviction that they were professionally equipped to recognize the inner truths that their clients, by virtue of their disease, tenaciously denied. And while Laura's portrayal of a typical assessment clearly reveals a native logic of addiction, an important question remains. That is, how might we account for the assessee's insistence that she has never used cocaine in relation to the evidence to the contrary procured from the very same client's body? Is client denial the only or even the most likely explanation?

The evidentiary yields of urinalysis aside, there are many alternative explanations for the assessee's refutations, explanations that all require a consideration of the social dimensions of speech.[6] For instance, remember that Laura had been called in to do the assessment by a case manager at the local domestic violence shelter, where the assessee had been staying. As was the case with all residential social services in the area at the time, clients agreed to abstain from drugs before receiving shelter and housing services. Although shelter managers were unlikely to immediately expel her for the apparent violation, the assessee may have feared such a dire consequence for having apparently breached the agreement.

As she sat down with Laura, perhaps the assessee also recalled the whispered stories of fellow clients who told of zealous social workers counting drug habits as evidence of "neglect" and placing calls to Child Protective Services. There were also the highly gendered cultural politics of victimhood and blame to consider (see Bennett and Lawson 1994; Kilpatrick et al. 1997). As many clients at the domestic violence shelter wisely ascertained, sometimes by way of the shelter's own corps of legal advocates, admission of drug habits could threaten their status not only as worthy service recipients but also as credible plaintiffs.

Of course, there was also the observable fact that four mornings a week, the Fresh Beginnings van arrived at the high-security shelter, picked up a group of mostly reluctant and usually grumbling women, and returned with them in the mid- to late afternoon. Having no doubt witnessed these comings and goings, and having likely (over)heard at least some of the grumbles, the assessee may have correctly concluded that if Laura diagnosed her as "chemically dependent" and admitted her to Fresh Beginnings, she too would have to ride that van or—as a matter of policy—lose her spot in the shelter. And, even if the assessee thought she might benefit from the group and individual therapy the treatment program offered, the demanding treatment schedule would interfere significantly with any attempts to secure or retain gainful employment, finish a GED, visit with children not in her custody, or attend classes at the local community college. So while perhaps the client knew full well that she had used cocaine, and perhaps did so habitually and problematically, she had plenty of reasons to trouble her therapist's aggressive attempts to distinguish truth and its denial.

In acknowledging the loaded institutional and cultural conditions of clinical assessments, which inevitably and profoundly shape what drug users do and do not say, we open up the possibility that Laura's assessee was defying therapeutic truisms, resisting the institutional authority they bolster, or strategically working to manage her difficult circumstances, rather than simply denying inner truths. However, in a symbolic economy in which only inner truth and its denial were recognized, the range of pressing reasons why clients might manage and edit their self-presentations —as we all regularly do, perhaps particularly in high-stake institutional circumstances—were effectively erased.

From Insightful Semantics to Motivating Speech Acts

Once admitted to Fresh Beginnings, Laura's assessees became her clients and discovered in their treatment an all-too-familiar theme: they were to see and speak what they were presumed to have denied. However, now they were expected to do so among a new set of denial-prone peers (see Carr 2006, 2011). During group therapy sessions, Laura and Susan highlighted the importance of "honesty, openness, and willingness" (or, HOW), which acronymically linked the practice of sober insight to the verbal revelation of its yields. With much at stake in their treatment, clients did their best to speak in accord with these psycholinguistic principles, whether or not they actually invested in them. After all, they knew that HOW was the primary marker of therapeutic achievement. Indeed, the therapists Laura and Susan ceremoniously awarded successful clients with "certificates of achievement" that read, for example, "For [Rhonda Smith] who is making a stronger commitment to her recovery, by demonstrating greater HOW (*honesty*, *openness*, and *willingness*), and for working to raise her awareness."

In espousing the virtues of HOW, Fresh Beginnings therapists not only operationalized the well-established clinical theory of addicted denial but they also drew on well-established cultural assumptions about the possibilities and value of clearly seeing and speaking inner truths. For, as I have argued elsewhere (Carr 2011), addiction treatment programs like Fresh Beginnings are cultural distilleries that process ideologies of language and personhood in pure and potent form. With this in mind, we must remember that Laura and Susan acted in close accord with the majority of Americans, who privilege the referential function of language and by extension evaluate a speaker's integrity, responsibility, and health by determining if his or her words correspond with what he or she already "truly" thinks or feels (Carr 2011; Hill 2000; Irvine 1989; Silverstein 1979, 1996; Woolard 1998). Thus, in enforcing a language ideology of inner reference—or the ideal of sober speaking—Fresh Beginnings therapists were engaged in fundamentally cultural work even though they framed this work in the distinctly clinical terms of addicted denial, the chief organizing heuristic of mainstream American addiction treatment.

To be sure, while American addiction science moves increasingly toward neuroscientific models, the project of using talk to treat denial and demonstrate insight remains remarkably consistent in the daily practice across the approximately thirteen thousand outpatient addiction treatment programs currently in operation in the United States, which provide services to about 1.1 million people annually (SAMHSA 2011). Consider also the famous Twelve Steps of Alcoholics and Narcotics Anonymous, which have prescribed a path to sobriety for millions of self-helping Americans since 1939. Consistent with Laura's lessons, these well-tread steps clearly advise that those who wish to manage addiction must cultivate insight through a rigorous process of internal inventory and verbal revelation:

Step 4—Made a searching and fearless moral inventory of ourselves.
Step 5—Admitted to God, to ourselves and to another human being the exact nature of our wrongs.
Step 10—Continued to take personal inventory and when we were wrong promptly admitted it. (Alcoholics Anonymous 1939)

In sum, the heuristics of addicted denial and sober insight are both so central to American addiction therapeutics and so firmly rooted in cultural ideologies of language that one can hardly imagine an alternative.

This is precisely why some recent developments in American addiction treatment initially seem so unfamiliar and almost exotic, even if a typical point of entry is a small, dully lit room in an unidentifiable building in an unidentifiable office park in an only semi-identifiable region of the United States, given the mass-produced rendition of a Navajo weaving hanging on the wall. Here, two metal-frame chairs are pulled so closely together that the lower limbs of the middle-aged white men sitting in them threaten to entwine. But it is their conversation that will soon bring them together in a very significant way.

It is not just any kind of conversation in which the two engage. It begins when one of the men, wearing business-casual garb along with a blond ponytail, confirms that he has been sent to the office-park room because he has failed a drug test administered by the company where he works long and hard, presumably as a middle manager. The second, heavily bearded man—who has gained a reputation as an expert communicator, a widely recognized social scientist, and something of a spiritual leader—expresses sympathy for the first man's predicament. Specifically, he underscores the ponytailed man's analysis that the drug test captured only the innocent fact that he was simply "blow[ing] off steam" after a long day at work. He even says, "It happens in your private life and, really, the company has no reason to be concerned about this," at one point adding, "It's none of their business really, in a way." The ponytailed man nods along, seemingly put at ease by his agreeable new companion.

In fact, the men seem to be in total agreement about each topic raised as they talk: the tedium and burdens of work, the worker's right to a private life, the enjoyment and relaxation offered by "smok[ing] a joint," the irritation of wives who complain about drinking with the boys. At times they even seem to revel in the camaraderie they have forged out of their talk. The ponytailed man goes so far to recount—as if to an old friend—some of his drug stories from high school. He also speaks fondly about recent fishing and camping trips with his buddies in which taking drugs is "just so much part of what [they] do."

But then something unexpected happens—at least from the perspective of the ponytailed man. Suddenly, he states that he uses drugs far more regularly than he initially let on to his new companion; that he uses not just marijuana but also cocaine and even heroin, and that his habits have "caused [him] a little internal conflict"—as they have his wife. Despite the bearded man's seeming support to the contrary, the ponytailed man now suggests that his wife and his boss have good reason to be concerned with his drug taking, and there are indeed some "changes [he's] going to need to make" even though he doubts his ability to do so. Just as he did in the early stages of their communication, the master communicator now agrees with everything the ponytailed man says, repeating it back to him in a very deliberate, even methodical way. However, now an air of sobriety fills a room that was once charged with drug-related camaraderie, and almost like magic, the man with the ponytail finds that he has *changed*.

Distributing Denial: The Rhetorical Art of Motivational Interviewing

Given the confrontational exchanges at Fresh Beginnings, which were characterized by therapists' steady insistence that they already knew the inner truths that addicted people denied, this agreeable exchange may seem quite refreshing. In this seemingly mundane office park, we have encountered an exemplar of a new therapeutic method—motivational interviewing (MI)—that was originally developed as an alternative to the confrontational approach of mainstream addiction treatment but is now practiced in an astonishing array of professional arenas, including primary care medicine, couples counseling, and child welfare practice in the United States, HIV risk prevention in northern Europe and sub-Saharan Africa, smoking cessation in China, corrections and parole in Singapore, and even water purification interventions in Zambia and Malawi. Across these fields of practice, MI casts as a special "way of being with people" that "can be likened to that of a dance, where the practitioner leads in a delicately balanced collaborative effort" (W. Miller and Rollnick 2002: 280).

Motivational interviewing was first developed in 1983 by William R. Miller, an emeritus professor of psychology at the University of New Mexico, a Christian spiritualist, and the author of more than forty books and four hundred articles that range from meta-analyses and randomized controlled trials of evidence-based therapies to meditations co-written with the "horse whisperer" Monty Roberts. Of all his writings, Miller most values a slim volume on what he once claimed can happen during a motivational interview (W. Miller 2009: 892)—that is, "sudden, dramatic, and enduring transformations that affect a broad range of personal emotion, cognition, and behavior" (W. Miller 2004: 453).[7] By far the most read, however, is his coauthored volume, *Motivational Interviewing: Preparing People for Change* (W. Miller and Rollnick 2002), otherwise known by some MI-insiders as the "MI Bible" and soon to be released in its much anticipated third edition.

Miller is also the bearded man in the scene described earlier, which is taken from one of the many clinical demonstration films he has produced with his colleagues to train people in the method he developed (CASAA 1998). In his writings and interviews, Miller explains that MI draws from and synthesizes two traditions of American psychology that have long been staked against each other: the client-centered approaches most prominently associated with Carl Rogers, and American behaviorism. Miller also claims that MI offers practitioners something new: an explicit theory and method of communication that is designed to facilitate change in the interviewee. And while MI requires substantial rhetorical skill on the part of the practitioner, Miller is careful to underscore that MI is "not a bag of tricks for getting people to do what they don't want to do" (W. Miller and Rollnick 2002: 25). Indeed, what an ethnographer of MI casts as the grammar and poetics of MI, a practitioner of MI understands as its skill and spirit. By either framing, learning how to properly conduct a motivational interview requires substantial time, significant devotion, and rigorous training, as two years of ethnographic fieldwork in MI training settings have made perfectly clear.

However, at first blush, the method demonstrated in the film (which is known in the field as "Ponytail John" for the client-actor who is ritually changed by Miller's brand of therapeutic communication) seems deceptively facile. Through a large part of their conversation, Miller seems to simply repeat, in somewhat altered but always affirmative terms, all that Ponytail John says. Strikingly, these "reflections" are consistently offered regardless of whether the client is reminiscing about his drug-addled, party-filled past or indicating regret and concern about it.[8] This produces the sense that Miller is faithfully enacting the client-centered tradition of "unconditional positive regard" (Rogers 1961). Although Miller seems to merely follow along with Ponytail John's narrative, he is in fact engaging in a finely tuned, very subtle, but highly directive rhetorical process that involves carefully "select[ing] what to reflect and what to leave unsaid" and periodically amplifying "the content offered or implied in the person's speech" by repeating it back to them in somewhat exaggerated or elaborated terms (W. Miller and Rollnick 2002: 88, 8). This is clearly the case when Miller says to Ponytail John, "So, you have a lot of responsibilities. The job you have, you're working with a lot of people, you oversee a lot of people, you've got—not a family yet—but a marriage, and you're responsible there. And in some ways, this is a pull to feel free of that, at least for a little while—to feel free of that responsibility" (CASAA 1998: 5).[9]

While we may be surprised to find that the narrative content that Miller reflects is precisely the list of reasons that Ponytail John "frees" himself with drugs, he does so with an agenda to change this behavior from the start. To this end, the master motivational interviewer deploys his trademark set of rhetorical strategies to prompt the client to articulate this prochange agenda, and he does so—paradoxically—by arguing alongside Ponytail John for *the maintenance* of his drug habit. The idea is that "an ambivalent person may respond with the opposite when you seem to be taking up one side of the argument" (W. Miller and Rollnick 2002: 89); thus, the interviewer's seeming defense of the status quo (i.e., using drugs) is actually an attempt to institute change (i.e., sobering up). As Miller and Stephen Rollnick advise their followers, "Always keep in mind that the overall purpose here is for the client to voice the change side of the conflict and, ultimately, to move in that direction" (89). And since the motivational interviewer's effectively directive statements are poetically crafted as sympathetic affirmations, and are therefore likely interpreted and experienced by the client as such, the interviewer's normative agenda is rendered virtually invisible.

Certainly, not all clinical practitioners would approach Ponytail John as "ambivalent," given his seemingly steadfast portrayal of drug use as enjoyable, steam-releasing, private business during the first half of the recorded interview. And, surely, mainstream addiction counselors like Laura would see in Ponytail John both a classic case of denial and willful determination to continue his habit unabated. However, Miller and the practitioners who follow him take human ambivalence as a practical point of departure. Rather than portraying ambivalence as a characterological trait or a pathological tendency—indeed, a theory of human subjectivity or particular pathologies is tellingly scant in the MI literature—ambivalence is conceptualized as the range of alignments human beings have with the circumstances of their existence (see chapter 2 of Miller and Rollnick 2002). It is not that drug users (or their sober brethren, for that matter) deny internal or external realities, proponents of MI propose. It is that we all align ourselves in multiple and sometimes conflicting ways with those realities —for instance, blowing off steam with drugs, on the one hand, and worrying with and about them, on the other.

The motivational interviewer's central task, then, is to identify and then verbally amplify any potential signs of these contradictory stances, all while seeming to support the client's stated resolution to maintain the status quo. MI proponents call this "developing discrepancy," suggesting that while ambivalence may be a natural human tendency, it can also be rhetorically manufactured. Thus, when Ponytail John hears his own description of "blow[ing] off steam after a long day at work" amplified by Miller ("And that's . . . I hear there's a little more than just partying or having a good time. As you've said, need; that there's a sense of—it might be hard to deal with all that if you didn't have these drugs to use; that in a way, you need these to break the tension, to get away from the stress and the responsibility"), he responds by saying, "That's true. That's how I've been using those substances all along now for quite awhile, and I can't envision not, you know, so it's hard to say how I would function if I couldn't or didn't" (CASAA 1998: 5). So, through a steady string of affirmations, Miller has carefully managed the course of the interview so that initial statements like "I believe that this is something I do on my own time, in my own life" have morphed into clearly articulated and clinically resonant expressions of concern.

Thus, in the recorded interview with Ponytail John, Miller demonstrates how to motivate (and, some might say, manipulate) the clients being interviewed to articulate statements such as, "Maybe it's time I cut back a little." Known in MI as a "change statement," such utterances are thought to have powerful force of their own and not because they reveal what the client already truly thinks, feels, or believes, as Fresh Beginnings therapists would have it. Rather, in MI, change statements have what the linguist J. L. Austin (1962) called *illocutionary force*—that is, they *do* something in the very act of saying something (such as issuing a promise of future behavioral change or making that change real in the mind of the speaker). Thus, according to Miller and his followers, when a client says, "Maybe it's time I cut back a little," he performs an action, and he does so whether he really believes his statement to be true.

Furthermore, for the practitioner of MI, change statements have what linguists call "perlocutionary force" in that they precipitate other actions (such as actually "cutting back a little"). In the case at hand, because Ponytail John's prochange statement has instantiated the belief that perhaps he really should cut back on his drinking and drug taking, it is more likely that he will do just that once he leaves the office park—or so Miller and his brethren claim. Indeed, drawing on the social psychologist Daryl Bem's (1967, 1972) thesis that *people believe what they hear themselves say*, Miller emphasizes that what counts in motivational interviewing is the

semiotic linkage of clients' talk to future social action rather than to existing internal states. In other words, practitioners of MI do not feel it is
important if Ponytail John is really worried about his drug use when he
says he is. Instead, it is Ponytail John's articulation of a "change statement"
that matters, precisely because that statement constitutes both an act in
itself and precipitates other, and presumptively positive, acts toward sobriety.

Thus, the "motivation" in motivational interviewing is conceived as the
potential product of the interview as a speech event, rather than a latent
quality of the client-speaker. Accordingly, MI practitioners understand
their practice as a matter of producing efficacious verbal acts rather than
eliciting accurate referents of inner states. To be sure, this way of thinking
about language has roots in American pragmatism, is mobilized in American forms of rhetoric, and enjoys a privileged role in some other professional milieux, including the street-level bureaucracies with which addiction professionals regularly interact (see Carr 2009). It nevertheless
represents a striking departure from the dominant language ideology of
mainstream America—that is, the ideology of inner reference—and its
scripting of mainstream American addiction therapeutics since the 1930s.

As MI gains ground, more is at stake than clinical iterations of native
theories of language (see table 6.1). Indeed, as I have demonstrated at
greater length elsewhere (Carr 2006, 2009, 2011), the linguistic ideologies
operationalized in American addiction treatment have far-reaching material and symbolic consequences for the clients who are treated, for the
professionals who craft and deploy forms of expertise, and for active drug
users who must contend with cultural portraiture so stark and overdetermined that there seems little room to legitimately represent themselves outside its frame. Let us consider some of the consequences of a
shift in clinical language ideology in turn.

First, consider that MI's performative theory of language entails a radical
reworking of the American addiction treatment's central heuristic—that is,
denial. Whereas mainstream addiction professionals conceptualize denial
as a denotational impasse within the addicted psyche, MI proponents understand denial as the discursive product of a clinical encounter gone wrong.
Almost as if in reference to the standoff Laura described earlier, Miller and
Rollnick explain: "Some people believe that resistance occurs because of a
client's character armor. . . . Primitive defense mechanisms such as denial
were once believed to be an inherent part of, even diagnostic of, alcohol

TABLE 6.1 A Comparison of Mainstream Addiction Treatment and Motivational Interviewing

THERAPEUTIC MODALITY	LANGUAGE IDEOLOGY	CLINICAL HEURISTIC	LINGUISTIC RITUAL	THEORY OF THERAPEUTIC AGENCY	PRIMARY THERAPEUTIC PRODUCTS	PRIMARY PROFESSIONAL PRODUCTS
Mainstream addiction treatment	Language functions to denote existing inner states; speech is evidence of insight	Denial and insight	Self-inventory and narrative account Confessional monologues	I see, therefore I say; I say therefore I am	The insightful subject Inner truth	Clinical authority
Motivational interviewing	Language is the grammar of (inter)action; speech is action and functions to facilitate future action	Ambivalence and motivation	Developing discrepancy and client "change talk" Collaborative dialogues	I speak, therefore I see; I speak therefore I act	Motivation Speech acts	Clinical skill and reflexivity

ism. In this way of thinking, resistance walks through the door with the client. We question this view, which attributes resistance primarily to the client. Instead, we emphasize that, to a significant extent, resistance arises from the interpersonal interaction between counselor and client" (2002: 98). Thus, Miller and Rollnick do not only extract denial from the "character" of the addict. They go further to suggest that denial cannot belong to any one individual, but rather "arises from interpersonal interaction," thereby implicating the therapist as much as the client. This means that when a client "denies" a positive drug test, as was "classically" the case at Fresh Beginnings, she is indexing and indicting a therapeutic interaction gone wrong rather than displaying a quality of addicted subjectivity. Indeed, once practitioners theorize language as a social practice and product rather than as an unmediated channel of self-reference, properties once attributed to individual psyches must be redistributed.

Furthermore, MI's philosophy of language institutes a novel form of addiction expertise, one that is characterized by acute reflexivity. For if client speech is seen as indexing the "skills" and "spirit" of the interviewer as much as the inner state of the speaker, MI practitioners begin to read themselves in what their clients say. This conclusion is borne out in my ethnography of MI training settings, where professional novices are conditioned by their trainers to continuously monitor their own practice by charting the statements of their interviewees. Note that this professional habitus stands in stark contrast to the one inhabited by Laura, who routinely distrusted and dismissed clients' claims, objections, insistences, and deferrals as signs of their own unexamined inner states, while leaving her own contributions to these clinical stalemates almost entirely unexamined. Indeed, while mainstream addiction treatment professionals commonly project an authoritative knowledge of reality by asserting their clients' denial of it, MI practitioners suggest that signs of client resistance index that the interviewer is not quite expert enough. Hence, the MI community's intensive focus on professional training and the continuous cultivation of what they call "skills" and "spirit," a central focus of my research on the method.

In examining mainstream addiction therapeutics and MI side by side, one can certainly question how much really changes in the normative goals, not to mention the outcomes, of treatment.[10] Just like Laura and Susan, Miller and Rollnick are surely invested in the production of sober bodies, if not in the ideal of sober speakers. However, arguably, MI practitioners deploy a set of rhetorical practices that funnel their agendas through the mouths of clients, who can then talk *themselves* into professionally authorized ends. After all, cajoled by what seems to be a steady string of affirmations, MI clients like Ponytail John are not privy to their interviewers' attempts to "develop discrepancy" within their very own words. By contrast, there is nothing furtive in the rituals of mainstream addiction treatment, where clients are explicitly and often aggressively exhorted to see and speak their inner truths. In programs like Fresh Beginnings, clients have ample opportunity to read their therapists' agenda, if not the chance to directly or immediately challenge it in a way that will be heard. They therefore commonly turn to their own furtive rhetorical art of flipping the script—that is, speaking in what their therapists consider to be sober terms without investing in the content of what they are saying (see Carr 2011, chapter 6).

My research in dueling modalities of American addiction therapeutics indicates that the experience of the clinical encounter differs significantly, with clients and practitioners of MI alike enjoying a sense of collaboration that is all too rare in mainstream addiction treatment. Considering the well-documented rates of burnout in the helping professions, on the one hand, and the equally high relapse rates that help "revolve [the] door" of American addiction treatment programs, on the other, any positive shift in the day-to-day experience of treatment will surely be welcome. As an anthropologist of addiction treatment, my interests extend out from the dynamics of clinical encounter, following its myriad products and gauging their cultural, political, and personal effects along the way. And, if American addiction treatment produces particular types of people, with a special interest in generating sober ones, it does so largely because it reproduces and refines the representational media available to American speakers.

In the end, of course, there is no perfectly sober way to speak in any sort of language. The ethnography of American addiction treatment must therefore carefully examine what clients, professionals, and laypersons can do and say when speaking in a therapeutic tongue.

Conclusion: Toward a Semiotic Anthropology of Addiction

From a linguistic anthropological perspective, the competing schools of clinical thought reviewed in this chapter evidence an active tension between two prominent ways that contemporary Americans theorize the value and function of language. The ethnography of American addiction therapeutics indeed demonstrates that the reflexive rationalizations that native speakers make about language—which linguistic anthropologists call "language ideology"—are mutable and multiple, and sometimes go head-to-head not only within that wide set of practices known as "culture" but also within specific domains of cultural expertise. Indeed, while insight-oriented therapies are still clearly holding ground as the dominant mode of treating American drug users, and the language ideology of inner reference continues to dominate the American imagination, MI's inroads into an ever-growing number of professional fields suggest a potentially significant shift in the representational media available to American speakers. Linguistic anthropologists, then, may soon need to reexamine the contemporary United States as a linguistic ideological terrain. At the very least, we should expect that MI will continue to baptize a growing group of Americans who are authorized to produce as well as denote truths when they speak.

Understanding itself first and foremost as a theory and method of communication, motivational interviewing also challenges medical anthropologists to more fully account for the semiotic dimensions of clinical practices, traditions, and institutions. Indeed, the linguistically sensitive ethnography of American addiction treatment illustrates how clinical ideas and practices are not just underwritten but also generated and justified by specifiable philosophies of language. And since professional ideas about language manifest in clinical heuristics and spawn specific modes of clinical expertise, language ideology affects how practitioners and clients alike engage in and experience treatment. What if anthropologists, like MI proponents, understood the treatment of addiction as, in essence, semiotic? At the very least, medical anthropologists should more fully account for our reasons to cling to the analysis of addicted subjectivity when an increasing number of clinical practitioners—who have born witness to the dangers of doing just that—work in accord with a far more pragmatic ethic.

Though my interest in MI expands well beyond its interface with American addiction treatment, I have worked here to chart the possible effects of an approach to addiction that understands itself as a theory and practice of productive communication rather than an analysis and treatment of pathological subjectivity. After all, the advent of motivational interviewing raises particularly pointed questions about how addiction as a social pathology, and the "addict" as cultural figure, are collectively imagined and clinically treated. Amazingly, after almost a century of clinical practice, American addiction therapeutics is beginning to turn away from the iconic figure of the denying addict and the attendant idea that drug users must be taught to speak a purely presupposing and socially unmediated—or sober—language. Freed from this arguably impossible charge, American drug users will surely begin to say new and unexpected things, and American addiction professionals will have to find ways to respond. If and when these professionals "learn from" their clients, as MI proponents claim to do, they will certainly become more reflexive and rigorous about their methods. In this particular regard, anthropologists of addiction will want to follow suit.

Notes

The following people contributed to this chapter, though its shortcomings remain my own: Nick Bartlett, Marianne Brennan, Jessica Cattelino, Julie Chu, Jennifer Cole, Judith Farquhar, William Garriott, Nicholas Harkness, Daniel Listoe, Constantine Nakassis, and Yvonne Smith. Deep gratitude is owed to my informants, including of course, William R. Miller, for helping me to understand their vision of practice. Versions of this chapter were presented at the Anthropology Colloquium at Notre Dame University; the Culture, Power, and Social Change Series in the Anthropology Department at the University of California, Los Angeles; the Department of Anthropology's 2011–12 Colloquia Series at Northwestern University; the Working Group on Anthropology and Population Spring Seminar Series at Brown University; and the Medicine, Body, Practice workshop at the University of Chicago. I thank members of those audiences for their stimulating questions and responses. Special thanks are due to William Garriott and Eugene Raikhel for their patience, support, and inspiration in bringing this volume together.

1. See also Alcoholics Anonymous 1939; Chafetz 1997 [1959]; Davidson 1977; Denzin 1993; Doweiko 1996; Fewell and Bissell 1978; Flores 1997a, 1997b; Hazelden Foundation 1975; V. Johnson 1980; Kaufman 1994; Kearney 1996; Lemanski 2001; Morgan 2006; O'Dwyer 2004; Peterson et al. 2003; Rinn et al. 2002; Rosenfeld 1994; Spiegel and Fewell 2004; Tiebout 1953; Wallace 1978; Walters 1994; Wurmser 1978, 1985, 1987, 1992.

2. As is well known, Freud posited that a group of ego operations (or "defenses") function to ward off threats to the integrity of the individual psyche. In 1924, Freud began using the term *Verleugnung*—which has been translated as "disavowal" as well as "denial"—and he elaborated on it in "An Outline of Psychoanalysis" (Freud 1938). However, Freud never distinguished denial from other closely related defenses and therefore cannot be said to have developed a theory of denial (Laplanche and Pontalis 1973: 118). This work would be left to his daughter, Anna, who delineated two kinds of denial defenses: "denial in fantasy," in which daydreams are used to substitute or reverse painful realities, and "denial in word

and act," which requires collaboration with an audience that responds to a dramatization contrary to social facts. Anna Freud stressed that whereas denial is a normal feature of children's psychic development, it is pathological in adults, because to maintain a state of denial the individual ego must sacrifice both its synthesizing function and its capacity to recognize and critically test reality (Freud 1937; see also Altschul 1968). Nonetheless, most psychoanalysts hold that denial, like all defense mechanisms, can be adaptive, helping the denier to hold painful realities at bay so he or she can function in the here and now, or maladaptive and even psychotic, constricting normal adult development.

3. For instance, in his classic genealogical paper "The Discovery of Addiction," Harry Levine (1978: 494) identifies Locke's differentiation between desire and will as the seed for the modern concept of addiction: "In the 19th and 20th century versions, addiction is seen as a sort of disease of the will, an inability to prevent oneself from drinking." According to Levine, Benjamin Rush, the earliest American addictionologist and signer of the Declaration of Independence, identified addiction as a "disease of the will."

4. Of course, ideas about privacy are embedded in the larger conceptual constellation that we call "subjectivity" and, more particularly, in the culturally and historically variable line drawn between "person" and "public." In his study of Thomas Jefferson and eighteenth-century rhetorical practices, Jay Fliegelman (1993: 2) has brilliantly described the advent of "a new affective understanding of the operations of language, one that reconceives all expression as a form of self-expression, an opportunity as well as an imperative to externalize the self, to become self-evident." In line with Fliegelman's treatment of Jefferson as "an especially sensitive register of the social costs and benefits of such a view of language" (Fliegelman 1993: 2), I suggest that clients' careers at Fresh Beginnings demonstrate the material and symbolic consequences of particular modes of self-expression that have their roots in the "natural language" of the Jeffersonian era and have continued to expand and exploit the region of "the private" thanks in large part to the contemporary recovery movement (see also Hacking 1975; Lowney 1999).

5. Mikhail Bakhtin (1984) describes double voicing as both part and parcel of discourse, as an utterance never belongs to a single author. He also indicates that double voicing is a linguistic strategy in which a speaker brackets part of his or her speech with quotations to demarcate the voice of another.

6. This is not to mention the fact that forensic traces of drugs or alcohol do not necessarily signal that the person in question is a regular or problematic drug user, but simply that he or she had used a particular substance within a particular timeframe. This accounted for the fact that recreational users often sat next to chronic users in that circle of donated loveseats at Fresh Beginnings (see Carr 2011).

7. On the subject of quantum change, Miller more specifically suggests that "what is happening in the motivational interview is like the same thing on a small scale, around a particular behavior" (W. Miller 2009: 892). The statement was made in an interview, published in the journal *Addiction*, and was later confirmed in an ethnographic interview with me.

8. Notably, reflections are common in American psychotherapies and are especially well developed in client-centered therapies, where they enjoy a central function. According to Rogers, reflections are ways to check "whether my understanding of the client's inner world is correct" (1986: 375), and as such, are also demonstrations of the therapist's attunement to the client—or client centeredness—at the expense of the projection of authoritative knowledge. The explicitly directive mobilization of reflections is, arguably, one of MI's most important innovations (see Carr and Smith, n.d.).

9. There is a poetics to the practice of motivational interviewing that prominently features a distinct pattern of punctuated speech, or pause, that cannot be captured by a simple verbatim transcript. The poetic dimensions of MI in particular, and pscyhotherapeutic practice more generally, are the subject of a forthcoming article (Carr and Smith, n.d.).

10. There is, of course, a massive literature devoted to the study of client outcomes in various treatment modalities, including those that eventually gain the coveted status of an "evidence-based practice," as MI has.

SEVEN   EUGENE RAIKHEL

PLACEBOS OR PROSTHESES FOR THE WILL?
Trajectories of Alcoholism Treatment in Russia

While interviewing patients at the Municipal Addiction Hospital in St. Petersburg, I met Vyacheslav, a portly factory worker in his fifties.[1] He was, in some ways, a typical patient, although unlike many others he lived in a communal apartment with his wife. As we sat under the cracked and graying plaster walls of a small examination room, Vyacheslav told me that his son had died in the army six years earlier, but more recently his daughter had given birth to children. Vyacheslav gestured toward his motivation for sobriety in describing his new familial role: "I'm already a grandfather, but still I continue to drink." He described his stay at the hospital as part of a yearly cycle. Each year he would go on a drinking binge, at the end of which he would be persuaded by his wife to return to the hospital. There he underwent a week of intensive pharmacological procedures aimed at detoxifying his body. At the end of each stay, he received an injection (colloquially known as a "torpedo") that, he was told, would keep disulfiram, an alcohol antagonist, in his bloodstream over the course of a year. Fearing the negative effects of drinking with the substance in his body, Vyacheslav explained, he always waited until the course of the torpedo was over before embarking on another binge. While he felt that abstaining from alcohol noticeably dampened his social life, he also argued that he and his family had successfully learned to manage his tendency to indulge in drink.

As I learned in conversations with physicians at the hospital, many (and perhaps the majority) of patients like Vyacheslav who believe that they are receiving disulfiram are in fact injected with chemically neutral substances. While narcologists (as specialists in addiction medicine are known in Russia) represent this therapy to patients as *khimzashchita* (which translates literally as "chemical protection")—a potent pharmacological treatment that renders their bodies unable to process alcohol— privately they often describe the method as "placebo therapy" and emphasize its reliance on mechanisms of suggestion (*vnushenie*). Such clinical techniques have been used in Russia since the 1950s and, according to some sources, khimzashchita and closely related methods currently make up the majority of long-term interventions for alcoholism offered by narcologists (Mendelevich 2005; Sofronov 2003).

Such therapies are also highly contested in Russia and condemned on a variety of clinical, ethical, and political grounds. They are criticized by proponents of Twelve Step therapies for ignoring the underlying emotional and spiritual roots of alcoholism and by advocates of harm reduction for being wrongly represented as "cures" for a chronic disease (Mendelevich 2005). Even many clinicians who administer khimzashchita point out that while it is often successful in facilitating short-term remissions, patients rarely see the need to supplement it with longer-term psychosocial interventions, leading to a cycle of decreasingly successful and increasingly short remissions (Sofronov 2003). Not surprisingly, critiques made by visiting Western European and North American physicians often have focused on the disregard that such treatments seem to show for a normative model of patient autonomy; instead of treating patients as autonomous, rational, and (potentially) self-knowing individuals, these methods are said to rely on "people's ignorance" and their "belief" to frighten them into sobriety and foster their dependence on the clinician (Fleming et al. 1994; Parfitt 2006a).[2] According to such accounts, the mechanism underlying khimzashchita is very simple; it consists of the physician convincingly telling his patient, "If you drink—you die" (Chepurnaya and Etkind 2006).

In this chapter, I draw on historical and ethnographic research to examine why, despite such critiques, khimzashchita remains a popular form of treatment among physicians and patients in contemporary Russia. I argue that one reason for this popularity may be the fact that methods such as khimzashchita do not attempt to transform patients' subjectivities or "inner selves." I trace how this particular form of disulfiram treatment in Russia has been shaped by a clinical style of reasoning specific to Soviet and post-Soviet psychiatry, itself the product of contested Soviet intellectual and institutional politics over the knowledge of the mind and brain.[3] I argue that this style of reasoning has facilitated narcologists' understanding of disulfiram as a behavioral, rather than a pharmacological, treatment and has disposed them to amplify patients' responses through attention to the performative aspects of the clinical encounter as well as through management of khimzashchita's broader reputation as an effective therapy. Moreover, rather than transforming patients' subjectivities, these methods work by harnessing their preexisting ideas, affects, and motivations. The end result, I suggest, is that such methods act—at least, in some cases—as a kind of prosthesis for the will, allowing for a change in behavior without a change in self.

Disulfiram's therapeutic trajectory in the Soviet and post-Soviet Russian context stands in counterpoint to a widely circulated argument about the emergence of a neurobiological idiom of selfhood in the early twenty-first century. Over the past two decades, scholars have traced how the biologization of psychiatry and the production of new neuroscience knowledge—along with the neoliberal transformation of healthcare in many countries—has facilitated a growing emphasis on pharmaceutical interventions for mental illnesses (Biehl 2004; Dumit 2003; Kirmayer and Gold 2012; Lakoff 2006; Luhrmann 2000; Martin 2007; Rose 2007). While, as discussed at length in the introduction to this volume, this narrative has been more complex in the case of addiction, recent decades have seen the emergence of a neurobiological model of addiction, as well as a renewed emphasis on the potential of pharmacological treatments for substance dependence. These developments have been interpreted by many observers as signs of biological psychiatry's increasingly global hegemony over knowledge of and intervention on the mind and brain. Others, particularly Nikolas Rose, have argued that as neurobiological ways of thinking about and acting on human beings move beyond the laboratory, a somatic understanding of the self will displace the psychological subject of the twentieth century (Rose 2003a, 2007; Vrecko 2006, 2010b). Moreover, Rose links this "neurochemical personhood" to a particularly neoliberal way to govern pathological behavior and—in the case of addiction—desire. According to this argument, the new norm is not just the self-maximizing individual but one who internalizes governing functions once carried out by the state or social institutions, assuming responsibility for the management of his or her own susceptibilities and desires (Rose 2003a). The difference between the figure of the person that is said to inhere in such pharmacological treatments and that underlying psychotherapeutic ones is illustrated by Scott Vrecko in an article on the opiate-antagonist naltrexone. Vrecko (2006: 302) quotes a naltrexone user on an online forum who calls herself "endorphin-challenged," rejecting the category of the "addict," with its implications of essentialized identity and chronicity ("Once an addict, always as addict") and instead conceiving of herself as "targeting and controlling specific elements of neurochemistry."

Such arguments, which ascribe an epochal shift in personhood and self-governance to neuroscience and psychiatry largely in relation to contemporary Anglo-American societies, may risk ignoring the specific therapeutic trajectories charted by interventions as they move from bench to bedside or from one cultural setting to another. Numerous ethnographic studies have traced how nosological categories (most often those of the DSM), psychopharmaceuticals, and their attendant ways to understand mental distress have moved far beyond the North American and European settings in which they were developed, articulating in varying ways with differences in national and local styles of psychiatric reasoning (Kitanaka 2008; Lakoff 2006; Lee 1999), domestic economies (Biehl 2004), and institutional and political economic conditions (Ecks and Basu 2009; Jain and Jadhav 2009). Even in the postindustrial societies where brain-based modes of conceptualizing and managing distress have become ubiquitous, they have continued to mesh in unforeseen ways with lay explanatory models, forms of identification and sociality (Dumit 2003; Martin 2007), and longstanding patterns of marginalization (Oldani 2009). The Russian practice of khimzashchita is particularly significant to these debates because it so clearly calls into question a number of distinctions that prevail in North American clinical practice, as well as in much of the social science literature: not only the distinctions between pharmacology and psychotherapy and between medication and placebo, but also between the somatic and the psychological, as distinct categories of knowledge and intervention.

A Hybrid Discipline

During the time this research was being carried out, St. Petersburg's Narcological Service consisted of dispensaries in each of the city's administrative districts (*raiony*) and a central five-hundred-bed Gorodskaia Narkologicheskaia Bol'nitsa (Municipal Addiction Hospital) to which patients like Vyacheslav were sent for hospitalization. While many aspects of addiction treatment in Russia were radically transformed during the 1990s, the overall structure of the state-funded network had not changed significantly since the 1970s, when the Soviet narcological system was established. This Soviet system had been a hybrid, made up both of medical institutions run by the Ministry of Health and penal/therapeutic ones administered by the Ministry of Internal Affairs, the seat of Soviet police organs. While these institutions were instantiations of distinct disciplinary and professional ideologies about the nature, etiology, and appropriate treatments of alcoholism, the notion of alcoholism as a problem of public order saturated the entire system (Babayan and Gonopolsky 1985). Noncriminal alcoholics and those who resisted the "compulsory treatment" (*prinuditel'noe lechenie*) of hospitals and clinics could be committed for one to two years in explicitly penal institutions called Lechebno-Trudovye Profilaktorii (Therapeutic Labor Profilactories; LTPs), which were modeled on labor colonies and prison camps (Tkachevskii 1974: 39).[4] Beginning in the late 1970s, the narcological system grew rapidly, reaching its peak of funding and access to resources during the final Soviet anti-alcohol campaign in 1985–88.

By the time of my first visit to the Municipal Addiction Hospital in 2003, certain elements of the narcological system had changed profoundly, while others reflected a striking continuity with the Soviet period. Shortly after the fall of the Soviet Union, the Russian Federation had moved to dismantle the explicitly punitive elements of the system. The LTPs were formally disbanded in 1994, the same year that involuntary hospitalization for noncriminal alcoholics was outlawed (Entin et al. 1997; S. White 1996). Indeed, patients at the Municipal Addiction Hospital in 2003–4 generally needed only to inform their physicians in writing to end their treatment and be discharged.

Physicians at the hospital recounted how, through the 1990s and early 2000s, they had struggled to manage the increasing numbers of alcoholic patients, as well as the sudden rise of injected heroin, which was accompanied by a rapid spread of HIV infection (Heimer et al. 2007; Leon et al. 2007). These efforts were made all the more difficult by the severe budgetary cutbacks the system experienced in connection with the dismantling of the Soviet-administered economy generally and the restructuring of the healthcare sector in particular (Egorov 1997; Twigg 1998). This meant that while basic treatment remained free of charge, the hospital had begun to charge for various additional services. Shortages of medications and staff were also common. Physicians often complained about having to spend more than half their time on paperwork because they lacked computers or administrative support.

At the same time, narcology had offered physicians opportunities for profit during the period of intense economic depression. In 2004, narcologists in the state service were paid more than many of their colleagues in other specialties—this was meant to be official remuneration for the difficulty of their work—while the potential for profit in commercial narcology (or unofficial services in the state sector) was so great that competition between physicians and clinics occasionally turned into violent commercial war, with the involvement of mafia groups (Raikhel 2009: 227 n. 1). For physicians or medical researchers whose small salaries were often delinquent or delayed for months at a time, the promise of a specialty with even a modestly higher pay scale was clearly attractive. While most of the narcologists I spoke to had entered medicine with a variety of motivations, almost all explained that they had chosen to specialize in narcology for financial reasons.

A final change that swept narcology during the 1990s was the loss of the near-monopoly over the clinical knowledge and treatment of addiction that it had held during the Soviet period. Narcologists now found themselves competing with a number of methods and movements, some "imported," such as Alcoholics Anonymous (AA) and Scientology, and others "homegrown," such as the Orthodox Church (Critchlow 2000; Lindquist 2005; Zigon 2010). While many nonbiomedical practitioners borrowed heavily from narcological therapies, hybridizing them and thereby blurring the clear distinctions between official narcology and "alternative medicine," others, like some proponents of AA, were either only grudgingly tolerant of the state-run service or, like the Scientologists, were devoted to an explicitly antipsychiatric and antinarcological agenda.

Nonspecific Pharmacology

When I brought up khimzashchita (the treatment Vyacheslav received) in my conversations with narcologists, some initially represented it as a pharmacological treatment while others depicted it as "psychotherapy." Irina Valentinovna, a narcologist in the acute ward of the Municipal Addiction Hospital explained it this way: "Khimzashchita is a psychotherapeutic method. In principle, we give a regular—you can give a placebo—

this depends on the personality of the patient—and either we use a placebo or the chemical. . . . I give you this medication. I give you a prohibition [*zapret*] through personal psychotherapy [*lichnostnaia psikhoterapiia*]: for a certain period of time you don't have the right to consume alcohol [*spirt-noe*]. If he waits through the period, then we do another one. His self-image rises."

While it was clear that khimzashchita was meant to help facilitate what narcologists called periods of "remission" (sobriety) for patients, it seemed, based on Valentinovna's description, that the chemical content of the medication (disulfiram or "placebo") mattered less than the meanings enacted by the narcologist and her clinical tools. I found myself both troubled by the deception that this blithe equation of "placebo" and disulfiram seemingly entailed and fascinated by the questions it raised. Was khimzashchita a somatic or a psychological treatment? More important, why did the distinction seem to matter so little to the narcologists I spoke to?

While the literature on placebo phenomena shows clearly that *all* medications induce both specific and nonspecific effects, disulfiram's mode of therapeutic action makes these interactions particularly clear (Price et al. 2008). Often referred to in Russia as teturam, Esperal, or Antabuse,[5] disulfiram prevents the body from fully processing alcohol. By blocking the action of aldehyde dehydrogenase, a key enzyme in the metabolic pathway of ethanol, the drug causes the toxic byproduct acetaldehyde to build up, with extremely unpleasant consequences for patients. Rather than the pleasurable effects of alcohol intoxication, people with active disulfiram in their bodies experience flushing, nausea, and high blood pressure soon after drinking—referred to in the medical literature as a disulfiram-ethanol reaction, or DER (Eneanya et al. 1981; Kenna et al. 2004; Mann 2004). Thus, as the authors of one review explain, "When taken in an adequate dose, disulfiram usually deters the drinking of alcohol *by the threat or experience of an unpleasant reaction*" (C. C. Brewer et al. 2000: 329; emphasis added). Often recommended as an adjunct to psychosocial treatment programs, disulfiram is used to facilitate periods of sobriety during which patients can develop a "sober life-style" (C. C. Brewer et al. 2000: 329).

Although many studies have shown disulfiram therapy to be a potentially effective means of increasing the lengths of patients' remissions, adherence represents the major obstacle to efficacy (Suh et al. 2006). Once ingested, the medication remains at chemically active levels for only several days, which means that patients must take the drug regularly for the threat of an adverse reaction to alcohol to remain (C. C. Brewer et al. 2000: 331; Eneanya et al. 1981). While this may not represent a problem for highly motivated patients, for many others the challenge of adhering to the treatment is as great as that of abstaining from alcohol itself (Valverde 1998: 99). Not surprisingly, disulfiram therapy seems to be most effective when a relative or clinician is able to monitor or supervise the patient's consumption of the medication (C. C. Brewer et al. 2000). The issue of compliance has also been addressed by embedding disulfiram treatment into a number of institutional structures and coupling it with behavioral technologies in which patients' agency is closely delimited or curtailed— such as parole, probation, or dispensation of the drug at specialized clinics (C. Brewer et al. 2000: 332–36; W. White 1998: 227).

In a different attempt to manage the problem of adherence to treatment, the method of implanting capsules of disulfiram subcutaneously was developed in France during the 1950s (Kline and Kingstone 1977; W. White 1998: 228). Here, agency for adherence was shifted from the patient or his caretaker and structured into the implant, which was meant to release the chemical gradually into the bloodstream. However, clinical studies have shown that no disulfiram or aldehyde dehydrogenase inhibition is detectable in patients soon after the commercially available implants are inserted (C. Brewer et al. 2000; Johnsen and Morland 1992). In other words, after the first week following the implanting of the disulfiram, patients are highly unlikely to suffer from a DER. At the same time, since the early 1970s, researchers studying disulfiram implants have noted their effectiveness relative to unsupervised oral disulfiram, and most have agreed that such effects were due to a "psychological rather than a pharmacological deterrent" (Kline and Kingstone 1977; Malcolm et al. 1974: 488). The authors of one review summarize the clinical findings on implants this way: "All pharmacological treatments have nonspecific or placebo effects as well as pharmacological effects. Disulfiram is no exception" (C. Brewer et al. 2000: 331).

As a pharmacological therapy that seems to work primarily by nonpharmacological means, disulfiram occupies an uneasy position in the biomedical literature and clinical practice. With a few exceptions, most researchers writing in the English-language literature refer to disulfiram as having "nonspecific or placebo effects" with some trepidation or as evidence for its overall *ineffectiveness*. In part, this has to do with the deeply ambivalent attitude that most of the biomedicine community has taken toward treatment outcomes that cannot be attributed to a specific material cause, as well as to the subjective dimensions of human experience (Harrington 2006, 2008; Kirmayer 2006). In the case of disulfiram, this epistemological ambiguity is compounded by the fact that, unlike placebo analgesia or changes mediated by the immune system, the locus of disulfiram's "nonspecific" effect is particularly unclear. Sobriety that results from disulfiram therapy is a change in behavior that can be conceptualized as mediated both by conscious and unconscious mental processes.

Clinical phenomena variously described as "suggestion," "placebo," or "nonspecific effects" have long posed an epistemological challenge for a somatically grounded biomedicine. So it was striking that many of the narcologists I spoke to in St. Petersburg emphasized precisely these aspects of disulfiram treatment. Narcologists such as Valentinovna explicitly described khimzashchita as "placebo therapy" or as a treatment that depends on the mechanisms of suggestion (vnushenie). As one physician working in a commercial addiction clinic put it, "In addition to the purely chemical effect [of disulfiram], there is a suggestive effect [*effekt vnushenia*]." Why were narcologists seemingly less troubled by the epistemological problems posed by placebo therapy than many of their Western European and North American peers? I suggest that we cannot answer this question without examining khimzashchita as a product of Soviet narcology's neurophysiological logic and a particular clinical style of reasoning. Indeed, I will argue that narcologists' clinical reasoning is shaped, at least in part, by a Russian/Soviet genealogy of ideas about suggestion and healing that is radically different from its counterpart in the English-speaking world.

A Logic of Reflexes

While narcology was developed as a distinct subspecialty only during the 1970s, many of its therapeutic methods and styles of thought were developed much earlier, under the aegis of Soviet psychiatry. Along with other sciences of the mind and brain in the Soviet Union, psychiatry had been deeply affected by the politically shaped dominance of Pavlov's theory of "higher nervous activity." During the early Soviet period, the relationship between physiology and psychology was an extremely contentious ideological issue, primarily because it represented a sphere of knowledge in which Marxists hoped to link their understanding of human beings as historical actors with an objective science of humans as material beings (Joravsky 1989; R. Smith 1992: 191). This was largely approached through the concepts of dialectical materialism. In this context, Pavlov's reflex theory was not simply an example of a concrete behavioral mechanism, but a way to conceptualize the "dialectical" relationship between human biology and the environment (Graham 1987: 163; Joravsky 1989; Petryna 2002: 162). In practice, however, this may often have meant a reduction of psychology to physiology, of mind to brain—or, more precisely, of person-hood to reflex action.

The ascendance of Pavlovian theory in the Soviet sciences of the mind and brain began during the late 1920s and culminated in the early 1950s, when Pavlov's doctrine was declared the objective foundation for the Soviet "psy-" sciences at a series of conferences on physiology, psychiatry, and psychology (Calloway 1992; Joravsky 1989: 413; Todes 1995; Windholz 1997). While a resurgence of interest in psychology and theories of consciousness took place following Stalin's death, the influence of Pavlovian doctrine on clinical psychiatry extended well past the early 1950s, in part due to the prominent institutional posts held by its adherents and in part simply to the persistence of certain clinical interventions. For example, the dominance of Pavlov's theories had a number of infrequently discussed—and presumably unintended—consequences in that it legitimated hypnosis and other suggestion-based practices by providing a coherent explanation for them in scientific terms as forms of inhibition (Chertok 1981: 11). Pavlov described inhibition, along with excitation and equilibrium, as a fundamental process that takes place in the nervous system. Inhibition encompassed all processes that weakened conditioned reflexes and could be distinguished into the categories of "external inhibition," "internal inhibition," and the inhibition associated with sleep (R. Smith 1992: 200–201). Hypnosis resulted when the inhibitory process that led to sleep occurred to a less extensive degree; it was also a state of consciousness that facilitated suggestibility (Pavlov 1994 [1925]: 84; Platonov 1959).

Whether one interpreted such accounts as reduction to physiology or as "dialectical," Pavlov's theories helped to render hypnosis scientifically legitimate, allowing it to be incorporated into mainstream psychiatry (Babayan and Gonopolsky 1985; Babayan and Shashina 1985). In helping to legitimate hypnosis, the Pavlovian dominance in psychiatry led to the development of multiple suggestion-based interventions categorized as "psychotherapy." Indeed, with a few notable exceptions, as well as a strong tradition of "rational psychotherapy," most interventions identified as psychotherapy during the Soviet period employed hypnosis and suggestion (Etkind 1997; Lauterbach 1984; Wortis 1950: 88). These methods included various types of individual and group hypnosis; "direct suggestion," in which the patient remains in a waking state and is aware of the procedure; "indirect suggestion," which included the use of placebos; and techniques of autosuggestion and the "autogenous training" developed by German therapists (Lauterbach 1984: 81). As I describe, such methods made up the majority of long-term interventions used to treat alcoholism in the Soviet Union.

Disulfiram's Soviet Trajectory

The Danish developers of disulfiram therapy initially employed it as a form of aversion therapy, and that style of treatment fell on particularly fertile ground in the Soviet Union (Hald and Jacobsen 1948; Martensen-Larsen 1948). Soviet medical researchers first began to experiment with disulfiram during the late 1940s (contemporaneously with researchers in Scandinavia and North America); their model for thinking about treatment for "chronic alcoholism," however, was a method developed some fifteen years earlier: conditional-reflex therapy,[6] sometimes referred to as "apomorphine treatment." While the idea of inducing a physical aversion to alcohol in patients was not new in itself, Soviet medical researchers had grounded their efforts in Pavlov's theories. After initial attempts using electrical shock, they settled in 1933 on the use of emetics such as apomorphine to condition subjects to experience a nausea reflex when they tasted or smelled alcohol (Sluchevsky and Friken 1933; Zhislin and Lukomskii 1963). Between the 1940s and the 1980s in the Soviet Union, conditional-reflex therapy was a recommended mode of clinical treatment for alcoholism, given pride of place in textbooks as a first-line therapy for use after detoxification and mandated in LTPs and other penal institutions (Babayan and Gonopolsky 1985).[7] Even following the post-Stalin liberalization of science, conditional-reflex therapy remained prevalent in Soviet psychiatry and narcology because it complemented the needs of planners and administrators.[8]

When disulfiram was introduced in the Soviet Union its use was modeled after that of conditional-reflex therapy. Patients were not simply told about the potential negative effects of drinking alcohol while on the drug; the effects were demonstrated to them in "tests" administered by physicians (Babayan and Gonopolsky 1985; Strel'chuk 1952). Moreover, disulfiram treatment was seen by early Soviet researchers as developing a "negative conditioned reflex to alcohol" in the patients, and this reflex was observed even in "patients who had not taken Antabuse in nearly a year" (Strel'chuk 1952: 49). In other words, the notion that patients might have the intended physiological reaction to disulfiram in absence of the drug itself was present almost from the inception of its use in the Soviet Union. By the late 1960s, Soviet researchers were reporting clinical experiments with the use of placebo therapy: the replacement of the drug with a saline solution or vitamins (Ialovoi 1968). Originally intended for patients for whom the drug was contraindicated, such placebo therapy became increasingly widespread over the following decades. By the 1990s (and perhaps earlier), it was entirely commonplace (Fleming et al. 1994).

Subdermal implants of the French Esperal quickly became the most popular application of disulfiram: patients would have a capsule implanted behind the shoulder blade and would be warned about possible adverse effects from using alcohol for a period from one to five years (Fleming et al. 1994). While other placebo therapies were also used, such as the "tablet" and the "torpedo" (represented to patients as oral and intravenous forms of "long-acting" disulfiram, respectively), implantation was by far the most popular (Chepurnaya and Etkind 2006). Among patients and relatives, the therapy was referred to colloquially as an "implant" (*podshivka*), and patients would commonly say, "I was implanted" (*menia podshili*). Narcologists referred to all of these variants of disulfiram or placebo therapy as khimzashchita. Such treatment remained extremely common among patients I spoke to in 2004, and some returned regularly for repeat implantations.

Disulfiram treatment was first conceptualized in the Soviet Union as an aversive treatment like conditional-reflex therapy. Its transformation into khimzashchita involved several key shifts. Where conditional-reflex therapy hinged on patients' bodily memories of past experiences, khimzashchita worked on their anticipation of potential future consequences. Moreover, while conditional-reflex therapy depended on a behavioral response to stimuli administered within the walls of the clinic, khimzashchita transposed the source of this stimulus into patients' own bodies. Underlying these was an even more fundamental conceptual shift: whereas conditional-reflex therapy depicted the patient as a body responsive to inherently meaningless stimuli, khimzashchita assumed a subject replete with expectations, emotions, and beliefs.

Most narcologists described khimzashchita as a form of psychotherapy and emphasized its parallels with a type of hypnosis known as emotional-stress psychotherapy, or "coding" (*kodirovanie*). Developed in the 1970s by Alexander Romanovich Dovzhenko, a physician working in Crimea, coding was a variation on other forms of hypnotic treatment for alcoholism (see, e.g., Rozhnov and Burno 1987). It became popular as a "rapid" form of therapy during the 1980s and 1990s, often in an extremely commercialized form, where it was depicted as a magic-bullet cure (Dovzhenko et al. 1988). Like khimzashchita, coding is a therapy designed to keep patients from drinking seemingly by convincing them that their brains have been altered to make the consumption of alcohol harmful or fatal. Unlike khimzashchita, coding does not involve the ingestion, injection, or implantation of any substance at all; it is the therapist who "alters" the patient's brain through his or her actions. Narcologists and patients alike often implicitly acknowledged the similarities between khimzashchita and coding by classifying them together. Proponents of the therapies have called them "mediating psychotherapy" (*oposredovannaia psikhoterapiia*) in print, and many patients refer to both types of treatment as coding (Entin 1991: 132). In addition to highlighting the fact that purportedly disulfiram-based treatments are viewed as entirely suggestion-based (rather than physiologically active) therapies, this classification also foregrounds a number of formal similarities between these clinical techniques.

"A Small Ritual": Making Placebo Therapy Effective

I asked Anton Denisovich, the young physician who ran the ward where Vyacheslav was being treated, to explain khimzashchita as he would to a patient:

> We inject the medication disulfiram. It comes in different forms: intravenous, capsule form or subdermal implantation. All of these forms are long-acting. If the medication is taken intravenously or orally, it dissolves in the stomach and ends up in the bloodstream and then enters the body's tissues, combines with proteins in the liver . . . and for a certain period of time this medicine remains in the bloodstream. This medication cannot be taken with alcohol, as it blocks the enzymes that

break down alcohol. If a patient on this medication drinks and alcohol enters his bloodstream, the possible side effects are dangerous to his health or life-threatening. It can be anything from a flushing or reddening of the face to serious or crippling consequences or even death. . . . This is told to the patient, and he signs a paper explaining that he understands the procedure. And then the procedure takes place.

As Anton Denisovich himself acknowledged, this statement was often untrue in a referential sense, as he often used placebos in place of disulfiram. Like other narcologists, he treated the statement as a perlocutionary speech act meant to foster in the patient a particular belief (that a chemical agent in his body has made the consumption of alcohol potentially deadly), an accompanying affective state (that of fear, stress, or concern), and a consequent behavioral change (abstinence). Perhaps most important, a central idea implicit in such treatments is that clinical effectiveness depends on patients' belief in this "truth" about their bodies, a condition that the statements are meant to bolster. Even the "paper" patients signed to acknowledge that they understand the procedure often functioned performatively, as a prop that aids the physician in delivering the intended effect, as much as a contract meant to inform the patient and verify his consent.

Following these key preliminary steps, the clinical interaction at the core of khimzashchita takes place. Alexander Sergeevich, a narcologist at the Municipal Addiction Hospital, explained in strikingly clear terms how a clinical performance is central at this stage of khimzashchita (and related treatments): "Everything hinges on one short action, either in coding or in our methods of placebo therapy—in other words, a small ritual [*malen'kii ritual'chik*]. A touching of hands to the head, some kind of words, the use of some substance that gives a sensation: maybe a local anesthetic is poured into the throat. This ritual just signifies a point in time when the period of sobriety begins. This exists in all versions of psychotherapy."

It is worth noting that, like others at St. Petersburg's Municipal Addiction Hospital, Sergeevich regarded himself not as an "alternative" practitioner but, rather, as a mainstream psychiatrist-narcologist. His account further highlights the degree to which the disciplinary assumptions of narcology attuned clinicians to view performance as part of their practice. Sergeevich emphasized the importance of ritual form over content (physical contact, words, and substance are interchangeable) in producing a meaningful temporal demarcation of a new "period of sobriety" for patients. Following this logic, narcologists' and patients' preference for implantations and injections to daily self-administered tablets takes on additional significance, since such methods of application allow for yearly or half-yearly markings of "sober time."[9]

Many of the patients with whom I discussed khimzashchita repeatedly spoke about the material aspects of the treatment: the size of the ampules, the place on their bodies where the Esperal was implanted, the mode of administration—patients ascribed particular meanings to all of these characteristics, which in turn mediated their assumptions about the potential efficacy of the therapy. "They have ampules about this size [*indicating the size with his fingers*] and bigger ones," Vyacheslav explained when I asked him to describe the treatment. Torpedo injections were typically dyed bright pink or blue to signify their chemical potency (Fleming et al. 1994: 360). The mode of administration was certainly important, as well: that patients and their families generally preferred implants to injections, which, in turn, they preferred to tablets, suggesting that more physically invasive methods of administration may have also been associated with greater efficacy or potency. At the same time, as they replaced disulfiram with vitamin C, saline, or other neutral substances, narcologists used various methods to reinforce patients' interpretation of the treatment as chemically potent. A narcologist interviewed by Alexander Etkind and Olga Chepurnaya (2006) explained that he sometimes carried out sham surgery on patients—making and sewing up an incision without implanting anything—and then prescribed chemically active disulfiram tablets, telling the patient he or she was taking an antibiotic.

Patients also recognized the objects and substances used in khimzashchita as commodities and often linked the drug's efficacy and value to its geographical point of production, ascribing greater potency to implants imported from France or elsewhere than to their domestic equivalents. One patient recounted the choice he had heard a doctor offering an acquaintance: "[The narcologist] says, 'I can give you our domestic [*otechestvennaia*] khimzashchita—it costs 1,900 rubles [about $65]. I can't guarantee that it will work—that if you drink, something will happen. Or I can put in the French one—that one costs [significantly more]. This is the 100 percent option [guaranteed to work].'" In ascribing greater potency to imported disulfiram than to the Russian-made variety, physicians and patients employed a common form of post-socialist consumer judgment that links material value to an object's place of production (Patico 2005). Moreover, they implicitly translated commodity value into a judgment of potential clinical value or efficacy.

Secrets and the Management of Belief

Khimzashchita was a delicate topic for many narcologists. While some spoke about the use of "placebo therapy" without trepidation, in other cases, bringing up the topic of placebos led to awkward pauses, attempts to circumvent the question, or insistence that the difference between using chemically active disulfiram and a neutral substance was merely a "professional nuance." Once they knew I was in on their secret, narcologists offered a number of explanations for why they chose to give patients neutral substances in place of disulfiram, suggesting a subtle moral and social calculus that underlay their reasoning about clinical effectiveness. Anton Denisovich explained: "All patients cannot take these substances, in part because some of them won't wait out the entire period, and this will just be dangerous for them. So it's better to give him a placebo and give him the gift of several months of sober life than to inject the real medication." Such decisions to administer neutral substances were underpinned by judgments about particular patients and their capacity for adherence. A strong DER could indeed be deadly to some patients, and narcologists often sought to mitigate risks to their patients, as well as their own potential liability, by using placebo therapy. Although most verifiable accounts of patients dying from a DER seemed to be clear cases of negligence of the part of physicians, narcologists at the hospital framed noncompliant patients as the primary source of risk.[10]

Judgments about potential for adherence, in turn, drew on a categorization of patients based on their familial resources, as well as an ascribed level of "social decline." In a recent textbook, Russia's head narcologist, Nikolai Ivanets (2001: 113–14), recommends using disulfiram only for the small contingent of patients who remain "socially conserved" (*sotsial'no sokhranen*) and argues against its use for the vast majority, which he characterizes as "the asocial type [*asotsial'nyi tip*] of alcoholic." Narcologists I spoke to articulated a similar logic. This way of thinking rendered the physicians' perceptions of respectability and social status clinically relevant, as indices of a patient's potential adherence. "Socially conserved" patients included those who had not (yet) lost their jobs or contact with their family members; they were viewed as having greater motivation for sobriety but also as possessing greater social and familial resources to facilitate adherence. "The real medications have so many side effects," explained one narcologist. "We give it if there is a mother or a wife who strictly makes sure that the patient is taking the medication." In other words, the use of chemical disulfiram in the clinic was often seen as dependent on a complementary (typically gendered) arrangement for its management in a domestic space.

Using disulfiram entailed certain risks for a particular category of patients. The efficacy of placebo therapy, however, was also seen by narcologists as highly variable. Some argued that placebo therapy was more effective among particular types of patients who typically could be identified via certain psychological characteristics. Narcologists conceptualized patients' suggestibility as either an individual disposition or a generational characteristic. Older patients, or "Soviet people," were often described as being more suggestible than younger people, an ascription that draws on a common stereotype of the *sovok* (or *homo Sovieticus*) as conformist and prone to manipulation through political propaganda.

At times, such patients were described in terms of their tendency or capacity for belief or faith (*vera*). Indeed, narcologists partook of a particular concept of belief that, as Byron Good (1994: 5) has argued, is central to the empiricist paradigm underlying the "folk epistemology" of biomedicine. Implicitly dichotomizing belief and knowledge, most narcologists cast themselves as rational actors who "know," in contrast to patients, who merely "believe." The disciplinary assumptions and clinical techniques of narcologists may have fostered a particular attention to the relationship between this "belief" and the effectiveness of khimzashchita and other therapies.

Even further, some physicians characterized "belief" in particular therapies as a sort of resource requiring careful management. In a paper, Alexander Sofronov (2003), a well-respected professor of psychiatry at the Military Medical Academy in St. Petersburg, argues that the popularity (among patients) of modes of treatment such as khimzashchita hinders the advancement of methods accepted throughout the world, particularly the Twelve Step program and the therapeutic community model. Sofronov describes clinical technologies of khimzashchita and similar methods as "explanatory medicine" (*ob'iasnennaia meditsina*), in which the patient's only source of knowledge or information is assumed to be the physician: "the way we explain it is how they'll be treated" (Sofronov 2003: 4). Despite his misgivings, Sofronov regarded methods such as khimzashchita in a highly pragmatic way. During a conversation in his office, Sofronov posed a rhetorical question about the popularity of such treatments. "Should we undermine this belief [vera]?" he asked. "Absolutely not!" While Sofronov thought that "explanatory medicine" blocked the growth of more effective modes of treatment, he also worried that those modes were not yet adequately developed or available to patients in Russia. Not only was it unethical to undermine patients' faith in khimzashchita under such conditions but, Sofronov implied, belief in the efficacy of treatments needed to be carefully managed.

In other words, the effectiveness of khimzashchita hinged partly on narcologists' skills of persuasion and performance in their face-to-face encounters with patients, but it was equally dependent—as the physicians saw it—on their successful management of its broader representation to various publics as a pharmacological treatment—and as an effective one, at that. This work of building and maintaining the treatment's legitimacy took place not only during narcologists' bedside chats with their patients, but also in conversations with family members, in debates on the pages of medical journals and newspapers, and in arguments or offhand remarks they made in our conversations.

For example, when I asked Vyacheslav's physician, Anton Denisovich, whether he ever administered chemical disulfiram, he replied, "You understand that we can't give every single person the placebo, because we'll discredit the method that way." Not only did this answer suggest widespread anxiety that khimzashchita might easily lose its effectiveness by becoming associated with placebo therapy among patients, his statement was itself aimed at maintaining the legitimacy of the therapy. Whether chemical disulfiram was ever used or not, it seemed to be important to tell me that it was used at least sometimes, lest I depict the entire therapy as a sham, as others had done.

In working to legitimate khimzashchita physicians used multiple strategies, ranging from quoting statistics of efficacy (typically percentages of patients achieving year-long sobriety) to constructing origin stories for treatment modalities that linked them to Russia and depicted them as culturally appropriate. For example, the argument was sometimes made that it was appropriate for physicians to employ their professional authority to frighten patients because this clinical relationship reflected a particularly "Russian" form of authority. Moreover, as narcology in 2003–4 was a thoroughly commercialized sphere of medicine, in which practitioners competed fiercely for patients, claims about the efficacy of one's methods and medications were often interspersed with disparaging comments about one's competitors as manipulators, cult leaders, quacks, or even mentally ill.

Doubts, Rumors, and Fears: Patients' Ideas about Khimzashchita

What effect did narcologists' efforts have on patients' understanding of khimzashchita? The answer often had to do both with a particular patient's prior experiences in treatment and with the broader social context of their life. While patients' descriptions of khimzashchita ranged from confused to compliant to defiant to desperate to cynical, it was most often the patients with jobs and intact families—those likely to be viewed as potentially compliant—who spoke about the treatment in a manner likely to be understood as "believing" by their physicians. For example, Gleb, a middle-aged working-class patient in Anton Denisovich's ward, explained that he had been given a torpedo in the past but had not been able to wait until it ran its course and had begun drinking. He added that nothing had happened as a result of his drinking during the course of the torpedo. Yet the fact that he had survived this relapse without any consequences, contrary to the warnings of his narcologist, did not lead Gleb to doubt the potential dangerousness of khimzashchita: "Before you take it, you sign a paper saying that if you drink, the doctors are not responsible for what happens to you. You get it for a year; then you have to wait it out for a year. If you do it, you want to live. It's fine if it kills you: better that than if it paralyzes you or something. *We don't know with these drugs.* That would be worse. So each person needs to use his brain" (emphasis added).

Gleb's description evokes the state of uncertainty many patients experience regarding the risks of khimzashchita. Indeed, many stories circulated in St. Petersburg about deaths caused by disulfiram. Some of the stories were offered by narcologists as condemnations of the rapacious commercial practices of their colleagues. Others had the quality of rumors or warnings: accounts by patients or the relatives of acquaintances who had died because of khimzashchita. I was also told apocryphal stories that attributed the death of the popular Soviet singer Vladimir Vysotsky in 1980 to a particularly serious disulfiram reaction. Many patients also spoke about the importance of having an implant removed before beginning to drink (Chepurnaya and Etkind 2006). Whatever the intentions of people who circulated such rumors, the narratives themselves played an important part in reinforcing the idea of khimzashchita's potency among laypeople.

However, for every story about the chemical potency of the treatment, there was another that attested to its *ineffectiveness* or that recounted a technique to counteract disulfiram's effects. Ironically, the patients who received placebo therapy because they were categorized as noncomplaint were the very ones who were least likely to give credence to the potential efficacy of narcology's treatments. Eduard, an unemployed man in his mid-thirties whom I met at the hospital, was one such patient. During the late Soviet period, Eduard had worked as a *fartsovshchik* (a black-market dealer of goods from capitalist countries, such as blue jeans), but he had been unable to maintain steady work for several years. When I spoke to him, his arm was bandaged from a burn he had received cooking while drunk. Eduard was doubtful of any therapies and described how he had seen another patient receive an Esperal implant, which her physician explained was a foolproof option: "If you don't want to live, you can just drink a glass of beer, and you won't be here any longer." However, Eduard continued, "*one week later* [after the patient's discharge], they bring her back—after a week-long binge already! Almost comatose. So all these khimzashchity are complete nonsense." Eduard easily could have interpreted his acquaintance's serious condition when she returned to the hospital as an indication that the disulfiram had been active and potent. Instead, he emphasized that she had survived her binge—however narrowly—despite the assurances of her physician and took that as evidence that the treatment was "complete nonsense." It is particularly interesting to compare this account with that of Gleb, who did not doubt the potential dangerousness of khimzashchita even though he had experienced no physiological effects as a result of a previous torpedo. Unlike Eduard, who was living on the margins of homelessness, Gleb resided with his family. Like Vyacheslav, Gleb had integrated khimzashchita into his domestic life.

As the contrasting accounts of Gleb and Eduard suggest, patients' dispositions toward the efficacy of khimzashchita may be shaped more by the overall contexts and trajectories of their lives, their motivations, and their hopes for sobriety and the legitimacy that they accord to medical institutions than by specific experiences of efficacy or lack thereof. Indeed, if the standard account suggested that khimzashchita relied on patients' fear, which in turn depended on their belief in its potency, most narcologists also emphasized that the treatment worked only for patients who, like Gleb and Vyacheslav, were adequately motivated for other reasons.

For instance, Alexander Sergeeivich explained that patients can use fear as part of a process of self-management. "The mechanism [underlying khimzashchita] is simply fear," he explained, but added that one also needed a motivation to become sober: "If he doesn't have this, then even fear won't hold him back." Part of the physician's work, as Sergeeivich saw it, was rendering this fear meaningful to the patient, making sure that it took hold. He added, "Many of [the patients], either openly or not, approach the doctor with the request, 'Put this fear of consuming [alcohol] into me,' because many of them understand that nothing else will hold them back—only this kind of fear." Not only physicians made such arguments. For example, Grigorii, a Twelve Step counselor, described to me how he had once voluntarily returned to a psychiatric hospital for a repeat of a sulfazine injection,[11] which he described as "punishment" rather than "treatment": "I said, do this thing to me one more time. I ask him voluntarily; I want to remember this state [*sostoianie*], this horrible state, I want to experience it and remember it, so that I'll always remember it." Such an account suggests that the model patient for narcology's methods may not be the unknowing dupe of narcologists but the successfully self-disciplining subject. In their use of treatments and the institutions surrounding them to "actualiz[e] programmatic fantasies of a supposed autonomy," these patients are not unlike the poor and middle-class Brazilians who, as described by João Biehl and his colleagues (2001), returned for multiple HIV tests and counseling sessions, despite testing negative each time.

Conclusion: Prostheses for the Will

Throughout this chapter, I have traced the reasons for the continued prevalence of khimzashchita and other suggestion-based methods of treatment for alcoholism in Russia. There is, however, a caveat in that despite khimzashchita's continued prevalence, many narcologists described it as "a thing of the past." The collapse of the Soviet Union and the subsequent reintegration of narcologists into transnational professional networks, brought them into contact not only with psychosocial models of addiction treatment but also with the biologizing trends sweeping global psychiatry. Even as various forms of talk therapy have experienced an efflorescence in post-Soviet Russia (Matza 2009), broadly biological styles of reasoning in Russian psychiatry have been reinforced by this dovetailing of geopolitical rupture and disciplinary shift. Thus, it was not so surprising that some narcologists I spoke to articulated a disdain for khimzashchita and a hope for therapies that would "cure" alcoholism through biological means. When I asked Anton Denisovich (Vyacheslav's doctor) which methods of treatment or rehabilitation he found most effective, he explained, "Out of what now exists in the sphere of rehabilitation—these are all palliative measures, not radical ones. The future is certainly with psychopharmacology in this situation, as I see it. If we look far ahead, either neurosurgery or genetics, I don't know, but with some kind of radical measures. Psychotherapy can only more or less lengthen the remission."

Anton Denisovich's future-oriented notion of "radical measures," which might completely "cure" addiction, echoed many North American biological psychiatrists' hopes for an effective pharmacological treatment of addiction.[12] However, the tension between this hope and Denisovich's daily work at the Municipal Addiction Hospital, where he continued to employ khimzashchita regularly, paralleled the uneasy and paradoxical disposition of many narcologists in regard to their clinical techniques. Whatever their aspirations, narcologists in Russia continue to work in a setting shaped by institutional, political-economic, and cultural vectors conducive to the persistence of methods such as khimzashchita.

What broader conclusions can we then draw from the case of disulfiram therapy in Russia? For one, this narrative calls into question the argument that a somatic notion of the self follows from a thoroughly biologically based psychiatry. In the Russian case, a style of reasoning that privileged biological explanations did not produce treatments that encouraged patients to think of their drinking problems as chemical imbalances to be modulated. Nor did most patients who received narcology's behavior-modification treatments articulate an illness-based addict identity, as advocated by Twelve Step programs. Vyacheslav certainly did not speak of himself as an "alcoholic"; rather, he spoke of himself as someone who was managing drinking binges. Indeed, the treatments employed by Russian narcology stand in an ambivalent relationship to the interiority of the patients who undergo them, somewhat like that of the motivational interviewing described by Summerson Carr in this volume. While these treatments clearly assume and depend on a certain set of psychological mechanisms, they are uninterested in interiority in any explicit terms.

Indeed, I suggest that patients like Vyacheslav, who return year after year to renew their disulfiram implants, perhaps find those clinical techniques attractive precisely because they do not work through a wholesale transformation of their persons. While this may make such treatments appear "less effective" from the standpoint of North American addiction medicine, for many post-Soviet citizens, this is exactly what makes them attractive. For patients like Vyacheslav, disulfiram (or placebo) injections or implants were seen less as quick fixes than as what one might call prostheses for the will: pragmatic aids for the care of the self that bolster personal motivations for sobriety.

Ultimately, patients' different experiences and understandings of khimzashchita had less to do with anything specific to the treatment protocol than with the broader configuration of institutions and relationships (both inside and outside the clinic) within which any particular instance of the treatment took place. It is in this sense that the case of Russian disulfiram treatment also demonstrates vividly that "chemical" and "placebo" effects, or the social and pharmacological lives of medicines, cannot be disentangled as easily as some anthropologists have suggested (Whyte et al. 2002). The addiction therapies discussed here highlight how the efficacy of *all* ostensibly pharmacological treatments is shaped by elements, including chemical effects and patients' interpretations of those effects, clinical performances and relationships, clinicians' styles of reasoning and local research traditions, and the institutional and political economic settings of treatment. Moreover, such a perspective suggests how partial and incomplete an understanding of any clinical intervention is when it is reduced to a therapeutic protocol, a reduction that depends on the assumption that clinical technologies are discrete, portable, and transposable between contexts with little transformation.[13] As the movement of clinical knowledge, substances, and techniques becomes ever more ubiquitous and far-reaching, it is increasingly important for anthropologists of medicine and psychiatry to explore the processes and mechanisms that link patients' treatment experiences to the material, discursive, performative, and institutional elements of which all interventions are composed.

Notes

My deepest thanks go to the patients and narcologists in St. Petersburg who agreed to share their stories with me. The fieldwork described in this paper was generously funded by a Fulbright-Hays Doctoral Dissertation Research Abroad Fellowship, and much of the writing was supported by a Postdoctoral Fellowship funded by the Canadian Institutes of Health Research Strategic Training Program in Culture and Mental Health Services Research, Division of Social and Transcultural Psychiatry, McGill University. I thank the participants in the Social Science Research Council Eurasia Dissertation Development Workshop in 2006 and in the Comparative Human Development workshop at the University of Chicago and the Anthropologies of Addiction workshop in Montreal in April 2009 for their many helpful comments. This chapter has also benefited greatly from the readings and suggestions of Lauren Ban, Iris Bernblum, João Biehl, John Borneman, Colin C. Brewer, Carol Greenhouse, Hanna Kienzler, Laurence Kirmayer, Anne Lovell, Kelly McKinney, Alessandra Miklavcic, Kavita Misra, Tobias Rees, Jamie Saris, Roger Schoenman, Ian Whitmarsh, and Allan Young.

An earlier version of this chapter appeared as "Post-Soviet Placebos: Epistemology and Authority in Russian Treatments for Alcoholism," *Culture, Medicine, and Psychiatry* 34, no. 1 (2010): 132–68. Reprinted with permission from Springer Science and Business Media.

1. This chapter is based on fourteen months of fieldwork in a number of addiction treatment facilities in St. Petersburg, Russia, conducted in 2002–4. Most of the material presented here was drawn from interviews and observations conducted in the municipal Narcological Service. They included thirty interviews with patients and twenty-four with physicians, as well as numerous informal interactions and conversations; in addition, I conducted fieldwork at one commercial addiction clinic and a charitable Twelve Step–based rehabilitation center. I also interviewed and observed the practice of a number of narcologists, psychiatrists, and healers in private practice; sat in on a series of training lectures on narcology for physicians; and attended open sessions of AA.

   The project was approved by the institutional review board of my home institution at the time (Princeton University), as well as by the St. Petersburg Department of Public Health. To ensure the confidentiality of informants, all of the patients and physicians I interviewed in the Narcological Service have been given pseudonyms or general appellations (i.e., "older narcologist"), and some identifying details have been changed. While I refer to several physicians who have made their views known in previous publications by their real names (Alexander Sofronov, Eugene Zubkov), in these cases I do not ascribe to these physicians any statements substantively beyond those they have made in print.

2. Peter Finn, "Russia's One-Step Program: Scaring Alcoholics Dry," *Washington Post*, October 2, 2005.

3. Throughout this chapter, I use the notion of "style of reasoning" drawn from the work of Ludwik Fleck (1979 [1935]) by Ian Hacking (1992) and further elaborated by Allan Young (2000). A style of reasoning, Young (2000: 158) writes, "is composed of ideas, practices, raw materials, technologies and objects. . . . It is a characteristically self-authenticating way of making facts, in that it generates its own truth conditions."

4. These close institutional links to the state created a paradoxical set of conditions

for Soviet physicians and for narcologists in particular. While their ability to call on the state's means of coercion gave narcologists a way of managing patients, it also undermined physicians' "legitimacy as healers" (Rivkin-Fish 2005: 26). Several narcologists who had practiced during the Soviet period with patients undergoing "compulsory treatment" explained the extremely deleterious effect that such perceptions had on their attempts to establish trusting relationships with patients, especially those with histories of detention.

5. Derived from the full chemical name tetraethylthiuram disulfide, "teturam" and "tiuram" are names used for disulfiram in Russia (Eneanya et al. 1981; Sereiskii 1952). Antabuse is the trademarked name of disulfiram. Esperal is a brand name for disulfiram produced by the French pharmaceutical company Sanofi-Aventis, but in Russia, "Esperal" typically refers specifically to disulfiram implants.

6. While *uslovnyi refleks* is often translated into English as "conditioned reflex," historians of science have argued that "conditional reflex" more closely approximates the Russian term (Joravsky 1989).

7. The use of apomorphine treatment was not confined to the Soviet Union, although its use was less widespread elsewhere (W. White 1998: 106–8).

8. By the time of my fieldwork, apomorphine therapy was no longer in use in St. Petersburg.

9. This temporal aspect of the treatment also complemented the way in which the heavy consumption of alcohol was conceptualized by many patients in St. Petersburg. Patients I met in various institutions rarely spoke in terms of "consuming" or "drinking" alcohol. Most referred to "entering" and "exiting" drinking binges (*zapoii*) in a way that suggested a separate time and space. While the phenomenon of drinking binges is prominent in international medical literature on alcoholism, this local vernacular understanding of a binge—and the set of practices it described—was clearly distinct from the medical one.

10. Most of the cases of patients' deaths after disulfiram therapy involved commercial enterprises that offered at-home disulfiram treatment. The procedure was sometimes carried out without checking a patient's current blood alcohol level, and the house-call teams often left immediately after completing the treatment.

11. Injecting sulfazine, another relatively common practice in Soviet psychiatry and narcology, caused excruciating pain and fever and was used as a form of aversion therapy.

12. Of course, as the chapters by Carr, Hansen, Meyers, and Garriott in this volume demonstrate, English-language addiction medicine, like Russian narcology, is hardly a homogenous field of practice.

13. I thank Anne Lovell for pushing me to clarify the distinction between therapeutics per se and interventions more broadly conceived.

"YOU CAN ALWAYS TELL WHO'S USING METH"
Methamphetamine Addiction and the Semiotics
of Criminal Difference

In the spring of 2007, Dwight Tanner, a white working-class man
in his early forties, pled guilty in a rural West Virginia court to
four counts of grand larceny. According to court documents,
Dwight had committed numerous acts of breaking and entering
and burglary over the course of the previous year, including the
theft of the contents of an entire household—everything from
the coffeemaker to the washer and dryer and the old tractor,
which he used to haul the bigger items out of the house. The four
counts of grand larceny to which Dwight pled guilty accounted
for fewer than half of the crimes for which he had been indicted,
which were dismissed as part of his plea agreement with the state,
and they represented only a fraction of the total number of
crimes he was assumed to have committed in his lifetime. Indeed,
this was not Dwight's first arrest but his third, each time on
charges of breaking and entering and burglary.

Dwight was arrested after the owner of the house saw him
riding her tractor around his own property. A state trooper came
to investigate. When the trooper asked why he had committed
the crimes, Dwight replied obliquely, "I got in a bind, a financial
bind. Picked a dumb way to try to make some money." Awaiting
sentencing at the regional jail, he elaborated on this explanation
to the county probation officer: "I was breaking into places to

support my drug habit. I was using Crystal Meth every day. I got to the point I didn't have any more money. So the guy I was getting my Meth from was trading me Meth for anything I could bring him.... It started out with little things, and with time, my drug habit got worse. I wish I could turn back time and stay away from the drugs.... I'm not the same person when I'm not on drugs."

People like Dwight have begun to fill courthouses and jails in rural communities around the United States. "Sex offenders and drug addicts, that's about all I see around here," said Rose Hinkle, the local probation officer. Often, methamphetamine is the source of these "drug addicts'" criminality. Many, like Dwight, have been arrested for property crimes committed to obtain money with which to buy methamphetamine. Others have been arrested for participating more directly in the drug economy, for producing or selling meth. And some have never been arrested but live as marginal and "dangerous" members of the community who "everybody knows" are selling drugs.

In 2006–7, I conducted ethnographic research looking at the impact of methamphetamine on the rural community of Baker County, West Virginia (Garriott 2011). For more than a year, I combed through archives, spoke with local residents, and observed the impact meth was having on the local community. I focused particularly on the workings of the criminal justice system: the efforts of police officers, judges, and administrators at the regional jail. But I also focused on everyday social relationships such as kinship networks, neighboring practices, and exchanges of rumor and gossip to see how these, too, were being reoriented around the growing concern over meth.

I watched as prosecuting priorities of the courts shifted toward meth offenders, increasing caseloads and bringing new people into the criminal justice system; as community groups advocated for expanded drug testing in schools, causing tension between teachers and students, parents and children; as rumors circulated over who had been seen going to receive treatment for addiction at the local mental health facility; and as addicts, driven into lives of crime by their use of methamphetamine, were sent to overcrowded regional jails and state prisons, where they received little medical treatment. Upon their release, they struggled to find a place for themselves in their communities, where they lived with the double stigma of their criminal record and their addiction.

The events taking place in Baker County, while locally unique, were nevertheless part of a broader history of struggle in the United States with illicit drugs. The War on Drugs, now entering its fourth decade, is America's longest-running war. Its impact continues to be profound. But the most significant impact, perhaps, has been the deepening of the fundamental association between drugs, addiction, and crime in U.S. legal and political culture.

This association has come to define thinking about crime in the United States. Lawrence Friedman, for instance, wrote in 1993: "Many people [in the United States] sincerely believe that addicts are responsible for most of our violent crime: they rob to get money for a high; and on this high they rape and rob and kill, wantonly, cruelly" (Friedman 1993: 356–57). It has also shaped thinking about addiction. The entry for the term "substance abuse" (which replaced "addiction") in the DSM-IV, for instance, lists "recurrent substance-related legal problems (e.g., arrests for disorderly conduct)" as one of its defining "symptoms" (Bourgois 2000). Thus, to put it simply, the association between drugs, crime, and addiction, though itself an artifact of U.S. drug control policies, has become a social fact in the United States.

The U.S. criminal justice system has been rightly criticized for its less than adequate efforts to address addiction, which is often the root cause of many drug offenders' criminality. So have drug laws and enforcement practices that criminalize addiction. However, simply viewing the problem from this perspective overlooks the myriad ways in which knowledge of addiction and its relationship to drugs and crime has been incorporated into the everyday workings of the criminal justice system itself—constituting new avenues through which the system's traditional punitive mandate may be carried out and complicating easy dichotomies between treatment and punishment, sickness and badness, retribution and rehabilitation. The incorporation of knowledge of addiction into U.S. criminal justice practice has been the most pronounced in three key areas: the explanation of crime; the identification of criminals; and the staging of interventions.

With regard to the explanation of crime, knowledge of addiction has provided the criminal justice system with a working theory of criminal behavior. According to this theory, criminality is a symptom of addiction; drug users are driven by their addiction to commit acts of criminality in the constant and singular pursuit of more drugs. These crimes could include anything from property crimes to forgery and participation in the drug economy itself. Thus, "drugs"—and, more specifically, "drug addiction"—provide a common explanation for a variety of otherwise unrelated types of crimes.

Knowledge of addiction has also served as a resource to assist in the identification of criminals. Members of the criminal justice system in Baker County often used the physical and behavioral symptoms of addiction as a lens through which to read the criminal body and address what David Garland (2001: 137) has called "the chimeral obscurity of criminal difference." The symptoms of methamphetamine addiction provided a particularly robust resource in this regard, given the striking effects that methamphetamine use can have on the body. These include everything from scabs and missing teeth to psychosis and paranoia—even the "symptom" of criminality itself. Using the symptoms of addiction in this way fed into the longstanding desire within the criminal justice system—and in popular culture more generally—to use scientific insights for forensic purposes, to uncover the signs of criminality on the very body of the criminal (Horn 2003; Valverde 2006).

Finally, addiction has provided a medium for the staging of interventions aimed at addressing criminality. Addiction is notable for the diverse range of interventions it supports. They include everything from investigation, arrest, and punishment to treatment, education, and prevention, as well as the broad array of practices aimed at "offender management" in prisons and during probation. Taken as a whole, these techniques and practices make up a significant portion of the local drug enforcement apparatus, which is thus sustained by the common concern with addiction.

In this way, the figure of the methamphetamine addict functioned in Baker County as a potent "figure of criminality" (Rafael 1999) in the local juridical imaginary. Anthropologists have noted the importance of such criminal figures in the making of contemporary social and political orders (Comaroff and Comaroff 2006; Parnell and Kane 2003; Rafael 1999; Siegel 1998). Such figures often become the object of collective anxiety, representing the intrusion of the dangerous, the threatening, the unknown, or the unexpected into everyday life. The potency of these figures derives not only from their capacity to invoke law (they are, after all, *criminal* figures and thus products of the legal order itself), but also because they test the limits of law's efficacy: its powers of recognition and retaliation, as well as its claims to legitimacy and to act in the name of collective opinion (Rafael 1999: 12–13). In this regard, such figures become the focus of collective action, the locus around which a common response may be carried out. Notably, although the specific figures of criminality in question vary from time to time and from place to place, they seem nevertheless to be a common element in a diverse array of contemporary political regimes. As Jean Comaroff and John Comaroff (2006: 279) have written, "In sum, the figure of the archfelon, albeit culturally transposed, seems to be doing similar work in many places, serving as the ground on which a metaphysics of order, of the nation as a moral community guaranteed by the state, may be entertained, argued for, even demanded."

The methamphetamine addict—and the drug addict more generally—has become such a potent figure of criminality because it represents a dangerous conflation of moral, legal, and biological forms of deviance and difference. The use of the drug that begins the addiction is construed as both an immoral and an illegal act that, in turn, sets in motion the chronic, neurobiological condition of addiction. The addiction then embroils the individual in further illegality, driving her or him into continued drug use and related criminal acts, eroding her or his physical and mental well-being in the process. The chronic character of addiction and high rates of relapse mean that the addict is viewed as perpetually inclined toward criminality, making her or him a constant threat (cf. Garcia, this volume).

This stereotypical understanding of the addict's life course fed into the popular representation of drugs as inherently criminogenic and justified the targeting of methamphetamine addicts both in Baker County and nationally. More significantly, it provided members of the criminal justice system with a common medium to address perennial concerns, such as explaining crime, identifying criminals, and intervening to punish and prevent past and future criminality. In what follows, I examine how knowledge of addiction sustained everyday criminal justice practice in Baker County. Rather than inspire a more rehabilitative approach to the methamphetamine problem, knowledge of the signs and symptoms of methamphetamine addiction were incorporated seamlessly into standard criminal justice practice, where they functioned ultimately as a semiotics of criminal difference.

Drug-Crime Connections

I was not initially concerned with the criminal dimension of methamphetamine. As originally conceived, my project was to examine the treatment experiences of addicts working to overcome their addiction to meth.

What I did not appreciate at the time, however, was that this therapeutic dimension of meth addiction could not be understood outside the criminal context.

This quickly became evident as I began speaking to those who worked in therapeutic services related to addiction. I began with Carl Ferguson, the head addiction counselor at the local mental health clinic. I met him at his office in the small brick building that housed the clinic. He was younger than I had expected, seeming at most to be forty. Stills from *The Andy Griffith Show* hung on the walls, providing the only decoration.

"How in the world did you end up here?" he asked, smiling, as we sat down. Carl began to explain in detail all of the problems the clinic and the community were having with meth. He estimated that, at best, the clinic had a 30 percent success rate treating meth addicts. In his experience, treatment worked only when people really wanted to stop using the drug. Meth was so addictive that users rarely got to that point and thus rarely sought treatment on their own; the clinic probably would not see any meth users if the court system did not send them. Indeed, the court played a vital role in the work of the clinic. "The court is the hammer that keeps them in treatment," Carl said.

This movement from the clinic to the court (and back again) became a theme that recurred in my early conversations. A group of professionals in the social service field—social workers, community organizers, the high school guidance counselor—met regularly at the local hospital. I began attending their meetings. They suggested, however, that I speak to the local deputy sheriff, Daryl Montgomery. He was the real expert on methamphetamine.

Daryl's expertise had come from two years of working as part of a Federal Drug Task Force in the area. He estimated that well over half of all of the crime that occurred in the county was somehow drug-related (others put the figure closer to 90 percent). The spread of meth in the area had played a significant role in this transformation. I asked him why he thought that had happened. "It's so addictive," he replied quickly.

I asked Daryl if addicts ever received treatment instead of incarceration. "They all want treatment when they get caught," Daryl said. But few stayed with it. "I see treatment as an easy getaway," he continued. "Some people call me hardcore, but I think jail's the best treatment for them." The prosecuting attorney for the county shared Daryl's view and was very aggressive in obtaining felony convictions for drug offenders. "We're very lucky," Daryl stated.

I called Baker County's prosecuting attorney, Daniel Gardner, at his office one morning. After two rings, a man with a decidedly un–West Virginian accent picked up the phone and briskly said, "Hello?" I introduced myself to him and explained my interests. "Uh-huh," he said, distractedly. I could hear papers rustling in the background. "I was wondering if you could tell me about some cases in which drugs were involved," I said. "I don't really have time to do that," he answered, papers still rustling. "Just go to the circuit clerk's office and start looking through files. If you have any questions about specific cases, let me know."

This was the first of many brushoffs I received during my fieldwork—or so I thought. I followed his instructions and went to the circuit clerk's office, where all of the criminal case files for the county were housed. "Could I see the files for any cases in which drugs were involved?" I asked. "I'd be particularly interested in seeing any related to methamphetamine." The clerk looked back, silently, lips pursed as though she was about to say something. I could not tell whether her expression was annoyance, confusion, or both. I braced myself for another brushoff. Then she spoke. The problem, she explained, was that so much of the crime they saw was drug-related. Of course, there were the cases of possession and distribution, crimes in which drugs were explicitly involved. But the crimes committed with more regularity—breaking and entering, theft, domestic abuse— were often drug related too, even though this was not reflected in the charges. She concurred with the prosecuting attorney's suggestion: the best thing to do was simply go through the file drawers. It would not take long to find drug-related cases.

Arthur Cravens had been the judge for Baker County for thirty years. When we spoke about methamphetamine, he echoed the prevailing sentiments at the courthouse. Methamphetamine was everywhere; as a result, meth users were fixtures in his courtroom. Meth's addictiveness was to be blamed for much of this. "I thought heroin was the most addictive [drug]," he reflected, "but they say meth is even more addictive; that you can be hooked after trying it just once." He paused before adding, with a slight smile, "But, then, that's what they said about heroin."

Rose Hinkle, the probation officer for Baker County, likewise stated that drug offenders were a major focus of her work. In most cases, their criminality was rooted in their addiction. Indeed, Rose was consistently amazed by the lengths to which people would go to satiate their addictions, including the commission of crimes. "They'll sit right there and tell me about the urges," she said. Rose saw the lack of viable treatment options in the area as part of the problem. The nearest in-patient treatment center was one hundred miles away. Being admitted as a patient was often difficult. This left most with outpatient options. In addition to the classes and counseling offered at the local mental health clinic, Alcoholics Anonymous and Narcotics Anonymous meetings took place in the community. But none of this was adequate, in Rose's view: most drug offenders needed in-patient treatment with constant care and supervision.

The closest thing to in-patient treatment available to those ensnared in the criminal justice system in Baker County was the program at the regional jail, but it served only eight inmates at a time, and access was competitive. Moreover, it lasted only as long as the person was incarcerated—the juridical rationale of the institution always trumped the rehabilitative efforts contained within. Thus, by the time addicted inmates reached Rose as probationers, they could no longer participate in the program. And all of this was overshadowed by the sad fact that one had to be arrested to gain access to the treatment program in the first place.

Rose was constantly frustrated by these contradictions and inadequacies within the system. Yet what she found most challenging—and depressing—was the sheer magnitude of drug use and crime in the community. "I had no clue what went on [in Baker County] until I got this job," Rose said, noting that many of the people on probation were her former high school classmates. "It's really hard to see people I know on drugs."

These early conversations revealed the power of the association between drugs, addiction, and crime in the local juridical imaginary. These associations sustained—and were sustained by—an institutional infrastructure in which the criminal justice system was the most powerful and visible local embodiment of the state—the primary distributor of state services and sanctions. Treatment resources, such as those I had set out to study at the beginning of my research, for the most part were part of the wider drug enforcement apparatus, so it was this apparatus that became the focus of my research. Tracing this apparatus involved looking at everything from police officers' efforts to raise the community's awareness to the addiction treatment program in the jail and the prosecutorial practices of the local court system. Each element was united in its use of knowledge of addiction to do the work of drug enforcement.

Pedagogies of Policing

Law enforcement's understanding of the link between drugs, crime, and addiction was most explicitly articulated during the public presentations given by police officers to various groups within the community. Officers regularly gave presentations on the dangers of methamphetamine and viewed this pedagogical work as part of their more general efforts at drug prevention. In the presentations, the officers combined materials they received during training seminars with their own personal experience. The presentations frequently received local newspaper coverage, allowing them to reach a broader audience. This could have a very tangible impact on police. For instance, when he heard Deputy Sheriff Daryl Montgomery's account of the methamphetamine problem, one resident donated $6,000 toward the purchase of a microphone to be used in undercover investigations.

State Trooper Frank Fields regularly gave presentations on methamphetamine to community groups. He worked exclusively on drug cases. When I made arrangements to interview him, he responded by offering to let me view his PowerPoint presentation. This move was partly an attempt to deflect attention away from the details of his undercover police work, which he was somewhat reluctant to share with me, but it also reflected a sincere belief that the PowerPoint presentation contained the most relevant information for understanding methamphetamine.

Frank's presentation, which he had given to a variety of community organizations, employed a largely biomedical idiom to explain the experience of using methamphetamine and the eventual onset of addiction. "Methamphetamine is a powerful central nervous system stimulant," the presentation began, going on to describe the ease with which meth could be made, the pleasurable feelings it produced, and the "state of high agitation that in some individuals can lead to violent behavior." Another slide stated, "The rush and high are caused by the release of very high levels of the neurotransmitter dopamine into areas of the brain that regulate feelings of pleasure." Later slides continued in this vein, explaining the difficulty users experience when they try to stop using methamphetamine and the resulting high likelihood of relapse.

Frank said little as I clicked through the presentation until I reached a slide titled "Physical Effects of Meth Use." "This one's pretty interesting," he said. The slide depicted the impact of methamphetamine use on the body, using graphic images to illustrate the effects of both "short-term" and "long-term" use. Short-term use was illustrated by a picture of an arm with severe open sores, the likely result of the person picking at imaginary "meth bugs" under his or her skin. Long-term use was illustrated with a series of mugshots depicting the physical decline of a woman who appeared relatively "normal" in 1998 and grossly disfigured by 2002, her hair thin and greasy, her face gaunt and pale, and her body covered with scabs and sores.

These images were the prelude to a more detailed explanation of long-term methamphetamine abuse in which "addiction" was explicitly defined:

> Long-term methamphetamine abuse results in many damaging effects, including addiction. Addiction is a chronic, relapsing disease, characterized by compulsive drug-seeking and drug use which is accompanied by functional and molecular changes in the brain. In addition to being addicted to methamphetamine, chronic methamphetamine abusers exhibit symptoms that can include violent behavior, anxiety, confusion, and insomnia. They also can display a number of psychotic features, including paranoia, auditory hallucinations, mood disturbances, and delusions (for example, the sensation of insects creeping on the skin, which is called "formication"). The paranoia can result in homicidal as well as suicidal thoughts.

This was the first of three slides explaining the long-term effects of methamphetamine use. Each slide used images of meth-ravaged bodies to illustrate the topic. On a slide picturing the arms of a man with open, bloody sores, the phenomenon of "tolerance" was discussed. It explained how excessive users must regularly increase their use of the drug to achieve the same effects. Use quickly became "chronic abuse," which "can lead to psychotic behavior, characterized by intense paranoia, visual and auditory hallucinations, and extremely violent behavior." The man's mangled arm was an illustration of this process. The next slide, showing a picture of a mouth missing most of its teeth (representing the condition known as "meth mouth"), further explained the "symptoms" that occurred when someone stopped using meth, including "depression, anxiety, fatigue, paranoia, aggression, and an intense craving for the drug."

The rest of the presentation continued in this vein. Although the presentation made frequent references to the negative effects associated with methamphetamine use, it was not until the very last slide that the presentation explicitly addressed the issue of criminality. That slide was simply titled "CRIME" and stated:

> Meth labs along with the selling of the drug can breed crime, including burglaries, thefts and even murder. Both teenagers and adults addicted to the drug and who have no income to pay for their habit may steal valuables from their own homes or even their friends' homes. High on meth, there's no telling what a person would do if provoked—people have been killed for not owning up to a drug payment or coming through on a transaction. This type of crime requires a great deal of attention from the police, for which a town may not have the funding or the resources to spare.

This culminating slide provided the understanding of the drugs-addiction-crime relationship from the police point of view. It gave legal meaning to what until then had been a strictly clinical account of the onset, effects, and symptoms of methamphetamine addiction. It stated unequivocally that methamphetamine was a major source of crime (even using the biological metaphor of "breeding") and that the majority of crimes were committed to appease users' addiction. Moreover, it suggested that such addiction-induced criminality was a "type of crime [that] requires a great deal of attention from the police," but "for which a town may not have the funding or the resources to spare." Thus, the detailed, biomedical account of methamphetamine addiction was marshaled in support of more funding for the police.

Cognitive Models of Crime and Addiction

Police were not the only members of the criminal justice system in Baker County to focus on the signs and symptoms associated with methamphetamine addiction. Administrators at the regional jail also focused on meth addiction in their work. "You can always tell who's using meth," said Bobby Lively, the warden at the regional jail. He described how meth users often looked decades older than they actually were. They were agitated and aggressive, "practically climbing the walls."

Drug use was so common among inmates at the jail that detox had become part of the intake procedure for every new inmate, regardless of whether the offense was drug-related. Bobby could always tell the meth users by how they reacted to the detox. Meth users experienced nightmares and sweats and paced and dug at themselves. And they begged for some kind of medication to help them sleep or feel less anxious or depressed. It was jail policy to refuse any request for medication out of concern for inducing an overdose, but one might speculate that the overarching penal logic of the institution made this suffering institutionally tolerable, as well.

Shelly Carson, a licensed addiction counselor in charge of the jail's addiction treatment program, echoed Bobby's sense of the prevalence of drug problems at the facility and its deep ties to criminality. "[Their] crimes [are] usually committed under the influence of something," Shelly stated. Right now, that something tended to be meth. The most common charges among women, for instance, were related to money, such as fraud and writing bad checks. "Basically drugs," she said.

Shelly's approach to addiction treatment emphasized cognitive-behavioral therapy, which framed both addiction and crime as problems of thinking. According to Shelly, most of the inmates at the jail displayed both "criminal and addictive thinking." The two were closely correlated according to the treatment curriculum—the one, in fact, driving the other like two perfectly aligned gears, as illustrated by a diagram taken from the treatment curriculum's workbook (see figure 8.1).

Criminal and addictive thinking drove each other in many ways. For instance, thinking about theft—stealing something to support your addiction—was a classic example of criminal and addictive thinking working in tandem. The two forms of thinking were broken down in the program into sets of complementary traits and subtraits. Thus, where addictive thinking "Controls with Deceit," criminal thinking "Controls with Power." Similarly, where addictive thinking is "Pleasure Focused," criminal thinking is "Excitement Focused." Both forms of thinking, according to the curriculum, displayed a tendency to be "Irresponsible."

The institutional significance of the jail's treatment program lay less in providing treatment to addicts (it served only eight inmates at a time) than in creating an authoritative discourse to explain criminal behavior—one that represented the relationship between addiction and crime as a set of interlocking cognitive-behavioral processes. Addiction and criminality were so closely aligned, in fact, that they blurred into one single (bio)behavioral reality.

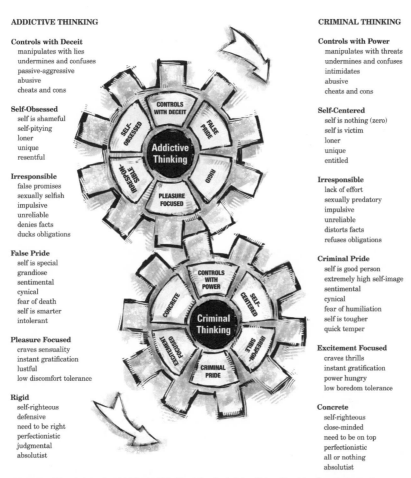

Controls with Deceit
manipulates with lies
undermines and confuses
passive-aggressive
abusive
cheats and cons

Self-Obsessed
self is shameful
self-pitying
loner
unique
resentful

Irresponsible
false promises
sexually selfish
impulsive
unreliable
denies facts
ducks obligations

False Pride
self is special
grandiose
sentimental
cynical
fear of death
self is smarter
intolerant

Pleasure Focused
craves sensuality
instant gratification
lustful
low discomfort tolerance

Rigid
self-righteous
defensive
need to be right
perfectionistic
judgmental
absolutist

Controls with Power
manipulates with threats
undermines and confuses
intimidates
abusive
cheats and cons

Self-Centered
self is nothing (zero)
self is victim
loner
unique
entitled

Irresponsible
lack of effort
sexually predatory
impulsive
unreliable
distorts facts
refuses obligations

Criminal Pride
self is good person
extremely high self-image
sentimental
cynical
fear of humiliation
self is tougher
quick temper

Excitement Focused
craves thrills
instant gratification
power hungry
low boredom tolerance

Concrete
self-righteous
close-minded
need to be on top
perfectionistic
all or nothing
absolutist

FIGURE 8.1 "How Criminal and Addictive Thinking Drive Each Other." From Hazelden Foundation and Minnesota Department of Corrections, A New Direction: A Cognitive-Behavioral Treatment Curriculum, Criminal and Addictive Thinking (Copyright 2002 by the Hazelden Foundation). Reprinted by permission of Hazelden Foundation, Center City, Minn.

Administrators lamented the program's small size as one more example of the state's reluctance to invest in mental health. But they made strategic use of it, as well. For instance, the opportunity to participate in the treatment program was used as an incentive through which to induce compliance with the behavioral expectations of the institution. Admittance to the treatment program was competitive, based less on need (which was excessive) than on merit (which was not). Addicted inmates had to spend months distinguishing themselves through exemplary behavior even to be considered for the program. Thus, targeting drugs and addiction in the jail worked on multiple levels to assist administrators in carrying out the jail's penal mandate.

Addiction and Police Work

Police officers not only invoked the signs and symptoms of methamphetamine addiction when they were engaging in community education. They also operationalized such knowledge during more routine police work. As noted earlier, when I asked Daryl why methamphetamine was causing so many problems, his answer was, "It's so addictive." He underscored meth's addictiveness by contrasting it with marijuana, another common drug in the area. "With marijuana you're just gonna sit at home and eat chips or something," Daryl said with a smile. In fact, marijuana was of such little concern that local police had practically decriminalized it: they spent no time trying to locate marijuana users or dealers; nor did they suspect marijuana when a criminal offense was committed.

The same could not be said about methamphetamine. Meth's association with crime was so strong that police work was virtually unimaginable apart from it. Again, this link with criminality was articulated in terms of meth's addictiveness, which, Daryl explained, was driving the local drug economy itself, as users turned to dealing to support their addiction. The prosecuting attorney offered an outline of how addiction fueled the local drug economy during the trial of a local drug dealer:

> Your Honor, I think the Court's aware of the problem that this community has had with methamphetamine in the past few years . . . and the Court's well aware of the effect that we've had as a result of that. And the effect is you have individuals like [the one in this case] who buys methamphetamine . . . [and] because of the high price and the fact that it's so addictive—he keeps some of it and sells it to somebody in order to pay and support his habit. So it's a pyramid, Your Honor, and it's a pyramid that keeps going on and on and on and due to the fact that it's very expensive there's only two ways to do it. You either sell to support your habit or you have to commit some type of criminal offense to support your habit.

The prosecutor's statement regarding addiction's central role in driving the drug economy echoed that made in Frank's PowerPoint presentation. Deputy Casey Phillips expressed a similar view. He had returned to active police duty in 2000 after a brief stint in the military and had since witnessed the methamphetamine problem grow exponentially. Like Daryl, Casey attributed this to its addictiveness, as well as to the ease with which it could be made. The proof of meth's addictiveness was the fact that anyone was susceptible. "Meth is no respecter of person," he said. "It doesn't matter if you're high status or low class, living in a nice house or a trailer."

Casey went on to describe meth's impact on policing in the community. His small department had always had to function as a "one-stop shop" of police work. One day, the officers might be doing routine traffic patrol; the next, they might be answering domestic disturbance calls or carrying out criminal investigations. These activities had once seemed largely unrelated, but now there was a common denominator: methamphetamine. Routine traffic stops were increasingly producing methamphetamine or related paraphernalia; domestic disturbances were often caused or fueled by meth; and the vast majority of the crimes they investigated—property crimes in particular—ultimately were determined to be connected to methamphetamine.

I asked the officers how they could tell who was using methamphetamine, given that, as Casey stated, "Meth is no respecter of person." Casey explained how easy it was to spot meth users based on their physical appearance. He would see people on the street who had lost a lot of weight or just looked high. He would stop and ask them if they were using meth. Many admitted to using it. Some even asked to be taken to jail, according to Casey, so they could detox and try to beat their addiction. Similarly, seeing a crater or another significant scab or wound on the face of a driver would provide enough "reasonable suspicion" to pull the person over and perform a search, particularly if she or he was also driving as though she or he was intoxicated. According to Casey, such stops frequently produced drugs or drug paraphernalia.

Daryl painted a similar picture. He regularly encountered people who displayed the symptoms of methamphetamine addiction: "They'll have open sores from digging at 'meth bugs'; their teeth will be falling out." Daryl explained that police at times approached people in this condition and tried to "bluff" them, threatening them with arrest unless they cooperated. This was part of a more general tactic of threatening low-level drug users with penal sanctions to "flip" them and turn them into confidential informants to aid in criminal investigations of other drug users and dealers. In this way, the symptoms of methamphetamine addiction were read by police officers as signs of criminal involvement and used to make arrests or coerce drug users to cooperate with police operations.

Police officers were quick to mobilize their knowledge of addiction during criminal investigations, as well. Late one evening in the spring of 2006, police officers set out to arrest Burt Culper and Mandy Swift at their home on the outskirts of Meadville. Over the previous year, numerous homes, businesses, and construction sites had been burglarized throughout Baker County. Police had come to believe that the burglaries were linked, and Burt and Mandy, two known meth users in the community, were the primary suspects.

Four police officers arrived at Burt and Mandy's apartment, and Burt was immediately taken to the police station for questioning. Mandy was questioned for more than two hours. Nervously, Mandy explained to the officer that although Burt had instigated the crimes, she had always helped. They had walkie-talkies, and she served as the lookout while he committed the burglaries. Mandy was standing watch, for instance, when Burt broke into the mental health clinic to steal a computer, remaining there even when, in the midst of the burglary, he went to the clinic's kitchen and used the microwave to make a bowl of soup.

Periodically, the officer inquired into the motivation behind Burt's criminal behavior. Each time the officer asked, Mandy gave the same response: it was Burt's need to constantly find quick sources of cash to pay for more meth that drove his criminality. This seemed to confirm the officers' suspicions, as did the meth found in Burt and Mandy's bedroom. It was the officer, then, who raised the possibility that Burt was an addict. This came out over the course of the interview, culminating with this exchange toward the end:

> **Police Officer:** Another thing to elaborate on that would kind of help me out maybe, ah, you made, you made a number of comments about that [Burt] is selling some of his stuff to obtain drugs. Ah, help me out on, ah, he's not only a user? Would you . . . say that he's an addict?
> **Mandy:** Yeah.
> **Police Officer:** How often does, how often are you aware of him using narcotics?
> **Mandy:** Daily.
> **Police Officer:** Daily. What . . . type of narcotics, ah, or drugs or anything does he use?

Mandy: Um, what do you call it? Meth? Crank? Crank.[1]

Police Officer: And how . . . many days, or how long have you known him?

Mandy: Um, Burt and I have been together since last September. So it's been approximately a year.

Police Officer: And correct me if I'm wrong; you're saying that he used drugs every day since you've known him?

Mandy: I can think of maybe three days of that amount of time that he hasn't.

Recognition that an individual was an addict could play out in other ways. Recall Dwight Tanner's case. Dwight broke into a local vacation home and stole everything that was in the house. It was only after his arrest that Dwight's criminality was openly acknowledged to be the result of his "drug habit," when Dwight stated that he was stealing items to sell or trade for methamphetamine. Dwight's "drug habit" was mentioned frequently during the court proceedings: the probation officer cited it repeatedly during her pre-sentencing investigation, as did the judge during the conviction and sentencing hearings. Both referred to Dwight as having a "severe drug addiction" and affirmed his need for treatment.

At no point, however, was Dwight's drug addiction taken to excuse his crimes. Nor was it seen to justify an alternative to incarceration. On the contrary, Dwight's "severe drug addiction" was cited specifically as a reason to expedite his incarceration. In her final report before the sentencing hearing, Dwight's probation officer stated explicitly:

> In talking with the Defendant regarding his crime he genuinely appears remorseful for his actions and is accepting [of] the fact that he has a severe drug problem. He also appears to understand what a problem his drug use has caused himself, his family and his friends. . . . The Defendant acknowledges that he needs some type of treatment for his drug abuse and is willing to accept treatment. Based upon [this] information . . . , *the undersigned believes that the Defendant is not a good candidate for probation at this time due to his inability to keep clean from drugs. The undersigned believes that the Defendant would not be able to comply with the standard terms of probation.* (Emphasis added)

After acknowledging Dwight's "severe drug problem" and need for treatment, the probation officer recommended incarceration. Ironically, the severity of Dwight's addiction made him a poor candidate for the available treatment programs, which were outpatient programs administered in the context of probation: they required a degree of self-monitoring and self-control that Dwight, as an addict, was seen to be incapable of managing. In particular, his inability to control his desire for meth made him likely to violate the key requirement of probation: refraining from further criminality. Thus, Dwight's incarceration was figured as a means of preventing future crimes from taking place in the community through the incapacitation of an individual who, because of his addiction, was seen as being at high risk to "reoffend."

The same themes recur in the case of Eddie Curtis. He was in his midtwenties when he was arrested on multiple counts of breaking and entering and burglary. In the winter of 2005, during an interview with police, Eddie admitted to breaking into a dentist's office once, a local insurance company twice, and two private cabins multiple times. In each case, he took whatever cash he could find, a sum totaling about $1,400. In the process of breaking into the homes and businesses, which typically involved kicking down a back door or breaking through a window, he caused close to $4,000 in damage. Police photographs revealed homes and businesses thrown into complete disarray by Eddie's apparently frantic search for cash.

Eddie was taken into custody based on information provided to the police by an unnamed confidential informant. Officers picked him up at his house and took him to the sheriff's department for questioning. Eddie was questioned specifically about the places he was suspected of burglarizing, and, like Dwight, he admitted to committing each crime. The police repeatedly asked Eddie, "What did you do with the money?" Each time, Eddie provided an answer that linked his criminality back to his drug use: "I spent it on methamphetamine."

After obtaining a detailed confession for each of the burglaries and discovering that Eddie had spent all of the money on meth, the police asked him about the motivations for his crimes. "Why did you break into all these places?" Deputy Ted Thomas asked. "For cash to buy drugs," Eddie replied. This led to an extended inquiry into Eddie's drug use, in which he admitted to a $300-a-week meth habit. And though he did not name names, Eddie also revealed the location of his dealer, providing directions to the trailer park where he lived.

Eddie's case bears a striking resemblance to Mandy and Burt's and to Dwight's. Eddie had committed a series of property crimes to obtain "cash to buy drugs." In addition, these acts were part of a long history of proven and suspected criminality, much of which could be linked to chronic drug use. Although this was his first felony, Eddie had been arrested for several misdemeanors, including charges for domestic violence and possession of methamphetamine. Eddie was not incarcerated for those offenses but had incurred numerous fines.

Eddie, too, was seen to be a poor candidate for probation. The prosecuting attorney, Daniel Gardner, wrote a letter to Eddie's court-appointed attorney to negotiate a plea agreement in which he stated, "The State will strongly oppose any probation or reconsideration of any sentence. It is the State's intent that the Defendant [Eddie Curtis] go to prison." He concluded the letter this way: "I have dealt with the Defendant for a number of years. . . . He has numerous cases which he has failed to pay. In fact, he would owe in excess of $6,500.00 to clear those cases. He was told many times that he needed to obtain employment and honor his responsibilities. He has shown no initiative in the past. Therefore, the State does not find him to be suitable for any leniency."

As a result of the plea agreement, Eddie received a sentence of two to twenty-five years. But Eddie fought against this outcome. He wrote a series of letters to the judge requesting a new attorney and contesting the state's narrow account of his subjectivity. Each letter also asked for a reconsideration of his sentence. Of the four letters he wrote, only one mentioned drug use, stating, "I know Also [sic] that I had a problem of drug abuse, and realize I do need treatment." Notably, Eddie made this statement in a letter complaining about the lack of treatment and other rehabilitative services available at the regional jail. (Because of overcrowding in the state penitentiary system, Eddie remained at the regional jail well beyond the time he was scheduled to be transferred.) For Eddie, the lack of treatment services for a well-acknowledged problem justified reconsideration of his sentence and reassignment (such as probation) that would allow him greater opportunity to seek treatment.

Letters such as these were familiar to administrators in the criminal justice system. It was not uncommon for incarcerated people to write to judges asking that their sentences be reconsidered. However, the officials tended to hold such efforts in low regard. Most saw them as insincere attempts to avoid punishment by trying to gain sympathy or convince those in power that they had changed. Thus, these efforts were rarely taken seriously. Not surprisingly, Eddie's letters had no effect on the judge, who never reconsidered his sentence. Eddie's long history of domestic violence, combined with his criminal history, most likely made his pleas to be released from prison for the sake of his family ring hollow.

These cases illustrate in part why police focused their efforts on arresting meth offenders. All were meth users who, by their own admission, committed a series of property crimes in support of a drug habit. In this regard, the trajectory of their addition conformed approximately to the stereotypical accounts offered within the criminal justice system: drug use gave way to drug addiction which pushed the user/addict into criminality. In arresting these individuals, the police saw themselves as both responding to crimes that had been committed and preventing future crimes from taking place, thereby fulfilling two fundamental police functions simultaneously. The opportunity to have such a broad impact through single arrests increased the incentive to focus on meth offenders. Furthermore, in prosecuting Dwight, Eddie, and Mandy and Burt, the state cited their addiction as a reason to incarcerate them rather than pursue alternatives (such as probation). This allowed the state to likewise fulfill the dual objective of punishing crimes committed and preventing (whether through deterrence, rehabilitation, or incapacitation) the commission of future crimes. Thus, strong institutional incentives existed to target methamphetamine users throughout the criminal justice system.

A Body on Drugs

As I concluded my interview with Daryl and Casey, I walked with them back to the sheriff's office. The office was small, and the gray cinderblock walls were free of any decoration, so I was surprised to see a poster taped next to the entrance. The poster was large, white, and cluttered with text and images. The text was tiny and impossible to read from a distance, and the images were likewise difficult to make out from far away. Closer inspection revealed it to be composed of pictures of parts of bodies—arms, legs, hands, mouths, faces, and even brains—in various states of sickness, injury, and decay. The arms and legs had open sores; the hands were scabbed and bandaged; the mouths were missing teeth; the brains showed signs of malfunction; and the faces were prematurely aged. Small capital letters at the top of the poster stated its theme: A BODY ON DRUGS (see figure 8.2).

Here were all of the physical markers of methamphetamine manufacturing, use, and addiction the deputies had just been describing, as well as

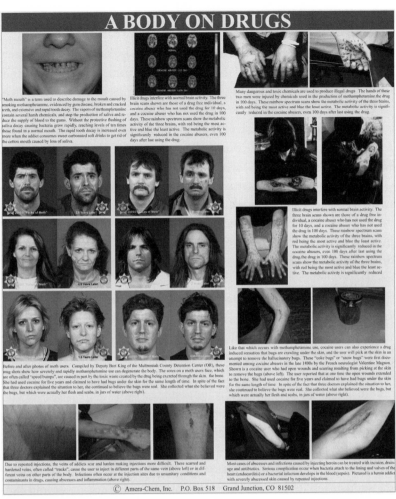

FIGURE 8.2 "A Body on Drugs." Reprinted with permission of Amera-Chem, Inc., James Mock and Brookhaven National Laboratory. Faces of Meth Mug Shots © Used with permission of the Multnomah County Sheriff's Office.

physical symptoms associated with the use of other drugs, such as heroin and cocaine. The facial portraits were the most striking, partly because they were images with which I was already familiar. I knew them from other drug awareness campaigns, as well as from a *Frontline* documentary on methamphetamine. They were compiled by Deputy Bret King of the Multnomah County Detention Center in Multnomah County, Oregon, and deployed as part of the "Faces of Meth" campaign. Some of the images had appeared in Frank's PowerPoint presentation and at seminars I had attended on methamphetamine in Baker County and other parts of the state.

Even if one did not know the origin of the images, it was obvious they were mugshots. This immediately implicated the drug use and addiction of those pictured in criminality. Although their crimes were not specified, the passage of time implied by the juxtaposition of the "before" and "after" images suggested a narrative of progressive physical and social deterioration brought on by the addiction and punctuated by recurrent encounters with police. In this regard, the poster served the opposite function of the classic "Wanted" poster. Rather than drawing attention to an individual criminal wanted for particular crimes, this poster drew attention to a generic *type* of criminal and the signs by which that type of criminal could be identified. Such a reading of the criminal body was made possible by understanding both physical appearance and criminality as symptoms of addiction.

In its focus on the features of the criminal body, the poster was reminiscent of the catalogues of criminals from which Cesare Lombroso sought to discern the distinctive features of congenital criminality (Horn 2003): both the poster and Lombroso's catalogues expressed an "anxious faith" in the body, particularly "the idea that the bodies of criminals—or potential criminals—give themselves away, testifying to their own dangers" (Horn 2003: 6, 23). Although sharing this concern with general physical markers of criminality, the poster in the sheriff's office portrayed a different reading of the criminal body. In no way did it suggest that any of the individuals pictured were "born criminals." On the contrary, through its focus on the sudden and progressive deterioration of the subject's body and concomitant slide into criminality under the influence of drugs, it conveyed the opposite message: that these were "normal" people whose progressive physical and social deterioration had been set in motion by nothing other than their use of, and inevitable addiction to, methamphetamine and other drugs.

The poster was a topic of much discussion the following week at a meeting of the Substance Abuse Prevention Coalition, a local community action group. "Have any of you all been up to the sheriff's office to pay your taxes?" asked a brown-haired woman in her forties, whom I later learned was the school guidance counselor. "There's a poster up there that shows what happens to you when you get addicted to meth." The woman went on to describe an encounter she had had with a young girl who was also looking at the poster. With a knowing smile, she recounted their conversation: "She said, 'I know people who use meth, and they don't look like that.' I looked at her and said, 'Yeah, *not yet* they don't.'" This brief exchange was a testimonial to the poster's effectiveness, indicating that it conveyed a particular vision of the temporality of drug use, criminality, and addiction—one that was progressive, deteriorative, and inevitable.

The guidance counselor went on to describe the program of which the posters were part. Apparently, the sheriff's office had ordered a number of the posters and was planning to put them up in various places throughout the community, including at the hospital, in factories, and in schools. The hope was that the posters would make people more aware of the signs of methamphetamine use and that this, in turn, would enable them to both recognize drug users and stay away from drug use themselves.

The members of the Substance Abuse Prevention Coalition saw the poster campaign as a positive development, particularly as they often complained that the police were not doing enough to deal with the methamphetamine problem. The police were aware of these perceptions. They argued that the extent of the problem exceeded their capacity to address it. Without more funding or more officers, they stood little chance of doing more than containing it.

These feelings of inadequacy revealed an underlying lack of faith in the ability of the criminal justice system—and the state more generally—to address drug problems through the punitive management of the addicted offender population. They also pointed to the consequences of making addicted criminals the target of police activity. While targeting addicted criminals did provide a certain coherence to criminal justice work in Baker County, it also threatened to undermine that work by making the problem seem greater than the state's ability to manage it.

Conclusion: The Paradox of the War on Drugs

This points to a paradox at the heart of America's recent drug enforcement efforts. Even as the power and resources of the criminal justice system have been built up and extended through the focus on drug enforcement, the continued focus on drug offenders appears to be having an erosive effect, chipping away at rather than galvanizing faith in public institutions and their capacity to justly solve social problems—even among those who work in those institutions.

Indeed, one of the most striking findings of my research was the pessimistic light in which residents viewed efforts to address methamphetamine. This was true not just among citizens, but also among those given the task of dealing directly with the meth problem. I asked Frank if he thought what he and his fellow officers were doing was having any effect. He smiled slightly and shook his head no. "All we can do is try and contain it," he said. "But we'll never get rid of it." Daryl echoed this sentiment. After explaining in detail all he had done to locate and arrest local methamphetamine dealers, he sighed and with a slight grin wistfully concluded, "Yeah, but we'll never win the war. We're just a nation of drug users."

Perhaps the most telling comment came during an early interview I conducted with Rose Hinkle, Baker County's probation officer. Reflecting on the cases of the many individuals who had ended up sitting in her office because of their involvement with meth, she finally declared, exasperated, "Meth is impossible. *What do you do with them*?"

Those affected by meth thus appear to have inherited the ambivalent attitude toward the War on Drugs documented by public opinion research. A poll conducted in 2001, just as methamphetamine was starting to gain national attention, found that nearly three-fourths of the population (74 percent) believed that the United States was "losing the drug war." Moreover, the same percentage stated that the drug war could not succeed, agreeing with the statement, "Demand is so high we will never stop drug use" (Pew Research Center for the People and the Press 2001: 1).

Yet despite this pessimism, little interest was expressed in stopping the drug war or even considering alternative strategies. Indeed, even the de-escalation of certain components of the drug war (such as the rolling back of mandatory minimum sentences for nonviolent drug offenders) received only tepid endorsement. Ultimately, the American public still seems to view criminalization as the best policy, despite the fact that it is viewed less favorably than it was even a decade ago. This, then, is the paradox: the majority of Americans appear committed to fighting a war they feel cannot be won, using a strategy in which they no longer believe.

"Meth is impossible. *What do you do with them*?" I am still haunted by Rose's question, in part because I know what happens in the meantime. Communities like Rose's are still looking to the criminal justice system to address the problems associated with drugs. Legislators continue to create regulations that affect wide swaths of the population, regardless of their proximity to the drug problem. And, most important, people like

Dwight, whose story began this chapter, remain incarcerated for crimes committed to support their use of drugs.

Indeed, a fundamental goal of my research into methamphetamine has been to understand the fate of people like Dwight. As I write today, Dwight remains incarcerated in a state penitentiary, serving time for crimes committed as a result of his inability to control his addiction to methamphetamine. It is my central contention that, to understand Dwight's story—and the stories of so many like him—it is necessary first to understand the perceptions, experiences, and anxieties of the people who surround him, particularly those representatives of the state whose actions carry the force of law. As a result of the ongoing War on Drugs, knowledge of addiction is now at the heart of how those perceptions, experiences, and anxieties take shape.

Notes

Sincerest thanks to the people of Baker County who shared their lives with me and made this research possible. The research on which this chapter is based was funded by the National Science Foundation (NSF). I thank the NSF for its support. Many people provided feedback on the chapter. In addition to the participants at the Anthropologies of Addiction workshop and contributors to this volume, I thank João Biehl, James Boon, Carol Greenhouse, Joseph Masco, Dawn Moore, Lawrence Rosen, and Mariana Valverde. This chapter is reprinted from William Garriott, *Policing Methamphetamine: Narcopolitics in Rural America* (New York: New York University Press, 2011).

1. Crank is a commonly used term for methamphetamine.

NINE   NANCY D. CAMPBELL

"WHY CAN'T THEY STOP?"
A Highly Public Misunderstanding of Science

Visualizing subjective states as they happen: this power of neuro-
imaging technologies is reverentially affirmed by those seeking to
cultivate respect for "addiction," the complex disorder they study.
Although definitional disputes abound in the substance abuse
research arena, the conviction that pharmacotherapy will eventually be the best way to "treat," "manage," or even prevent the
onset of addiction is widely shared. Addiction was redefined in
the late twentieth century as a "chronic, relapsing brain disease," a
conceptual and practical move that attracted neuroscientists to
the scientific puzzle of addiction and gave their knowledge paradigm entrée to a field not formerly populated by a critical mass of
neuroscientists (Campbell 2007, 2010). They brought imaging
technologies that ranged from positron emission tomography to
functional magnetic resonance imaging (FMRI).[1] Driven by a fervent pharmacological optimism, neuroscientists speak of their
work as practically translating into treatment medications that
temporarily change the brain in ways that produce socially appropriate behavior and displace those deemed deviant, unproductive, or antisocial (Vrecko 2010b).

Altering the brain for lifelong biomedical management raises
ethical and political dilemmas; neuroscience cannot abstract itself from the social and political meanings projected onto the
figures of "addicts" as a heterogeneous social class. The move to

redefine addiction as a brain disorder arose from scientists' perception that the condition should be distanced from older cultural lexicons of moral turpitude, stigma, and weak will. Given the tenacity of this moral lexicon, how did brain images gain sway over how "addiction" is conceptualized? What assumptions go into the making, interpretation, and circulation of the new neuro-imagery of addiction? How do older discourses about addiction and recovery converge with or diverge from the ever new "pharmacological optimism" of the neurosciences? Finally, how will these new discursive moves fit with or diverge from popular notions that recovery is based on abstinence and the continued maintenance of a drug-free state?

My book *Discovering Addiction* (Campbell 2007) told a tale in which neuro-imaging appeared to be the latest technology deployed in a series of successive attempts to "discover addiction." Far from seeing neuroscience as a culmination of these efforts, I am fascinated with how the optimistic belief that a pharmacotherapy to prevent relapse will arise from the "translation" of knowledge derived from neuro-imagery persists. This chapter is an ethnography of pharmacological optimism that picks up where *Discovering Addiction* left off, looking ethnographically at one of the most publicly prominent contributors of a small group of neuroscientists who are acting as "moral entrepreneurs" or "moral pioneers" to change public policy and shift popular perceptions of what the problem of "addiction" means in the United States of the early twenty-first century.[2] Neuro-imagery has come to be used by moral-scientific pioneers as a powerful persuasive technology for gaining moral traction in a campaign to reframe notions of will, choice, compulsion, and self-control in the addiction arena.

Proponents of recovery discourse clashed with neuroscientists over the haunting problem of relapse in *Addiction*, a series aired on HBO in March 2007, and on the episode of *The Oprah Winfrey Show* broadcast on April 9, 2007.[3] Relapse has been contentious since it first became an object of research.[4] For instance, G. Alan Marlatt advocates a cognitive behavioral approach to managing relapse that encourages people to identify "risky situations" and plan how they will handle them.[5] Such efforts are premised on intentionally avoiding "people, places, and things" that might trigger drug or alcohol use. Others believe such approaches—which are premised on abstinence or avoidance—will not help people to better cope with cravings they encounter in actual social situations. At the Treatment Research Center (TRC) in Philadelphia, Anna Rose Childress finds the recovery community's advice to avoid risky situations unrealistic because her patients live where illegal drug markets are unavoidable. Instead of counseling them to avoid the "triggers" surrounding them, she urges them to cope with their cravings.

Trained at Bryn Mawr as a behavioral pharmacologist, Childress is a "hybrid" in that she embodies elements of neuroscientific approaches that regard "the brain" as the locus of addiction, but she also draws on the conceptual methodologies of the previously dominant behavioral paradigm that shifted with the advent of neuroscience. Trying to characterize what happens neurologically during relapse, Childress began to conduct neuro-imaging studies in combination with her clinical work for the Veterans Administration Medical Center in Philadelphia. In these studies, she repurposes psychological tasks developed by her behaviorally oriented colleagues for real-time use in the magnet.[6] Neuro-imaging studies are designed to visualize "craving" states when they occur; the hope is that this will enable understanding of the neurobiochemical events that lead up to relapse and someday help prevent or control it. As a clinician, Childress has followed some of her patients' patterns of relapse for decades. She easily spins stories across their life course without reference to charts or notes, offering impromptu case histories (without specifics to protect privacy and confidentiality). She knows their families and treasures their homemade gifts, which are strewn about her office. She voices a complex amalgam of behavioral, neuronal, and clinical lexicons, one reason, surely, that reporters from the mainstream media have sought her out as an articulate spokesperson for the science of addiction research.

Speaking for Science: Addiction and Relapse on HBO

Public engagement has become important to neuroscientists studying addiction; most feel the disorder is widely misunderstood. For instance, Childress participated in Bill Moyers's special *Close to Home* (1998) and a decade later was featured in "The Science of Relapse," the third episode of HBO's *Addiction* series, making follow-up appearances on *Good Morning, America* and *Oprah* to further explain her views. The opening sequences of the HBO series illustrated the complex amalgamation of behavioral and neuronal lexicons at work in the reframing of addiction that is under way. One of the leading members of the group of neuroscientists, Nora Volkow, who was then at the Brookhaven National Laboratory and is now the executive director of the National Institute on Drug Abuse (NIDA), was depicted as asking, "How can we comprehend the concept of a person that wants to stop doing something and they cannot despite catastrophic consequences, and yet they cannot control their behavior?" Among the most publicly prominent neuro-imagers working on addiction, Volkow became the executive director of NIDA shortly after the sequence was shot. As in her subsequent scientific work, Volkow's depiction of addiction in the HBO series is of an unexplainable, almost irrational, abnormal behavior, a disruption of volition or an example of neurobiology going awry.[7] "The Science of Relapse" shows Volkow pointing to her computer screen while counseling a methamphetamine addict about her belief that brain imaging will someday aid subjects in stopping the damage they are doing to their brains. Well in advance of actual translation into clinical practice, such claims credit "brain imaging science" with providing the missing support for self-control. The hope is that, by making visible where the urge to use a drug occurs in the brain, specific targets for medications will emerge. "When a person who has this disease is exposed to cues or stimuli that remind them of or have previously been associated with the use of a drug," comments Charles P. O'Brien, director of the TRC, in the opening sequence of the episode, "there is an uncontrollable reflex that happens very quickly in the brain. We can see it in brain imaging. The person doesn't have the ability to stop it. As a matter of fact, it may happen before they're even conscious of it." O'Brien's last statement is an obvious reference to work performed by Childress, who has worked in the laboratory he heads since the late 1970s.[8]

At the TRC, the "uncontrollable reflex" to relapse is considered so integral to addiction that the disorder cannot be defined without reference to that impulse. Speaking words that foreshadowed *Oprah*, Childress said, "Patients say, 'Why can't I just stop? I've lost so much. I've paid such a high price.' Parents say, 'Why can't they just stop? They've completely wrecked their lives. Why can't they just stop?' What we're beginning to understand now at the level of the brain is that there are a lot of cards that are stacked in the wrong direction here."[9]

Childress conveys the strength of the situational context within which drug use takes place. Strength of moral character is simply not enough to control "parts of the brain . . . that think that when they see these signals for the drug that that's as important as a relationship, as the best food you ever saw. It's a trick that's played on the brain and in a way that tends to leave out this decision making part of your brain."[10] This trickery is part of an evolutionary argument that Childress mobilizes as she explains the activation of an "ancient GO circuit for helping us to respond to natural rewards that are so important for our survival." The frontal lobe system that "evolved to help us weigh the consequences of our impulses" is not active during relapse. This form of argumentation is controversial given the recent critical pressure on two immensely popular and problematic neuroscientific constructs: the "triune brain" and the "limbic system" (Maclean 1952). Her patients, Childress says, have brains in which the STOP and GO systems are "functionally disconnected. It is as though the GO system is running off on its own, has become a rogue system now and is not interacting in a regular, seamless, integrated way with the STOP system." The evolutionary argument is connected with a historical argument, neatly illustrated by an abrupt segue to William, an African American man interviewed on the streets of Philadelphia. "This is the trigger, all of this around me," he says. "You can turn around and look at all of that, because all of this is where I'm from, and I've always used in this area. So you imagine, the trigger is here. The trigger is not only up here (points to head). The trigger is when I walk out, open my eyes, and what I see."[11]

"The STOP system doesn't enter this picture, which is all about GO," according to Childress. We next see William in the sterile environment of a scanner and learn that Childress is trying to find out whether the connections between STOP and GO systems have somehow been broken in her patients. To do this, she is studying the very shortest cues imaginable —so short that their content cannot be consciously recognized—that spark a "conversation" that triggers relapse in the brain. Patients, she says, sometimes cannot point to the cue that set off a craving state because the moment arises so quickly. Thus, she is searching for a pharmacotherapy to calm the brain, quiet the conversation, "bring things into a manageable range," or otherwise "turn down the volume on the GO system" to reduce its activity. Here the analogy is made to turning down the volume of a conversation as the necessary precursor to short-circuiting an episode of relapse.

Red spots on a brain scan are said to represent craving. When a scan of William's brain was shown, Childress explained that the scan was a visual representation of "Let's go for it" and noted the intense "dialogue" depicted by "these very hot spots." As contrast, she showed a scan of a patient on the candidate treatment drug. "It's not that the brain is dead," she said. "There's activity, but instead of 'Go! Go! Go!,' it's, 'I don't know, doesn't seem like it's worth going.'" Here the camera cuts to William stating that he does not "want to be an addict, to live my life in the grips of addiction. I will be an addict probably all my life but I want to not be an addict using." The hopes voiced by Volkow, O'Brien, Childress, and other members of the small band of neuroscientists who speak publicly about the need to destigmatize addiction are proponents of pharmacotherapies that do not completely block or "silence" the conversations that constitute episodes of "craving" within the brain but do reduce their volume to a whisper. What are we to make of this hope, of the persistent testimony to the potential of pharmacological optimism to deliver us from the history of unexplainable failures to consider future consequences?

On the HBO special, we see compassionate scientists and caring clinicians testify to the power of "disrupted volition," cues "outside awareness," conversations between STOP and GO systems, and consequent relapse. Their beliefs in the truth of what they are saying are as fervent as those who believe in the power of abstinence in the recovery community; both groups mobilize intense affect, but the two contending rhetorics clash with each other.[12] In *Using Women* (Campbell 2000), I argued that the difference between "affective realism" and "empirical realism" resided in the unstable rhetorical power of testimonials, citing the work of the feminist philosopher Lorraine Code: "Testimony is an ambiguous sort of evidence that links emotion with authenticity to produce an affective realism that differs from the empirical realism of those whose claims to authority are not grounded in the evidence of experience. The spoken truths of testimony pass through a social process of validation and acquittal, or condemnation and dismissal" (Code 1995: 58). In the rhetorical space of *The Oprah Winfrey Show* that I discuss in the next section, a form of testimony underpinned by "science," which attributes the capacity to act to "the brain" and not the person, was rendered literally incredible. Yet some witnesses achieved credibility by stabilizing the interpretive process and getting their stories to accord with the "facts" and "values" prevailing within that rhetorical space.

Elsewhere I have suggested that we inhabit a "relapse society,"[13] in which many people understand themselves to live on the cusp of relapse, holding this threat at bay by continually restaging their vigilance against relapse. Those who cannot do this embody a threatening moral contagion and thus are convenient others—even for themselves. Recovery narratives attest to the threatening possibility of an embodied state beyond redemption. Because of this, testimony typically consolidates prevailing relations between socially dominant and subordinate groups, keeping their positions intact relative to each other (Campbell 2000: 47). *The Oprah Winfrey Show* demonstrated a dynamic interplay between scientific constructs of craving and relapse as definitional to the disorder and testimonial constructs of craving and relapse that fall within the moral purview of recovery discourse. For those neuroscientists seeking to take the moralism out of "addiction," this dynamic represents a frustrating throwback to a time that "addiction" was considered a moral failure. Neuroscience is essentially offering a *new* morality, but it is doing so through an expert discourse in which a new set of pharmaceutical and imaging technologies testifies to the inadequacy of the old one.

Testifying to the Power of the Person: Brain Science on *Oprah*

When I arrived at the TRC on April 9, 2007, I learned that the schedule for the day included watching *The Oprah Winfrey Show*, on which Childress and one of her research subjects, William, appeared. We went to a nearby bar and convinced the bartender to let us watch *Oprah* on closed-captioned TV. This was one of my first encounters with *The Oprah Winfrey Show*. The program unfolded a productive contradiction between scientific and therapeutic expertise, the evidence of experience, and broader cultural meanings mobilized by "addiction." While viewing the show beside someone who has conducted decades of basic addiction research and has an unusually high level of therapeutic expertise (whereas most neuroscientists working on addiction at the time were relative newcomers to substance abuse research, and few had clinical experience), I learned that Childress views neuro-imaging technologies as ways to get inside her patients' heads. As I shadowed her throughout the week, I saw her constantly trying on multiple interpretations of her imaging data, as well as the evidence provided by the everyday experiences of her patients and subjects.

A scientist who thinks about science as a form of storytelling, Childress spends much time mentoring young scientists. When a postdoctoral researcher dropped by her office to talk about grant proposals to be submitted later that spring, the following interchange ensued:

Researcher: I'm writing about what ROI [regions of interest] mean what!
Childress: You making up stories?
Researcher: I'm not making up stories. I'm researching!

While budding scientists may well disavow that they are "making up sto-ries," Childress, it became clear to me, chafes at the constrained format of scientific publication. Her presentations are thickly laden with metaphor that sometimes raise the eyebrows—if not the blood pressure and pulse rate—of her audience. She illustrates talks about craving and desire not with drug cues but with photographs of chocolate and luscious desserts. Her persona militates against her separating "the brain" from "the person." Trained as a behavioral pharmacologist who worked with rats until she became allergic to them, Childress has a fondness for the "intact organ-ism," despite the sharply drawn separation between "the brain" and "the person" encouraged by the discourse of neuroscience. The stories she tells are stories about multidimensional people who happen to have drug prob-lems, through no fault of their own, because of something unusual about their brains. This capacity was evident in her discussion of the portion of the *Oprah* show in which William's brain images were displayed.

Animated through the techniques of neuro-imagery, the brain floated free of William, the person to whom it belonged, as Oprah drew Childress into joking about William's "very nice brain." M. R. Bennett and P. M. S. Hacker (2003) criticize major flaws in the current conceptual scheme of neuroscience, naming them the "mereological fallacy" and ongoing Carte-sian dualism. "Not only do neuroscientists hold that it is the brain that perceives, feels and thinks," they write, "but also that it is the brain that has desires. So it is the brain that wills, and the 'unconscious' acts of will of the brain . . . are the causes of the bodily movements that are constitutive of voluntary action" (M. Bennett and Hacker 2003: 113).

As the onscreen Childress tutored the audience, the image of William's brain floated above them, detached from William as a person who grew up on the streets of Philadelphia, a person who has difficulty disentangling the meaningful aspects of home from drug use. William's brain was taken to indicate that a candidate pharmacotherapy drug had reduced "craving" and lessened his state of "desire," a brain state that had overwhelmed him and "precipitated" relapse. Childress makes many statements about the need for pharmacological assistance in preventing desire or craving from overwhelming conscious controls. For her, it is not interior or subjective states that should be valorized during the recovery process but the assis-tance provided by another drug—and it is this that cuts against the grain of an audience schooled to view "recovery" as based on abstinence from any and all psychoactive substances.

While the central organizing frame around which *Oprah* unfolded restated Childress's scientific question, "What is it about their brains that makes stopping difficult for drug users?," the program was operating out of a discursive frame in which recovery is a *drug-free* process during which inner states of self-control, personal choice, responsibility, and self-forgiveness come to the fore for examination, self-reflection, and processing. Within the therapeutic mode that *Oprah* embodies, recovery requires a narrative of personal progress in which these inner states are given over to a higher power but ultimately become convergent with the person's worldly activities. Oprah Winfrey drew on her own experience of "food addiction" to make the point that people should be able to stop themselves from ingesting things that are bad for them. Her point was supported by numerous sub-narratives in which the relationship between person and substance was emplotted as a romance or Bildungsroman, a narrative of self-discovery in which the hero (or heroine) is engaged in an agonistic struggle with external forces that threaten to subsume his or her internal controls. Once beyond the immediate grip of those forces, however, the hero (or heroine) is continually threatened by "triggers" that set off "cravings" with which the subject must struggle. The degree to which this agonistic battle—almost a fight for the addict's soul—is conscious or unconscious is very much up for grabs. If there is something damaged in the brain of the hero or heroine, then *the person's* need to restrain *the brain* is even stronger.

"Why Can't They Stop?" The Central Organizing Frame

The episode of *The Oprah Winfrey Show* we watched was organized around the question "Why can't they stop?" Attempts to reframe the question, to substitute another question, or even to ask whether this is the right or wrong question by a few resistant talk-show participants and chat-room contributors met with active and passive resistance. Reframing was rebuffed first and foremost by Oprah herself, but others also conveyed the "rightness" of this question, which made sense to all participants, regardless of their position, social location, experiences, or stakes.[14] This question structured the situation, as the following excerpt indicates:

Oprah Winfrey *(host)*: Why can't you stop?

William *(abused drugs for 20 years)*: I don't actually know the answer.

Oprah Winfrey *(host)*: Why can't you stop if you know, and I ask this of all of you, why can't you stop? Why couldn't you stop? You know you have your two sons waiting for you back at home. You know your wife is depending upon you. You know your wife is depending on you and your three children. Why can't you stop?

Rick *(former reporter addicted to crack)*: I don't think, you don't have a choice. There's no choice to it.

William *(abused drugs for 20 years)*: If it was . . . as easy as that, I would've stopped in a heartbeat.

Oprah Winfrey *(host)*: You would've.[15]

Appearing skeptical that William would stop if he could, Oprah elicited her expected response from Rick—there is no choice in the realm of compulsion. Rick's insistence that "there's no choice to it" cued more powerful others, including Oprah and the star panelist, Cheryl, an African American woman whose compelling account of her own addictions repeatedly returned to the voluntary element. Despite showcasing neuroscientific and experiential evidence that willful decisions to stop often are insufficient, the discourse remained one of volitional choice and cognitive control. Deeply embedded cultural notions concerning the nature of compulsion are conditioned on the binary opposition drawn and redrawn in this arena between "choice" and "not choice."

Choice/Not Choice: The Construction of Compulsion

The Oprah Winfrey Show was a performative arena in which the display of "raw, emotional first person experiences provide a rare glimpse into the broken lives of people who just can't stop."[16] "Can't stop" marks a boundary between people who "can stop" or never made the "choice" to start, and those who just cannot stop. The boundary is drawn between those who are "broken," for whom there is no choice, and those who are whole, who are able to exercise self-control and unable to comprehend lack of choice at the heart of what appears to be an intentional, voluntary act. Since the 1930s, addiction researchers have suspected that there is something about "chronic drug administration" that makes it harder to stop once one has started but remains inaccessible to cognitive processes. Neuro-imaging is considered a technology by which to document that lack of intentionality or subjective "awareness" at work in relapse.

By setting up situations in which neuro-imaging can capture what is happening in the brains of drug users before they are subjectively aware that "cravings" have been triggered, Childress gathers data on "subjective response" to stimuli. In a scientific paper titled "Prelude to Passion," reviews of which were discussed at the laboratory when I was there, Childress and her colleagues (2008: 2) explain that the brain is "exquisitely sensitive" to reward signals, "not only for rewards with clear survival significance . . . but also for drug rewards with acquired, 'as if' biologic significance because of their actions on the same brain circuitry. Though the amygdala is better known for its rapid response to signals for danger, the response demonstrated here to "unseen" sexual and drug stimuli point to its importance in the processing of signals for reward, even when presented outside awareness." Rapid responses were interpreted to mean that "the brain can strike up a prelude to passion in an instant, outside awareness, and without heavy policing from frontal regulatory regions" (Childress et al. 2008: 2). Here "the amygdala" appears as shorthand for interconnected ROI, and the neuro-imaging paradigms that use "unseen cues" are claimed to be the basis for developing clinical practices to address the source of "problematic motivation."

I observed Childress's use of this neuro-imaging paradigm. A "forced choice categorization task" was administered while the subject was in the magnet. Lengthy neutral cues were used to "backward mask" very fast nonneutral cues that cannot be seen in real time but are cocaine-related, sexual, and aversive stimuli. Subjects complete an off-magnet "priming task" before the imaging is done and are tested two days later to determine their "affective valence" toward the cues. This FMRI experiment demonstrated that limbic brain activity increased in relation to "unseen" cocaine cues. This increase in activity was then shown to be related to positive affects that the subjects later attributed to "visible versions of the same cues in subsequent off-magnet testing" (Childress et al. 2008: 1). The Childress team used the discourse of "limbic activation" to challenge the discourse of choice and its attendant assumptions of cognitive control, "rational" behavior, and voluntarism.[17] Their results lend credence to the idea that something extra-cognitive—or, at least, beyond conscious awareness—precipitates relapse. The main lesson that can be drawn from their conclusions is that there is far more to relapse than flawed judgment, poor decision making, or lack of control. These attributions, it should be stated, are interpretations and translations: they are the meanings that the scientists generate as they seek to understand the images. Typically, neuro-imagers understand the flexible nature of the interpretations they produce during the production process, but when these are translated into public discourse, the interpretive flexibility often leaks away.

This lesson of interpretive flexibility was not lost on all of Oprah's panelists, some of whom understood that the scientific claims were at odds with the claims of recovery discourse. Cheryl directly contradicted the idea that behavior is not under completely conscious control. Cheryl was identified as a "cocaine abuser for fifteen years"; she insisted, "I . . . made a willing choice to get high, because I just didn't want to feel it anymore."[18] Cheryl strongly distinguished between her past self, who chose to get high because her "first drug was fear," and her present self, who chose recovery through abstinence. The discourse of choice was strong here despite the fact that the confessional narratives staged on *Oprah* are "feminine" texts, regardless of the gender of panelists who appear in them.[19] As she asked Cheryl to recount hitting bottom, Oprah consistently provided affirmations: "Yeah, isn't that what all addiction essentially is about? I mean, I, you know, have done these shows for years. And I've said on television I'm a food addict. And that's why I relate so closely to what you're saying because whether you gamble or whether you eat, whether you shop, whether you do drugs, it's all about manipulating and suppressing feelings." When Childress interrupted the flow of Cheryl's story to note that although many people use drugs to self-medicate uncomfortable feeling states, discomfort was far from the brain's only vulnerability, Oprah cut to a commercial break.

When "science" says something that cannot be heard within therapeutic discourse, it is because it counts for little in the confessional arena. This discounting made for a dynamic cultural clash; the subject position of "scientific expert" is unstable on *Oprah*. If expert analysis converges with Oprah's position, it is accepted as "true," legitimate, credible, and authoritative and relayed. Despite appearing to know something about addicts' brains—and to be able to illustrate the interior workings of subjective states—Childress was discursively positioned as knowing little of practical value. Appearing long after the experience-based testimonials of the panelists had established the confessional tone, she was identified as someone who "studies addiction and the brain." Although addressed respectfully, her words were not relayed for further sense making, and Oprah cut short her interactions with Childress, evidently frustrated about how brain images were ever going to help William.

Science and the Reordering of Social Interaction

Talk shows are highly scripted, and participants are prescribed certain rights and responsibilities. Their "interaction order" is tightly specified so that the host can contain any differences that erupt. According to Goffman, an interaction order is a syntax or "socio-logic" that sequentially orders actions. Any disruption of the interaction order could unsettle the host's authoritative claims and are hence disallowed or disavowed. For instance, in recovery discourse trauma is widely considered a salient cause of drug addiction and alcoholism. When Childress tried to disabuse Oprah of the commonsense idea that trauma is the *primary* cause of drug addiction, Childress upset the socio-logic. Having worked with the Veterans Administration to serve veterans suffering from post-traumatic stress disorder and addictions for decades, Childress is experienced with this population but does not generalize the link between trauma and addiction. The socio-logics on which the interaction order on *Oprah* was based reveal a pattern that adds up to a reassertion of the need for addicts to regain control over their situation by consciously making "good" choices. Because neuro-imaging is showing that something other than conscious volition may be at work in compulsive use, it does not fit in an orderly way with the discursive framework of *The Oprah Winfrey Show*. The following section shows three socio-logics in which the contradictions between this neuro-scientific discourse and the testimonial and confessional mode are displayed in the "relapse society."

Working from a pattern in which patients frequently made seemingly meaningless statements amounting to "I don't know what I was thinking" to explain continued drug use in the face of negative consequences,[20] Childress took seriously that her subjects actually did not know what was going on in such moments immediately preceding relapse. Rather than assuming they were "in denial" (cf. Carr, this volume), she said, "We knew that [thinking about the possible negative consequences of acting on craving] was hard for people long before we had an imaging device, long before we could actually see that there might be problems at the level of the frontal lobes. It was really exciting to be able to see that—but we suspected it for a long time because we could see that people were 'living the subcortical life.' They were basically very much in the throes, in the grips of this state that was very much a limbic state."

Decontextualized, such a statement may be taken as a primitivizing neurobiological determinism, especially if "living the subcortical life" is joined to accounts of "uncontrolled" drive states.[21] While some neurobiological determinism may be at work here, the notion of a brain state designated as a "limbic state" represents a bigger conceptual problem; indeed, all such designations are problematic for the history and ethnography of science. While there is raging debate about whether or not the amygdala can be said to exist or can be designated as a "unified object,"[22] it is clear that my informant, Childress, believes that the amygdala is meaningful and actively premises her science on its existence. I do not mean to participate in this debate so much as to provide an account for how the amygdala appears in the course of scientific reasoning and the socio-logics that lie at the basis of the practices of neuro-imaging.

After making this statement about the subcortical life, Childress moved quickly to get me—her white, professional-class, female interlocutor—to compare the "limbic state" of a drug addict about to relapse with my own experiential states when liqueurs or chocolate mousse are served after a full meal. In her presentations, Childress flashes luscious photographs of dessert onscreen while discussing "connectivity" between the frontal lobes and regions of interest in the so-called limbic or "reptilian" brain (for which she uses the term "amygdala"). By inducing subjective craving states (for legal drugs such as alcohol and chocolate) in her audience, she drives home the lesson that human beings are challenged when consequences are delayed because they are uncertain. She draws a parallel between middle-class gourmands who have limited exposure to mind-altering substances beyond chocolate and alcohol and those whose experiences with illegal drugs, such as cocaine, are wider. The latter may find that with chronic exposure, their neural circuitry is altered. The nonsubjective states that precede conscious craving have a different effect in social situations where cocaine is abundant and easily obtained. Such subjective states may be acted on with little conscious thought, just as the middle-class gourmand helps herself to dessert without thinking that she has been fully sated by dinner.

Underlying the notion of nonsubjective states is the metaphorical matter of neural circuitry. The metaphor of the "wired" brain—and addiction as a matter of "mis-wiring"—underlies the above reading of "I dunno" statements. Such statements are taken as indicating "short-circuiting": "If you don't have such great wiring in terms of these frontal regions talking downstream to the limbic regions, you may have an especially difficult time. Our patients' account to us all the time was, 'I don't know what I was thinking, I don't know what I was doing, it wasn't even me, how could I have done that, [taken] money from my grandmother's purse, what was I thinking?' It really is as though they feel that part of themselves is short-circuited and they really don't have help from the frontal lobes."

Childress's scientific quest is to clarify how long and under what conditions her patients or subjects start "living the subcortical life" and just which connections are disrupted when ROIS communicate with one another. Although she does not make the analytic move to associate living the subcortical life with what David Courtwright has called the globalization of "limbic capitalism," the connections are tantalizing.[23] Rather than locating deficient connectivity within individual brains, the onus might be placed on the proliferating forms of psychoactive commerce that induce subjective and nonsubjective craving states. For instance, the moral economy of Las Vegas might well be described as a form of "limbic capitalism" (see Schüll, this volume).[24]

While putting her scientific goals in terms of identifying a visible "brain signature," Childress sees hers as a clinical quest. "When I think about it, my studies are always guided by the problems I'm seeing in the clinic," she said. "The overall problem of relapse with this powerful craving that doesn't seem to be easily managed by our patients—we can now visualize in the brain and try to fix it. Just as soon as we can get a signature for it and see what it is, the clinical impulse is to see how to intervene on it, to really try to shape that with treatment."

Nonsubjective states designated by phrases such as "I don't know what I was thinking" became the basis for an entire research program using the tools of neuro-imaging to investigate what living the subcortical life looked like in *the brain*. Not only were the clinical implications lost on Oprah, but the show restaged what Childress referred to as an "extended cue exposure study" that clearly triggered symptoms of arousal and subjective states of craving for participants.

The discourse about "triggers" raises the question of what, if any, volitional control people have in response to them. The HBO special was accompanied by several independent films, two of which were excerpted on *Oprah*. The protagonist of one of the films, *Montana Meth*, was a woman aptly named Crystal; the other film, *TV Junkie*, was made by Rick Kirkman, a reporter with the news program *Inside Edition* who video-taped himself smoking crack cocaine. Footage from the films was projected onto a ten-by-twenty-foot screen so the panelists and audience could watch Crystal injecting meth into her carotid artery and, later, Rick igniting what he called a "trigger fire" while lighting up a crack pipe. These graphic representations of drug use were, in the language of learning and conditioning theory, lengthy "cues" or, in popular parlance, "triggers." Although Oprah warned of graphic footage to come, few could have been prepared for the length or content of the clip of Crystal injecting methamphetamine. Childress explained that cues only 0.33 milliseconds long can "get someone going." Then, she continued, "Oprah goes to [Rick], the reporter, and shows him using cocaine, close up, lighting his pipe. She noticed he was sweating a lot and asked how he felt when he saw this. He said, "It's been seven years, but I gotta say, I still feel something." When Oprah reached William, whose recovery was a matter of months, he told her that he simply could not watch the footage. Rick referred to the footage as igniting a "trigger fire," but Oprah did not make the connection between the footage, which was basically one long sequence of triggers and evocative drug cues of the type that Childress has made for her studies, and "triggers." Well aware that discursive constructions convey tacit assumptions, Childress said: "Oprah had done several programs by the seat of her pants where people tell their wrenching stories, and even used the word 'triggers.' Then there was 'footage' separate from the triggers. [This made me] so unsettled. The films were made a year and a half ago. . . . I didn't know how many years Rick had been abstinent. . . . I'm sure Oprah didn't intend [the show] to be sensational with regard to images of drug use. I'm sure it was supposed to be about science, desire, hope." The film segments unleashed an unpredictable and destabilizing set of triggers among panelists and the audience (many chat-room contributors commented on their desires for drugs having been kindled by the footage). Popular assumptions about the loss of control were fueled by the footage, and there was very little anyone could do about it.

Yet the science of desire staged on *Oprah* was billed as offering hope and "new strategies" for recovering addicts and alcoholics via the new technology of neuro-imaging. On the set, Childress noted that Oprah strayed from the pre-established questions and did not appear to grasp the significance of the brain images. She recalled Oprah turning to her staff during a commercial break and in frustration saying, "I don't get it; how's this supposed to help William?" The writers pointed out that William was in a study where he received "medication that blunts [desire for drugs]."

The breakdown in understanding concerned "translation" of results from neuro-imaging into treatment strategies: for acolytes of recovery discourse, pharmacotherapies sit uneasily alongside identities configured around abstinence and self-control. When Childress later explained to me how she saw neuro-imaging helping patients, she noted that her harshest critics are "people who have walked away, or struggled in recovery and think, 'If I did it, someone else can if they really want to.'" Recovery has given them a temporary certainty, but no permanent resolution to the fragile and uncertain ontological status of a disease now assumed to be unending, to place individuals at "perpetual risk" of relapse. As Angela Garcia reminds us in her poignant account of Alma's life and death in this volume, unintended moral and psychological repercussions follow from the redefinition of addiction as a chronic, relapsing disease state.

Neuro-imagers have remained committed to using their technology as a therapeutic tool despite the skepticism that their technologies will readily translate into pharmacotherapies. The promise of a technological fix offers them a degree of precision and control that clinicians typically lack. "It's the only way to help William that I have any control over," Childress said. "I can't control where he lives or who offers him cocaine that will interact with his vulnerability. The only thing I can control potentially is that state of his brain and the behaviors I can offer to try to help him control [his addiction]." Recognizing that social, environmental, and contextual factors are beyond control, Childress believes that a combination of anti-craving medications and cognitive behavioral therapy will offer clinicians, counselors, or therapists something more effective for people whose brains are like William's brain. Anti-craving medications appear as the ultimate means by which the fruits of neuro-imaging technologies can be "translated" from research to practice in the addiction research arena.[25] Yet the social contexts in which "translation" takes place shape the meanings of these therapies. As William Garriott's contribution to this volume clearly shows, police, judges, and other participants even in the very lowest reaches of the criminal justice system have institutionalized the neurobiological disease discourse of addiction in ways that lend scientific credibility to their accounts of criminality. While Garriott's police officers in rural West Virginia seem to have incorporated biomedical understandings into their own, they reproduce them in punitive contexts that illustrate what Craig Reinarman (2005) has called the "double-edged" character of the disease concept of addiction. The therapeutic and punitive states converge in the biomedicalization of addiction, and anti-craving technologies enable that convergence at the molecular level.

Neuro-imagers chart brain structures (particularly receptors) that serve as "molecular targets" for medications that intervene in neuro-chemical processes that sustain chronic use of drugs of abuse. Although there are medications currently marketed as "anti-craving" medications, there has not been wide social acceptance of these,[26] so others are being explored "off-label" to see if they can be adapted as treatment medica-tions. By comparing arousal states before and after exposure to drug cues, Childress started building an evidence base for Baclofen as a drug that might damp down "craving" after hearing an anecdotal account from a paraplegic former dealer of crack cocaine whose spinal cord was damaged from a gunshot wound incurred in the course of his work.[27] Prescribed Baclofen for its antispasmodic effects, this patient had indisputably suf-fered "negative consequences" from his "addiction." Yet one day when his mother was out, he made his way down several flights of stairs in his wheelchair. Knowing he could not make it back up those very stairs, he used cocaine—but to his surprise, it failed to have its usual effects. Upon hearing this story and reading other clinical reports, Childress began to explore Baclofen as an anti-craving agent.

While the value of the scientific quest to identify anti-craving agents might have been lost on Oprah, inquiries about "magic pills" such as Antabuse poured into the chat room and in direct emails to Childress. Discursive construction of anti-craving medications and treatment drugs differs across the alcohol and drug domains. Childress, who has worked primarily with opiate and crack-cocaine addicts from South Philadelphia and New Jersey, speaks of using a drug to rebalance or calm the "vulner-able brain"—literally, to "take the red out" of brain images showing ac-tivity in the amygdala and prefrontal regions, not to cure or make aversive but to dampen response to triggers. By "recovery," she means not absti-nence but lengthy periods with very occasional relapse. While many argue that "pills are not the answer," and some might see them as an ominous form of behavior control, anti-craving medications are typically figured in hopeful terms.[28] Ominous undertones of behavioral control are overshad-owed by happy constructs of magic pills that will give individuals control over subjective states.[29] Control, however, was most often equated with moral choice, as illustrated late in the show, when "choosing drugs over children" came to the fore as a control issue.

Rather than pursue triggers, and gripped by the confessional mode for which her name practically stands as a synecdoche, Oprah returned to Cheryl's story about missing her child's eighth birthday because of a cocaine binge. Cheryl held a garage sale to raise money for a party, but cash proved a "powerful trigger." Oprah admonished, "So you chose the drug over your children."[30] Childress reported feeling dumbfounded about the gendered and racialized dynamics involved:

> Oprah may be able to say this, but . . . when the head of [the National Institutes of Health] talked about studies showing animals would abandon their young and choose the drug over anything, it was interpreted as a racist comment. . . . [When Oprah asked each panelist], Why is it that you could choose the drug over all else? That's the conundrum, because, of course, they love their children. They're all saying, "I don't know how I could do that; I loathe myself." Then she comes back to me and says, "So, doctor, how is it they could do this?"

Putting Childress in the position of using science to explain a moral outrage (choosing drugs over children), Oprah neatly contained the threat that neuro-imaging poses to notions of volitional control and moral choice as the only means to recovery. If Childress affirms that a choice is being made, she contradicts her own scientific work showing that much of the "prelude to passion" takes place "outside awareness" and is not subject to conscious control through cognition.

Respect for the Disorder: Neuro-imaging Technologies and the Engendering of Empathy

Intuiting the discursive trap she was in as a result of disclaiming choice and cognition, Childress argued that responsibility should be reframed as "responsibility for getting treatment." The public discourse of personal responsibility as a counterbalance to dependence pervades social policy and is part of the problematic framing of public discourse on addiction.[31] To make sense of the incongruities she experienced as Oprah's guest, Childress figured the work in which she and others were engaged as using neuro-imaging technologies to engender empathy by getting people to recognize that "craving" may persist "outside awareness." Counselors who find their clients' behavior challenging are invited to empathize on the basis of science (the discourse of evidence-based or science-based treatment has saturated the therapeutic arena for the past decade). Neuro-imaging technologies are literally refashioned as tools of subjectivity—much in the way that LSD once enabled psychiatrists to identify with patients who were mentally ill (Dyck 2008). But in making that move, neuro-imagery can be seen as amplifying the importance of differences in brain structure and function, particularly connectivity, as the source of "addiction." The brain becomes the origin of addiction, as well as the "target" of medication.

What are the ethico-politics of localizing addiction—a complex social, economic, and political phenomenon that takes wildly differing forms across space and time—to the brain? What are the implications of a science that amplifies, rather than counteracts, myriad differences between "normal" and affected brains and bodies when a stigmatized condition is involved? When I posed this question to Childress, she answered, typically, with a question of her own: "So we've got different brains: does this mean you're defective, or possessed, depending on the language of the times? Having different behaviors and a different kind of brain could make you vulnerable to discrimination. How can we bring the science forward and have it resolve into what we hope will be a compassionate understanding of the biological constraints that we all struggle under to some degree, without it being turned against the patients, against the disorder?"

Addiction is here personified as a disorder that exacts respect from those who do not grant it status as a "real" disease worthy of scientific scrutiny or who fail to recognize its persistent nature. Moving rapidly from data produced via neuro-imaging to the persuasive value of images and potential clinical translations, Childress said, "When I [see the data, I] immediately and self-reflexively ask, 'Does that map onto anything I know [as a clinician]?' Before I even think about it, I have to feel it. It is clinically intuitive but it has something to do with having a deep and abiding knowledge, familiarity, and a respect for this disorder." There is a distinct way in which those who advocate sole reliance on conscious control or drug-free abstinence as the only path to recovery may in fact fail to "respect the disorder" from which they seek to dissuade themselves and others. It may be that the pharmacological optimism displayed by neuroscientists working in the domain of substance abuse signals not deterministic or reductionist contempt for the "disorder," but a more fulsome respect for the complexities represented by relapse. And it may be that the epistemic allergies that we witness between popular and neurobiological accounts of addiction force us to recognize that neuro-scientific accounts have limited potential for displacing deeply entrenched moral lexicons. While a dose of "pharmacological pessimism" may be in order, sacrificing pharmacological optimists' hard-won empathy, "respect for the disorder," and recognition that "addiction" is a likelihood rather than an individual defect within specific political, economic, and cultural geographies may be too high a price to pay.

Notes

I acknowledge the generosity of the College on Problems of Drug Dependence, Charles P. O'Brien, and Anna Rose Childress. I also thank Isaac Campbell Eglash, Grace Campbell Woodhouse, and Ned Woodhouse for giving me the time, space, and peace to write, and Eugene Raikhel and William Garriott for the invitation to participate in the conference that led to this volume.

1. Addressing the limitations of neuro-imaging technologies is not my focus in this chapter (cf. Dowty 2008; Dumit 2004). My focus is on how neuro-imaging technologies have been used to redefine addiction as a brain disorder in ways that validate neuroscience above other ways of knowing addiction.
2. The first term is drawn from Howard S. Becker's discussion in *The Outsiders* (1963) and is typically applied to those who promote new social norms and persuade others to adopt policies based on dominant forms of moral reasoning that co-construct forms of "deviance." Rayna Rapp (1987, 1999) uses the term "moral pioneers" throughout her work to describe those who invent new forms of moral or cultural reasoning in the face of new technologies.
3. Documents include transcripts and videos of talk-show panelists using drugs, which included street scenes, interior shots of them getting high, and graphic scenes of them shooting up, made for the prize-winning HBO series *Addiction*: see the website at http://www.hbo.com/addiction/thefilm/bios/651_jon_alpert.html.
4. The neurophysiologist Abraham Wikler conducted seminal studies of relapse in the late 1940s and through the 1950s and 1960s. For instance, Wikler (1965) recognized that "cues" to resume drug use were embedded in the social and cultural geography to which addicts returned after leaving the U.S. Public Health Service's Narcotics Hospital in Lexington, Kentucky, where he conducted research: see Acker 2002; Campbell 2007; Campbell et al. 2008.
5. Marlatt's extensive body of work, particularly *Alcoholism: New Directions in Behavioral Research and Treatment* (Nathan and Marlatt 1978), sets forth a taxonomy of "high-risk situations."
6. I thank Tobias Rees, whose comments on the version of this chapter that I gave at the "Anthropologies of Addiction" workshop emphasized my need to produce a genealogy of behavioral pharmacology separate from the genealogy of cognitive neuroscience in U.S.-based addiction research. Behavioral pharmacology as practiced in the United States is a variant of Skinnerian behaviorism that makes use of operant conditioning. Although it is a conceptually rich scientific field, its histor-

ical use as an industrial drug-screening technique led to its being viewed as an applied science: see interviews with Robert Balster, Joseph V. Brady, Roland Griffiths, Chris-Ellyn Johanson, C. Robert Schuster, Maxine Stitzer, and James H. Woods at http://sitemaker.umich.edu/substance.abuse.history/home (accessed August 15, 2012).

7. In "A Mother's Desperation," the second episode of *Addiction*, Volkow says, "Drug addiction is a disease of the brain that translates into abnormal behavior." On "disrupted volition," see Volkow and Li 2004, 2005.

8. The comment by Charles P. O'Brien is from the opening sequence of "The Science of Relapse," dir. Eugene Jarecki and Susan Froemke, *Addiction*, HBO. On the historical continuities between O'Brien's interest in relapse and that of Abraham Wikler, see Campbell 2007: 216–17.

9. Anna Rose Childress, quoted in Jarecki and Froemke, "The Science of Relapse."

10. This and all other quotes from Childress, unless noted otherwise, are from my recorded and transcribed field notes from the week of April 9–13, 2007.

11. William, quoted in Jarecki and Froemke, "The Science of Relapse."

12. I thank Dawn Moore for reminding me that confessions have more to do with moral status than with truth and making me think more deeply about the role of performative enactments of testimony in science.

13. I build on Arthur Frank's term "remission society," in which sickness and wellness are always becoming each other: Frank 1997: 8–10, quoted in Campbell 2000: 46–47.

14. In previous work I refer to "governing mentalities," the dominant discursive conditions out of which shared sense arises even among parties whose goals are antagonistic (Campbell 2000).

15. Transcript, "Addiction: Why Can't They Stop?," *The Oprah Winfrey Show*, April 9, 2007.

16. Transcript, 6.

17. "Limbic activation" and the very construct of the limbic system are deeply controversial. The term "limbic system" was first offered in 1952 by Paul Maclean in the context of the "triune brain," his attempt to make sense of the evolution of brain structure. According to Allan Young, the triune brain built in turn on an earlier conceptual platform offered by the British neurologist John Hughlings Jackson: see Young 2006. The outlines of this currently raging controversy are glaringly evident on the Wikipedia "talk page" at http://en.wikipedia.org/wiki/Talk:Limbic _system#This_article_is_severely_outdated. In this chapter, I use the term "limbic activation" as my informants do in their published and unpublished work, recognizing the historicity as well as the cultural work that the construct provides but also understanding it as a shorthand reference to heterogeneous elements.

18. Transcript, 18.

19. "Feminine" texts are open-ended accounts of never-ending struggles that rarely lead to closure. On feminine genre conventions, see Fiske 1988 (masculine action films versus feminine soap operatic conventions); Modleski 1982 (soap opera); Radway 1991 (reading the romance); D. Smith 1999 (femininity as discourse). The goal of critical discourse analysis is to use language as a way to get at the analysis of

social relations. This ethnographic use of language and discursive interaction as data provides a useful way into the study of socially situated subjectivity.

20. Analyzing strategic uses of "I dunno," Margaret Wetherall finds as much going on in seemingly meaningless utterances that disavow or disclaim knowledge as in utterances through which knowledge claims are made (Wetherall 2001: 14–28).

21. "Neuroscientific explanations of addictive behaviour explicitly formulate compulsions as arising out of primitive (which is in a sense to say 'uncivilized') urges that result when the lower brain, rather than the distinctively civilized one, exerts control over conduct. As a leading textbook on substance abuse and addictive behaviour puts it: 'The neurologic substrate for addiction is located in the limbic system. Within the limbic system is housed the biologically primitive circuitry for the drive states such as hunger, and thirst'" (Lowinson et al. 2005: 203, quoted in Vrecko 2010b).

22. The amygdala has a similarly checkered past and present. Barry J. Everitt and Trevor W. Robbins argue that neither "the" amygdala nor "the" central striatum can be viewed as a unitary structure; both are "neurochemically heterogeneous" (Everitt and Robbins 1992: 422). The work of Joseph E. LeDoux (1992) is insightful for understanding the trajectory of O'Brien's lab. LeDoux suggests that "emotional memories established through the amygdala are impervious to extinction and forgetting processes" (LeDoux et al. 1989). High degrees of "resistance to extinction" were attributed to "subcortical inputs," making it hard for the amygdala to "easily switch the emotional valence it assigns to a stimulus. . . . Other structures, such as orbitofrontal cortex, may have to intervene" (LeDoux 1992: 344). For further discussion of the amygdala, see Campbell 2010.

23. David Courtwright (2001b) argued that epidemic drug use indicated social circumstances out of sync with our "evolved natures." The mesolimbic dopamine reward system (which Courtwright calls "the NIDA paradigm") pushed him to recognize the fit between "limbic capitalism" and the commercialization of psychoactives: David Courtwright, personal communication, February 27, 2009. "I noticed that the most commercially popular drugs invariably affected, whether strongly or weakly, directly or indirectly, the reward system that neuroscientists now held to be central to both motivation and craving. That could not be a coincidence. Dopamine reward helped explain why an exotic, bizarrely consumed, seemingly diabolical drug like tobacco, which often met with fierce official resistance, caught on wherever it was introduced in the early modern world. Dopamine reward also helped explain why exposure mattered so much" (Courtwright 2009, 14).

24. There has been much debate in the relevant scientific communities about the desirability of eliminating craving states altogether, as opposed to dampening or reducing them. Seemingly "perfect" anti-craving medications such as naltrexone have not achieved the level of clinical or social acceptance addiction researchers assumed they would (O'Brien 2004). This puzzling lack of practical success may be attributed to lack of profit in generics. "Unlike antidepressants, in which there is a commercial reason for selective publication of positive studies, naltrexone is

generic and not highly profitable. Thus, negative trials of naltrexone for this complex disorder are just as likely to be published as are positive studies. Perhaps one of the reasons that medications are not routinely used to prevent alcohol relapse lies in the notion that total abstinence is the only desirable goal and a medication that blocks some of the rewarding properties of alcohol is dismissed as a 'crutch.' Given the devastation produced by repeated relapses and the accumulating evidence of a biological basis for many—if not most—forms of alcoholism, perhaps a crutch is medically and morally justified" (O'Brien 2004: 1742).

25. As argued by Scott Vrecko in his work on how naltrexone (marketed by DuPont Merck under the brand name ReVia) has been phased into a drug court in Butte County, California, a "specific assemblage of control—which may be referred to as 'penal psychopharmacology' has emerged as a form of 'somatic regulation' based on 'neurobiological modulation'" (Vrecko 2009: 229). Such programs illustrate the importance of understanding the context-dependent character of the meanings attributed to anti-craving medications.

26. My recent thinking about naltrexone has been shaped by my conversations with Larry D. Reid: see Reid 2009. Investment in naltrexone, former site of pharmacological optimism, now disappointed, may be glimpsed in Willette and Barnett 1981.

27. No doubt, Childress read clinical reports such as "Suppression of Symptoms of Alcohol Dependence and Craving Using High-Dose Baclofen" (Bucknam 2007). In response, the French cardiologist Olivier Ameisen wrote a letter to the editor hypothesizing that GHB deficits could explain some of the symptoms of alcoholism, including muscle tension, for which Baclofen could compensate. Ameisen, who was then at the Weill Cornell Medical College, adopted a once venerable tradition of self-administration in pharmacology, treating himself for alcoholism with Baclofen and calling for clinical trials in the pages of the *Journal of the American Medical Association*. He published a book in France titled *Le dernier verre*, translated into English as *The End of My Addiction*. The translation was released in the United States in December 2008, accompanied by media commentary. See also reports from Rome, where a randomized, placebo-controlled clinical trial showed that Baclofen could be used to control drinking in cirrhotic alcoholics. The results were published in the British medical journal *Lancet* 370 (2007): 1915–22, 1884–85. See also Addolorato et al. 2006.

28. Increasingly, the "right drugs" are used to modulate effects of the "wrong drugs." Recent work by Vrecko (2009) indicates that anti-craving medications are not confined to the realm of substance abuse, but are widely used to "treat" so-called behavioral addictions such as gambling, compulsive shopping, and eating.

29. This is not unlike how antidepressants and anxiolytics figure in popular culture according to David Herzberg (2009) and Andrea Tone (2009).

30. An enormous feminist literature on the cultural construction of drug-using women as archetypal "bad mothers" now includes Campbell 2000; Flavin 2009; Gomez 1997; Ladd-Taylor and Umansky 1998; Woliver 2002.

31. Another point of feminist intervention appears in analysis of the cultural work of

the term "dependence" in Fraser and Gordon 1994; Naples 2003; Schram 2006. For an example of the continued promotion of "personal responsibility" in the treatment field, see Sally Satel and Scott Lilienfeld, "Medical Misnomer: Addiction Isn't a Brain Disease, Congress," *Slate*, July 25, 2007, available online at http://www.slate.com/id/2171131.

COMMITTED TO WILL
What's at Stake for Anthropology in Addiction

I am a poet who has made it known that I do not give readings. I am a person who becomes quite a jackass when drunk, and when sober I don't have anything to say, so there weren't many knocks at the poet's cottage.
—**Charles Bukowski,** *Tales of Ordinary Madness*

Charles Bukowski, the bard of the beaten-down and the self-appointed voice for life's losers from my home town of Los Angeles, puts into a few lines some sophisticated ideas about the relationship of the intention of a subject, what a person *means* through an utterance or a practice, and the intension of their products—in other words, the web of postulates and agreed-on definitions that make such expressions of agency possible. The collection containing "My Stay in the Poet's Cottage" is titled *Tales of Ordinary Madness* (Bukowski 1983), the author using a metaphor at the edge of the disciplinary episteme of reason—that is, "madness"—to subvert the common sense of the striving mass in the United States (and, indeed, in many other parts of the world) that "we have plans." Thus, most of Bukowski's short stories and many of his poems explore the theme of control, with his protagonists seemingly always caught up in the grip of various systems—from psychological to economic—of which they only have fleeting glimpses and even less ability to influence. At best, according to Bukowski, "plans" (the horses, the hierarchies, the drinks, the relationships, and the jobs) have us, but they are indifferent and unpredictable, not even doing us the courtesy of *per-*

sonally afflicting us. Like freak waves, they can occasionally deposit us on higher ground, but, far more often than not, they sweep us remorselessly and relentlessly out to sea. Meanwhile, Bukowski's characters, like their creator, are nearly always connected to a mind-altering substance—routinely alcohol and nicotine, but commonly amphetamines and minor tranquillizers, as well. Their uncertain epiphanies, therefore, rarely come to an unmediated human mind; thus, the nature of their insight, and the locus of their enlightenment, is obscure.

So where, exactly, is the poetry in the poet's cottage? On the one hand, we could read the epigraph in a fairly traditional way—as separating the imaginative (perhaps especially in the throes of chemical enhancement) from the everyday, the poetic impulse from the quotidian (see Saris 2007). In my adopted home of Ireland, for example, the idea that some sort of intoxication is necessary for the creation of verbal art—in other words, that drunkenness was the standard mood of poetry (Ó'hÓgáin 1979)—needs little elaboration. Indeed, the Irish language possesses a very ancient word, *meisce* (drunkenness, frenzy, ectsasis) that generally requires a modifier to specify the vehicle that has taken one "out of one's mind" (e.g., *meisce mearachta*, as against *meisce leanna*, meaning the intoxication of madness as opposed to the intoxication of ale). On the other hand, the statement presents us with a conundrum as to the source, perhaps even the ontological status, of Bukowski's poetic voice. Does it require an intersubjective affirmation (an appreciative audience) to be? If so, then, to whom does it belong—to Bukowski, who alone has nothing to say; or to "Bukowski + alcohol," who is destructive-creative as a condition of his art; or maybe to all of us (i.e., including his audience)? In what sense, then, does one choose to create "Art" or to be "a jackass" or, indeed, to consume mind-altering substances regularly and to excess? Why should this assemblage be of public interest—never mind, of all things, to be assimilable to some understanding of aesthetics? What, in other words, does Bukowski "mean"?

The Will to Will

I am intrigued by this question for a variety of reasons. Professionally, of course, I am a cultural anthropologist, trained by scholars who took this question very seriously in a discipline that has filled up libraries on this very problematic. At the same time, I have largely spent my career with people who traditionally would be considered to inhabit spaces at the limits of meaningful behavior: folks with major mental illnesses and people with a fascination for illegal pharmaceuticals. Many of the latter engage in a wide variety of other criminal activities that routinely, almost monotonously, subject them to criminal sanctions, serious health risks, occasional violence, and even death. I suppose, with due deference to Mary Shelley and Lord Byron, one could chart my career to date as tracking between the mad and the bad. The "dangerous to know" bit is provided by something else: the gnawing sense that I have (at least some of the time) that I have no idea what they "mean" by certain critical actions or utterances; nor, it seems to me, do they. I want tentatively to suggest that this failure on my part develops out of the very different stakes that they and I have had in our interactions. To make this idea theoretically useful, though, I want to rethink (somewhat) the idea of "stakes." I then want to use this sense to interrogate some of the ways that "addiction" exists in the modern moment.

In a theoretically sophisticated reformulation of his (and, indeed, my) mentor's (Arthur Kleinman's) understanding of the *stakes* in anthropology, Lawrence Cohen (n.d.: 1) proposes an idea of "commitment" that I find fruitful in answering some of the issues that I laid out earlier: "By *commitment*, I mean (1) the giving of a body (2) to or for another (3) in a way that remakes the limit of that body's existence or horizon. . . . It gestures toward a broader program: what would it offer us to frame the stakes in anthropology in such terms of commitment?" Cohen is specifically interested in the physicality of bodies subjected to various types of surgery in present-day India—in particular, sterilization and organ transplantation. *Commitment* provides him a flexible conceptual apparatus insofar as, in the modern moment, it models two very different versions of the movement (spatial and conceptual) of bodies: that of total and selfless gifting (as in, ideally, Christian marriage) and that of involuntary seizing (as in, say, psychiatric commitment). In Cohen's data, these end points (e.g., an organ donated out of filial obligation as against the violated body, wrested of something with neither consent nor compensation to be sold in the developed world) are separated by a middle ground of the market, where specific cultural logics of marginal utility, mediated by currency, chance, and choice, produce the horizons of possibility for any particular body.

At a more abstract level, the movement of bodies that Cohen seeks to understand seems able to shift between three widely available folk models in English, which claim quite separate ideological spaces but seem to easily flow into one another in practice:

Gift ↔ Purchase/Sale ↔ Seizure[1]

In other words, I am arguing that most English-speakers understand that there are clear differences between these kinds of exchanges, and, indeed, the more intimate the exchange—say, sex in the context of (1) a committed relationship, (2) prostitution, and (3) rape—the stronger the ideological resistance would be to mixing these models and, therefore, the more striking their mixing is rhetorically.[2] The rhetorical power that derives from these frame shifts, of course, grows out of a largely tacit sense among these same speakers that many exchanges can in fact be understood, at least partially, from more than one of these vantage points. For the moment, though, I want to suggest that this triad gives us a way to approach the relationships between our neurochemistry and our context in discourses about "addicts" and "addiction" outside stale models of "internal" and "external," or deracinated "impulses," insofar as such discourses need to *commit* to certain crucial ideas (such as will or choice) as a precondition of their analysis of the phenomenon. At the same time, those subjectivities, substances, and, indeed, activities plot a trajectory through parts or all of this triad in everything from the macro-contexts of specific drugs (what Sjaak van der Geest and his colleagues [1996] call a drug biography) to the actual lives of users. Most importantly, however, the ways that the current understanding of "the addict" moves through this triad clearly challenges the liberal subject at the heart of most Western social-science explanation, in the process providing a unique opportunity for anthropology's own ongoing interrogation of this construct.

Back, then, to our author. By modern definitions, Bukowski was an alcoholic, and like many other artists, he insisted that he did not choose his art—instead, it chose him. As a starting point of this argument, I want to suggest that, in the modern moment, we are all Bukowski—probably not as colorful or, perhaps, as talented but facing a similar conundrum. Do we have a "choice" when the locus of that "choice," the humanistic subject, discursively excavated so brilliantly by Michel Foucault in *Les mots et les choses*, is being fundamentally destabilized by one of its constitutive discourses: biology, and in particular, the biology of addiction. At both a political and a philosophical level, then, we need to ask: What is our *commitment* to "choice" at this moment, and transitively, in what ways have the contours of our thinking been *committed to* (seized by) choice? The first of these, I argue, is a moral and political stance with a variety of ethical implications toward certain kinds of action in the world. The second, on the other hand, is a default theoretical stance that, I feel, has hindered anthropology's engagement with pressing social issues in biopsychiatry by vitiating some of the critical insights that have been uniquely made in our discipline.

I argue below that the condition of possibility of this question is crucially bound up with the way that "choice" has been revisioned in part through the burgeoning discursive production of "addiction." In other words, the connection of a subject with a substance and or an activity, such that within this *assemblage* (to [again] use Gilles Deleuze's and Félix Guattari's phrasing), *will* becomes impossible. Ironically, and at about the same time, *will* has become fetishized in other assemblages, very often involving the same compounds—notably, in the artful combination of drugs for specific, nontherapeutic effects, such as in so-called cosmetic pharmacology or where people endeavor to enhance their "normal" functioning through well-researched, if off-label, drug use (e.g., using Provigil to improve concentration at work). To pursue these questions, I briefly review some of the curious history of the words "addiction" and, especially, "addict" in English. I then briefly outline some of the history of the capture of this concept by biology, stressing how the modern construction of addiction constitutes particular frames around the *time* and *substance* of the addict. Finally, I will look at how anthropology might fit into this complex.

Finding the Addict in Addiction

Clearly, the phenomenon of bondage to a substance or an activity that overwhelms the will, even as it damages the body or the social person, has become a discipline in its own right, spawning entire research agendas and at least a dozen scholarly journals. It supports various disciplinary historians writing different histories about how all this came to be. (For a very approachable instance of this, see Courtwright 2001.) In the modern moment, the addict stands in stark contrast to the productive citizen, perhaps even more so than the criminal, because of the uniquely destructive ability she or he ostensibly possesses to tear up the social contract and to shred the social fabric: "Addicts are, by and large, incapable of maintaining relationships, because they cannot fulfil their responsibilities to others. They can't hold jobs. They can't support their families. They can't pay back loans and maintain credit. They can't maintain their personal health against the ravages of drug use. They drive stoned and endanger others on the highway just as much as drunk drivers. Addicts do not have a 'right' to this destructive behavior."[3] The addict, then, unlike even the criminal,[4] erodes the very conditions of possibility of the social contract: she or he is the bourgeois anti-subject. In other words, in any of the exchanges entangling the addict as subject—that is, the public economy of the market, the civil economy of rights and duties, and the domestic economy of affective obligation—no sure exchange is possible either between addicts or between an addict and a social person. Tellingly, neither sanction nor suasion can reach them.

Curiously, however, "addict," as a noun, is an unusual word, whose relatively shallow history in English is belied by the universalistic pretensions of the current biological knowledge base. As a noun, the term (almost always used with a modifier, such as "drug addict") was recognized by the *Oxford English Dictionary* only in 1920; with references earlier than 1900 being difficult to find. Addict, in this sense, appears to be part of a specific assemblage connected to the rise of the pharmaceutical industry in the late nineteenth century and early twentieth century (aspirin, for example, was patented only in 1899), along with the trauma and horror of the First World War, when morphine, among other opiates, was widely used to dull both physical agony and psychological horror. At about the same time, the initial legal framework to regulate pharmaceuticals, socially separating them as legal (and, in turn, subdividing them between over-the-counter and prescription varieties) and illegal comes into force, first in the United States and then in other developed countries. From a surprisingly early point, though, "addict" appeared in conjunction with other modifiers, such as "night club addict." This is clearly our sense of seizing or of involuntary commitment, as laid out earlier. The noun form, "addict," then becomes pejorative as such: the will is in chains, which makes questions such as "How comfortable is the prison?" or "Is it fun to go to night clubs every night?" secondary and somehow less relevant.[5]

As a participial adjective, though, "addict" has a much longer and, in some ways, more interesting pedigree in the language. In 1529, for example, John Frith (who was martyred a few years later), in a translation of the German tract "A Pistle to the Christen Reader," wrote, "Be not partially addict to the one nor to the other" (Frith 1529: 318).[6] This sense seems closer to our idea of "commitment" in terms of gift giving and voluntary dedication: it is advice not to fall between two stools, as it were, a call to fully commit oneself and a warning against half-measures. The term "addict" appears in numerous religious tracts connected to the Reformation, but the grammatical opportunity to turn it into a noun was not, seemingly, taken advantage of. Instead, the term describes a state of serious voluntary bonding (commitment in the "free giving" sense) that could be dissolved by circumstances or by the party who was "addict." Moralizing was confined to the object or idea to which the self had committed rather than to the state of being committed as such.[7]

Addiction, Biological Psychiatry, and Modern Life

By the middle of the twentieth century, however, "addict" as a noun had become ubiquitous, and the horizon of knowledge in which she or he is centered (i.e., addiction) is enjoying explosive growth. The older grammatical usage of "addict" is completely usurped (and all but forgotten), and the problem of addiction has moved from the assumption or imposition of external bonds to a state that is fundamentally internal and, probably, irresistible. One addresses the advice "be not *addict*" to an agent, but "an addict" is unreachable by such means. Neither persuasion nor compulsion now suffices. Indeed, in the modern moment, bonds need to be laid on an agent before addiction (i.e., "Just say no!" or the threat of criminal sanctions), and various cures are concocted to remove the stain of addiction involuntarily (legally enforced replacement therapy, cold-turkey withdrawal), to bring agency back. As in "commitment," then, there is a fundamental temporality in the modern sense of "addict," to which I will return.

For the moment, though, I want to address how the noun form of "addict" has become one of the main points at which cutting-edge theorizing in biochemistry has entered the warp and woof of everyday life. It has also become one of the best-funded meeting grounds for expansive theorizing in neurobiology. This trend was very much in evidence in May 2006, when an important conference on addiction was held at the Picower Institute for Learning and Memory at the Massachusetts Institute of Technology. Sponsored in part by the insurance company Cigna, which underwrites many state and corporate employee benefit plans in the United States, the conference was a select affair, inviting neuroscientists, clinicians, and policymakers, as well as the obligatory handful of folks "in recovery" (i.e., addicts), to an exhibition of what the lavishly funded institute was accomplishing in tackling what Nora D. Volkow, director of the National Institute on Drug Abuse, termed one of the great health threats facing modern America: "Addiction: Free Will Gone Awry." This condition, whatever its underlying "cause" or even its ontological status, also has the sort of profile that makes for social notice in the United States: by some estimates it affects more than 10 percent of the American public, and since some treatment is covered by most health plans, it burdens employers and insurance people with seemingly excess medical costs and apparently lost productivity. When expenses connected to the so-called War on Drugs are factored in, some estimates of the "cost" of addiction go as high as half a trillion dollars a year.

Both the institute and its director, Susumu Tonegawa, are justly famous in the world of biology and neuroscience. Tonegawa is a Nobel Prize winner; his reach in the life sciences is truly impressive. From his initial work in immunology, demonstrating how a limited number of genes can code proteins for a seemingly unlimited number of antibodies (much like how phonemes work in language), to work in the genetics of schizophrenia and, now, cutting-edge work on addiction, there seems to be no field in molecular biology to which he cannot make (or guide others to make) a substantial contribution. For example, his team generated a lot of media interest recently by producing a new model of addiction based on learning and salience rather than reward as such. This was an interesting reconceptualization of the activities and effects of one of the brain chemicals of great importance to biological psychiatry—that is, dopamine— away from a framework stressing its role as a simple reward in a pain-and-pleasure model to one discussing how it brings objects to attention within the stream of consciousness. Although such arguments as these are notoriously shallowly rooted in the history of disciplines (thus, such connections remain unmade), one could say (with only a hint of irony) that the current way that the Picower team is now thinking about the dopaminergic system now owes more to William James, even to Franz Boas, than to B. F. Skinner.

The Pharmakon and the Gift

Given how central the perceived danger of drugs has been for the explosive development of the discourse of biology from the 1960s onward, it is ironic how a discussion of drugs was also an important moment in the revolution of philosophy and much of the human sciences that goes under the banner of poststructuralism during the same period. In "Plato's Pharmacy," one of his early essays to be translated into English, Jacques Derrida spends some time unpacking Plato's notion of the pharmakon (ναρκωτικών) in the context of a debate about the nature and status of writing and meaningful philosophy. As most readers know, Derrida makes much of how the Greek word "pharmakon" means both remedy and poison (see also Martin 2006). Pharmakon challenged Plato and attracted Derrida precisely because it is neither a stable essence nor an ideal identity. It is a neither a simple thing (monoeidetic) nor a composite of other simple things. Indeed, it is itself only a remedy or a poison in relation to the human body. There can, then, be no "nature" of either remedies or poisons.

Although it is many other things, as well, "Plato's Pharmacy" is in large part Derrida's close reading of Plato's Phaedrus dialogue. In a crucial passage in that work, the god Theuth offers King Thamus the gift of writing as a medicine for wisdom and memory. The king rejects the gift as poison that will bring false wisdom and no real memory. Pharmakon, then, for both Plato and Derrida, is also associated with the gift and all of its world-building qualities, as well as all of the uncertainties entangling exchange and reciprocity.[8] I want to veer away from Derrida's critique of Plato's logocentrism in this work, however, and simply develop the connection between the gift and the drug, as it is central to understanding our commitments to the idea of the addict.

It is surprising that this relationship between the pharmakon and the gift is relatively underdeveloped theoretically, as it saturates (in my experience, at least) nearly every level of drug use. In the case of long-term maintenance, whether to antipsychotic or replacement therapies, for example, the sufferer commits (is addict) to such a course as a precondition to getting better. In practice, these interactions have a strong resemblance to gift giving. In the mental hospitals in which I have worked, nurses cajole psychiatric patients into taking their meds, either as desirable goods in themselves or as an offer of quasi-hospitality whose refusal would be in bad taste. In turn, outpatients express their gratitude to their physicians for their prescriptions, in the same way that psychoactive compounds are fundamental in establishing relationships through giving and receiving in many other settings in social life ("I'll buy this round!" or "Can I bum a cigarette?"). While the topic cannot be explored in great detail here, the theme of the gift also has saturated promotional, advertising, and educational literatures that pharmaceutical companies have produced for several decades. One can see this in the production of advertising that portrays biopsychiatry as the gift of knowledge to mankind. Finally, the ubiquity of gifts flowing from the pharmaceutical industry to various medical practitioners is too well known to deserve much comment here (see, among others, Tsai 2003; Wazana 2000). It has become enough of an issue that it has spawned its own ethical literature and a rash of policies prohibiting or severely regulating such interactions at certain elite medical schools.

It is not commonly appreciated, though, how important gift giving (very often from an intimate, in Schutz's [1967 (1932)] terms) is in establishing a relationship to a drug in extralegal settings. The following is from the recollection of "S," a young, often very chaotic heroin user I met some years ago and with whom I still maintain occasional contact. She has a history of being both the victim and the perpetrator of serious violence. She is a thin woman, and her flax-blue eyes convey a sense of being much older than her twenty-three years. We met for the first time at the drop-in center she was then attending weekly as part of her rehab (and as a condition of maintaining at least some access to her toddler, who was in foster care). In one of our early conversations about her first experience of "gear" (heroin), she developed a story about how the drug initially entered her life and body as an uncertain gift from her father. She spoke in a quiet, almost musical voice. As she fiddled with the string of her hoodie, we had the following exchange:

> **S:** Me da would say, "You're gonna fuck yourself up." And he'd go, "Here, you can have it. I'll share it with you, but you'r gonna fuck yourself up," he used to say . . .
> **Ethnographer:** And do you think . . . you'd have been better off if he didn't let you, or whatever? Or do you think you would have got it somewhere?
> **S:** I think I would have bought it somewhere anyway. But I don't think he should have gave it to me, even though I wanted it, like, 'cause I didn't have [*unclear*]. Like, that's all he ever said to me, the first time, and when he said, "Sure, fuck it! [and] the two of us get strung out together."

Here, substance is shared between bodies, and new (arguably more limited) horizons of possibilities are instantiated (see also Garcia 2010). *You* do/do not take this, which is something of *me*, which is bad, but we are/will be, one substance, so you, too, must/will be bad. There is both a tender intimacy in this sharing of a substance, the reproduction of a shared likeness in the moment, and a projection into the future, looking forward to the transfer of spoiled identity between generations: "You're gonna fuck yourself up [so you'll end up like me]."

The same assemblage of person plus drug plus context moves easily between therapy, enhancement, and dysfunction. Narratives of heroin as therapy, for example, in my experience are easy enough to elicit, the attraction of the drug narrated not as euphoria but as the sudden achieving of "normal": "[I felt] just brilliant [early on]. After the initial, kind of, 'wow,' you know that completely stoned feeling; instead, I just felt normal, like I felt as if I should have felt like this all my life because I'd always felt abnormal, kind of different from everyone else. I've been nervous, and I just felt that I should feel like this all the time. I bet other[s] feel like that all the time [*laughs*]; that's what it felt like. Then, anyway." At the same time, drugs whose "addictive potential" is considered to be fairly low, such as selective serotonin reuptake inhibitors (SSRIs), can be narrated as the cause of severe dependence problems that sound a lot like being seized by the drug—that is, addiction:

> [The doctor had me on] Prozac and things like that. They put an awful lot of weight on me, which lowered my mood even more. I was putting on so much weight my doctor was convinced I was bulimic, so he trebled the dose [laughs], so I put on even more weight. There is proof now that [those medications can] cause suicidal ideation, so I think that was part of it, and I'm naturally an impulsive and compulsive person, so I used to just turn off; my conscious mind would just turn off, and I'd have just one thought in my mind: "go off and take pills" [*laughs*]. Then I'd end up in [the emergency room].

This continuum—from a model of an individual enhancing his or her "normal" state to ones of ascribed or achieved deficits needing pharmacological correction for individual choice to function at all—are really different ways to understand "will." If earlier psychology took the will as a property of the human experience (e.g., William James in *The Principles of Psychology* [1890]) or as a sort of illusion (B. F. Skinner [1950]), then theorizing in both psychopharmacology and addiction increasingly has given us a sense of the will as an uncertain achievement, less of an essence and more an epiphenomenon of discrete processes that are subject to both degradation and enhancement (see Saris 2011).

It is not surprising, then, that current research on addiction is largely geared toward providing pharmacological workarounds for the metabolic mess that choice produces in certain users. In turn, from an early point, research in psychopharmacology has been comfortable with the idea that chronic mental illness would require long-term pharmacological workarounds for functional recovery to be maintained.

To put it another way, following Volkow: the dilemma of the modern understanding of addiction is that choice leads to a lack of choice, increasingly leading to a search for new compounds to repair the machinery of choice. The mirror image of this problem is found in psychopharmacology for major mental illness: a drug is needed not only for the possibility of choice or even minimal functioning, but also, more broadly, in the sense that pharmacology can alleviate ever less severe forms of psychological morbidity. Ideologically, in the "good" usage, the drug becomes, if not truly a magic bullet, at least something closer to it than its predecessors and, crucially, is waiting for its improved replacement. Again, any contact with long-term users of psychotropic drugs renders this valuation more complex, but theoretically, the drug is positively valued as making choice possible. Entangled with this sense of effective psychopharmacology, however, is a rejected identity of the compound bound up with both recreation and dependence (see Saris 2011). Not surprisingly, both popular and professional constructions of such off-label usage are often tightly bound together: recreational use is constituted as an unauthorized seizing by persons of the commanding heights of their psychic economy for the pursuit of pleasure, and dependence is seen as something of the just, if regrettable, desserts for such revolutionary hubris. Thus, the remedy that restores agentive functioning is always in danger of transforming into the poison that degrades the will outside the bounds of professionally sanctioned pharmacology.

In the Time of Addiction

This "poison" aspect of the pharmakon, then, produces a double temporality. The first is the history of the concept and its discursive production, some of which I have outlined and to which I will return. The second is the post facto horizon that the "addict" both discovers and instantiates. Thus, an increasingly individuated biochemistry and, increasingly, unique contextual histories have thrown up an interesting collective term—"predisposition"—whose usage, in contrast to that of "addict," has stayed remarkable stable in English going back to Francis Bacon. No matter what the drug or activity, not all are called to "be addict," and, indeed, not all who are called seem to answer the summons. "Predisposition," then, exists as a post facto concept: a flaw or a potentiality whose signature is legible only in retrospect. In the treatment of major psychiatric illnesses, it is the combination of person plus drug that becomes the condition of possibility for future agency; in predisposition, the temporality points in the opposite direction, toward an already unfolded biochemical history wherein a person's flaw existed as only potential until the connection to a drug or activity. The ontology of the first case might be conceived (with due credit to Byron Good [1977]) as existing in the subjunctive mood, while that of the addict's predisposition, in the tense of the historical present. But both take life history, behavioral environment, and temporal trajectory as difficult to separate.

The other aspect of this temporality is found in the social practices that produce and stabilize the legibility of this condition. Following Paul Rabinow (1992; see also Saris 2011), I see the current practices producing communities, in terms that we have come to know as biosociality (more on this later), but I am arguing that there is something we can learn from an earlier moment in the anthropological project about how these processes are occurring. To put it in its strongest form, I am arguing that the anthropological imaginary is less removed from (at least my reading of) the modern biochemical imaginary than is currently thought, and that this fact should both intrigue and worry us. I also wish to outline how an anthropology interested in, even appreciative of, modern research into the brain, might produce new understandings of such issues as communities and the role of the market in the production of the pharmaceutical self. All of these problems impinge on our understanding of "choice" in terms of our triad of Gift ↔ Purchase / Sale ↔ Seizure. To understand the connection between these states, however, we need to understand how addiction assumed its modern guise.

How We Became Addicted

Based on work begun in the late 1950s, Vincent Dole and Marie Nyswander formulated the concept of "metabolic lesion" as the root cause underlying the specific behaviour associated with heroin addiction (Courtwright 1997, 2001a). The key texts in this movement are, as scholars such as Michael Agar and David Courtwright have pointed out, two articles published by Dole and Nyswander in 1967, with a follow-up in 1976. In the articles, they state expressly what had only been implied in their previous work. Heroin addiction, they argued, was the result of a deeper "metabolic disease" that could potentially be stabilized through pharmacological intervention. Methadone, an opiate agonist, operates basically by getting to the μ-receptor ahead of heroin and, consequently, blocking the euphoric qualities associated with the drug. It also binds to the receptor for longer periods, thereby significantly reducing withdrawal symptoms (i.e., getting "dope sick"). Without such a workaround, the authors argue, the various sticks in an addict's life—from the social risk associated with illegal use to the actual physical dangers that surround the economic activity to pay for such use—simply did not serve as sufficient deterrents to heroin use.

The prototype of urban failure (at least in the United States), the junkie, could then be redefined as a sufferer with an unfortunately altered biochemistry. As Agar (1985: 176) puts it "'dope' became 'medication,' the 'addict' became a 'patient,' and 'addiction' became 'treatment.'" Methadone arguably is more physically addictive than that for which it substitutes, but because it is tolerated while stimulating opiate receptors to a point at which heroin's pleasure is supposedly removed, this is seen to be a fair exchange between treatment and side effect. Many former addicts credit methadone with saving their lives; many others are profoundly dissatisfied with the substitution of "one addiction for another." Dole and Nyswander more or less agreed with the temporality, if not the valence, of the latter statement, expressing pessimism that an addiction based on a metabolic lesion could really be "curable," instead suggesting that long-term methadone maintenance therapy was formally closer to treating a diabetic with insulin than to someone working through a brief course of antibiotics.

Clearly, the central theoretical correlate to the "metabolic lesion" is the concept of *predisposition*. Dole and Nyswander, for example, concede that a metabolic lesion was exposed by *some* agonists, only for *some* people; thus, addiction existed at the intersection between a substance, an individual's biochemistry, and, perhaps most important, a life history. Thus, a variety of substances, according to this logic, could in theory become "addictive," and further, the possibility that any strongly rewarding activity, such as sex or gambling, was addictive "like heroin" merely awaited the development of tools sophisticated enough to show specific biochemical dynamics. Thus, while Dole seemed little concerned with the linguistic history of his population of "addicts," he would not have been surprised, it seems to me, by the seemingly precocious usage (from his point of view) of "night club addict" in the 1920s.[9]

Addiction and the Market

In the recent past, of course, corporate pharmacological interest in addiction has grown apace with the increasingly variable relationships "addiction" can form with people—from specific psychoactive substances, such as alcohol or heroin, to strongly rewarding activities, and gambling and sex and "real" rather than metaphoric hunger—that is, excessive eating leading to obesity. From the early 1980s, of course, the cause for hunger as such has been something of the "holy grail" of this research. The hope that there might be something "like methadone" to deal with such hunger has produced a veritable tradition of research, genealogically connected to Dole's laboratory at Rockefeller University (see Shell 2003).

I am in firm agreement with Emily Martin (among other scholars) that the market is both the macro-context of our analysis and the source of some of our most powerful metaphors in this moment of biological psychiatry. "Addict" as a noun, for example, is clearly part of the modern institutional constellation of biochemical knowledge—that is, everything from laboratory research moving from the province of gentlemen amateurs toward more industrial production models and the rise of modern medical schools to moral panics about drug use and the development of progressive legislation aimed at "protecting" the consumer. No space remains to explore the various connections between this institutional establishment and the needs of the market, but it seems clear to me at least that if in the early moment, this institutionalization was aimed at making physical workers productive (and, to be sure, as comfortable as possible)— that is, something recognizably connected to a Foucauldian disciplinary episteme—the rise of the importance of knowledge work has produced a more Deleuzian problem of control, finely tuned and closely monitored feedback cycles of self-care, situational effervescence, and the management and hierarchizing of information. This uncomfortable connection between unfortunate desire and free will is what sponsors such an explosion of interest in addiction, in the hope of getting certain people's free will, as it were, back on track: "Addiction—whether to alcohol, to drugs or even to behaviors like gambling—appears to be a complicated disorder affecting brain processes responsible for motivation, decision making, pleasure seeking, inhibitory control and the way we learn and consolidate information and experiences. This new research, in turn, is fueling a vast effort by scientists and pharmaceutical companies to develop medications and vaccines to treat addiction. The National Institute on Drug Abuse and the National Institute on Alcohol Abuse and Alcoholism are studying, or financing studies on, more than 200 addiction medications."[10] The exercise of choice, the ontological basis of the market, then, produces bad results, which in turn produces a poisonous "black" market, as well as a remedial legal market for remedies, based on an alliance of government funding and corporate capitalism. This periodization of this cycle seems to be increasing as new drugs find off-label and black markets faster (buprenorphine, for example, can appear in both new clinical trials to treat heroin dependence and be emerging as a problem drug in its own right simultaneously), and old drugs (ketamine, MDMA and its derivatives) experience periodic cycles of therapeutic interest and off-label popularity (Saris 2011).

This sense of the ubiquitous presence of the market should encourage us to be critical, but only if we understand how our own subject position as observers and critics are bound up in these processes. There is now a sort of triple-prospecting occurring in Big Pharma, a crypto-biosociality, conducted by researchers with potentially multimillion-dollar stakes in descriptively integrating an overlap between a drug, a population, and a syndrome, wherein capital can profitably be reproduced. Not surprisingly, this corporate production of pharmaceutical knowledge produces hierarchies and naturalizes certain relationships. This organization of limited technical expertise, for example, helps to explain some of the most profound health inequalities today: why we have a veritable plethora of drugs treating people in advanced industrial societies for conditions at, what I have called in other places, "the profitable edge of the clinical imaginary" (Saris 2008), while until very recently the youngest drugs to treat, say, malaria were decades old, making malaria one of the most devastating diseases in the modern world and producing yet another population available to social science—those dying of "neglected diseases." Both of these social facts are reifications, yet an analysis that stops at the essential nonnecessity of this state of affairs must substantially fail. In postcolonial literature, for example, we have models for effectively contextualizing other kinds of reifications, connected to an older mode of production (say the East India Company's role in "fixing" caste and custom in India). It seems to me that the discovery and manipulation of such modern collectivities based on the corporate organization of scientific expertise can be productively analyzed within the same sort of frame as these new forms of crypto-bio-sociality are produced within a neoliberal market.

Conclusion: The Disciplinary Stakes

Neither our language nor our theoretical courage, it seems to me, has kept up with these advances in our object of study. Note, for example, that the "communities" I have discussed exist slightly outside of the frame of bio-sociality in Rabinow's sense of the forming of associational (largely civil society) groups to influence state policy and science (Rabinow 1992). They also exceed Veena Das's reformulation of this concept, which stresses how the presence of stigmatized conditions in the domestic domain can pit family against the kinship group or local community by separating the stigmatized individual and confining him or her to various practices of social exclusion (Das 2001). What we see instead is an emerging process where a seemingly hyper-individuated psychobiology produces surprisingly anthropologically available communities in the service of equations for both governmentality and corporate planning.

In the so-called developed world, this process is clearly part of one of the main forums for the reproduction of capital in the current configuration of capitalism—that is, "lifestyle." This has resulted in an interesting split between ends and means. For example, we now talk easily about lifestyle as a commodity or as a burden, but, oddly enough, we feel less and less that it is the result of our choice. On the other hand, we do not have to look hard in our culture for certain holes in our lifestyles that we expect to fill through enlightened pharmacology—better stress relief, better ability to concentrate, perhaps better relationships between stressed couples—through, we hope, better chemistry. These compounds can be expected to exist as remedies in certain discourses (and, indeed, for certain subjects) and as dependence-producing poisons for others. Yet, both lifestyle and the targets of such chemical manipulation (legal and illegal) also appear as weakly affiliated groups who share at least some needs and, perhaps, some other traits, as well. They look a lot like groups produced around different senses of alienation and control, and, as I have argued elsewhere (Saris 2011), a renewed anthropological interest in notions of fetish (perhaps even Lukács's sense of reification) might be a way toward understanding such processes.[11] At the same time, as social scientists, we should also be able to connect the uneven proliferation of this knowledge in the so-called developed world to a ruthlessly stratified global political system, where "neglected diseases" currently form one of the largest burdens for morbidity and mortality.

This is not happening at the level that it should, it seems to me, because our analyses and our critiques of biopsychiatry and Big Pharma often fail to distinguish between our commitment to will/choice (a viable ethical-political stance, provided it is consciously articulated) and how the contours of our thinking have been *committed* to (seized by) "choice" in the abstract. The latter stance smuggles in a standard average subject—deracinated, genderless, disembodied, disengaged from material conditions (from specific forms of work to the specifics of neurochemistry)—and, of course, a subject without history. This phantom, of course, vitiates the essential insight that mind-bodies and social relations make systems of meaning, power, and knowledge, which make mind-bodies and social relations, which make systems of meaning, power, and knowledge. In the absence of being able to provide an alternate embodied subjectivity to the standard average subject, even the predisposition model looks like it takes embodied historical context more seriously.

My point is that we are emerging into a moment in which cutting-edge research into biochemistry and psychopharmacology is surprisingly condign with an old, almost hoary anthropological postulate: the seeing eye is the organ of tradition. In other, less elegant phrasing: the physical apparatus, its scope and its field, emerges, within the broad band of human variation, in concrete contexts that are historically and materially produced. This is an old idea that Franz Boas had all the way back in "On Alternating Sounds" (1889) that preceded and in some sense formed the condition of the possibility of the culture concept (whose modern usage in English, by the way, emerges surprisingly in lockstep with the use of "addict" as a noun). Phenomena such as hearing and sight are constructed, and to this precise extent they become "real" in the sense of belonging to a particular embodied subject in concrete social-historical circumstances. This should give us some hope for understanding and perhaps improving our current condition, but we also need to understand the stakes involved.

The potential of the new biochemistry of addiction and a sophisticated theoretical treatment of the same phenomena to refract out these issues is very promising. The hyperproduction of will in cosmetic pharmacology and its complete absence in the biopsychological production of addiction can be seen as a sort of experimental moment for our understanding of the liberal subject. It is the same sort of productive conundrum that Bukowski sets for any potential interlocutor. This interrogation of the liberal subject will not give simple answers to questions such as "Where is poetry?" and, still less, to "What is will?" Instead, it will provide the necessary terms with which to engage an understanding of power in the ubiquity of what we might call mind-body in this moment. Its appetites, its interior states, the legitimate scope for its rescripting (and, therefore, its proper functions), its benchmarks (life, death, age-appropriate activities), and its new pathologies are at once implicated in new forms of subjectivity and new forms of aesthetics, as well as emerging as one of the main sources of developing economic value. We have stakes in this interaction as both citizens and researchers, but the rules of each of these games are increasingly different, and we pretend that they are not at the peril of both our analyses and our ability to effect change in the world.

Thus, an anthropology of the modern moment needs a sense for the ubiquity of these modes in several spheres of social life, not as separate issues, but as the social-material context of an increasingly shared modernity. As anthropologists, we need to engage with subject positions—good and bad—that this new moment throws up. Most importantly, we have to understand that "construction" works at the level of biology as much as it does at any other level, and, of course, that discursive ruptures could in principle be initiated by radically (re)visioned bodies and their horizon of possibilities as easily as they can be initiated by the discursive production of epistemic breaks. In this sense, drugs and new forms of gene therapy, among other interventions, could function as what Deleuze and Guattari (1987: 306) call a "quality," that is, "a line of de-territorialization of an assemblage, or [a means of] going from one assemblage to another," not just at an individual but a social level, as well. These interventions that potentially fundamentally reformulate the locus of choice are now increasingly available in a social formation that fetishizes "choice" as such. An anthropology of the modern moment needs to understand its commitments in this field as a precondition of its analysis, never mind its critique.

Notes

Versions of this work were presented at the Anthropology Seminar Series, National University of Ireland, Maynooth, in 2010, and at the Mind, Medicine, and Culture seminar series, University of California, Los Angeles. I am grateful for insightful comments I received at both sessions. Any mistakes and omissions are my own.

1. I am using "gift" in a natural language sense here. Of course, Marcel Mauss (1967 [1924]) finds all of these different aspects of reciprocity in the gift as a condition of it serving as a "total social fact." For Cohen, the stress in most Western countries on organ transplantation being a freely given, generally anonymous gift; the difficulty of broaching the subject of a market for organs; and the media attention paid to actual cases of illegal seizure tend to magnify such differences in the analysis of this phenomenon.

2. Think of the rhetorical positions around the statement that "all heterosexual relationships in patriarchy are rape" attributed at various times to Andrea Dworkin and Catherine MacKinnon: see http://www.snopes.com/quotes/mackinnon .asp.

3. "Legalizing Drugs Would Produce a Social Disaster," *Body Parts*, August 30, 2007, available online at http://shroudedindoubt.typepad.com/bodyparts/2007/08/le galizing-dr-1.html.

4. Here I am thinking of Durkheim's understanding of the relationship between law and law breaking.

5. See, among many others, Cole 1998; Derrida 1993; Lilienfeld and Oxford 1999; Sedgwick 1993. The noun "addiction," of course, has a much longer history, going back to Roman law. It meant a state of dedication or of swearing over increasingly, as Rome developed, to work off debts, often those one had accrued through gambling (see Schüll 2006, this volume). Again, though, one needs to get to the nineteenth century to find self-evidently pejorative uses, such as, "A man who causes grief to his family by addiction to bad habits": John Stuart Mill, *On Liberty* (1859), chap. 4, available online at http://www.bartleby.com/130. There is, of course, a critical literature that attacks the modern understanding of addiction from the perspective that it makes wrongheaded, "medicalized," or "therapeutic" excuses for bad decisions: see Courtwright 2005; Peele 1989, 2000; Rieff 1987. In my terms, these critiques are all made from a commitment to will/choice, but their theoretical usefulness is often vitiated by how naively their thinking is committed to will/choice.

6. This was one of the first anti-papal tracts to appear in English. Frith also translated continental Reformation writings into vernacular Scots: see Herbert Samworth, "John Frith: Forging the English Reformation," Sola Scriptura website, available online at http://www.solagroup.org/articles/historyofthebible/hotb_ 0011.html.

7. Compare this with the treatment of "belief" in Good 1994.

8. This idea is developed in an earlier moment in anthropology in Bailey 1971.

9. Philosophically, of course, the split can only be provisional between a "drug" addict and an "[insert activity here]" addict. John Searle and other contributors to *The Mystery of Consciousness* (1997) outline some of the peculiarities of the subject statement "I have a pain." These issues also pertain to the sensation states (and their representations) for the drug-using body. Like analyses of pain, we seek objective signatures to determine the nature of an experience while bypassing the particular locus of that experience. Whatever shape these "experience graphs"

will take, they will not quite have the sense of remove that Susan Sontag (2003) sees in photographs of war. They will be paired with their normalized counterpart at some point—theoretical endpoints in a therapeutic continuum that will have an interesting relationship to time—showing not just a "damaged" brain but the brain that hides a flaw that becomes apparent only after connection with an environmental insult. Joseph Dumit (2004) has driven the analysis of these technologies in anthropology.

10. Benoit Denizet-Lewis, "An Anti-addiction Pill?," *New York Times*, June 25, 2006, available online at http://www.nytimes.com.

11. Georg Lukács, "Reification and the Consciousness of the Proletariat," 1923, available online at http://www.marxists.org/archive/lukacs/works/history/hcc05 .htm.

FOLLOWING *ADDICTION TRAJECTORIES*

This volume enables us to look at the concept of addiction with ethnographic and historical eyes. We not only come to grasp the culturally entrenched (and hence often invisible) defining assumptions that permit the concept of addiction to do its work, but we also learn to see the distinct forms this powerful concept has taken in different times and places. The three trajectories that organize the volume—the epistemic, therapeutic, and experiential—work effectively separately and together. More often than not, the volume indicates how they intertwine. Every case study reveals motion and change in how the concept of addiction has been used and defined, how it has been treated, and how it is experienced. This is all the more remarkable an achievement in light of the common association of "addiction" with a person who is in the grip of an inexorable force, held rigidly in place. The tension captured in these essays between the poles of a condition involving fixity and the constant change in all social lives is what allows the book to make one of its most important contributions: showing how the figure of the addict confounds the liberal subject, that autonomous and free individual prominent in Euro-American culture since seventeenth-century liberal democratic theory and essential to most Western social-science explanation. The concept of the addict confounds the possibility of being a particular kind of person, the possibility of being an individual who is owner of himself and his capacities and independent of his surrounding social context.

The Will

Addiction has been memorably termed a "disease of the will," but maladies of the will are also central to many other mental conditions. In psychiatric parlance, too little will can tip a person into depression or addiction, and too much will can play a part in a person becoming manic or narcissistic. There is no question that losing control of one's will is one of the most dreaded psychiatric fates: psychotic separation from one's desires or inability to identify them are conditions that threaten dominant conceptions of rationality and personhood at their core.

The sciences of the mind have tried to define the proper degree of the will since the mid-nineteenth century, always in connection with the particular political and economic contexts surrounding them. For example, the models of mind promulgated by American behaviorist psychologists in the early twentieth century made subjects look like robots following the dictates of authoritarian structures. After the Second World War, implicitly looking for ways to distinguish open-minded and free-thinking Americans from the conforming masses of the Soviet Union, theories of how American minds worked had a different political dimension, arguing that "democratic people exhibit open-minded, tolerant, and flexible minds while authoritarian people are closed-minded and rigid" (Cohen-Cole 2005: 111). Marking "themselves as open-minded and behaviorists as authoritarian ideologues," they could defend their own thinking and simultaneously model how all humans think (Cohen-Cole 2005: 107). These investigators, opening up the field of cognitive science, looked to computers for "a model of autonomous human cognitive processes" (Cohen-Cole 2005: 125). The mind became imagined as a reasoning machine, operating flexibly in response to constantly changing environments. The will was dissolved into a multitude of well-calculated decisions.

Following a different historical trajectory, post-Soviet citizens struggling with alcohol found appeal in a materialist view of addiction therapies that did not insist on transformations in self-perception. The therapies left the self autonomous and thus could act as "prostheses for the will" (Raikhel, this volume). As the authors of the foregoing chapters show for Eastern European and North African migrants to France, Puerto Rican Pentecostal evangelists, U.S. support communities, rehabilitation centers, laboratories, courts, penal institutions, casinos, and pharmaceutical companies, the specific model of the addicted mind or brain that captivates people in any of these settings relies on broader cultural values that inform concepts of the ideal person and society.

The late twentieth-century move to find a biological mechanism in the brain to account for addiction, frequently encountered in the foregoing chapters, draws—in the case of the United States, at least—on a desire to insist that normal psychological functioning is free from authoritarian constraint. If a person becomes unable to resist the "authority" of a drug or the pull of a compulsive activity, that person must have a different kind of mind—which is to say, brain—that lacks the capacity to be creative, flexible, and constantly adaptive, now deemed the essential qualities of human nature. There is a certain compatibility between the idea that a free and flexible mind is an essential feature of modern democratic states and the robust growth of biological models of mental processes. Biological models can distract attention from social contexts. The stronger the appeal of the individual will, with full autonomy, free choice, and agency, the more it is possible to imagine that social structures—the state, the law, regulatory agencies—are only a hindrance to the individual's potential because they promote dependence. Seeing how "addict" takes its meaning from social contexts helps us to realize that all conceptions of personhood, even the liberal subject, are similarly indebted to the social contexts surrounding them.

Weakening of Social Fabric

Early in their training, cultural anthropologists learn from Durkheim's classic work that there "can be no full-fledged person standing apart from the 'moral,' as instituted in some historically constituted social setting" (Fields 1995: lv). This is an argument best made by demonstrating how social interactions constitute the person in particular settings, rather than from first principles, as this volume does in grand style. The authors are rightfully wary of ways biological models of addiction can erode understandings of social processes; at the same time, they are careful to allow that biological models of addiction can change social attitudes in ameliorative ways. For example, substantiating the biological basis of addiction can enable more people to regard addiction as a medical disorder that can be treated like any other medical disorder. Nonetheless, the authors clarify the most persistent logic of biological explanations of addiction, which is to place social processes at the feet of the brain. Seen as brain disorders, addictions are disease entities with specifiable physical locations, forms, and signatures. In this volume, we learn that addictions take shape as contingent outcomes that emerge from specific social settings in particular times and places.

Biological Categories

Anthropologists have long recognized that social categories that describe human beings (whether they result from ritual practices or scientific findings) have a way of affecting the perceptions of the persons so categorized. This means that when medical or biological sciences define a category such as "the addict" or "a person who is addicted," the category does not fly out like an arrow and strike the affected persons or groups into immobility. Rather, the process of categorization entails the likelihood that people will be "living under the description of" a category such as "addict." This "living under" is a complex social reality that involves some rigid and coercive aspects and some malleable and interpretive aspects. The process can be rigid and coercive: to be accepted into treatment programs, whether medical or legal, may require that one be labeled an "addict." The process can be malleable and interpretive: living under the description category of "addict" can mean many different things to different people. To live under the description of a social category, whatever its source, is to enter a world of experience in which daily life and interactions with others are colored in particular ways. Moreover, the person who has been living under the description of "addict" may reenter the clinic, the laboratory, or the therapeutic community bearing these social processes, and "looping back," to use Hacking's felicitous phrase, change circumstances at the category's point of origin (Hacking 1995). The rich case studies in this volume make clear how inadequate the distinction between compliance and noncompliance is. The person categorized is not passive, and the category is not stable. Being compliant is not a passive state, and being noncompliant is not the only way to be active. The biology of addiction can lead to new forms of self-identification as people actively engage with biological claims that we are our brains. Even Francis Crick's "Astonishing Hypothesis"—that "'you,' your joys and your sorrows, your memories and your ambitions, your sense of personal identity and free will, are in fact no more than the behavior of a vast assembly of nerve cells and their associated molecules"—can be taken up in creative ways that negate Crick's premise.

This volume demonstrates that the brain can do many kinds of work in the enterprises of self-making surrounding addiction. Some anthropologists who focus on the importance of social connections might want to question the ways people use the brain, ways that assume that neuronal-level processes can translate directly into social-level processes. We might wonder whether the neurological self some people imagine and desire around their addictions can be considered less rich and complex in its social dimensions than others. If we wanted to work toward changing the view that neuronal processes can be crystalline building blocks for social processes such as addiction, we would have to understand much more about why the brain-based view appeals to so many people. Are they sensing and trying to avoid new ways to govern that depend on our increasing knowledge of neural states? Are they clinging to the hope of self-actualization through choice and to a fantasy of individual uniqueness? Perhaps the self-making project that sees culture and brain as made up of the same sort of material is just as "social," just as "cultural," as a less reductive, more heterogeneous one. At the least, it is clear that the brain of someone living under the description of addiction is a plural thing, in cultural terms. The brain is an organ that is generating many kinds of self-making projects, even for the presumably will-disordered addict.

Contingencies

This volume makes plain the multiple forces—political, economic, medical, scientific, social, and legal—that come together or fail to come together in the course of making specific social categories under the heading of addiction. The conclusion that these forces always take hold in particular social milieux applies very widely. Another category, disorders of attention, could be said to be a close cousin of addiction. In the course of my research into the history of attention disorders, I was given a large box of materials accumulated during the career of a sales representative for Ciba-Geigy, the company that developed the stimulant drug methylphenidate, which came to be marketed as Ritalin. In the box, I found a set of films made by Ciba-Geigy (now merged with Sandoz in the corporation Novartis). In the 1970s, Ciba-Geigy sent thousands of copies of the film to doctors around the country to educate them about how to identify a malady they called minimum brain dysfunction (MDB). In the soundtrack of the film, during which two small boys interact with a doctor wearing a white coat, we hear doctors being taught the criteria for a new disorder of the brain. The narrator describes the standard neurological finger-to-nose test and says that it can reveal the signs of MDB. The doctor holds up his finger and asks the first boy to touch the doctor's finger and then his own nose. The boy touches his nose with the fingers of alternating hands and then laughs. The following dialogue ensues:

Doctor: Are you angry?

Boy: Yes.

Doctor: Why are you angry? [*Boy swings his hand aggressively.*] Can you say? [*Boy hits at doctor's hand with his hand.*]

Doctor: What are you angry about? OK, you want to give a sock? Give it a sock. [*The boy waves arms around, hits the doctor's hand, then recoils in pain, having hurt his own hand.*]

Doctor: Oh, boy—that hurt, didn't it? All right, can you try touching my finger? Now, go ahead, touch my finger, no, no touch it with your finger, don't give it a sock, that hurt. [*The boy hits at doctor's finger again, then grabs it.*]

Doctor: Touch it with your finger. Come on, now—touch your nose, touch your nose, now touch your finger—finger, nose.

The camera suddenly cuts to a different boy, who is calmly and attentively alternating between touching the doctor's finger and his own nose. The narrator summarizes: "Tests like finger-nose coordination may demonstrate the neurological deficits of minimal brain dysfunction—MBD. No special equipment is needed. When you suspect MBD, these tests should be part of your diagnostic workup, along with a comprehensive examination."

The film displays pathology (which could be described as an undisciplined will) in one boy in sharp contrast to the control and focus of a normal boy. The boy with MBD is seen as having a faulty brain that needs to be fixed with methylphenidate. What is significant is that the diagnosis "MBD" simply failed to take hold. The pharmaceutical's campaign to create the diagnosis came to naught, partly because of alarm raised by a congressional inquiry at the time in which fear was expressed about the addictive qualities of a drug (chemically similar to the amphetamines and cocaine) that would be prescribed to children. At that time, the specter of subjecting children to an addictive drug made both the diagnosis and Ciba's remedy largely unacceptable (Mayes et al 2009: 64 n. 62).[1]

In the 1980s, MBD was followed by another malady, attention deficit disorder (ADD), now expanded to attention deficit hyperactivity disorder (ADHD), used as a cover term for a host of performance problems for

children in schools and adults at work. How this happened is a complicated story that is highly differentiated by class, race, and ethnicity, but
one element, according to Lawrence Diller, was a revision of psychiatric
categories involving childhood hyperactivity by the early 1980s to greatly
broaden the group of children and adults who might qualify for the diagnosis. The line between children with 'normal' variations of temperament,
lively or spontaneous children who are sensitive to stimuli, and those who
have a 'disorder' had become increasingly blurred" (Diller 1996: 13). Diller,
a physician who is highly critical of the extent of Ritalin use in the United
States, argues that we are giving medication for a condition whose chief
trait is the failure to perform up to one's potential. We are engaged in
cosmetic psychopharmacology, done to enhance human potential. In the
current era, the specter of addiction has faded in the light of the need to
produce productive children who succeed at the disciplined kinds of behavior required by schools. But the possibility of children controlled into
discipline by an addictive drug continues to rankle. It did not take long for
the rebellious, mischievous side of the brain condition MBD, shown so
clearly in Ciba-Geigy's film, to emerge from ADHD and become a sought-
after trait. By the early 1990s, ADHD, especially when skillfully medicated,
became touted as an advantage—a talent, even—for chief executives and
political leaders. Attention deficit hyperactivity disorder underwent a dramatic revision in American middle-class culture, from being simply a
dreaded liability to being an especially valuable asset that can potentially
enhance one's life (Breeding 2003; Hartmann 1993; Palladino 1997).

Meanwhile, along similar lines, addiction, seen with a lens that draws
attention to its extreme and singular focus and its penchant for risk taking, its "hyperactive will" (Hansen, this volume), can also seem an advantage to powerful leaders and executives, as in this op-ed: "When we think
of the qualities we seek in visionary leaders, we think of intelligence,
creativity, wisdom and charisma, but also the drive to succeed, a hunger
for innovation, a willingness to challenge established ideas and practices.
. . . The risk-taking, novelty-seeking and obsessive personality traits often
found in addicts can be harnessed to make them very effective in the
workplace."[2] However much neurology and psychiatry try to stabilize the
categories of mental disorder, they bleed into each other and at times
mutate from deficits to assets. Now we have addiction bleeding into hyper
attention. In the helpful terms of this volume, the epistemic trajectory of

addiction is taking a swerve—in this case, drawing on energy from its close cousin "attention."

Addiction can also emerge from people's experience of everyday life, even when the medical community has not signaled its presence. Websites devoted to discussions among people with sleep problems abound with participants' testimony about how addictive the new prescription sleep aids (such as Ambien, Lunesta, or Sonata) are, even though drug dependence, tolerance, withdrawal, and addiction are scarcely mentioned in their advertisements and official descriptions of side effects:[3]

> I started taking Xanax about 7 years ago, then went to Ambien about 4 years ago. I thought that the little magical white pill was wonderful! What started out as short-term use turned into 4 long years of addiction to Ambien. How do I know that they are addictive? Because anytime that you would do anything to get an Ambien, panicking and not thinking you can make it through the night, then you are addicted. I literally panicked if I ran out of Ambien and forgot to get it filled. Also, Ambien or any other sleep med for that matter, builds up in your system over a period of time and you require more and more and eventually it just doesn't work anymore. . . .
>
> Hope I have helped. Please, Please, Please get off of sleeping meds. They will eventually lead to addiction, and then you have your insomnia to overcome as well as an addiction.[4]

The experience of Ambien, Sonata, or Lunesta as addictive is often a sequel of another kind of compulsion—the compulsion to work impossibly long hours, be impossibly productive, and remain impossibly flexible in the face of economic conditions that make life precarious. Sleep, in this extreme environment, comes to be defined as being inactive and unproductive for hours on end—an unaffordable luxury. At the least, if one cannot train oneself to do without it, one can corral it into predetermined hours and make sure one does it efficiently. Of course, the harder one tries to achieve sleep on demand, the more elusive it can become, and this is the entry point for drugs that promise immediate sleep with no side effects. Compelled to be a certain kind of working person, one ends up depending on a drug in a manner that some experience as addictive. This volume helps us follow and understand paradoxes like these: compelled to bend one's will to the demand for extreme productivity, one ends up enslaved.

The will is always an "uncertain achievement" (Saris, this volume). With *Addiction Trajectories* as our guide, we are well equipped to understand the category of addiction as a social achievement that depends on historically specific conceptions of what it means to be free.

Notes

1. Another reason was the association in the *DSM* between MDB and a psychoanalytic concept on the verge of going out of style: "hyperkinetic reaction of childhood" (Singh 2008: 351).

2. David J. Linden, "Addictive Personality? You Might Be a Leader," *New York Times*, July 24, 2011.

3. A TV ad for Ambien from 2003 says, "Patients who abuse prescription sleep aids may become dependent." An ad for Ambien CR in 2009 (after generic zolpidem was available) prints in faint letters at the bottom of the screen, "It has some risk of dependency."

4. Posted at Sleepnet.com, March 22, 1999, available online at http://www.sleepnet.com/insomnia2/messages/549.html (accessed November 12, 2005).

REFERENCES

Abbott, Max W. 2006. "Do EGMS and Problem Gambling Go Together Like a Horse and Carriage?" *Gambling Research* 18 (1): 7–38.

Acker, Caroline Jean. 2002. *Creating the American Junkie: Addiction Research in the Classical Era of Narcotic Control*. Baltimore: Johns Hopkins University Press.

Addolorato, Giovanni, Lorenzo Leggio, Ludovico Abenavoli, et al. 2006. "Baclofen in the Treatment of Alcohol Withdrawal Syndrome: A Comparative Study versus Diazepam." *American Journal of Medicine* 119 (3): 276.e13–18.

Agar, Michael. 1973. *Ripping and Running: A Formal Ethnography of Urban Heroin Addicts*. New York: Seminar.

———. 1985. "Folks and Professionals: Different Models for the Interpretation of Drug Use." *International Journal of the Addictions* 20 (1): 173–82.

Agar, Michael, Philippe Bourgois, John French, et al. 2001. "Buprenorphine: 'Field Trials' of a New Drug." *Qualitative Health Research* 11 (1): 69–84.

Alcoholics Anonymous. 1939. *Alcoholics Anonymous: The Story of How Many Thousands of Men and Women Have Recovered from Alcoholism*. New York: Works Publishing.

Altschul, Sol. 1968. "Denial and Ego Arrest." *Journal of the American Psychoanalytic Association* 16 (1968): 301–18.

Ameisen, Olivier. 2005. "Naltrexone for Alcohol Dependence." *Journal of the American Medical Association* 294 (8): 899–900.

American Psychiatric Association. 1980. *Diagnostic and Statistical Manual of Mental Disorders: DSM-III*, 3rd ed. Washington, D.C.: American Psychiatric Association.

———. 1994. *Diagnostic and Statistical Manual of Mental Disorders: DSM-IV*, 4th ed. Washington, D.C.: American Psychiatric Association.

Appleby, Louis. 2000. "Drug Misuse and Suicide: A Tale of Two Services." *Addiction* 95: 175–77.

Austin, John Langshaw. 1962. *How to Do Things with Words*. Cambridge: Harvard University Press.

Babayan, Eduard A., and M. H. Gonopolsky. 1985. *Textbook on Alcoholism and Drug Abuse in the Soviet Union.* New York: International Universities Press.

Babayan, Eduard A., and Yu G. Shashina. 1985. *The Structure of Psychiatry in the Soviet Union.* New York: International Universities Press.

Babcock, Barbara, and Victor Turner. 1978. *The Reversible World: Symbolic Inversion in Art and Society.* Ithaca: Cornell University Press.

Baer, Hans, Merrill Singer, and Ida Susser. 2003. *Medical Anthropology and the World System.* Westport, Conn.: Praeger.

Bailey, Frederick G., ed. 1971. *Gifts and Poison: The Politics of Reputation.* Oxford: Blackwell.

Bakhtin, Mikhail M. 1984. *Problems of Dostoevsky's Poetics*, trans. Caryl Emerson. Minneapolis: University of Minnesota Press.

Barry, Andrew. 2005. "Pharmaceutical Matters: The Invention of Informed Materials." *Theory Culture Society* 22 (1): 51–69.

Bateson, Gregory. 1972. "The Cybernetics of Self: A Theory of Alcoholism." In *Steps to an Ecology of the Mind: Collected Essays in Anthropology, Psychiatry, Evolution, and Epistemology.* New York: Ballantine.

Becker, Howard S. 1953. "Becoming a Marihuana User." *American Journal of Sociology* 59: 235–42.

——. 1963. *The Outsiders: Studies in the Sociology of Deviance.* New York: The Free Press.

Becker, Gay, and Sharon R. Kaufman. 1995. "Managing an Uncertain Illness Trajectory in Old Age: Patients' and Physicians' Views of Stroke." *Medical Anthropology Quarterly* 9: 165–87.

Béland, Daniel, and Randall Hansen 2000. "Reforming the French Welfare State: Solidarity, Social Exclusion and the Three Crises of Citizenship." *West European Politics* 23 (1): 47–64.

Bem, Daryl J. 1967. "Self-Perception: An Alternative Interpretation of Cognitive Dissonance Phenomena." *Psychological Review* 74 (3): 183–200.

——. 1972. *Self-Perception Theory.* New York: Academic Press.

Benedict, Marion, and Burton Benedict. 1982. *Men, Women, and Money in Seychelles.* Berkeley: University of California Press.

Benjamin, Walter. 2006. *On Hashish.* Cambridge: Harvard University Press.

Bennett, Larry, and Marie Lawson. 1994. "Barriers to Cooperation between Domestic Violence and Substance Abuse Programs." *Families in Society* 75 (5): 277–85.

Bennett, Linda A., Aleksandar Janca, Bridget F. Grant, et al. 1993. "Boundaries between Normal and Pathological Drinking: A Cross-Cultural Comparison." *Alcohol Health and Research World* 17: 190–95.

Bennett, Maxwell R., and Peter M. S. Hacker. 2003. *Philosophical Foundations of Neuroscience.* Malden, Mass.: Blackwell.

Benson, April Lane, ed. 2000. *I Shop, Therefore I Am: Compulsive Buying and the Search for Self.* Northvale, N.J.: Jason Aronson.

Benson, Peter. 2010. "Safe Cigarettes." *Dialectical Anthropology* 34 (1): 49–56.

Bernhard, Bo J. N.d. "Problem Gambling and Treatment in Nevada." Report. Available online at http://www.hr.state.nv.us/GMU/Reports/Gambling-Addiction.doc.

Berridge, V. 2001. "Altered States: Opium and Tobacco Compared." *Social Research* 68 (3): 655–75.

Berridge, Virginia, and Griffith Edwards. 1981. *Opium and the People: Opiate Use in Nineteenth-Century England*. London: St. Martin's Press.

Berthelot, Jean-Michel. 1999. "Préface." *Les règles de la méthode sociologique*. Paris: Flammarion.

Biehl, João. 2004. "Life of the Mind: The Interface of Psychopharmaceuticals, Domestic Economies, and Social Abandonment." *American Ethnologist* 31 (4): 475–96.

———. 2005. *Vita: Life in a Zone of Social Abandonment*. Berkeley: University of California Press.

———. 2010. "Human Pharmakon: Symptoms, Technologies, Subjectivities." *A Reader in Medical Anthropology: Theoretical Trajectories, Emergent Realities*, ed. Byron J. Good, Michael M. J. Fischer, Sarah S. Willen, and Mary-Jo DelVecchio Good, 213–31. West Sussex: Wiley-Blackwell.

Biehl, João, Denise Coutinho, and Ana Luzia Outeiro. 2001. "Technology and Affect: HIV/AIDS Testing in Brazil." *Culture, Medicine and Psychiatry* 25: 87–129.

Biehl, João, and Torben Eskerod. 2007. *Will to Live: AIDS Therapies and the Politics of Survival*. Princeton: Princeton University Press.

Biehl, João, Byron Good, and Arthur Kleinman, eds. 2007. *Subjectivity: Ethnographic Investigations*. Berkeley: University of California Press.

Biehl, João, and Peter Locke. 2010. "Deleuze and the Anthropology of Becoming." *Current Anthropology* 51: 317–51.

Block, Jerald J. 2008. "Issues for DSM-V: Internet Addiction." *American Journal of Psychiatry* 165 (3): 306.

Boas, Franz. 1889. "On Alternating Sounds." *American Journal of Psychology* 2 (3): 508.

Bobrova, Natalia, Ron Alcorn, Tim Rhodes, et al. 2007. "Injection Drug Users' Perceptions of Drug Treatment Services and Attitudes toward Substitution Therapy: A Qualitative Study in Three Russian Cities." *Journal of Substance Abuse Treatment* 33: 373–78.

Boltanski, Luc. 1968. *La découverte de la maladie. La diffusion du savior medical*. Paris: Centre de Sociologie Européenne.

Boothroyd, Dave. 2006. *Culture on Drugs: Narco-cultural Studies of High Modernity*. Manchester: Manchester University Press.

Bordreuil, Jean-Samuel, Raphaël Sage, and Gilles Suzanne. 2003. *Marseille et ses moments musicaux: Villes et scenes musicales*. Paris: Ministère de la Culture.

Borges, Jorge Luis. 1998. *Collected Fictions*. New York: Penguin Putnam.

Borovoy, Amy. 2001. "Recovering from Codependence in Japan." *American Ethnologist* 28 (1): 94–118.

———. 2005. *The Too-Good Wife: Alcohol, Codependency, and the Politics of Nurturance in Postwar Japan*. Berkeley: University of California Press.

Borrell, Jennifer. 2008. "A Thematic Analysis Identifying Concepts of Problem Gambling Agency: With Preliminary Exploration of Discourses in Selected Industry and Research Documents." *Journal of Gambling Studies* 22: 195–217.

Bourdieu, Pierre. 1986. "The Forms of Capital." *Handbook of Theory and Research for the Sociology of Education*, ed. John Richardson, 241–58. Westport, Conn.: Greenwood.

Bourgois, Philippe. 1995. *In Search of Respect: Selling Crack in el Barrio*. Cambridge: Cambridge University Press.

———. 2000. "Disciplining Addictions: The Bio-politics of Methadone and Heroin in the United States." *Culture, Medicine, and Psychiatry* 24 (2): 165–95.

———. 2007. "Intimate Apartheid: Ethnic Dimensions of Habitus among Homeless Heroin Injectors." *Ethnography* 8 (1): 7–31.

Bourgois, Philippe, Mark Lettiere, and James Quesada. 1997. "Social Misery and the Sanctions of Substance Abuse: Confronting HIV Risk among Homeless Heroin Addicts in San Francisco." *Social Problems* 44: 155–73.

Bourgois, Philippe, and Jeffrey Schonberg. 2009. *Righteous Dopefiend*. Berkeley: University of California Press.

Bozarth, Michael. 1990. "Drug Addiction as a Psychobiological Process." *Addiction Controversies*, ed. David M. Warburton, 112–34. London: Harwood Academic.

Brandes, Stanley H. 2002. *Staying Sober in Mexico City*. Austin: University of Texas Press.

Breeding, John. 2003. *The Wildest Colts Make the Best Horses: Defending the Development of Spirited Young People*. Essex: Chipmunka Publishing.

Breen, Robert B., and M. Zimmerman. 2002. "Rapid Onset of Pathological Gambling in Machine Gamblers." *Journal of Gambling Studies* 18 (1): 31–43.

Breiter, Hans C., Itzhak Aharon, and Daniel Kahnemann. 2001. "Functional Imaging of Neural Responses to Expectancy and Experience of Monetary Gains and Losses." *Neuron* 30: 619–39.

Brewer, Colin, Robert J. Meyers, and Jon Johnsen. 2000. "Does Disulfiram Help to Prevent Relapse in Alcohol Abuse?" *CNS Drugs* 14 (5): 329–41.

Brewer, Devon D., Richard F. Catalano, Kevin Haggerty, et al. 1998. "A Meta-analysis of Predictors of Continued Drug Use during and after Treatment for Opiate Addiction." *Addiction* 93 (1): 73–92.

Brodie, Janet Farrell, and Marc Redfield, eds. 2002. *High Anxieties: Cultural Studies in Addiction*. Berkeley: University of California Press.

Bruce, R. Douglas, Sergey Dvoryak, Laurie Sylla, et al. 2007. "HIV Treatment Access and Scale-Up for Delivery of Opiate Substitution Therapy with Buprenorphine for IDUs in Ukraine: Program Description and Policy Implications." *International Journal of Drug Policy* 18 (4): 326–28.

Brusco, Elizabeth. 1995. *The Reformation of Machismo*. Austin: University of Texas Press.

Buchman, Daniel Z., Judy Illes, and Peter B. Reiner. 2011. "The Paradox of Addiction Neuroscience." *Neuroethics* 4 (2): 65–77.

Bucknam, William. 2007. "Suppression of Symptoms of Alcohol Dependence and Craving Using High-Dose Baclofen." *Alcohol and Alcoholism* 42 (2): 158–60.

Bukowski, Charles. 1983. *Tales of Ordinary Madness*. San Francisco: City Lights Books.

Burke, Kenneth. 1969. *A Grammar of Motives*. Berkeley: University of California Press.

Butler, Judith. 2004. *Precarious Life: The Powers of Mourning and Violence*. London: Verso.

Cain, Carole. 1991. "Personal Stories: Identity Acquisition and Self-Understanding in Alcoholics Anonymous." *Ethos* 19 (2): 210–53.

Calloway, Paul. 1992. *Soviet and Western Psychiatry: A Comparative Study*. Keighley, Yorkshire: Moor Press.

Camí, Jordi, and Magí Farré. 2003. "Drug Addiction." *New England Journal of Medicine* 348 (10): 375–86.

Campbell, Nancy D. 2000. *Using Women: Gender, Drug Policy, and Social Justice*. New York: Routledge.

———. 2007. *Discovering Addiction: The Science and Politics of Substance Abuse Research*. Ann Arbor: University of Michigan Press.

———. 2010. "Towards a Critical Neuroscience of Addiction." *BioSocieties* 5 (1): 89–104.

Campbell, Nancy, J. P. Olsen, and Luke Walden. 2008. *The Narcotic Farm: The Rise and Fall of America's First Prison for Drug Addicts*. New York: Abrams.

Carr, E. Summerson. 2006. "'Secrets Keep You Sick': Metalinguistic Labor in a Drug Treatment Program for Homeless Women." *Language in Society* 35 (5): 631–53.

———. 2009. "Anticipating and Inhabiting Institutional Identities." *American Ethnologist* 36 (2): 317–36.

———. 2011. *Scripting Addiction: The Politics of Therapeutic Talk and American Sobriety*. Princeton: Princeton University Press.

Carr, E. Summerson, and Yvonne Smith. N.d. "The Poetics of Therapeutic Practice: Motivation Interviewing and the Powers of Pause." Unpublished manuscript.

CASA (The National Center on Addiction and Substance Abuse) at Columbia University. 2001. "Shoveling Up: The Impact of Substance Abuse on Federal, State, and Local Budgets." Report, January.

CASAA (Center on Alcoholism, Substance Abuse, and Addictions). 1998. Motivational interviewing professional training videotape series B, phase I, part 2. Albuquerque, N.M.

Castel, Robert. 1981. *La gestion des risques*. Paris: Les Editions du Minuit.

———. 2009. *La montée des incertitudes: Travail, protections, status de l'individu*. Paris: La Découverte.

Castellani, Brian. 2000. *Pathological Gambling: The Making of a Medical Problem*. Albany: State University of New York Press.

Center for a Healthy Maryland. 2007. "Improving Patient Access to Buprenorphine Treatment through Physician Offices in Maryland." Report, June.

Center for Substance Abuse Treatment. 2006. "Diversion and Abuse of Buprenorphine: A Brief Assessment of Emerging Indicators." Report, December. Available online at http://buprenorphine.samhsa.gov (accessed July 2, 2008).

Centers for Disease Control. 2001. "Basic Statistics—Ten States/Territories and Cities Reporting the Highest Number of AIDS Cases." Available online at www.cdc .gov/hiv/stats/topten.htm (accessed June 6, 2003).

Chafetz, Morris E. 1997 (1959). "Practical and Theoretical Considerations in the Psychotherapy of Alcoholism." *Essential Papers on Addiction*, ed. Daniel L. Yalisove, 20: 315–24. New York: New York University Press.

Chatterji, Roma. 1988. "An Ethnography of Dementia." *Culture, Medicine, and Psychiatry* 22 (3): 355–82.

Chen, Kevin, and Denise B. Kandel. 1995. "The Natural History of Drug Use from Adolescence to the Mid-Thirties in a General Population Sample." *American Journal of Public Health* 85 (1): 41–47.

Cheng, Anne Anlin. 2001. *The Melancholy of Race.* New York: Oxford University Press.

Chepurnaya, Olga, and Alexander Etkind. 2006. "Instrumentalizatsiia smerti: Uroki antialkogol'noi terapii" [The instrumentalization of death: Lessons of an anti-alcohol therapy]. *Otechestvennyie Zapiski* 2 (27): 201–13.

Chertok, Leon. 1981. *Sense and Nonsense in Psychotherapy: The Challenge of Hypnosis.* London: Pergamon.

Childress, Anna R., Ronald N. Ehrman, Ze Wang, et al. 2008. "Prelude to Passion: Limbic Activation by 'Unseen' Drug and Sexual Cues." *PLOS ONE* 3 (1): e1506.

Cioran, Emil. 1992. *Anathemas and Admiration.* London: Quartet.

Cleary, Edward R., and Hannah Stewart-Gambino, ed. 1997. *Power, Politics, and Pentecostals in Latin America.* Boulder, Colo.: Westview Press.

Code, Lorraine. 1995. *Rhetorical Spaces: Essays on Gendered Locations.* New York: Routledge.

Cohen, Lawrence. N.d. "Commitment." Paper presented at the Anthropology Guest Lecturer Series, National University of Ireland, Maynooth.

——. 1999. "Where It Hurts: Indian Material for an Ethics of Organ Transplantation." *Daedalus* 128 (4): 135–65.

Cohen-Cole, Jamie. 2005. "The Reflexivity of Cognitive Science: The Scientist as Model of Human Nature." *History of the Human Sciences* 18 (4): 107–39.

Cole, Cheryl L. 1998. "Addiction, Exercise, and Cyborgs: Technologies of Deviant Bodies." *Sport and Postmodern Times*, ed. Geneviève Rail, 261–75. Albany: State University of New York Press.

Collier, Stephen J., and Andrew Lakoff. 2005. "On Regimes of Living." *Global Assemblages: Technology, Politics, and Ethics as Anthropological Problems*, ed. Aihwa Ong and Stephen J. Collier, 22–39. Malden, Mass.: Blackwell.

Collier, Stephen J., and Aihwa Ong. 2005. "Global Assemblages, Anthropological Problems." *Global Assemblages: Technology, Politics, and Ethics as Anthropological Problems*, ed. Aihwa Ong and Stephen J. Collier, 3–21. Malden, Mass.: Blackwell.

Colson, Elizabeth, and Thayer Scudder. 1988. *For Prayer and Profit: The Ritual, Economic, and Social Importance of Beer in Gwembe District, Zambia, 1950–1982.* Stanford: Stanford University Press.

Comaroff, Jean, and John Comaroff. 2006. *Law and Disorder in the Postcolony.* Chicago: University of Chicago Press.

Conférence de Consensus. 2004. "Stratégies thérapeutiques pour les personnes dépendantes des opiacés: place des traitements de substitution." *Textes des recommendations*, 44. Lyon: Agence Nationale d'Accréditation et d'Évaluation de la Santé and Fédération Française d'Addictologie.

Corbin, Juliet, and Anselm L. Strauss. 1987. "Accompaniments of Chronic Illness: Changes in Body, Self, Biography, and Biographical Time." *Sociology of Health Care*, vol. 6, ed. Julius Roth and Peter Conrad, 249–82. Greenwich, Conn.: JAI Press.

Courtwright, David T. 1997. "The Prepared Mind: Marie Nyswander, Methadone Maintenance, and the Metabolic Theory of Addiction." *Addiction* 92 (3): 257–65.

———. 2001a. *Dark Paradise: A History of Opiate Addiction in America*, 2nd ed. Cambridge: Harvard University Press.

———. 2001b. *Forces of Habit: Drugs and the Making of the Modern World.* Cambridge: Harvard University Press.

———. 2005. "Mr. ATOD's Wild Ride: What Do Alcohol, Tobacco, and Other Drugs Have in Common?" *The Social History of Alcohol and Drugs* 20: 105–40.

———. 2009. "The NIDA Brain-Disease Paradigm: History, Resistance, and Spinoffs." Keynote address, Addiction, the Brain, and Society Conference, Emory University, Atlanta, February 26–28.

Cox, Harvey. 1994. *Fire from Heaven: The Rise of Pentecostal Spirituality and the Reshaping of Religion in the Twenty-First Century.* New York: Addison-Wesley Publishing Company.

Critchlow, Patricia. 2000. "First Steps: AA and Alcoholism in Russia." *Current History* 99 (639): 345–49.

Dackis, Charles, and Charles O'Brien, 2005. "Neurobiology of Addiction: Treatment and Public Policy Ramifications." *Nature Neuroscience* 8 (11): 1431–36.

Das, Veena. 2000. "The Act of Witnessing: Violence, Poisonous Knowledge, and Subjectivity." *Violence and Subjectivity*, ed. Veena Das, Arthur Kleinman, Mamphela Ramphele, and Pamela Reynolds, 205–55. Berkeley: University of California Press.

———. 2001. "Stigma, Contagion, Defect: Issues in the Anthropology of Public Health." Paper presented at Stigma and Global Health: Developing a Research Agenda, Bethesda, Md., September 5–7. Available online at http://www.stigma conference.nih.gov/FinalDasPaper.htm.

Das, Veena, and Ranendra K. Das. 2007. "How the Body Speaks: Illness and the Lifeworld among the Urban Poor." *Subjectivity: Ethnographic Investigations*, ed. João Biehl, Byron Good, and Arthur Kleinman, 66–97. Berkeley: University of California Press.

Davidson, Virginia. 1977. "Psychiatry's Problem with No Name: Therapist-Patient Sex." *American Journal of Psychoanalysis* 37 (1977): 43–50.

de Certeau, Michel. 1988. *The Practice of Everyday Life*, vol. 1. Berkeley: University of California Press.

Deleuze, Gilles. 2007. "Two Questions on Drugs." *Two Regimes of Madness*, ed. David Lapoujade, 151–55. Cambridge: MIT Press.

Deleuze, Gilles, and Félix Guattari. 1987. *A Thousand Plateaus: Capitalism and Schizophrenia*, trans. Brian Massumi. Minneapolis: University of Minnesota Press.

Denzin, Norman K. 1993. *The Alcoholic Society: Addiction and Recovery of the Self.* New Brunswick, N.J.: Transaction.

De Quincey, Thomas. 1822. *Confessions of an English Opium Eater.* http://supervert.com/elibrary/thomas_de_quincey.

Derby, Karen. 1992. "Some Difficulties in the Treatment of Character-Disordered Addicts." *The Chemically Dependent: Phases of Treatment and Recovery*, ed. Barbara C. Wallace, 115–26. New York: Psychology Press.

Derrida, Jacques. 1981. "Plato's Pharmacy." *Dissemination*, ed. Barbara Johnson, 61–171. Chicago: University of Chicago Press.

———. 1993. "The Rhetoric of Drugs." *differences* 5: 1–25.

———. 1995. *Points . . . Interviews, 1974–1994.* Stanford: Stanford University Press.

Desjarlais, Robert. 1997. *Shelter Blues: Sanity and Selfhood among the Homeless.* Philadelphia: University of Pennsylvania Press.

———. 2003. *Sensory Biographies: Lives and Deaths among Nepal's Yolmo Buddhists.* Berkeley: University of California Press.

Dickerson, Mark. 2003. "Exploring the Limits of Responsible Gambling: Harm Minimization or Consumer Protection?" *Gambling Research* 15: 29–44.

Dietler, Michael. 2006. "Alcohol: Anthropological/Archaeological Perspectives." *Annual Review of Anthropology* 35: 229–49.

Dietz, James. 1986. *Economic History of Puerto Rico: Institutional Change and Capitalist Development.* Princeton: Princeton University Press.

———. 2003. *Puerto Rico: Negotiating Development and Change.* Boulder, Colo.: Lynne Rienner.

Diller, Lawrence H. 1996. "The Run on Ritalin: Attention Deficit Disorder and Stimulant Treatment in the 1990s." *Hastings Center Report* 26: 12–18.

Dingel, Molly, and Barbara A. Koenig. 2008. "Tracking Race in Addiction Research." *Revisiting Race in a Genomic Age*, ed. Barbara A. Koenig, Sandra Soo-Jin Lee, and Sarah S. Richardson, 172–200. New Brunswick, N.J.: Rutgers University Press.

Dole, Vincent P., and Marie E. Nyswander. 1967. "Heroin Addiction: A Metabolic Disease." *Archives of Internal Medicine* 120: 19–24.

———. 1976. "Methadone Maintenance Treatment: A Ten-Year Perspective." *Journal of the American Medical Association* 235: 2117–19.

Douglas, Mary. 1987. *Constructive Drinking: Perspectives on Drink from Anthropology.* Cambridge: Cambridge University Press.

Dovzhenko, Alexander R., A. F. Artemchuk, Z. N. Bolotova, et al. 1988. "Stressopsikhoterapiia bol'nikh alkogolizmom v ambulatornykh usloviiakh" [Outpatient stress psychotherapy of patients with alcoholism]. *Zhurnal Nevropatologii i Psikhiatrii Imeni S. S. Korsakova* 88 (2): 94–97.

Doweiko, Harold. 1996. *Concepts of Chemical Dependency.* Pacific Grove, Calif.: Brooks/Cole.

Dowty, Rachel. 2008. "The Boundaries between Your Brain and Me: Mental Categories in the Cognitive Neurosciences." PhD diss., Rensselaer Polytechnic Institute, Troy, N.Y.

Duff, Cameron. 2011. "Reassembling (Social) Contexts: New Directions for a Sociology of Drugs." *International Journal of Drug Policy* 22 (6): 404–6.

Dumit, Joseph. 2002. "Drugs for Life." *Molecular Interventions* 2: 124–27.

——. 2003. "Is It Me or My Brain? Depression and Neuroscientific Facts." *Journal of Medical Humanities* 24 (1): 35–47.

——. 2004. *Picturing Personhood: Brain Scans and Biomedical Identity*. Princeton: Princeton University Press.

——. 2012. *Drugs for Life: How Pharmaceutical Companies Define Our Health*. Durham: Duke University Press.

Durkheim, Émile. 1995 (1912). *The Elementary Forms of Religious Life*, trans. Karen E. Fields. Glencoe, Ill.: Free Press.

Dyck, Erika. 2008. *Psychedelic Psychiatry: LSD from Clinic to Campus*. Baltimore: Johns Hopkins University Press.

Eber, Christina E. 1995. *Women and Alcohol in a Highland Maya Town: Water of Hope, Water of Sorrow*. Austin: University of Texas Press.

Ebright, Malcolm. 1994. *Land Grants and Law Suits in Northern New Mexico*. Albuquerque: University of New Mexico Press.

Ecks, Stefan, and Soumita Basu. 2009. "The Unlicensed Lives of Antidepressants in India: Generic Drugs, Unqualified Practitioners, and Floating Prescriptions." *Transcultural Psychiatry* 46 (1): 86–106.

Eggert, Kurt. 2004. "Truth in Gaming: Toward Consumer Protection in the Gaming Industry." *Maryland Law Review* 63: 217–86.

Egorov, V. F. 1997. "O sostoianii narkologicheskoi sluzhby v Rossii i problemakh ee sovershenstvovaniia" [On the state of the narcological service in Russia and problems of its improvement]. *Voprosy Narkologii* 1: 9–18.

Ehrenberg, Alain. 1995. *L'individu incertain*. Paris: Hachette Littératures.

Elovich, Richard, and Ernest Drucker. 2008. "On Drug Treatment and Social Control: Russian Narcology's Great Leap Backwards." *Harm Reduction Journal* 5: 23.

Eneanya, Dennis I., Joseph R. Bianchine, Dumar O. Duran, et al. 1981. "The Actions and Metabolic Fate of Disulfiram." *Annual Reviews in Pharmacology and Toxicology* 21 (1): 575–96.

Eng, David L., and David Kazanjian. 2003. *Loss: The Politics of Mourning*. Berkeley: University of California Press.

Entin, Gennadii M. 1991. "Eshche raz k voprosu o stresspsikhoterapii alkogolizma po metodu A. R. Dovzhenko" [More remarks on the problem of stress psychotherapy of alcoholism by the A. R. Dovzhenko method]. *Zhurnal Nevropatologii i Psikhiatrii Imeni S. S. Korsakova* 91: 132–33.

Entin, Gennadii M., A. G. Gofman, A. V. Grazhenskii, et al. 1997. "O sovremennom sostaianii narkologicheskoi pomoshchi v rossii" [On the contemporary state of narcological help in Russia]. *Voprosy Narkologii* 1: 68–76.

Epstein, Joan F., and Joseph C. Gfroerer. 1997. *Heroin Abuse in the United States.* Rockville, Md.: Office of Applied Studies, Substance Abuse and Mental Health Services Administration.

Etkind, Alexander M. 1997. "There Are No Naked Thoughts: Psychoanalysis, Psychotherapy, and Medical Psychology in Russia." *Psychology in Russia: Past, Present, Future,* ed. Elena L. Grigorenko, Patricia Ruzgis, and Robert J. Sternberg, 59–82. Hauppauge, N.Y.: Nova.

Everitt, Barry J., and Trevor W. Robbins. 1992. "Amygdala-Ventral Striatal Interactions and Reward-Related Processes." *The Amygdala: Neurobiological Aspects of Emotion, Memory and Mental Disfunction,* ed. John P. Aggleton, 421–29. New York: Wiley.

Fairbanks, Robert P., II. 2009. *How It Works: Recovering Citizens in Post-welfare Philadelphia.* Chicago: University of Chicago Press.

Fassin, Didier. 2001. "The Biopolitics of Otherness: Undocumented Foreigner and Racial Discrimination in French Public Debate." *Anthropology Today* 17 (1): 3–7.

———. 2005. "Compassion and Repression: The Moral Economy of Immigration Policies in France." *Cultural Anthropology* 20 (3): 362–87.

———. 2009. "Another Politics of Life Is Possible." *Theory, Culture, and Society* 26 (5): 44–60.

Fatseas, Mélina, and Marc Auriacombe. 2007. "Why Buprenorphine Is So Successful in Treating Opiate Addiction in France." *Current Psychiatry Reports* 9 (5): 358–64.

Ferentzy, Peter. 2001. "From Sin to Disease: Differences and Similarities between Past and Current Conceptions of Chronic Drunkenness." *Contemporary Drug Problems* 28: 363–74.

Feroni, Isabelle, and Anne M. Lovell. 2007. "Les dispositifs de regulation publique d'un medicament sensible: Le cas du Subutex, traitement de substitution aux opiaces." *Revue Française des Affaires Sociales* 61 (3): 153–65.

Fewell, Christine H., and Leclair Bissell. 1978. "The Alcohol Denial Syndrome: An Alcohol-Focused Approach." *Social Casework* 59: 6–13.

Fields, Karen. 1995. "Translator's Introduction." *The Elementary Forms of Religious Life,* by Emile Durkheim. New York: Free Press.

Fiellin, David A., and Patrick G. O'Connor. 2002. "New Federal Initiatives to Enhance the Medical Treatment of Opioid Dependence." *Annals of Internal Medicine* 137 (8): 688–92.

Fischer, Michael. 1999. "Worlding Cyberspace: Toward a Critical Ethnography in Time, Space, and Theory." *Critical Anthropology Now: Unexpected Contexts, Shifting Constituencies, Changing Agendas,* ed. George E. Marcus, 245–304. Santa Fe: School of American Research Press.

———. 2001. "Emergent Forms of Life, Ethical Plateux, Risk Society, and Deep Plays: Technoscience and Social Critique." Paper presented at the Annual Meeting of the Society for the Social Studies of Science, Cambridge, Mass., November 1–4.

———. 2003. *Emergent Forms of Life and the Anthropological Voice.* Durham: Duke University Press.

Fiske, John. 1988. *Television Culture.* New York: Routledge.

Flavin, Jeanne. 2009. *Our Bodies, Our Crimes: The Policing of Women's Reproduction in America.* New York: New York University Press.

Fleck, Ludwik. 1979 (1935). *Genesis and Development of a Scientific Fact.* Chicago: University of Chicago Press.

Fleming, Philip M., Artak Meyroyan, and I. Klimova. 1994. "Alcohol Treatment Services in Russia: A Worsening Crisis." *Alcohol and Alcoholism* 29 (4): 357–62.

Fliegelman, Jay. 1993. *Declaring Independence: Jefferson, Natural Language, and the Culture of Performance.* Stanford: Stanford University Press.

Flores, Phillip J. 1997a. *Group Psychotherapy with Addicted Populations: An Integration of Twelve-Step and Psychodynamic Theory,* 2nd ed. New York: Psychology Press.

——. 1997b. "Psychoanalytic Considerations of the Etiology of Compulsive Drug Use." *Essential Papers on Addiction,* ed. Daniel L. Yalisove, 87–108. New York: New York University Press.

Foddy, Bennett, and Julian Savulescu. 2010. "A Liberal Account of Addiction." *Philosophy, Psychiatry, and Psychology* 17 (1): 1–22.

Foucault, Michel. 1965. *Madness and Civilization: A History of Insanity in the Age of Reason.* New York: Pantheon.

——. 1966. *Les mots et les choses.* Paris: Éditions Gallimard.

——. 1984. "What Is Enlightenment?" *The Foucault Reader,* ed. Paul Rabinow, 32–50. New York: Random House.

——. 1988. "Technologies of the Self." *Technologies of the Self: A Seminar with Michel Foucault,* ed. Luther H. Martin, Huck Gutman, and Patrick H. Hutton, 16–49. Amherst: University of Massachusetts Press.

——. 1990. *The History of Sexuality, Volume 3: The Care of the Self.* New York: Vintage.

Frank, Arthur W. 1997. *The Wounded Storyteller: Body, Illness, and Ethics.* Chicago: University of Chicago Press.

Franklin, Sarah. 2000. "Life Itself: Global Nature and the Genetic Imaginary." *Global Nature, Global Culture,* ed. Sarah Franklin, Celia Lury, and Jackie Stacey, 188–227. London: Sage.

Fraser, Nancy, and Linda Gordon. 1994. "A Genealogy of 'Dependency': Tracing a Keyword of the U.S. Welfare State." *Signs* 19 (2): 309–36.

Freud, Anna. 1937. *The Ego and the Mechanisms of Defense.* London: Hogarth.

Freud, Sigmund. 1938. "An Outline of Psycho-analysis." *The Standard Edition of the Complete Psychological Works of Sigmund Freud,* ed. James Strachey, 23: 144–207. London: Hogarth.

——. 1955 (1939). *Moses and Monotheism.* New York: Vintage.

——. 1960 (1923). *The Ego and the Id.* New York: W. W. Norton.

——. 1961 (1920). *Beyond the Pleasure Principle.* New York: W. W. Norton.

——. 1973 (1926). "Inhibitions, Symptoms, and Anxiety." *The Standard Edition of the Complete Psychological Works of Sigmund Freud,* ed. James Strachey, 20: 75–175. London: Hogarth.

——. 1989 (1917). "Mourning and Melancholia." *The Freud Reader*, ed. Peter Gay, 584–85. New York: W. W. Norton.

Friedman, Lawrence. 1993. *Crime and Punishment in American History*. New York: Basic.

Frith, John. 1529. "A Pistle to the Christen Reader: The Revelation of Antichrist; Antithesis, wherein Are Compared Togeder Christes Actes and Oure Holye Father the Popes." In *The Whole Works of W. Tyndall, John Frith, and Dr. Barnes, Three Worthy Martyrs*, 3 vols. London: Walter H. Parker Society.

Gandhi, Devang H., Jerome H. Jaffe, Scot McNary, et al. 2003. "Short-Term Outcomes after Brief Ambulatory Opioid Detoxification with Buprenorphine in Young Heroin Users." *Addiction* 98: 453–62.

Gandhi, Devang H., Greg J. Kavanagh, and Jerome H. Jaffe. 2006. "Young Heroin Users in Baltimore: A Qualitative Study." *American Journal of Drug and Alcohol Abuse* 32: 177–88.

Garcia, Angela. 2010. *The Pastoral Clinic: Addiction and Dispossession along the Rio Grande*. Berkeley: University of California Press.

Gardner, Richard. 1970. *¡Grito! Reies Tijerina and the New Mexico Land Grant War of 1967*. New York: Harper Colophon.

Garland, David. 2001. *The Culture of Control: Crime and Social Order in Contemporary Society*. Chicago: University of Chicago Press.

Garriott, William. 2011. *Policing Methamphetamine: Narcopolitics in Rural America*. New York: New York University Press.

Garro, Linda. 1992. "Chronic Illness and the Construction of Narrative." *Pain as Human Experience: An Anthropological Perspective*, ed. Mary-Jo DelVecchio Good, Paul E. Browdin, Byron Good, and Arthur Kleinman, 100–37. Berkeley: University of California Press.

Gaudillère, Jean-Paul. 2005. "Introduction: Drug Trajectories." *Studies in History, Biology, Philosophy, and Biomedical Sciences* 36: 603–22.

GLS Research. 1995. "1994 Clark County Resident's Study: Survey of Leisure Activities and Gaming Behavior." Report for the Las Vegas Convention and Visitors Authority.

——. 2009. "2008 Clark County Resident's Study: Survey of Leisure Activities and Gaming Behavior." Report for the Las Vegas Convention and Visitors Authority.

Golub, Alex, and Kate Lingley. 2008. "'Just Like the Qing Empire': Internet Addiction, MMOGs, and Moral Crisis in Contemporary China." *Games and Culture* 3 (1): 59.

Gomart, Emilie. 2002. "Methadone: Six Effects in Search of a Substance." *Social Studies of Science* 32 (1): 93–135.

——. 2004. "Surprised by Methadone: In Praise of Drug Substitution Treatment in a French Clinic." *Body and Society* 10 (2–3): 85.

Gomez, Laura E. 1997. *Misconceiving Mothers: Legislators, Prosecutors, and the Politics of Prenatal Drug Exposure*. Philadelphia: Temple University Press.

Gonzales, Phillip. 2003. "Struggle for Survival: The Hispanic Land Grants of New Mexico, 1848–2001." *Agricultural History* 77 (2): 293–324.

Good, Byron J. 1977. "The Heart of What's the Matter: The Semantics of Illness in Iran." *Culture, Medicine, and Psychiatry* 1 (1): 25–58.

———. 1994. *Medicine, Rationality, and Experience.* Cambridge: Cambridge University Press.

Good, Byron J., Carla Manchira, Nida Ul Hasanat, et al. 2010. "Is 'Chronicity' Inevitable for Psychotic Illness? Studying Heterogeneity in the Course of Schizophrenia in Yogyakarta, Indonesia." *Chronic Conditions, Fluid States: Chronicity and the Anthropology of Illness,* ed. Lenore Manderson and Carolyn Smith-Morris, 54–76. New Brunswick, N.J.: Rutgers University Press.

Good, Byron J., Subandi, and Mary-Jo DelVecchio Good. 2007. "The Subject of Mental Illness: Psychosis, Mad Violence, and Subjectivity in Indonesia." *Subjectivity: Ethnographic Investigations,* ed. João Biehl, Byron J. Good, and Arthur Kleinman, 243–72. Berkeley: University of California Press.

Goodman, Robert. 1995. *The Luck Business: The Devastating Consequences and Broken Promises of America's Gambling Explosion.* New York: Free Press.

Gootenberg, Paul. 2008. *Andean Cocaine: The Making of a Global Drug.* Chapel Hill: University of North Carolina Press.

Gordon, Colin. 1991. "Governmental Rationality: An Introduction." *The Foucault Effect: Studies in Governmentality,* ed. Graham Burchell, Colin Gordon, and Peter Miller, 1–52. Chicago: University of Chicago Press.

Gorski, Terrence. 2000. *Denial Management Counseling Professional Guide: Advanced Clinical Skills.* New York: Herald Publishing.

Graham, Loren R. 1987. *Science, Philosophy, and Human Behavior in the Soviet Union.* New York: Columbia University Press.

Grant, Jon E., Suck Won Kim, and Marc N. Potenza. 2003. "Advances in the Pharmacological Treatment of Pathological Gambling." *Journal of Gambling Studies* 19 (1): 85–109.

Grant, Jon E., Marc N. Potenza, Eric Hollander, et al. 2006. "Multicenter Investigation of the Opioid Antagonist Nalmefene in the Treatment of Pathological Gambling." *American Journal of Psychiatry* 163 (2): 303–12.

Greene, Jeremy A. 2004. "Therapeutic Infidelities: 'Noncompliance' Enters the Medical Literature, 1955–1975." *Social History of Medicine* 17 (3): 327–43.

Gremillion, Helen. 2001. "In Fitness and in Health: Crafting Bodies in the Treatment of Anorexia Nervosa." *Signs* 27 (2): 381–414.

Griffiths, Mark. 1993. "Fruit Machine Gambling: The Importance of Structural Characteristics." *Journal of Gambling Studies* 9 (2): 101–20.

———. 1999. "Gambling Technologies: Prospects for Problem Gambling." *Journal of Gambling Studies* 15 (3): 265–83.

Gusfield, Joseph R. 1996. *Contested Meanings: The Construction of Alcohol Problems.* Madison: University of Wisconsin Press.

Hacking, Ian. 1975. *Why Does Language Matter to Philosophy?* New York: Cambridge.

———. 1992. "'Style' for Historians and Philosophers." *Studies in History and Philosophy of Science* 23: 1–20.

———. 1995. "The Looping Effects of Human Kinds." *Causal Cognition: A Multidisci-plinary Debate*, ed. Dan Sperber, David Premack, and Ann James Premack, 351–83. New York: Oxford University Press.

———. 2002. *Historical Ontology*. Cambridge: Harvard University Press.

Haddad, P. M. 2001 "Antidepressant Discontinuation Syndromes: Clinical Relevance, Prevention and Management." *Drug Safety* 24 (3): 183–97.

Hald, Jens, and Erik Jacobsen. 1948. "A Drug Sensitizing the Organism to Ethyl Alcohol." *Lancet* 2 (26): 1001–4.

Hamid, Ansley, Richard Curtis, Kate McCoy, et al. 1997. "The Heroin Epidemic in New York City: Current Status and Prognoses." *Journal of Psychoactive Drugs* 29 (4): 375–91.

Hansen, Helena. 2005. "Isla Evangelista, a Story of Church and State: Puerto Rico's Faith-Based Initiatives in Drug Treatment." *Culture, Medicine, and Psychiatry* 29 (4): 433–56.

Hansen, Helena, Carole Siegel, Brady Case, et al. n.d. "Buprenorphine and Methadone in New York City: Two Tiers of Treatment?" Unpublished manuscript.

Harrington, Anne. 2006. "The Many Meanings of the Placebo Effect: Where They Came From, Why They Matter." *Biosocieties* 1 (2): 181–93.

———. 2008. *The Cure Within: A History of Mind–Body Medicine*. New York: W. W. Norton.

Hartmann, Thom. 1993. *Attention Deficit Disorder: A Different Perception*. Grass Valley, Calif.: Underwood.

Hazelden Foundation, ed. 1975. *Dealing with Denial*. Center City, Minn.: Hazelden.

Heath, Dwight B. 1958. "Drinking Patterns of the Bolivian Camba." *Quarterly Journal of Studies on Alcohol* 19: 491–508.

———. 1987. "Anthropology and Alcohol Studies: Current Issues." *Annual Reviews in Anthropology* 16: 99–120.

———. 2004. "Camba (Bolivia) Drinking Patterns: Changes in Alcohol Use, Anthropology, and Research Perspectives." *Drug Use and Cultural Contexts "Beyond the West": Tradition, Change, and Post-colonialism*, ed. Ross Coomber and Nigel South, 119–36. London: Free Association Books.

Heimer, Robert, Michael Merson, Kevin Irwin, et al. 2007. "HIV and Drug Use in Eurasia." *HIV/AIDS in Russia and Eurasia*, vol. 1, ed. Judyth L. Twigg, 141–64. New York: Palgrave Macmillan.

Herzberg, David. 2009. *Happy Pills in America: From Miltown to Prozac*. Baltimore: Johns Hopkins University Press.

Heyman, Gene M. 2009. *Addiction: A Disorder of Choice*. Cambridge: Harvard University Press.

Hill, Jane H. 2000. "'Read My Article': Ideological Complexity and the Overdetermination of Promising in American Presidential Politics." *Regimes of Language: Ideologies, Polities, and Identities*, ed. Paul V. Kroskrity, 259–91. Santa Fe: School of American Research Press.

Horn, David. 2003. *The Criminal Body: Lombroso and the Anatomy of Deviance*. New York: Routledge.

Hser, Yih-Ing, Douglas Longshore, and M. Douglas Anglin. 2007. "The Life Course Perspective on Drug Use: A Conceptual Framework for Understanding Drug Use Trajectories." *Evaluation Review*, 31: 515–47.

Human Rights Watch. 2006. *Rhetoric and Risk: Human Rights Abuses Impeding Ukraine's Fight against HIV/AIDS*. New York: Human Rights Watch.

Hunt, Alan. 2003. "Risk and Moralization in Everyday Life." *Risk and Morality*, ed. Richard V. Erickson and Aaron Doyle, 165–92. Toronto: University of Toronto Press.

Hunt, Geoffrey, and Judith C. Barker. 2001. "Socio-cultural Anthropology and Alcohol and Drug Research: Towards a Unified Theory." *Social Science and Medicine* 53: 165–88.

Hyde, Sandra. 2011. "Migrations in Humanistic Therapy: Turning Drug Users into Patients and Patients into Healthy Citizens in Southwest China." *Body and Society* 17 (2–3): 183–204.

Hyman, Steven E. 2005. "Addiction: A Disease of Learning and Memory." *American Journal of Psychiatry* 162 (8): 1414–22.

———. 2007. "The Neurobiology of Addiction: Implications for Voluntary Control of Behavior." *American Journal of Bioethics* 7 (1): 8–11.

Ialovoi, A. Ia. 1968. "Zamena alkogol'no-antabusnoi probyi pri lechenii alkogolizma platsebo" [Substitution of the alcohol-antabuse test with a placebo in the treatment of alcoholism]. *Zhurnal Nevropatologii i Psikhiatrii Imeni S. S. Korsakova* 68: 593–96.

Insel, Thomas R., and Remi Quirion. 2005. "Psychiatry as a Clinical Neuroscience Discipline." *Journal of the American Medical Association* 294 (17): 2221–24.

Irvine, Judith. 1989. "When Talk Isn't Cheap: Language and Political Economy." *American Ethnologist* 16 (2): 248–67.

Ivanets, Nikolai N. 2001. "Sovremennaia kontseptsiia terapii narkologicheskikh zobolevanii" [Contemporary conceptions of therapy for addictive disorders]. *Lektsii po narkologii* [Lectures on addiction medicine], ed. Nikolai N. Ivanets, 105–16. Moscow: Medica.

Jackson, Jean. 2005. "Stigma, Liminality, and Chronic Pain: Mind–Body Borderlands." *American Ethnologist* 32 (3): 332–53.

Jacobs, Durand F. 1988. "Evidence for a Common Dissociative-Like Reaction among Addicts." *Journal of Gambling Behavior* 4: 27–37.

———. 2000. "Response to Panel: Jacob's General Theory of Addiction." The eleventh International Conference on Gambling and Risk-Taking, Las Vegas, June 12–16.

Jaffe, Jerome, and Charles O'Keeffe. 2003. "From Methadone Clinics to Buprenorphine: Regulating Opioid Agonist Treatment in the United States." *Drug and Alcohol Dependence* 20 (2): S3–S11.

Jain, Sumeet, and Sushrut Jadhav. 2009. "Pills That Swallow Policy: Clinical Ethnography of a Community Mental Health Program in Northern India." *Transcultural Psychiatry* 46 (1): 60–85.

James, William. 1890. *The Principles of Psychology*. New York: Henry Holt and Company.

Jameson, Fredric. 2004. "The Politics of Utopia." *New Left Review* 25: 35–54.

Jasinski, Donald R., Jeffrey S. Pevnick, and John D. Griffith. 1978. "Human Pharmacology and Abuse Potential of the Analgesic Buprenorphine." *Archives of General Psychiatry* 35 (4): 501–16.

Jernigan, David H. 1997. *Thirsting for Markets: The Global Impact of Corporate Alcohol*. San Rafael, Calif.: Marin Institute for the Prevention of Alcohol and Other Drug Problems.

Johnsen, Jon, and Jorg Morland. 1992. "Depot Preparations of Disulfiram: Experimental and Clinical Results." *Acta Psychiatrica Scandinavica* 86 (s369): 27–30.

Johnson, Rolley E., Eric C. Strain, and Leslie Amass. 2003. "Review: Buprenorphine, How to Use It Right." *Drug and Alcohol Dependence* 70: s59–s77.

Johnson, Vernon. 1980. *I'll Quit Tomorrow: A Practical Guide to Alcoholism Treatment*. New York: Harper and Row.

Johnston, Lloyd D., Patrick M. O'Malley, Jerald G. Bachman, et al. 2009. "Monitoring the Future National Results on Adolescent Drug Use: Overview of Key Findings, 2008." National Institutes of Health publication no. 09-7401, National Institute on Drug Abuse, Bethesda, Md.

Joravsky, David. 1989. *Russian Psychology: A Critical History*. London: Blackwell.

Joseph, Herman, Sharon Stancliff, and John Langrod. 2000. "Methadone Maintenance Treatment (MMT): A Review of Historical and Clinical Issues." *Mount Sinai Journal of Medicine* 67 (5–6): 347–64.

Kalivas, Peter W., and Nora D. Volkow. 2005. "The Neural Basis of Addiction: A Pathology of Motivation and Choice." *American Journal of Psychiatry* 162 (8): 1403–13.

Kaufman, Edward. 1992. "Countertransference and Other Mutually Interactive Aspects of Psychotherapy with Substance Abusers." *American Journal on Addictions* 1 (3): 185–202.

——. 1994. *Psychotherapy of Addicted Persons*. New York: Guilford.

Keane, Helen. 2002. *What's Wrong with Addiction?* Melbourne: Melbourne University Publishing.

Keane, Helen, and Kelly Hamill. 2010. "Variations in Addiction: The Molecular and the Molar in Neuroscience and Pain Medicine." *Biosocieties* 5 (1): 52–69.

Kearney, Robert J. 1996. *Within the Wall of Denial: Conquering Addictive Behaviors*. New York: W. W. Norton.

Keller, Mark. 1972. "On the Loss-of-Control Phenomenon in Alcoholism." *British Journal of Addiction* 67 (3): 153–66.

Kenna, George A., John E. McGeary, and Robert M. Swift. 2004. "Pharmacotherapy, Pharmacogenomics, and the Future of Alcohol Dependence Treatment, Part 1." *American Journal of Health-System Pharmacy* 61 (21): 2272–79.

Kilpatrick, Dean G., Ron Acierno, Heidi S. Resnick, et al. 1997. "A Two-Year Longitudinal Analysis of the Relationships between Violent Assault and Substance Use in Women." *Journal of Consulting and Clinical Psychology* 65 (5): 834–47.

Kirmayer, Laurence J. 2006. "Toward a Medicine of the Imagination." *New Literary History* 37 (3): 583–605.

Kirmayer, Laurence J., and Ian Gold. 2012. "Re-socializing Psychiatry: Critical Neuroscience and the Limits of Reductionism." *Critical Neuroscience: A Handbook of the Social and Cultural Contexts of Neuroscience*, ed. Suparna Choudhury and Jan Slaby. Chichester, West Sussex: Wiley-Blackwell.

Kirmayer, Laurence J., and Eugene Raikhel. 2009. "From Amrita to Substance D: Psychopharmacology, Political Economy, and Technologies of the Self." *Transcultural Psychiatry* 46 (1): 5–15.

Kitanaka, Junko. 2008. "Diagnosing Suicides of Resolve: Psychiatric Practice in Contemporary Japan." *Culture, Medicine, and Psychiatry* 32 (2): 152–76.

Kleinman, Arthur. 2006. *What Really Matters: Living a Moral Life amidst Uncertainty and Danger.* Oxford: Oxford University Press.

Kline, Stephen A., and Eddie Kingstone. 1977. "Disulfiram Implants: The Right Treatment but the Wrong Drug?" *Canadian Medical Association Journal* 116 (12): 1382–83.

Klingemann, Harald. 2001. "The Time Game: Temporal Perspectives of Patients and Staff in Alcohol and Drug Treatment." *Time and Society* 10: 303–28.

Knorr-Cetina, Karin. 1999. *Epistemic Cultures.* Cambridge: Harvard University Press.

Kohrmann, Matthew, and Peter Benson. 2011, "Tobacco." *Annual Review of Anthropology* 40: 329–44.

Kosek, Jake. 2006. *Understories: The Political Life of Forests in Northern New Mexico.* Durham: Duke University Press.

Kunitz, Stephen J., Jerrold E. Levy, and Tracy J. Andrews. 1994. *Drinking Careers: A Twenty-Five-Year Study of Three Navajo Populations.* New Haven: Yale University Press.

Kushner, Howard I. 2006. "Taking Biology Seriously: The Next Task for Historians of Addiction?" *Bulletin of the History of Medicine* 80 (1): 115–43.

———. 2010. "Toward a Cultural Biology of Addiction." *Biosocieties* 5 (1): 8–24.

Ladd-Taylor, Molly, and Lauri Umanksy, eds. 1998. *"Bad" Mothers: The Politics of Blame in Twentieth-Century America.* New York: New York University Press.

Lakoff, Andrew. 2006. *Pharmaceutical Reason: Knowledge and Value in Global Psychiatry.* Cambridge: Cambridge University Press.

Lalander, Philip. 2003. *Hooked on Heroin: Drugs and Drifters in a Globalized World.* Oxford: Berg.

Laplanche, Jean, and Jean-Bertrand Pontalis. 1973. *The Language of Psycho-analysis,* trans. Donald Nicholson-Smith. New York: W. W. Norton.

Lauterbach, Wolf. 1984. *Soviet Psychotherapy.* London: Pergamon.

LeDoux, Joseph E. 1992. "Emotion and the Amygdala." *The Amygdala: Neurobiological Aspects of Emotion, Memory, and Mental Dysfunction,* ed. John P. Aggleton, 339–51. New York: Wiley-Liss.

LeDoux, Joseph E., Lizabeth Romanski, and Andrew Xagoris. 1989. "Indelibility of Sub-cortical Emotional Memories." *Journal of Cognitive Neuroscience* 1 (3): 238–43.

Lee, Sing. 1999. "Diagnosis Postponed: Shenjing Shuairuo and the Transformation of Psychiatry in Post-Mao China." *Culture, Medicine, and Psychiatry* 23 (3): 349–80.

Lemanski, Michael. 2001. *History of Addiction and Recovery in the United States.* Tucson, Ariz.: Sharp.

Le Marcis, Frederic. 2004. "The Suffering Body of the City," trans. Judith Inggs. *Public Culture* 16 (3): 453–77.

Lemke, Thomas. 2000. "Foucault, Governmentality, and Critique." Paper presented at the Rethinking Marxisim Conference, Amherst, Mass., September 21–24.

Lende, Daniel H. 2005. "Wanting and Drug Use: A Biocultural Approach to the Analysis of Addiction." *Ethos* 33 (1): 100–24.

———. 2012. "Addiction and Neuroanthropology." *The Encultured Brain*, ed. Daniel H. Lende and Greg Downey, 339–62. Cambridge: MIT Press.

Leon, David A., Lyudmila Saburova, Susannah Tomkins, et al. 2007. "Hazardous Alcohol Drinking and Premature Mortality in Russia: A Population Based Case-Control Study." *Lancet* 369: 2001–9.

Leshner, Alan I. 1997. "Addiction Is a Brain Disease, and It Matters." *Science* 278 (5335): 45.

Lesieur, Henry, and Richard Rosenthal. 1991. "Pathological Gambling: A Review of the Literature." *Journal of Gambling Studies* 7 (1): 5–39.

Levine, Harry G. 1978. "The Discovery of Addiction. Changing Conceptions of Habitual Drunkenness in America." *Journal of Studies on Alcohol* 39: 143–74.

Lilienfeld, Jane, and Jeffrey Oxford. 1999. *The Languages of Addiction.* New York: St. Martin's Press.

Lindesmith, Alfred R. 1938. "A Sociological Theory of Drug Addiction." *American Journal of Sociology* 43: 593–613.

Lindquist, Galina. 2005. *Conjuring Hope: Magic and Healing in Contemporary Russia.* New York: Berghahn.

Livingstone, Charles, and Richard Woolley. 2007. "Risky Business: A Few Provocations on the Regulation of Electronic Gaming Machines." *International Gambling Studies* 7 (3): 361–76.

Lock, Margaret, and Vinh-Kim Nguyen. 2010. *An Anthropology of Biomedicine.* Malden, Mass.: Wiley-Blackwell.

Lovell, Anne M. 2001. "Ordonner les risques: L'individual et le pharmaco-sociatif face à l'injection de drogues." *Critique de la santé publique: Une approche anthropologique*, ed. Jean-Pierre Dozon and Didier Fassin, 309–41. Paris: Balland.

———. 2006. "Addiction Markets: The Case of High-Dose Buprenorphine in France." *Global Pharmaceuticals: Ethics, Markets, Practices*, ed. Adriana Petryna, Andrew Lakoff, and Arthur Kleinman, 136–70. Durham: Duke University Press.

Lovell, Anne M., and Sandrine Aubisson. 2008. "'Fuitage pharmaceutique,' usages détournés et reconfigurations d'un médicament de substitution aux opiacés ["Pharmaceutical leakage," diversion and the reconfiguration of a pharmaceutical for opiate substitution]. *Drogues, Santé et Société* 7 (1): 297–355.

Lovell, Anne M., and Isabelle Feroni. 1998. "'Sida-toxicomanie': Un objet hybride de la nouvelle santé publique" [AIDS-drug addiction: A hybrid object of the new public health]. *Les figures urbaines de la santé publique. Enquêtes sur des expériences locales* [The urban figures of public health: Investigations of local experiences], ed. Didier Fassin, 203–38. Paris: La Découverte.

———. 2005. "Medicalizing Drug Treatment in France: The Normalization of an Addiction Pharmaceutical." *1er congrès international sur la chaîne du médicament (30 Août–2 Septembre 2005),* edited by Francine Dufort and Anne-Laure Saives, 299–308. Montréal: GEIRSO (Groupe d'étude sur l'interdisciplinarité et les représentations sociales), 2006.

Lovern, John D. 1991. *Pathways to Reality: Erickson-Inspired Treatment Approaches to Chemical Dependency.* Philadelphia: Brunner/Mazel.

Lowinson, Joyce H., Pedro Ruiz, Robert B. Millman, et al. 2005. *Substance Abuse: A Comprehensive Textbook.* Philadelphia: Lippincott Williams and Wilkins.

Lowney, Kathleen S. 1999. *Baring Our Souls: TV Talk Shows and the Religion of Recovery.* New York: Aldine deGruyter.

Luhrmann, Tanya M. 2000. *Of Two Minds: The Growing Disorder in American Psychiatry.* New York: Alfred A. Knopf.

———. 2004. "Metakinesis: How God Becomes Intimate in Contemporary U.S. Christianity." *American Anthropologist* 106 (3): 518–28.

———. 2007. "Social Defeat and the Culture of Chronicity: Or, Why Schizophrenia Does So Well over There and So Badly Here." *Culture, Medicine, and Psychiatry* 31: 135–72.

MacAndrew, Craig, and Robert B. Edgerton. 1969. *Drunken Comportment: A Social Explanation.* Boston: Walter De Gruyter.

Maclean, Paul D. 1952. "Some Psychiatric Implications of Physiological Studies on the Fronto-temporal Portion of the Limbic System (Visceral Brain)." *Electroencephalography and Clinical Neurophysiology* 4: 407–18.

MacNeil, Ray. 2009. "Government as Gambling Regulator and Operator: The Case of Electronic Gambling Machines." *Casino State: Legalized Gambling in Canada,* ed. James F. Cosgrave and Thomas Klassen, 140–60. Toronto: University of Toronto Press.

Mäkelä, Klaus, Ilkka Arminen, Kim Bloomfield, et al. 1996. *Alcoholics Anonymous as a Mutual-Help Movement: A Study in Eight Societies.* Madison: University of Wisconsin Press.

Malcolm, M. T., J. S. Madden, and A. E. Williams. 1974. "Disulfiram Implantation Critically Evaluated." *British Journal of Psychiatry* 125 (588): 485–89.

Malins, Peta. 2004. "Machinic Assemblages: Deleuze, Guattari, and an Ethico-aesthetics of Drug Use." *Janus Head* 7 (1): 84–104.

Mandelbaum, David G. 1965. "Alcohol and Culture." *Current Anthropology* 6 (3): 281–93.

Mann, Karl. 2004. "Pharmacotherapy of Alcohol Dependence: A Review of the Clinical Data." *CNS Drugs* 18 (8): 485–504.

Marcus, George E. 1995. "Ethnography in/of the World System: The Emergence of Multi-sited Ethnography." *Annual Review of Anthropology* 24: 95–117.

Marks, Harry. 1997. *The Progress of Experiment: Science and Therapeutic Reform in the United States, 1900–1990.* New York: Cambridge University Press.

Marsch, Lisa A., Warren K. Bickel, Gary J. Badger, et al. 2005. "Buprenorphine Treatment for Opioid Dependence: The Relative Efficacy of Daily, Twice and Thrice Weekly Dosing." *Drug and Alcohol Dependence* 77: 195–204.

Marshall, Mac. 1979. *Weekend Warriors: Alcohol in a Micronesian Culture*. Palo Alto, Calif.: Mayfield.

———. 1982. *Through a Glass Darkly: Beer and Modernization in Papua New Guinea*. Boroko, Papua New Guinea: Institute of Applied Social and Economic Research.

Marshall, Mac, Genevieve M. Ames, and Linda A. Bennett. 2001. "Anthropological Perspectives on Alcohol and Drugs at the Turn of the New Millennium." *Social Science and Medicine* 53 (2): 153–64.

Marshall, Mac, and Leslie B. Marshall. 1990. *Silent Voices Speak: Women and Prohibition in Truk*. Florence, Ken.: Wadsworth.

Martensen-Larsen, Oluf. 1948. "Treatment of Alcoholism with a Sensitizing Drug." *Lancet* 2 (6539): 1004.

Martin, Emily. 2004. "Taking the Measure of Moods." Paper presented at the Annual Meeting of the Society for Social Studies of Science, Paris, August.

———. 2006. "The Pharmaceutical Person." *Biosocieties* 1 (3): 273–87.

———. 2007. *Bipolar Expeditions: Mania and Depression in American Culture*. Princeton: Princeton University Press.

Matthews, J. Rosser. 1995. *Quantification and the Quest for Medical Certainty*. Princeton: Princeton University Press.

Matza, Tomas. 2009. "Moscow's Echo: Technologies of the Self, Publics, and Politics on the Russian Talk Show." *Cultural Anthropology* 24 (3): 489–522.

Mauss, Marcel. 1967 (1924). *The Gift: Forms and Functions of Exchange in Archaic Societies*. New York: W. W. Norton.

May, Carl. 2001. "Pathology, Identity, and the Social Construction of Alcohol Dependence." *Sociology* 35 (2): 385–401.

Mayes, Rick, Catherine Bagwell, and Jennifer Erkulwater. 2009. *Medicating Children: ADHD and Pediatric Mental Health*. Cambridge: Harvard University Press.

McDowell, David M., and Henry I. Spitz. 1999. *Substance Abuse: From Principles to Practice*. Philadelphia: Brunner/Mazel.

McLellan, A. Thomas, David C. Lewis, Charles P. O'Brien, et al. 2000. "Drug Dependence: A Chronic Medical Illness: Implications for Treatment, Insurance, and Outcomes Evaluation." *Journal of the American Medical Association* 284: 1689–95.

Medawar, Charles. 1997. "The Antidepressant Web: Marketing Depression and Making Medicines Work." *International Journal of Risk and Safety in Medicine* 10 (2): 75–126.

Meléndez, Irene, Héctor Manuel Colón, Rafaela Robles, et al. 1998. "Puerto Rico Substance Abuse Needs Assessment Program: Treatment Capacity Survey Final Results." Mental Health and Anti-addiction Services Administration, Commonwealth of Puerto Rico.

Mendelevich, Vladimir D. 2005. "Sovremennaia rossiiskaia narkologiia: Paradoksal'nost' printsipov i nebezuprechnost' protsedur" [Contemporary Russian narcology: The paradoxicality of principles and imperfection of procedures]. *Narkologiia* 5 (1): 56–64.

Midanik, Lorraine T. 2006. *Biomedicalization of Alcohol Studies: Ideological Shifts and Institutional Challenges.* New Brunswick, N.J.: Transaction.

Miller, Peter. 2001. "Governing by Numbers: Why Calculative Practices Matter." *Social Research* 68 (2): 379–96.

Miller, William R. 2004. "The Phenomenon of Quantum Change." *Journal of Clinical Psychology* 60 (5): 453–60.

———. 2009. "Conversation with William R. Miller." *Addiction* 104 (6): 883–93.

Miller, William R., and Stephen Rollnick. 2002. *Motivational Interviewing: Preparing People for Change.* New York: Guilford.

Mintz, Sidney W. 1985. *Sweetness and Power: The Place of Sugar in Modern History.* New York: Viking.

Missaoui, Lamia. 1999. *Gitans et santé de Barcelone à Turin* [Gypsies and health from Barcelona to Turin]. Canet, Spain: Llibres del Trabucaire.

Modleski, Tania. 1982. *Loving with a Vengeance: Mass-Produced Fantasies for Women.* Hamden, Conn.: Archon.

Moore, Dawn. 2007. *Criminal Artifacts: Governing Drugs and Users.* Vancouver: University of British Columbia Press.

Morgan, Thomas J. 2006. "Behavioral Treatment Techniques for Psychoactive Substance Abuse Disorders." *Treating Substance Abuse: Theory and Technique,* ed. J. M. Frederick Rotgers, Daniel S. Keller, and Jonathan Morgenstern, 190–216. New York: Guilford.

Muñoz, José E. 1997. "Photographies of Mourning: Melancholia and Ambivalence in Van Der Zee, Mapplethorpe, and Looking for Langston." *Race and the Subject of Masculinities,* ed. Harry Stecopoulos and Michael Uebel, 337–60. Durham: Duke University Press.

Musto, David. 1999. *The American Disease: The Origins of Narcotic Control.* New York: Oxford University Press.

Nabokov, Peter. 1970. *Tijerina and the Courthouse Raid.* Palo Alto, Calif.: Ramparts.

Naples, Nancy A. 2003. *Feminism and Method: Ethnography, Discourse Analysis, and Activist Research.* New York: Routledge.

Nathan, Peter, and G. Alan Marlatt. 1978. *Alcoholism: New Directions in Behavioral Research and Treatment.* New York: Springer.

Nestler, Eric. 2004. "Cellular and Molecular Mechanisms of Drug Addiction." *Neurobiology of Mental Illness,* ed. Dennis Charney and Eric Nestler, 698–702. New York: Oxford University Press.

Nguyen, Vinh-Kim. 2005. "Antiretroviral Globalism, Biopolitics, and Therapeutic Citizenship." *Global Assemblages: Technology, Politics, and Ethics as Anthropological Problems,* ed. Aihwa Ong and Stephen J. Collier, 124–44. Hoboken, N.J.: Wiley-Blackwell.

———. 2009. "Government-by-Exception: Enrolment and Experimentality in Mass HIV Treatment Programmes in Africa." *Social Theory and Health* 7: 196–217.

Nichter, Mark, Gilbert Quintero, Mimi Nichter, et al. 2004. "Qualitative Research: Contributions to the Study of Drug Use, Drug Abuse, and Drug Use(r)-Related Interventions." *Substance Use and Misuse* 39 (10–12): 1907–69.

Nicolet, Claude. 1982. *L'idée républicaine en France: Essai d'histoire critique* [The republican idea in France: A critical history]. Paris: Editions Gallimard.

Nietzsche, Friedrich. 1974. *Gay Science*. New York: Vintage.

——. 1997. "On the Uses and Disadvantages of History for Life." *Untimely Meditations*, ed. Karl Ameriks, 57–124. Cambridge: Cambridge University Press.

Niezen, Ronald. 1997. "Healing and Conversion: Medical Evangelism in James Bay Cree Society." *Ethnohistory* 44 (3): 463–91.

Nolan, James L., Jr. 2001. *Reinventing Justice: The American Drug Court Movement*. Princeton: Princeton University Press.

O'Brien, Charles P. 2004. "The Mosaic of Addiction." *American Journal of Psychiatry* 161: 1741–42.

O'Brien, Charles P., Nora Volkow, and T-K Li. 2006. "What's in a Word? Addiction versus Dependence in DSM-V." *American Journal of Psychiatry* 163 (5): 764.

Observatoire Français des Drogues et des Toxicomanies. 2003. "Phénomènes émergents liés aux drogues en 2002" [Emerging drug trends of 2002]. Quatrième rapport national du dispositif TREND, Observatoire français des drogues et des toxicomanies, Paris.

——. 2004. "Phénomènes émergents liés aux drogues en 2003" [Emerging drug trends of 2003]. Quatrième rapport national du dispositif TREND, Observatoire français des drogues et des toxicomanies, Paris.

——. 2007. "Phénomènes émergents liés aux drogues en 2005" [Emerging drug trends of 2005]. *Tendances récentes et nouvelles drogues* [Recent trends and new drugs]. Paris: Observatoire Français des Drogues et des Toxicomanies.

O'Dwyer, Phillip. 2004. "Treatment of Alcohol Problems." *Clinical Work with Substance-Abusing Clients*, ed. Shulamith L. A. Straussner, 171–86. New York: Guilford.

Office of Applied Studies. 2001. "Year Emergency Room Data from the Drug Abuse Warning Network." Drug Abuse Warning Network (DAWN) Series D-18, U.S. Department of Health and Human Services publication no. (SMA) 01-3532, Substance Abuse and Mental Health Services Administration, Rockville, Md.

——. 2005. "Treatment Episode Data Set (TEDS), 2002: Discharges from Substance Abuse Treatment Services." DASIS Series S-25, U.S. Department of Health and Human Services publication no. (SMA) 04-3967, Substance Abuse and Mental Health Services Administration, Rockville, Md. Available online at http://wwwdasis.samhsa.gov (accessed October 10, 2007).

Ogien, Albert. 1995. *Sociologie de la déviance* [Sociology of deviance]. Paris: Armand Colin.

Ó'hÓgáin, Dáithí. 1979. "The Visionary Voice: A Survey of Popular Attitudes to Poetry in Irish Tradition." *Irish University Review* 9 (1): 44–61.

Oldani, Michael. 2009. "Uncanny Scripts: Understanding Pharmaceutical Emplotment in the Aboriginal Context." *Transcultural Psychiatry* 46 (1): 131–56.

O'Malley, Pat. 1996. "Risk and Responsibility." *Foucault and Political Reason: Liberalism, Neo-liberalism, and Rationalities of Government*, ed. Andrew Barry, Thomas Osborne, and Nikolas Rose, 189–208. Chicago: University of Chicago Press.

O'Malley, Pat, and Mariana Valverde. 2004. "Pleasure, Freedom, and Drugs: The Uses of 'Pleasure' in Liberal Governance of Drug and Alcohol Consumption." *Sociology* 38 (1): 25.

O'Nell, Theresa D. 1996. *Disciplined Hearts: History, Identity, and Depression in an American Indian Community*. Berkeley: University of California Press.

O'Nell, Theresa D., and Christina M. Mitchell. 1996. "Alcohol Use among American Indian Adolescents: The Role of Culture in Pathological Drinking." *Social Science and Medicine* 42 (4): 565–78.

Ong, Aihwa. 2006. *Flexible Citizenship: The Cultural Logics of Transnationalism*. Durham: Duke University Press.

Ong, Aihwa, and Stephen Collier, eds. 2005. *Global Assemblages: Technology, Politics, and Ethics as Anthropological Problems*. Malden, Mass.: Blackwell.

Orford, Jim. 2005. "Complicity on the River Bank: The Search for the Truth about Problem Gambling: Reply to the Commentaries." *Addiction* 100: 1226–39.

Orlova, Alexandra. 2009. "The Russian 'War on Drugs': A Kinder, Gentler Approach?" *Problems of Post-Communism* 58 (1): 23–34.

Page, J. Bryan, and Merrill Singer. 2010. *Comprehending Drug Use: Ethnographic Research at the Social Margins*. New Brunswick, N.J.: Rutgers University Press.

Paillard, Bernard. 1994. *L'épidémie: Carnets d'un sociologue* [Epidemic: A sociologist's notebook]. Paris: Stock.

Palladino, Lucy Jo. 1997. *The Edison Trait: Saving the Spirit of Your Nonconforming Child*. New York: Times Books.

Pandolfi, Mariella. 2001. "L'industrie humanitaire: Une souveraineté mouvante et supracoloniale; Réflexions sur l'expérience des Balkans" [The humanitarian industry: A mobile and supracolonial sovereignty; Reflections on the Balkan experience]. *Multitudes* 3: 97–105.

Pandolfo, Stephania. 1998. *Impasse of Angels: Scenes from a Moroccan Space of Memory*. Chicago: University of Chicago Press.

Paolino, Ronald M. 1991. "Identifying, Treating, and Counseling Drug Abusers." *Drug Testing: Issues and Options*, ed. Robert H. Coombs and Louis. J. West, 215–34. New York: Oxford University Press.

Parfitt, Tom. 2006a. "Putin Urged to Address 'Russia's Curse.'" *Lancet* 367 (9506): 197–98.

———. 2006b. "Vladimir Mendelevich: Fighting for Drug Substitution Treatment." *Lancet* 368 (9532): 279.

Parnell, Philip, and Stephanie Kane. 2003. *Crime's Power: Anthropologists and the Ethnography of Crime*. New York: Palgrave Macmillan.

Parquet, Jean-Philippe. 1998. *Pour une prévention de l'usage des substances psychoactives* [For the prevention of psychoactive substance use]. Paris: Ministre de la Santé.

Patico, Jennifer. 2005. "To Be Happy in a Mercedes: Tropes of Value and Ambivalent Visions of Marketization." *American Ethnologist* 32 (3): 479–96.

Paugam, Serge, ed. 1996. *L'exclusion: L'état des savoirs* [Exclusion: The state of knowledge]. Paris: La Découverte.

Pavlov, Ivan P. 1994 (1925). "Relations between Excitation and Inhibition, Delimitation between Excitation and Inhibition, Experimental Neuroses in Dogs." *Psychopathology and Psychiatry*, ed. Ivan P. Pavlov, 72–86. New York: Transaction.

Peele, Stanton. 1989. *Diseasing of America: How We Allowed Recovery Zealots and the Treatment Industry to Convince Us We Are Out of Control.* San Francisco: Jossey-Bass.

——. 2000. "What Addiction Is and Is Not: The Impact of Mistaken Notions of Addiction." *Addiction Research* 8 (6): 599–607.

Peterson, Vincent, Bernard Nisenholz, and Gary Robinson. 2003. *A Nation under the Influence: America's Addiction to Alcohol.* Boston: Allyn and Bacon.

Petry, Nancy M. 2006. "Should the Scope of Addictive Behaviors Be Broadened to Include Pathological Gambling?" *Addiction* 101: 152.

Petryna, Adriana. 2002. *Life Exposed: Biological Citizens after Chernobyl.* Princeton: Princeton University Press.

——. 2007. "Experimentality: On the Global Mobility and Regulation of Human Subjects Research." *Political and Legal Anthropology Review* 30: 288–304.

——. 2009. *When Experiments Travel: Clinical Trials and the Global Search for Human Subjects.* Princeton: Princeton University Press.

Petryna, Adriana, Andrew Lakoff, and Arthur Kleinman. 2006. *Global Pharmaceuticals: Ethics, Markets, Practices.* Durham: Duke University Press.

Pew Research Center for the People and the Press. 2001. "Interdiction and Incarceration Still Top Remedies: 74 Percent Say Drug War Being Lost." Pew Research Center for the People and the Press, Washington, D.C., March 21.

Platonov, Konstantin I. 1959. *The Word as a Physiological and Therapeutic Factor: The Theory and Practice of Psychotherapy according to I. P. Pavlov.* Moscow: Foreign Languages Publishing.

Porter, Roy. 1985. "The Drinking Man's Disease: The 'Pre-history' of Alcoholism in Georgian Britain." *Addiction* 80 (4): 385–96.

Potenza, Mark. 2001. "The Neurobiology of Pathological Gambling." *Seminars in Clinical Neuropsychiatry* 6: 217–26.

Poznyaka, Vladimir B., Vadim E. Pelipas, Anatoliy N. Vievski, et al. 2002. "Illicit Drug Use and Its Health Consequences in Belarus, Russian Federation, and Ukraine: Impact of Transition." *European Addiction Research* 8: 184–89.

Price, Donald D., Damien G. Finniss, and Fabrizio Benedetti. 2008. "A Comprehensive Review of the Placebo Effect: Recent Advances and Current Thought." *Annual Review of Psychology* 59: 565–90.

Productivity Commission. 1999. "Australia's Gambling Industries." Report no. 10, AusInfo, Canberra.

Prussing, Erica. 2007. "Reconfiguring the Empty Center: Drinking, Sobriety, and

Identity in Native American Women's Narratives." *Culture, Medicine and Psychiatry* 31 (4): 499–526.

Quintero, Gilbert. 2000. "'The Lizard in the Green Bottle': 'Aging Out' of Problem Drinking among Navajo Men." *Social Science and Medicine* 51 (7): 1031–45.

Rabinow, Paul. 1992. "Artificiality and Enlightenment: From Sociobiology to Biosociality." *Zone 6: Incorporations*, ed. Jonathan Crary, 181–93. Cambridge: MIT Press.

———. 1996. *Essays on the Anthropology of Reason.* Princeton: Princeton University Press.

———. 1999. *French DNA: Trouble in Purgatory.* Chicago: University of Chicago Press.

———. 2003. *Anthropos Today: Reflections on Modern Equipment.* Princeton: Princeton University Press.

Radway, Janice. 1991. *Reading the Romance: Women, Patriarchy, and Popular Literature.* Chapel Hill: University of North Carolina Press.

Rafael, Vicente. 1999. *Figures of Criminality in Indonesia, the Philippines, and Colonial Vietnam.* Ithaca: Cornell South East Asia Program Publications.

Raikhel, Eugene. 2009. "Institutional Encounters: Identification and Anonymity in Russian Addiction Treatment (and Ethnography)." *Being There: The Fieldwork Encounter and the Making of Truth*, ed. John Borneman and Abdellah Hammoudi, 201–36. Berkeley: University of California Press.

———. 2010. "Post-Soviet Placebos: Epistemology and Authority in Russian Treatments for Alcoholism." *Culture, Medicine, and Psychiatry* 34 (1): 132–68.

Rapp, Rayna. 1987. "Moral Pioneers: Women, Men and Fetuses on a Frontier of Reproductive Technology." *Women and Health* 13 (1–2): 101–16.

———. 1999. *Testing Women, Testing the Fetus: The Social Impact of Amniocentesis in America.* New York: Routledge.

Rasmussen, Sandra. 2000. *Addiction Treatment: Theory and Practice.* Newbury Park, Calif.: Sage.

Raviola, Giuseppe, M'Imunya Machoki, Esther Mwaikambo, et al. 2002. "HIV, Disease Plague, Demoralization and 'Burnout': Resident Experience of the Medical Profession in Nairobi, Kenya." *Culture, Medicine, and Psychiatry* 26 (1): 55–86.

Reckitt Benckiser Pharmaceuticals. 2009. "Powering Ahead: Annual Report and Financial Statements 2009." Available online at http://annualreport2009.rb.com/Home (accessed April 28, 2012).

———. 2010. "Driving Innovative Growth: Annual Report and Financial Statements 2010." Available online at http://www.rb.com/Investors-media/Investor-information/Online-Annual-Report-2010 (accessed April 28, 2012).

Reid, Larry D. 2009. "Opioid Antagonists and Ethanol's Ability to Reinforce Intake of Alcoholic Beverages: Preclinical Studies." *Opiate Receptors and Antagonists: From Bench to Clinic*, ed. Reginald Dean, Edward J. Bilsky, and S. Stevens Negus. New York: Humana.

Reinarman, Craig. 2005. "Addiction as Accomplishment: The Discursive Construction of Disease." *Addiction Research and Theory* 13: 307–20.

Reith, Gerta. 2004. "Consumption and Its Discontents: Addiction, Identity and the Problems of Freedom." *The British Journal of Sociology* 55: 283–300.

———. 2007. "Gambling and the Contradictions of Consumption: A Genealogy of the 'Pathological' Subject." *American Behavioral Scientist* 51 (1): 33.

Rheinberger, Hans-Jörg. 1997. *Toward a History of Epistemic Things: Synthesizing Proteins in the Test Tube.* Stanford: Stanford University Press.

Rhodes, Tim, Merrill Singer, Philippe Bourgois, et al. 2005. "The Social Structural Production of HIV Risk among Injecting Drug Users." *Social Science and Medicine* 61: 1026–44.

Rhodes, Tim, Louise Watts, Sarah Davies, et al. 2007. "Risk, Shame and the Public Injector: A Qualitative Study of Drug Injecting in South Wales." *Social Science and Medicine* 65: 572–85.

Richaud, Hervé, and Didier Febvrel. 2005. "Santé mentale et conduites addictives: Proximité et réduction des risques" [Mental health and addictive behavior: Proximity and risk reduction]. *Villes et toxicomanies: Quelles preventions?* [Cities and addiction: What preventions?], ed. Michel Joubert, Pilar Giraux, and Chantal Mougin, 240–47. Ramonville-Saint-Agne: Erès.

Rieff, Philip. 1987. *The Triumph of the Therapeutic: Uses of Faith after Freud.* Chicago: University of Chicago Press.

Rinn, William, Nitigna Desai, Harold Rosenblatt, and David R. Gastfriend. 2002. "Addiction Denial and Cognitive Dysfunction: A Preliminary Investigation." *Neuropsychiatry Clinical Neuroscience* 14 (1): 52–57.

Rivkin-Fish, Michele R. 2005. *Women's Health in Post-Soviet Russia: The Politics of Intervention.* Bloomington: Indiana University Press.

Roberts, Bruce D. 2000. "Always Cheaply Pleasant: Beer as a Commodity in a Rural Kenyan Society." *Commodities and Globalization: Anthropological Perspectives*, ed. Angelique Haugerud, M. Priscilla Stone, and Peter D. Little, 179–96. New York: Rowman and Littlefield.

Roberts, Ken, Irina Predborska, and Katya Ivaschenko. 2003. "Youth Transitions in East and West Ukraine." *European Sociology Review* 20 (5): 403–13.

Robins, L. N. 1993. "Vietnam Veterans' Rapid Recovery from Heroin Addiction: A Fluke or Normal Expectation?" *Addiction* 88, no. 8 (1993): 1041–54.

Rogers, Carl R. 1961. *On Becoming a Person: A Therapist's View of Psychotherapy.* Boston: Houghton Mifflin.

———. 1986. "Reflection of Feelings." *Person-Centered Review* 1 (4): 375–77.

Roizen, Ron. 1991. "The American Discovery of Alcoholism, 1933–1939." PhD diss., University of California, Berkeley.

Room, Robin. 1983. "Sociological Aspects of the Disease Concept of Alcoholism." *Research Advances in Alcohol and Drug Problems* 7: 47–91.

———. 1984. "Alcohol and Ethnography: A Case of Problem Deflation?" *Current Anthropology* 25 (2): 169–78.

———. 1998. "Alcohol and Drug Disorders in the International Classification of Diseases: A Shifting Kaleidoscope." *Drug and Alcohol Review* 17 (3): 305–17.

———. 2003. "The Cultural Framing of Addiction." *Janus Head* 6 (2): 221–34.

——. 2004. "What If We Found the Magic Bullet?" *From Science to Action? One Hundred Years Later: Alcohol Policies Revisited*, ed. Richard Müller and Harald Klingemann, 153–62. New York: Springer.

Rosanvallon, Pierre. 2000 (1995). *The New Social Question: Rethinking the Welfare State*. Princeton: Princeton University Press.

Rose, Nikolas. 1999. *Powers of Freedom: Reframing Political Thought*. Cambridge: Cambridge University Press.

——. 2003a. "The Neurochemical Self and Its Anomalies." *Risk and Morality*, ed. Richard V. Ericson and Aaron Doyle, 407–37. Toronto: University of Toronto Press.

——. 2003b. "Neurochemical Selves." *Society* 41 (1): 46–59.

——. 2007. *The Politics of Life Itself: Biomedicine, Power, and Subjectivity in the Twenty-First Century*. Princeton: Princeton University Press.

Rosenberg, Charles. 1997. "Banishing Risk: Continuity and Change in the Moral Management of Disease." *Morality and Health: Interdisciplinary Perspectives*, ed. Allan M. Brandt and Paul Rozin, 35–52. New York: Routledge.

Rosenfeld, Joseph. 1994. "Denial: Reports of Its Death Are Premature." Editorial. *Behavioral Health Management* 14 (5): 44–45.

Rothschild, Debra. 1995. "Working with Addicts in Private Practice: Overcoming Initial Resistance." *Psychotherapy and Substance Abuse: A Practitioner's Handbook*, ed. Arnold M. Washton, 192–203. New York: Guilford.

Rozhnov, Vladimir. E., and Mark E. Burno. 1987. "Sistema emotsional'no-stressovoi psikhoterapii bol'nykh alkogolizmom" [A system of emotional-stress psychotherapy for alcoholism patients]. *Sovetskaia Meditsina* 8: 11–15.

Rush, Benjamin. 1805. *Inquiry into the Effects of Ardent Spirits upon the Human Body and Mind*. Philadelphia: Bartam.

Ruti, Mari. 2005. "From Melancholia to Meaning: How to Live the Past in the Present." *Psychoanalytic Dialogues* 15 (5): 637–60.

Sacks, Peter. 1985. *The English Elegy: Studies in the Genre from Spencer to Yeats*. Baltimore: Johns Hopkins University Press.

SAMHSA (Substance Abuse and Mental Health Services Administration). 2011. "National Survey of Substance Abuse Treatment Services (N-SSATS): 2010. Data on Substance Abuse Treatment Facilities." DASIS Series S-59, HHS Publication No. (SMA) 11-4665. Rockville, Md.: Substance Abuse and Mental Health Services Administration.

Sarang, Anya, Raminka Stuikyte, and Roman Bykov. 2007. "Implementation of Harm Reduction in Central and Eastern Europe and Central Asia." *International Journal of Drug Policy* 18: 129–35.

Saris, A. Jamie. 2007. "Culture, Inequality, and the Bureaucratic Imagination: States and Subjects for a New Millennium." *Irish Journal of Anthropology* 10 (2): 54–60.

——. 2008. "An Uncertain Dominion: Irish Psychiatry, Methadone, and the Treatment of Opiate Abuse." *Culture, Medicine, and Psychiatry* 32 (2): 259–77.

——. 2011. "The Addicted Self and the Pharmaceutical Self: Ecologies of Will,

Information, and Power in Junkies, Addicts, and Patients." *Pharmaceutical Self and Imaginary: Studies in Psychopharmacology and Globalisation*, ed. Janis Jenkins, 209–30. Santa Fe: School for Advanced Research.

Satel, Sally. 1999. "What Should We Expect from Drug Abusers?" *Psychiatric Services* 50 (7): 861.

Schaler, Jeffrey A. 2000. *Addiction Is a Choice*. Chicago: Open Court.

Schaub, Michael, Emilis Subata, Victor Chtenguelov, et al. 2009. "Feasibility of Buprenorphine Maintenance Therapy Programs in the Ukraine: First Promising Treatment Outcomes." *European Addiction Research* 15 (3): 157–62.

Schellinck, Tony, and Tracy Schrans. 2003. "Nova Scotia Gambling Prevalence Study: Measurement of Gambling and Problem Gambling in Nova Scotia." Final report submitted to the Atlantic Lottery Corporation, Focal Research Consultants, Halifax, Nova Scotia.

Scheper-Hughes, Nancy. 1992. *Death without Weeping: The Violence of Everyday Life in Brazil*. Berkeley: University of California Press.

———. 2000. "The Global Traffic in Human Organs." *Current Anthropology* 41 (2): 191–224.

———. 2003. "Commodity Fetishism in Organs Trafficking." *Commodifying Bodies*, ed. Nancy Scheper-Hughes and Loïc Wacquant, 31–62. Thousand Oaks, Calif.: Sage.

Schram, Sanford. 2006. *Welfare Discipline: Discourse, Governance, and Globalization*. Philadelphia: Temple University Press.

Schüll, Natasha Dow. 2005. "Digital Gambling: The Coincidence of Desire and Design." *Annals of the American Academy of Political and Social Science* 597: 65–81.

———. 2006. "Machines, Medication, Modulation: Circuits of Dependency and Self-Care in Las Vegas." *Culture, Medicine, and Psychiatry* 30 (2): 223–47.

———. 2012. *Addiction by Design: Machine Gambling in Las Vegas*. Princeton: Princeton University Press.

Schuster, Charles R. 2004. "Conversation with Charles R. Schuster." *Addiction* 99 (6): 667–76.

Schutz, Alfred. 1967 (1932). *Phenomenology of the Social World*, trans. George Walsh and Frank Lehnert. Evanston, Ill.: Northwestern University Press.

Scott, Christy K., Mark A. Foss, and Michael L. Dennis. 2005. "Pathways in the Replace–Treatment–Recovery Cycle over Three Years." *Journal of Substance Abuse Treatment* 28: s63–s72.

Scott, Cynthia G. 2000. "Ethical Issues in Addiction Counseling." *Rehabilitation Counseling Bulletin* 43 (4): 209–14.

Scott, Joan W. 1991. "The Evidence of Experience." *Critical Inquiry* 17: 773–97.

Searle, John R. 1997. *The Mystery of Consciousness*. New York: New York Review of Books.

Seddon, Toby. 2007. "Drugs and Freedom." *Addiction Research and Theory* 15 (4): 333–42.

Sedgwick, Eve Kosofsky. 1992. "Epidemics of the Will." *Incorporations*, ed. Jonathan Crary and Sanford Kwinter, 582–95. New York: Zone Books.

Sereiskii, M. Ia. 1952. "Lechenie khronicheskogo alkogolizma Tiuramom" [Treatment of chronic alcoholism with Tiuram]. *Zhurnal Nevropatologii i Psikhiatrii Imeni S. S. Korsakova* 52 (4): 51–57.

Seremetakis, Nadia. 1991. *The Last Word: Women, Death, and Divination in Inner Mani.* Chicago: University of Chicago Press.

Shaffer, Howard J., Matthew N. Hall, and Joni Vander Bilt. 1999. "Estimating the Prevalence of Disordered Gambling Behavior in the United States and Canada: A Research Synthesis." *American Journal of Public Health* 89: 1369–76.

Shah, Nina. 2006. "Overdose Surveillance in Hospital Departments in Northern New Mexico: A Pilot Study." *New Mexico Epidemiology* 2006 (3): 1–5.

Shell, Ellen. 2003. *Fat Wars: The Inside Story of the Obesity Industry.* New York: Atlantic Books.

Shoemaker, Stowe, and Dina Marie Zemke. 2005. "The 'Locals' Market: An Emerging Gaming Segment." *Journal of Gambling Studies* 21 (4): 379–410.

Shorter, Edward. 1998. *A History of Psychiatry: From the Era of the Asylum to the Age of Prozac.* New York: Wiley.

Siegel, James T. 1998. *A New Criminal Type in Jakarta: Counter-Revolution Today.* Durham: Duke University Press.

Silver, Hillary. 1994. "Social Exclusion and Social Solidarity: Three Paradigms." *International Labour Review* 133 (5–6): 531–78.

Silverman, Kaja. 2000. *World Spectators.* Stanford: Stanford University Press.

Silverstein, Michael. 1979. "Language Structure and Linguistic Ideology." *The Elements: A Parassession on Linguistic Units and Levels*, ed. Paul Clyne, William Hanks, and Carol Hofbauer, 193–247. Chicago: Chicago Linguistics Society.

———. 1996. "Monoglot Standard in America: Standardization and Metaphors of Linguistic Hegemony." *The Matrix of Language: Contemporary Linguistic Anthropology*, ed. Donnald Brenneis and Ronald K. S. Macauly, 284–306. Boulder, Colo.: Westview.

Simpson, Jeff. 2000. "Evening the Odds: Station Casinos Helps Fund Clinic for Problem Gamblers." *Las Vegas Review Journal*, February 7.

Singer, Merrill. 2001. "Toward a Bio-cultural and Political Economic Integration of Alcohol, Tobacco, and Drug Studies in the Coming Century." *Social Science and Medicine* 53 (2): 199–213.

———. 2006. *The Face of Social Suffering: The Life History of a Street Drug Addict.* Long Grove, Ill.: Waveland.

———. 2008. *Drugging the Poor: Legal and Illegal Drugs and Social Inequality.* Long Grove, Ill.: Waveland.

Singh, Ilana. 2008. "ADHD, Culture, and Education." *Early Child Development and Care* 178 (4): 347–61.

Skinner, B. F. 1950. "Are Theories of Learning Necessary?" *Psychological Review* 57: 193–216.

Skolnik, Sam. 2011. *High Stakes: The Rising Costs of America's Gambling Addiction.* Boston: Beacon.

Sluchevsky, I. F., and A. A. Friken. 1933. "Lechenie khronicheskogo alkogolizma

Apomorfinom" [On the treatment of chronic alcoholism with Apomorphine]. *Sovetskaia Vrachebnaia Gazeta* 12: 557–61.

Smith, Dorothy E. 1999. *Writing the Social: Critique, Theory, and Investigations.* Toronto: University of Toronto Press.

Smith, Garry, and H. J. Wynne. 2004. "VLT Gambling in Alberta: A Preliminary Analysis." Report. Alberta Gaming Research Institute. Available online at http://hdl.handle.net/1880/1632 (accessed August 2008).

Smith, Roger. 1992. *Inhibition: History and Meaning in the Sciences of Mind and Brain.* Berkeley: University of California Press.

Sofronov, Alexander G. 2003. "Aktual'nye problemy razvitiia otechestvennoi narkologii" [Issues in the development of a domestic narcology]. *Narkologiia* 3: 2–6.

Sontag, Susan. 2003. *Regarding the Pain of Others.* New York: Picador.

Spicer, Paul. 1997. "Toward a (Dys)Functional Anthropology of Drinking: Ambivalence and the American Indian Experience with Alcohol." *Medical Anthropology Quarterly* 11 (3): 306–23.

——. 1998. "Narrativity and the Representation of Experience in American Indian Discourses about Drinking." *Culture, Medicine and Psychiatry* 22 (2): 139–69.

Spiegel, Betsy R., and Christine Fewell. 2004. "Twelve-Step Programs as a Treatment Modality." *Clinical Work with Substance Abusing Clients*, ed. Shulamith L. A. Straussner, 125–45. New York: Guilford.

Spradley, James. 1970. *You Owe Yourself a Drunk: An Ethnography of Urban Nomads.* Boston: Little, Brown.

Stanton, Arlene, Caroline McLoed, Bill Luckey, et al. 2006. "SAMHSA/CSAT Evaluation of the Buprenorphine Waiver Program: Expanding Treatment of Opioid Dependence; Initial Physician and Patient Experiences with the Adoption of Buprenorphine." Paper presented at the American Society of Addiction Medicine, May 5. Available at http://buprenorphine.samhsa.gov/ASAM_06 _Final_Results.pdf (accessed September 10, 2012).

Stebbins, Kenyon Rainier. 2001. "Going Like Gangbusters: Transnational Tobacco Companies 'Making a Killing' in South America." *Medical Anthropology Quarterly* 15 (2): 147–70.

Strauss, Anselm, Shizuko Fagerhaugh, Barbara Suczek, et al. 1982. "Sentimental Work in the Technologized Hospital." *Sociology of Health and Illness* 4: 254–78.

Strel'chuk, Ivan V. 1952. "Dal'neishie nabliudeniia za lecheniem chronicheskogo alkogolizma Antabusom (Tetraetiltiuramdisul'firadom)" [Continued observations on the treatment of chronic alcoholism with Antabuse (Tetraethylthiuram disulfide)]. *Zhurnal Nevropatologii i Psikhiatrii Imeni S. S. Korsakova* 52 (4): 43–50.

Suggs, David N. 1996. "Mosadi Tshwene: The Construction of Gender and the Consumption of Alcohol in Botswana." *American Ethnologist* 23 (3): 597–610.

Suh, Jesse J., Helen M. Pettinati, Kyle M. Kampman, et al. 2006. "The Status of Disulfiram: A Half of a Century Later." *Journal of Clinical Psychopharmacology* 26 (3): 290–302.

Taber, Julian Ingersoll. 2001. *In the Shadow of Chance: The Pathological Gambler.* Reno: University of Nevada Press.

Tarrius, Alain. 2001. *Fin de siècle incertaine à Perpignan: Drogues, pauvreté, communautés d'étrangers, jeunes sans emplois, et renouveau des civilités dans une ville moyenne française.* Canet de Rosselló, France: Trabucaïre.

Temime, Emile. 2006. *Histoire de Marseille.* Marseille: Éditions Jeanne Lafitte.

Ticktin, Miriam. 2006. "Where Ethics and Politics Meet." *American Ethnologist* 33 (1): 33–49.

Tiebout, Harry M. 1953. "Surrender versus Compliance in Therapy, with Special Reference to Alcoholism." *Quarterly Journal of Studies on Alcohol* 14 (1): 58–68.

Tkachevskii, Yu. M. 1974. *Pravovye Mery Bor'by s Pianstvom* [Legal means in the struggle with drunkenness]. Moscow: Moscow University Press.

Todes, Daniel P. 1995. "Pavlov and the Bolsheviks." *History and Philosophy of the Life Sciences* 17 (3): 379–418.

Tone, Andrea. 2009. *The Age of Anxiety: A History of America's Turbulent Affair with Tranquilizers.* New York: Basic Books.

Tsai, Alexander C. 2003. "Policies to Regulate Gifts to Physicians from Industry." *Journal of the American Medical Association* 290 (13): 1776.

Twigg, Judyth L. 1998. "Balancing the State and the Market: Russia's Adoption of Obligatory Medical Insurance." *Europe-Asia Studies* 50 (4): 583–602.

U.S. Drug Enforcement Administration. 1997. DEA congressional testimony before the Subcommittee on National Security, International Affairs, and Criminal Justice, July 17.

Vaillant, George E. 1971. "Theoretical Hierarchy of Adaptive Ego Mechanisms." *Archives of General Psychiatry* 24: 107–18.

Valverde, Mariana. 1997 "'Slavery from Within': The Invention of Alcoholism and the Question of Free Will." *Social History* 22 (3): 251–68.

——. 1998. *Diseases of the Will: Alcohol and the Dilemmas of Freedom.* Cambridge: Cambridge University Press.

——. 2006. *Law and Order: Signs, Meanings, Myths.* New Brunswick, N.J.: Rutgers University Press.

van der Geest, Sjaak, Susan R. Whyte, and Anita Hardon. 1996. "The Anthropology of Pharmaceuticals: A Biographical Approach." *Annual Review of Anthropology* 25 (1): 153–78.

Van Zee, Art. 2009. "The Promotion and Marketing of OxyContin: Commercial Triumph, Public Health Tragedy." *Journal of the American Public Health Association* 99 (2): 221–27.

Vocci, Frank, Jane Acri, and Ahmed Elkashef. 2005. "Medication Development for Addictive Disorders: The State of the Science." *American Journal of Psychiatry* 162 (8): 1432–40.

Vocci, Frank, and Walter Ling. 2005. "Medications Development: Successes and Challenges." *Pharmacology and Therapeutics* 108: 94–108.

Volberg, Rachel A. 2001. "Gambling and Problem Gambling in Nevada." Report to the Nevada Department of Human Resources. Gemini Research, Northampton, Mass.

———. 2004. "Fifteen Years of Problem Gambling Prevalence Research: What Do We Know? Where Do We Go from Here?" *Journal of Gambling Studies* (10): 1–19.

Volkow, Nora, and T-K Li. 2004. "Drug Addiction: The Neurobiology of Behavior Gone Awry." *Nature Reviews: Neuroscience* 12: 963–70.

———. 2005. "The Neuroscience of Addiction." *Nature Neuroscience* 8: 1429–30.

Volkow, Nora D., and Charles P. O'Brien. 2007. "Issues for DSM-V: Should Obesity Be Included as a Brain Disorder?" *American Journal of Psychiatry* 164 (5): 708.

Vrecko, Scott. 2006. "Folk Neurology and the Remaking of Identity." *Molecular Interventions* 6 (6): 300–303.

———. 2008. "Capital Ventures into Biology: Biosocial Dynamics in the Industry and Science of Gambling." *Economy and Society* 37 (1): 50–67.

———. 2009. "Therapeutic Justice in Drug Courts: Crime, Punishment and Societies of Control." *Science as Culture* 18 (2): 217–32.

———. 2010a. "Birth of a Brain Disease: Science, the State, and Addiction Neuropolitics." *History of the Human Sciences* 23 (4): 52–67.

———. 2010b. "'Civilizing Technologies' and the Control of Deviance." *BioSocieties* 5: 36–51.

Wakefield, Jerome K. 1997. "Diagnosing DSM-IV—Part I: DSM-IV and the Concept of Disorder." *Behaviour Research and Therapy* 35: 633–49.

Walby, Kevin. 2008. "Hunting for Harm: Risk-Knowledge Networks, Local Governance, and the Ottawa Needle Hunter Program." *Canadian Journal of Law and Society* 23 (1–2): 161–78.

Waldorf, Dan. 1973. *Careers in Dope.* New York: Prentice Hall.

Wallace, John. 1978. "Working with the Preferred Defense Structure of the Recovering Alcoholic." *Practical Approaches to Alcoholism Psychotherapy*, ed. Sheldon Zimberg, John Wallace, and Sheila B. Blume, 19–29. New York: Springer.

Walters, Glenn D. 1994. *Escaping the Journey to Nowhere: The Psychology of Alcohol and Other Drugs.* Bristol, Penn.: Taylor and Francis.

Warner, Jessica. 1994. "'Resolv'd to Drink No More': Addiction as a Preindustrial Construct." *Journal of Studies on Alcohol* 55 (6): 685–91.

Waterston, Alisse. 1993. *Street Addicts in the Political Economy.* Philadelphia: Temple University Press.

Wazana, Ashley. 2000. "Physicians and the Pharmaceutical Industry: Is a Gift Ever Just a Gift?" *Journal of the American Medical Association* 283: 373–80.

Weber, Max. 1958. *The Protestant Ethic and the Spirit of Capitalism.* New York: Charles Scribner's Sons.

———. 1978. *Economy and Society: An Outline of Interpretive Sociology.* Berkeley: University of California Press.

Weinberg, Darin. 2002. "On the Embodiment of Addiction." *Body and Society* 8 (4): 1–19.

———. 2011. "Sociological Perspectives on Addiction." *Sociology Compass* 5 (4): 298–310.

Wetherall, Margaret. 2001. "Themes in Discourse Research: The Case of Diana." *Discourse Theory and Practice: A Reader*, ed. Margaret Wetherall, Stephanie Taylor, and Simeon J. Yates, 14–28. Thousand Oaks, Calif.: Sage.

White, Stephen. 1996. *Russia Goes Dry: Alcohol, State and Society*. Cambridge: Cambridge University Press.

White, William L. 1998. *Slaying the Dragon: The History of Addiction Treatment and Recovery in America*. Bloomington, Ill.: Chestnut Health Systems and Lighthouse Institute.

Whyte, Susan R., Sjaak van der Geest, and Anita Hardon. 2002. *Social Lives of Medicines*. Cambridge: Cambridge University Press.

Wiener, Carolyn. L., and Marilyn J. Dodd. 1993. "Coping amid Uncertainty: An Illness Trajectory Perspective." *Scholarly Inquiry for Nursing Practice* 7 (1): 17–31.

Wikler, Abraham. 1965. "Conditioning Factors in Opiate Addiction and Relapse." *Narcotics*, ed. Daniel M. Wilner and Gene G. Kassebaum, 85–100. New York: McGraw-Hill.

Wilcox, Danny M. 1998. *Alcoholic Thinking: Language, Culture, and Belief in Alcoholics Anonymous*. Westport, Conn.: Praeger/Greenwood.

Willette, Robert E., and Gene Barnett, eds. 1981. *Narcotic Antagonists: Naltrexone Pharmacochemistry and Sustained Release Preparations*. NIDA Research Monograph 28, National Institute of Drug Abuse, Rockville, Md.

Williams, Raymond. 1977. *Marxism and Literature*. Oxford: Oxford University Press.

———. 1985. *Keywords: A Vocabulary of Culture and Society*. New York: Oxford University Press.

Windholz, George. 1997. "The 1950 Joint Scientific Session: Pavlovians as the Accusers and the Accused." *Journal of the History of the Behavioral Sciences* 33 (1): 61–81.

Winger, G., J. H. Woods, C. M. Galuska, and T. Wade-Galuska. 2005. "Behavioral Perspectives on the Neuroscience of Drug Addiction." *Journal of the Experimental Analysis of Behavior* 84, no. 3 (2005): 667.

Winick, Charles. 1962. "Maturing Out of Narcotic Addiction." *Bulletin on Narcotics* 14 (1): 1–7.

Wiseman, Jacqueline P. 1970. *Stations of the Lost: The Treatment of Skid-Row Alcoholics*. Chicago: University of Chicago Press.

Woliver, Laura R. 2002. *The Political Geographies of Pregnancy*. Champaign: University of Illinois Press.

Woo, Grace M. 1998. "UNLV Las Vegas Metropolitan Poll." Cannon Center for Survey Research, University of Las Vegas.

Woolard, Kathryn. 1998. "Introduction: Language Ideology as a Field of Inquiry." *Language Ideologies: Practice and Theory*, ed. Bambi B. Schiefflin, Kathryn Woolard, and Paul V. Kroskrity, 3–47. Oxford: Oxford University Press.

Wortis, Joseph. 1950. *Soviet Psychiatry*. Baltimore: Williams and Wilkins.

Wurmser, Leon. 1978. *The Hidden Dimension: Psychodynamics in Compulsive Drug Use*. New York: Jason Aronson.

———. 1985. "Denial and Split Identity: Timely Issues in the Psychoanalytic Psycho-therapy of Compulsive Drug Users." *Journal of Substance Abuse Treatment* 2 (1985): 89–96.

———. 1987. "Shame: The Veiled Companion of Narcissism." *The Many Faces of Shame*, ed. Donald Nathanson, 64–92. New York: Guilford.

———. 1992. "Psychology of Compulsive Drug Use." *The Chemically Dependent: Phases of Treatment and Recovery*, ed. Barbara Wallace, 92–114. Bristol, Penn.: Taylor and Francis.

Yoshino, Kenji. 2002. "Covering." *Yale Law Journal* 111: 769–939.

Young, Allan. 1995. *The Harmony of Illusions: Inventing Post-traumatic Stress Disorder*. Princeton: Princeton University Press.

———. 2000. "History, Hystery, and Psychiatric Styles of Reasoning." *Living and Working with the New Medical Technologies: Intersections of Inquiry*, ed. Margaret Lock, Allan Young, and Alberto Cambrosio, 135–64. Cambridge: Cambridge University Press.

———. 2006. "Pathologies of the Social Brain." Unpublished manuscript. Available online at http://isik.zrc-sazu.si/doc2009/kpms/anthropology_of_the_social_brain.pdf (accessed April 10, 2011).

———. 2007. "America's Transient Mental Illness: A Brief History of the Self-Traumatized Perpetrator." *Subjectivity: Ethnographic Investigations*, ed. João Biehl, Byron Good, and Arthur Kleinman, 155–78. Berkeley: University of California Press.

Zanni, Guido R. 2007. "Review: Patient Diaries, Charting the Course." *Consultant Pharmacist* 22: 472–76, 479–82.

Zhislin, S. G., and I. I. Lukomskii. 1963. "30 let uslovnoreflektornoi terapii alkogolizma" [30 years of conditioned reflex therapy of alcoholism]. *Zhurnal Nevropatologii i Psikhiatrii Imeni S. S. Korsakova* 63: 1884.

Zigon, Jarrett. 2010. "'A Disease of Frozen Feelings.'" *Medical Anthropology Quarterly* 24: 326–43.

CONTRIBUTORS

NANCY D. CAMPBELL is a professor of science and technology studies at Rensselaer Polytechnic Institute, Troy, New York. She is the author (with Elizabeth Ettorre) of *Gendering Addiction: The Politics of Drug Treatment in a Neurochemical World* (2011). She is also the author of *Discovering Addiction: The Science and Politics of Substance Abuse Research* (2007) and *Using Women: Gender, Drug Policy, and Social Justice* (2000), and (with J. P. Olsen and Luke Walden), the coauthor of *The Narcotic Farm: The Rise and Fall of America's First Prison for Drug Addicts* (2008).

E. SUMMERSON CARR is an associate professor in the School of Social Service Administration, University of Chicago, where she is also affiliated with the Center for Gender Studies and the Department of Anthropology. She is the author of *Scripting Addiction: The Politics of Therapeutic Talk and American Sobriety* (2010).

ANGELA GARCIA is an assistant professor in the Department of Anthropology, Stanford University. She is the author of *The Pastoral Clinic: Addiction and Dispossession along the Rio Grande* (2010).

WILLIAM GARRIOTT is an assistant professor in the Department of Justice Studies and affiliate member of the Department of Sociology and Anthropology, James Madison University, Harrisonburg, Virginia. He is the author of *Policing Methamphetamine: Narcopolitics in Rural America* (2011).

HELENA HANSEN is an assistant professor in the Anthropology Department and in the School of Medicine's Psychiatry Department, New York University. She teaches, practices, and researches in both medical anthropology and clinical addiction psychiatry.

ANNE M. LOVELL, an anthropologist and senior research scientist at the Institut National de la Santé et de la Recherche Médicale, Cermes 3, Université de Paris René Descartes, has published extensively on narrative and mental illness, pharmaceuticals and globalization, and the social body after disaster. Her current project concerns the shaping of psychiatric epidemiology as an international discipline.

EMILY MARTIN teaches anthropology at New York University. She is the author of *The Woman in the Body: A Cultural Analysis of Reproduction* (1987), *Flexible Bodies: Tracking Immunity in American Culture from the Days of Polio to the Age of* AIDS (1994), and *Bipolar Expeditions: Mania and Depression in American Culture* (2007). Her current work is on the history and ethnography of experimental psychology.

TODD MEYERS is an assistant professor of medical anthropology at Wayne State University, Detroit. He is the author of *The Clinic and Elsewhere: Addiction, Adolescents, and the Afterlife of Therapy* (2013).

EUGENE RAIKHEL is an anthropologist and assistant professor in the Department of Comparative Human Development, University of Chicago. His work examines the circulation of new forms of knowledge and clinical intervention produced by biomedicine, neuroscience, and psychiatry.

A. JAMIE SARIS is a senior lecturer in the Department of Anthropology, National University of Ireland, Maynooth, and the cochair of the Combat Diseases of Poverty Consortium. He has been working for more than fifteen years in medical and psychological anthropology in Ireland, North America, and South Africa, where he has researched and published on such diverse issues as the social life of mental hospitals, the experience of major mental illness, colonialism and its aftermath, poverty and structural violence, drug abuse, and HIV risk and treatment.

NATASHA DOW SCHÜLL is a cultural anthropologist and associate professor in the Program in Science, Technology, and Society, Massachusetts Institute of Technology. She is the author of *Addiction by Design: Machine Gambling in Las Vegas* (2012), which explores the feedback between the technological configuration of gambling activities and the experience of addiction.

INDEX

AA (Alcoholics Anonymous), 6–7, 10, 12, 18, 24, 30, 33n8, 193

abstinence, 33n5, 110–11, 149, 239, 243, 245, 249, 254, 257, 260n24

Academia Nueva Fé. *See* New Faith Bible Academy

Acker, Caroline Jean, 34n15

actuarial selfhood, 71–73, 81–82, 85n15, 85n21, 86n23

ADD (attention deficit disorder), 73, 289–90

addict, 11, 32, 43, 160–61, 191, 217, 238–39, 246, 266–68, 271, 275, 284, 287; as anti-subject, 268; discourse about, 45, 266; etymology of, 268–69, 276–77

addicted denial, 160, 162, 174

addiction: anthropological inquiry, and, 1, 5–6, 9–10, 19, 30, 32, 34n14, 163, 184, 281; behavioral model of, 11–13, 240; biomedicalization of, 1, 2, 3, 6–7, 13–18, 22, 33n8, 44, 45, 84n14, 108–9, 114, 118, 122, 124, 174, 190, 217, 238–41, 254–55, 280, 286–88; and choice, 15–16, 22, 34n13, 44–45, 60n4, 111, 246–49, 255–56, 266–67, 273–74, 278–80, 282n4; chronicity of, 10, 12–14, 17, 29–30, 37, 39, 43–45, 56, 70, 100, 114, 121, 141, 189, 191, 217, 231, 238, 254–55; criminalization of, 7, 17, 22, 45, 136, 139–40, 163–64, 214–15,

235–37; criminality and, 17, 150, 214–21, 223–32, 234–35, 254, 265; diagnosis of, 9, 13–14, 19, 63–64, 83, 111, 160; disease of the will as, 165, 186n3, 285; genealogy of, 6–7, 11–12, 14, 26, 84n12, 267; heritability of, 44, 60n5, 61–62, 69, 274–76; as moral struggle, 16, 22, 33n8, 37, 56, 90, 108–9, 111, 118, 141, 165, 217, 238–39, 243–44, 256; neurological basis of, 6, 16–17, 18, 44, 221, 240; psychological model of, 6, 12, 14–15, 18, 21, 64, 141, 191, 208; as public health threat, 93, 95–96, 105n10, 126, 128, 132, 145; scope of, 14, 67–70, 84n12, 84n14, 276; stigma associated with, 15–16, 114, 120, 243, 257; and trauma, 163, 250, 268

Addiction (HBO series), 109, 239–41, 243, 252, 258n3, 259n7, 259n8

addiction trajectories, 2, 5, 7–11, 19, 28–32, 232, 284

addiction-treatment cycle, 26, 40, 45, 56, 100, 188–89

ADHD (attention deficit hyperactivity disorder), 70, 289–90

adolescent drug use, 28–29, 88–89, 96, 100, 102, 104n2, 104n3

Agar, Michael, 275–76

agency, 16, 122–24, 195, 263, 269, 284, 286

alcohol antagonist. *See* disulfiram

Alcoholics Anonymous (AA), 6–7, 10, 12, 18, 24, 30, 33n8, 193

alcoholism, 11–12, 24, 33n5, 33n8, 189, 192, 198, 200, 208–9, 212n9, 261n24; and sobriety, 108, 174, 188–89, 194, 196, 201–4, 207–8, 210

Alcoholism Movement, 33n7

Ambien, 291, 292n3. *See also* insomnia

ambivalence, 178–79, 181

Ameisen, Olivier, 261n27

American Academy of Addiction Psychiatry, 94

American addiction paradigm, 13, 23–24, 32n1, 124, 143, 156, 160–63, 165, 174, 180, 183–85, 210, 285. *See also* behaviorism

American Psychiatric Association, 13, 82n4

American Society of Addiction Medicine, 155n3

amphetamines, 73, 137, 154, 158n10, 264, 289

amygdala, 248, 251, 255, 260n22

anger, 171–72, 289

Antabuse. *See* disulfiram

anti-craving medications, 254–55, 260n24, 261n25, 261n28

anti-opioid medication, 36, 47

anxiety, 73–77, 109

apomorphine treatment. *See* conditional-reflex therapy

assemblages, 5, 11, 25, 27, 74, 128–32, 142, 148, 152, 261n25, 264, 267–68, 273, 281. *See also* Deleuze, Gilles; Guattari, Félix

attention deficit disorder (ADD), 73, 289–90

attention deficit hyperactivity disorder (ADHD), 70, 289–90

Austin, J. L., 179

Babayan, Eduard, 138

baclofen, 255, 261n27

Bahktin, Mikhail, 186n5

Baker County: court system, 214, 216, 218–21, 229–31, 235; drug-related crime in, 213–14, 217–20, 223–32; jail treatment program, 220–21, 223–26; law enforcement, 221–23, 226–28, 232, 235–36; methamphetamine use in, 213–14, 216–20, 223–24, 226–28, 232–37; treatment options in, 218, 220, 224–25, 229–31

Baltimore Sun, The, 91–95, 101–3, 105n10

Bateson, Gregory, 23, 86n24

Bayer Pharmaceuticals, 115

Becker, Howard S., 258n2

behaviorism, 161, 177, 258n6, 285. *See also* American addiction paradigm

Bem, Daryl, 179–80

Benjamin, Walter, 27

Bennett, M. R., 245

Biehl, João, 10, 123, 208

biological markers, 14–15

biopolitics, 30–31, 129, 132–33, 147–49, 154–55

biopower, 123

biosociality, 121–22, 275, 278–79

biosolidarity, 142, 146–52, 154

bled, the, 133, 152

Boas, Franz, 270, 280

"Body on Drugs, A," 232–35

Borges, Jorge Luis, 53–54

Bourdieu, Pierre, 113

Bourgois, Philippe, 22, 25, 86n27. *See also* Schonberg, Jeffrey

Bukowski, Charles, 263–64, 266, 281

Buprenex, 89–90, 92, 104n4, 116. *See also* buprenorphine

buprenorphine, 3–4, 6, 19, 21–22, 27, 109, 141, 155n3, 278; abuse and diversion of, 20, 92–95, 101–3, 105n9, 105n10, 154; as analgesic, 89–90, 92, 104n4, 116; Baltimore, use in, 91–94, 102; clinical trials of, 88, 90, 93, 98, 104n4, 158n19; demographics of use, 117–18; FDA approval of, 108, 114; history of, 115–16; New York City, use in,

117–20, 122; prescribing practices of, 93, 105n9, 119–20, 123; seizure of, 93–94; withdrawal from, 123
burnout, 48, 58, 183
Bush, George H. W., 114
Bush, George W., 108, 110

Campbell, Nancy, 13–18, 30
Carr, E. Summerson, 15, 21, 23–24, 209, 212n12
Castel, Robert, 143
Catholicism, 54–55, 110, 113, 142–44
Chatterji, Roma, 89
Chepurnaya, Olga, 202
Child Protective Services, 172
Childress, Anna Rose, 16, 239–58, 261n27
chronic illness, 9, 45, 56, 114
chronic pain, 117
Ciba-Geigy, 288–90
Cioran, Emil, 57
citizenship, 128–29, 140–46, 148–49, 154–55; biological, 4, 30–31, 129, 132, 147, 150; therapeutic, 130–31, 147–48
Clark, H. Westley, 93
clinical encounter, 24, 180, 183, 190
clinical reasoning, 29, 34n14, 89–90, 96, 99–100, 196
Code, Lorraine, 243
coding (kodirovanie), 200–201
cognitive-behavioral therapy, 18, 161, 224–25, 239, 254
Cohen, Lawrence, 265–67, 282n1
Comaroff, Jean, 217
Comaroff, John, 217
compliance, 11, 195, 225, 287
compulsivity, 7, 13, 64, 67–70, 75, 78, 247, 250, 260n21, 269, 286, 291
conditional-reflex therapy ("apomorphine treatment"), 198–200, 212n6, 212n7
Consumer Lifestyle Index, 67–68, 79, 83n10, 85n21
Controlled Substances Act, 105n8
cosmetic pharmacology, 267, 280–81, 290

Courtwright, David, 87n29, 252, 260n23, 275–76. See also limbic capitalism
craving, 13, 37, 65, 77, 90, 97, 135, 222, 244, 250; scales, 71–71; state, 16, 239–48, 251–52, 255–56, 260n23, 260n24, 277
Crick, Francis, 287
"criminal and addictive thinking," 224–25
criminal body, 216, 234
criminal justice system, 17, 214–17, 220, 223, 231–32, 235–37, 254
culto, 113–14, 120–21

Das, Veena, 279
DEA (Drug Enforcement Administration), 105, 118
Decade of the Brain, 114
Deleuze, Gilles, 10, 28, 75, 129, 132, 267, 277, 281. See also assemblage; Guattari, Félix
denial, 23, 56, 160–74, 178, 180–82, 185n2, 250
depression, 109, 224, 285
DER (disulfiram ethanol reaction), 194–95, 203
Derby, Karen, 170
Derrida, Jacques, 78, 160, 271. See also pharmakon
descanso (resting place), 40–42
detoxification, 37, 46–47, 50, 139, 188, 223–24
Diagnostic and Statistical Manual of Mental Disorders (DSM), 9, 13, 111; pathological gambling, classification of, 82n4; substance abuse, classification of, 215
Diller, Lawrence, 290
disulfiram, 19, 24, 188–90, 203–5, 209–10, 255; as behavioral treatment, 190; development of, 198–99; efficacy, 194–96, 207; implant, 195, 199–200, 202, 210, 212n5; injection, 188, 200, 202; negative conditioned reflex and, 199–200; nonspecific effect of, 195–

44; pharmaceutical industry in, 141, 155n3; Revenu Minimal d'Insertion, 144, 159n22; Solidarity and, 142–45, 153; Third Republic, 142; universal health care and, 128, 142–44

Frank, Arthur, 259n13

Freidman, Lawrence, 215

Fresh Beginnings, 162–68, 172–74, 182, 186n4

Freud, Anna, 185n2

Freud, Sigmund, 38–39, 58–59, 160, 185n2. *See also* melancholy

Frith, John, 268–69, 282n6

frontal lobes, 242, 250, 252, 255; and relapse, 242

GA. *See* Gamblers Anonymous

Gamblers Anonymous (GA), 31, 62, 63, 64–66, 83n7

gambling: convenience, 62, 82n2; industry, 62, 65, losses, 62, 71–72, 282n5; machine, 20–21, 31, 62–66, 74, 81, 82n3; technology, 62–63, 65; video poker, 65, 77, 81

gambling addiction, 7, 14, 20–21, 63–64, 82n4; Las Vegas and, 63–65; machine gambling and, 20, 31, 63–65, 73–74, 81; online forum for, 74–75; recovery from, 71–72; self-care and, 71–78; zone, 65–66, 72–78, 86n23

Garcia, Angela, 10–11, 20, 22, 30, 102–3, 254

Gardner, Daniel, 219, 231

Garland, David, 216

Garriott, William, 17–18, 27, 102–3, 254

gift giving, 271–72, 282n1; and drug use, 272–73

global flows, 130–33

Goffman, Erving, 250

Good, Byron, 43, 60n6, 204, 275

Gordon, Colin, 87n32

Gorski, Terrence, 161

Greene, Jeremy A., 96, 99

group therapy, 67, 72, 97–98, 163–65, 173

Guattari, Félix, 129, 132, 267, 281. *See also* Deleuze, Gilles

Hacker, P. M. S., 245

Hacking, Ian, 11, 33n4, 211n3, 287

Hansen, Helena, 22, 104n4

harm reduction, 4, 25, 119, 128, 140–41, 189; needle-exchange programs, 7, 24, 128, 134

Harrison Act of 1914, 108, 115

hepatitis-B, 150

hepatitis-C, 135–36, 149–50

heroin, 3, 20, 28–29, 43, 93–94, 97, 98, 115, 192, 219, 272–73; and accidental poisoning, 48; brown, 136; heroin chic, 116–17; history of, 20, 115; intentional overdose by, 58; overdose, 36, 58; as therapy, 273; white, 136; withdrawal, 36–37, 47, 50, 97

Hinkle, Rose, 219–20, 236

HIV/AIDS, 25, 116; and intravenous drug use, 94, 111, 140, 192; prevention, 119; testing, 123

Holy Spirit, 111–14, 121, 123

honesty, openness, and willingness (HOW), 173–74

hypnosis, 197–99

ideology of inner reference, 162, 164, 167, 173–74, 180

illness narratives, 9–10, 32n2, 43

illness trajectories, 8–10, 32n2

illocutionary force, 179. *See also* Austin, J. L.

immutable mobiles, 130–31

incarceration, 17, 136, 139, 214, 218–20, 223–24, 229–32, 236–37

informal economy, 114, 121–22

injecting dyads, 133, 272–73

insomnia, 38–39, 50, 53–54, 56–57, 222, 224, 291

intergenerational drug use, 44

interiority, 23, 154, 209, 245, 249, 281

International Classification of Diseases, 13

Internet addiction, 34n14, 67

Internet forums, 70, 74–75, 78–79, 191

Intervention (A&E show), 161

intravenous drug use, 2–3, 25, 91, 93–95, 111, 119, 121, 127–28, 130, 133–34, 136–37, 140, 154, 155n3, 192, 252–53

Ivanets, Nikolai, 203

Jackson, Jean, 45

Jaffe, Jerome, 115, 125n2

James, William, 273

Jameson, Frederic, 84n12

Jasinski, Donald, 92, 104n4

Jefferson, Thomas, 186n4

Jellinek, E. M., 33n7

Johnson, Rolley "Ed," 91–92, 105n10

Johnson, Vernon, 161

junkie, the, 101, 276

Kaufman, Edward, 160

Keane, Helen, 87n30

khimzashchita, 24, 189–91, 193–94, 198–99, 201–8; adherence to, 203–4; as behavioral treatment, 190, 194; and fear, 189, 194, 207–8; perceived potency of, 202–3, 205–7; as pharmacological treatment, 205; and placebo therapy, 196, 201–4

King, Bret, 233. *See also* "Faces of Meth" campaign

Kirkman, Rick, 252–53

Kleinman, Arthur, 59, 265

Lalander, Philip, 131–32

language ideology, 163, 183–84

Las Vegas, 62–64, 79, 86n28, 252; rates of gambling in, 62, 82n2, 82n3; therapeutic network in, 64–65, 83n6

LeDoux, Joseph E., 260n22

Lende, Daniel, 30

Levine, Harry, 33n5, 186n3

limbic activation, 248, 250–51, 259n17

limbic capitalism, 87n29, 252, 260n23. *See also* Courtwright, David

Lombroso, Cesare, 234

Lord Byron, 265

Lovell, Anne M., 2, 8, 10, 20, 27, 30–31, 78

Lovern, John, 161

Luhrmann, Tanya, 112–13

Luongo, Peter, 95

Mann, Marty, 33n7

marijuana, 34n12, 68, 117, 175; addictiveness of, 226

Marlatt, G. Alan, 239, 258n5

Marseillais, 126, 145, 152–54, 157n11

Marseille, 4, 126–27, 133, 145, 155n1; Canebière, the, 134, 154; drug treatment in, 4, 128–29, 140–41, 145–47, 151; methadone bus, 127–28, 133–34, 137, 140, 151; needle-exchange automats, 128; poverty, 151–52; Public Health Department, 127; reputation of, 126, 128, 155n1; toxicomanes, 127, 134, 141–44, 146–47, 151, 154, 158n19; transnational drug use, and, 126–27, 133, 141, 147, 153

Martin, Emily, 85n16, 85n20, 277

Marxists, 196–97

Mauss, Marcel, 282n1. *See also* gift giving

May, Carl, 14

McCance-Katz, Elinore F., 94

McDowell, David, 161

MDB. *See* minimum brain dysfunction

medical tourism, 130

melancholy, 38–39, 52, 58–59; subject, 39, 58

message boards (Internet), 70, 74–75, 78–79, 191

metabolic lesion, 275–77

methadone, 3–4, 19, 20, 25, 86n27, 92, 104n4, 115, 276; abuse and diversion, 128; clinical trials of, 104n4; clinic-based maintenance therapy, 21; injection of, 133; non-injectable, 127–28

methamphetamine, 17, 214, 217, 221; addictiveness of, 219, 227; criminal dimen-

Oxycodone, 117
OxyContin, 29, 95, 109, 115, 117; FDA approval of, 117

Partnership for a Drug Free Puerto Rico, 109
patient autonomy, 118, 189, 208
Pavlovian theory, 196–98
Paxil, 75, 77
perlocutionary force, 179–80
perlocutionary speech act, 201
personal inventory, 67–68, 71, 83n10, 85n21, 174, 181
Petryna, Adriana, 147. *See also* citizenship: biological
pharmaceutical industry, 268, 271–72, 277–79; and the gift, 271–72
pharmaceutical leakage, 20, 78, 96, 128
pharmaceutical self, 275
pharmacological optimism, 238–39, 257–58
pharmakon, 78, 132, 271, 274; poison, aspect of, 274
Picower Institute for Learning and Memory, 269–70
"placebo therapy." See *khimzashchita*
Plato, 271
poetry, 263–64
post-Soviet addiction medicine, 3, 32n1, 140, 189–90, 208–9, 285
post-traumatic stress disorder, 250
prescription drug addiction, 34n11, 95, 117
prescription sharing, 89
Prohibition, 12, 33n7
psychiatry, 14; biologization of, 6, 19, 190, 208, 280
psychoanalysis, 3, 32n1, 38, 141, 156n6, 160–61, 185n2
psychotropic medications, 20, 74–78, 85n19, 85n25, 209, 274; and gambling addictions, 75–78, 86n25
Puerto Rico, 22, 108, 110–11; drug trafficking in, 110; Mental Health Law in, 108; unemployment in, 110–11
Purdue Pharma, 117

Rabinow, Paul, 275, 279
Raikhel, Eugene, 23, 24, 27, 102–3, 159n26, 285
Rapp, Rayna, 258n2
Reckitt Benckiser Pharmaceuticals, 91–93, 108, 114–17, 123, 125n2
recovery, 44–45; as abstinence, 245–46, 249; and cure, 20, 25, 29, 99; discourse of, 239, 243–44, 249–50, 255; industry, 65; willful, 163, 249
regions of interest (ROIS): 244–45, 248, 252
Reinarman, Craig, 33n7, 254
relapse, 16, 37, 45, 217, 240–41, 243, 252, 254, 257; neurobiological basis of, 242–43, 252; uncontrollable reflex and, 241
residential treatment, 97, 102, 111
resting place. See *descanso*
Rheinberger, Hans Jörg, 27
Ritalin, 288, 290
Robaxin, 47
Robbins, Trevor W., 260n22
Roberts, Monty, 176
Rock Christian Fellowship, 54–56
Rogers, Carl, 177, 187n8
Rohypnol, 3, 135
ROIS. *See* regions of interest
Rollnick, Stephen, 178, 182
Roman Law, 11, 84n12, 182n5
"Room, The," 134, 146, 149, 151
Rose, Nikolas, 81–82, 84n14, 85n16, 85n18, 85n19, 102, 190–91
Rush, Benjamin, 33n5, 186n3
russes, les, 30–31, 126–27, 129–30, 133–34, 137, 141, 152–54
Russia: addiction treatment in, 23, 32n1, 139, 189, 192; Lechebno-Trudovye Profilaktorii (Therapeutic Labor Profilactories), 192, 198; Ministry of Health, 139, 192; Ministry of the Interior, 139, 192; toxicomania registry in, 135, 139, 149, 157n12; unemployment in, 139. See also *khimzashchita*
Russian Orthodox Church, 193

treatment, 18–19, 45; federally funded, 45, 108, 115; follow-up, 25; in-patient, 25, 220; pharmacological, 2, 6, 14–15, 19–21, 34n13, 96, 190, 238–39, 242, 245, 254; stigma related to, 114, 116–17; talk-based, 21

Treatment Research Center (TRC), 239–41, 244

Treaty of Guadalupe Hidalgo, 52

triggers, 16, 30, 60n4, 72, 79, 239–40, 242, 246, 252–53, 256

Trimeridian Resources for Problem Gambling, 65, 67, 72, 83n8, 83n9

Turner, Victor, 112

TV Junkie, 252–53

twelve-step programs: 6, 10, 15–16, 18, 21, 33n8, 34n14, 44–45, 70, 85n17, 124, 174, 189, 204. *See also* Alcoholics Anonymous (AA); Gamblers Anonymous (GA); Narcotics Anonymous (NA)

urine screen, 118, 168–69, 186n6

Valium. *See* diazepam

Valverde, Mariana, 124

Van der Geest, Sjaak, 266

Vietnam War, 46, 112, 115

Volkow, Nora, 240–41, 243, 259n7, 270, 274

Vrecko, Scott, 85n19, 86n25, 87n31, 191, 261n25, 261n28

Vysotsky, Vladimir, 206

War on Drugs, the, 215, 236–37, 270

Weber, Max, 162

Welsh, Christopher, 94

Wetherall, Margaret, 260n20

WHO (World Health Organization), 13, 140

Wikler, Abraham, 258n4

will, 165, 267, 273, 277, 280, 286, 290

Williams, Raymond, 42–43

Winfrey, Oprah, 16, 239, 240, 243–50, 252–53, 255–56

withdrawal, 3, 13, 50, 112, 135, 276; "cold turkey," 139

World Health Organization (WHO), 13, 140

Wurmser, Leon, 165

Xanax, 77–78, 291

Yoshino, Keiji, 153–54

Young, Allan, 211n3, 259n17

Zoloft, 76–77. *See also* selective serotonin reuptake inhibitors

Zyprexa, 65, 83n9, 86n25